Reign of Error

Reign of Error

The Hoax of the Privatization Movement
and the Danger to America's Public Schools

Diane Ravitch

ALFRED A. KNOPF · NEW YORK · 2013

THIS IS A BORZOI BOOK
PUBLISHED BY ALFRED A. KNOPF

www.aaknopf.com

Library of Congress Cataloging-in-Publication Data
Ravitch, Diane.
   Reign of error : the hoax of the privatization movement
and the danger to America's public schools / Diane Ravitch.
      pages cm
ISBN 978-0-385-35088-4
1. Privatization in education—United States.
2. School choice—United States.   3. Education and state—
United States.   I. Title.
   LB2806.36.R38 2013
   379.3—dc23
                    2013015275

Jacket design by Jason Booher

Manufactured in the United States of America
First Edition

This book is dedicated with love to Mary

What the best and wisest parent wants for his own child, that must the community want for all of its children. Any other ideal for our schools is narrow and unlovely; acted upon, it destroys our democracy. All that society has accomplished for itself is put, through the agency of the school, at the disposal of its future members. All its better thoughts of itself it hopes to realize through the new possibilities [are] thus opened to its future self.

—JOHN DEWEY, 1907

The whole people must take upon themselves the education of the whole people and be willing to bear the expenses of it. There should not be a district of one mile square, without a school in it, not founded by a charitable individual, but maintained at the public expense of the people themselves.

—JOHN ADAMS, 1785

Contents

CHAPTER 17   Trouble in E-land   180

CHAPTER 18   Parent Trigger, Parent Tricker   198

CHAPTER 19   The Failure of Vouchers   206

CHAPTER 20   Schools Don't Improve if They Are Closed   214

CHAPTER 21   Solutions: Start Here   224

CHAPTER 22   Begin at the Beginning   227

CHAPTER 23   The Early Years Count   230

CHAPTER 24   The Essentials of a Good Education   234

CHAPTER 25   Class Size Matters for Teaching and Learning   242

CHAPTER 26   Make Charters Work for All   247

CHAPTER 27   Wraparound Services Make a Difference   253

CHAPTER 28   Measure Knowledge and Skills with Care   261

CHAPTER 29   Strengthen the Profession   274

CHAPTER 30   Protect Democratic Control of Public Schools   278

CHAPTER 31   The Toxic Mix   290

CHAPTER 32   Privatization of Public Education Is Wrong   300

CHAPTER 33   Conclusion: The Pattern on the Rug   313

                Appendix   327

                Acknowledgments   353

                Notes   355

                Index   379

Introduction

The purpose of this book is to answer four questions.

First, is American education in crisis?

Second, is American education failing and declining?

Third, what is the evidence for the reforms now being promoted by the federal government and adopted in many states?

Fourth, what should we do to improve our schools and the lives of children?

In this book, I show that the schools are in crisis because of persistent, orchestrated attacks on them and their teachers and principals, and attacks on the very principle of public responsibility for public education. These attacks create a false sense of crisis and serve the interests of those who want to privatize the public schools.

My last book sought to show that many of the policies promoted by the Bush administration, the Obama administration, and the nation's largest foundations had meager evidence to support them, and in some cases no evidence at all, and were likely to harm public education without improving the schools. In this book, I report additional evidence about the failure of the Bush-Obama "reforms."

In the spring of 2011, I decided to write this book as a result of a conversation with David Denby, who was writing an article about me that would eventually be published in *The New Yorker* magazine. At the time, we were riding in a car from New Jersey, where I had just given a lecture at the Education Law Center, to New York City, where we both live. Denby writes about American film and American culture, not education, so he came to the issues without any preconceptions. In addition to engaging in long discussions with me, following me to lectures, and reading my books, he interviewed critics of my work. He said to me, "Your critics say you are long on criticism but short on answers."

I said, "You have heard me lecture, and you know that is not true."

He suggested that I write a book to respond to the critics.

So I did, and this is that book.

I do not contend that the schools are fine just as they are. They are not. American education needs higher standards for those who enter the teaching profession. It needs higher standards for those who become principals and superintendents. It needs stronger and deeper curriculum in every subject. Schools need freedom from burdensome and intrusive regulations that undermine professional autonomy. They need the resources to meet the needs of the children they enroll. But they cannot improve if they are judged by flawed measures and continually at risk of closing because they do not meet an artificial goal created and imposed by legislators.

Schools need stability, adequate resources, well-prepared and experienced educators, community support, and a clear vision of what good education is. The purpose of elementary and secondary education is to develop the minds and character of young children and adolescents and help them grow up to become healthy, knowledgeable, and competent citizens.

I believe that privatizing our public schools is a risky and dangerous project. I believe it will hurt children, shatter communities, and damage our society. That is why I wrote this book.

Reign of Error

CHAPTER 1

Our Schools Are at Risk

In the early years of the twenty-first century, a bipartisan consensus arose about educational policy in the United States. Right and left, Democrats and Republicans, the leading members of our political class and our media elite seemed to agree: Public education is broken. Our students are not learning enough. Public schools are bad and getting worse. We are being beaten by other nations with higher test scores. Our abysmal public schools threaten not only the performance of our economy but our national security, our very survival as a nation. This crisis is so profound that half measures and tweaks will not suffice. Schools must be closed and large numbers of teachers fired. Anyone who doubts this is unaware of the dimensions of the crisis or has a vested interest in defending the status quo.

Furthermore, according to this logic, now widely shared among policy makers and opinion shapers, blame must fall on the shoulders of teachers and principals. Where test scores are low, it is their fault. They should be held accountable for this educational catastrophe. They are responsible because they have become comfortable with the status quo of low expectations and low achievement, more interested in their pensions than in the children they teach.

In response to this crisis, the reformers have a ready path for solving it. Since teachers are the problem, their job protections must be eliminated and teachers must be fired. Teachers' unions must be opposed at every turn. The "hoops and hurdles" that limit entry into teaching must be eliminated. Teachers must be evaluated on the basis of their students' test scores. Public schools must be evaluated on an "objective" basis, and when they are failing, they must be closed. Students must be given choices other than traditional public schools, such as charter schools, vouchers, and online schools.

In Hollywood films and television documentaries, the battle lines are clearly drawn. Traditional public schools are bad; their supporters are apologists for the unions. Those who advocate for charter schools, virtual schooling, and "school choice" are reformers; their supporters insist they are championing the rights of minorities. They say they are leaders of the civil rights movement of our day.

It is a compelling narrative, one that gives us easy villains and ready-made solutions. It appeals to values Americans have traditionally cherished—choice, freedom, optimism, and a latent distrust of government.

There is only one problem with this narrative.

It is wrong.

Public education is not broken. It is not failing or declining. The diagnosis is wrong, and the solutions of the corporate reformers are wrong. Our urban schools are in trouble because of concentrated poverty and racial segregation. But public education as such is not "broken." Public education is in a crisis only so far as society is and only so far as this new narrative of crisis has destabilized it. The solutions proposed by the self-proclaimed reformers have not worked as promised. They have failed even by their own most highly valued measure, which is test scores. At the same time, the reformers' solutions have had a destructive impact on education as a whole.

Far from being progressive, these changes strike at the heart of one of our nation's most valued institutions. Liberals, progressives, well-meaning people have lent their support to a project that is antithetical to liberalism and progressivism. By supporting market-based "reforms," they have allied themselves with those who seek to destroy public education. They are being used by those who have an implacable hostility toward the public sector. The transfer of public funds to private management and the creation of thousands of deregulated, unsupervised, and unaccountable schools have opened the public coffers to profiteering, fraud, and exploitation by large and small entrepreneurs.

As a historian of American education, I have seen, studied, and written about waves of school reforms that came and went. But what is happening now is an astonishing development. It is not meant to reform public education but is a deliberate effort to replace public education with a privately managed, free-market system of schooling. Public education, established in America's towns and villages in the mid-nineteenth century, born of advocacy and struggle, is now in jeopardy. This essential institution, responsible for producing a democratic citizenry and tasked with providing equality of educational opportunity, is at risk. Under the cover of "choice" and "freedom," we may lose one of our society's greatest resources, our public school system—a system whose doors are open to all.

I was not always a critic of test-based accountability and choice. For many years, I too agreed that our public schools were in crisis. I wanted them to be far better. I worried about the content of the curriculum. I worried about low standards for students and for teachers. As a graduate of the public schools of Houston, I was an ambivalent supporter of school choice and certainly had no desire to replace public education with a voucherized, privately managed system of schools. In 1991–93, I served as assistant secretary of education in the administration of President George H. W. Bush, and I was in charge of the U.S. Department of Education's Office of Educational Research and Improvement. I was a strong supporter of standards, testing, and accountability. It was only after I saw the corrosive effects of No Child Left Behind that I reconsidered my long-held beliefs. In 2010, I published *The Death and Life of the Great American School System: How Testing and Choice Are Undermining Education*. In that book, I recanted my earlier support for what is now known as the "reform" agenda in education: high-stakes testing, test-based accountability, competition, and school choice (charters and vouchers). When the book appeared, it was widely reviewed, hailed by most experienced educators, and predictably scorned by advocates of these policies.

Their most typical complaint was that while I was long on criticism, I offered no solutions. They, on the other hand, had solutions.

I contend that their solutions are not working. Some are demonstrably wrong. Some, like charter schools, have potential if the profit motive were removed, and if the concept were redesigned to meet the needs of the communities served rather than the plans of entrepreneurs. It is far better to stop and think than to plunge ahead vigorously, doing what is not only ineffective but wrong. We must always be open to trying new ideas in the schools, but we should try them first on a small scale and gather evidence before applying and mandating new ideas nationwide. When evidence is lacking, we should not move forward with a sense of urgency. The reformers are putting the nation's children on a train that is headed for a cliff. This is the right time to stand on the tracks, wave a lantern, and say, "Wait, this won't work. Stop the train. Pick a different route." But the reformers say, "That's no solution. Full speed ahead," aiming right for the cliff.

What began as a movement for testing and accountability has turned into a privatization movement. President George W. Bush's No Child Left Behind, with its unrealistic goals, has fed the privatization frenzy. The overreliance on and misuse of testing and data have created a sense of crisis, lending credibility to claims that American public education is failing and in decline. Yes, we have problems, but those problems are concentrated where poverty and racial segregation are concentrated. The reformers say they care about poverty, but they do not address it other than to insist upon private management of the schools in urban districts; the reformers ignore racial segregation altogether, apparently accepting it as inevitable. Thus, they leave the root causes of low academic performance undisturbed. What began as a movement to "save minority children from failing schools" and narrow the achievement gap by privatizing their schools has not accomplished that goal, but the movement is undaunted. It is now intent on advancing into middle-income districts in the cities and suburbs as well. This is already happening.

In this book, I will show why the reform agenda does not work, who is behind it, and how it is promoting the privatization of public education. I will then put forward my solutions, none of which is cheap or easy, none of which offers a quick fix to complicated problems. I have no silver bullets—because none exist—but I have proposals based on evidence and experience.

We know what works. What works are the very opportunities that advantaged families provide for their children. In homes with adequate resources, children get advantages that enable them to arrive in school healthy and ready to learn. Discerning, affluent parents demand schools with full curricula, experienced staffs, rich programs in the arts, libraries, well-maintained campuses, and small classes. As a society, we must do whatever is necessary to extend the same advantages to children who do not have them. Doing so will improve their ability to learn, enhance their chances for a good life, and strengthen our society.

So that readers don't have to wait until the later chapters of this book, here is a summary of my solutions to improve both schools and society. Schools and society are intertwined. The supporting research comes later in the book. Every one of these solutions works to improve the lives and academic outcomes of young people.

Pregnant women should see a doctor early in their pregnancies and have regular care and good nutrition. Poor women who do not receive early and regular medical care are likely to have babies with developmental and cognitive problems.

Children need prekindergarten classes that teach them how to socialize with others, how to listen and learn, how to communicate well, and how to care for themselves, while engaging in the joyful pursuit of play and learning that is appropriate to their age and development and that builds their background knowledge and vocabulary.

Children in the early elementary grades need teachers who set age-appropriate goals. They should learn to read, write, calculate, and explore nature, and they should have plenty of time to sing and dance and draw and play and giggle. Classes in these grades should be small enough—ideally fewer than twenty—so that students get the individual attention they need. Testing in the early grades should be used sparingly, not to rank students, but diagnostically, to help determine what they know and what they still need to learn. Test scores should remain a private matter between parents and teachers, not shared with the district or the state for any individual student. The district or state may aggregate scores for entire schools but should not judge teachers or schools on the basis of these scores.

As students enter the upper elementary grades and middle school and high school, they should have a balanced curriculum that includes not only reading, writing, and mathematics but the sciences, literature, history, geography, civics, and foreign languages. Their school should have a rich arts program, where students learn to sing, dance, play an instrument, join an orchestra or a band, perform in a play, sculpt, or use technology to design structures, conduct research, or create artworks. Every student should have time for physical education every day. Every school should have a library with librarians and media specialists. Every school should have a nurse, a psychologist, a guidance counselor, and a social worker. And every school should have after-school programs where students may explore their interests, whether in athletics, chess, robotics, history club, dramatics, science club, nature study, Scouting, or other activities. Teachers should write their own tests and use standardized tests only for diagnostic purposes. Classes should be small enough to ensure that every teacher knows his or her students and can provide the sort of feedback to strengthen their ability to write, their noncognitive skills, their critical thinking, and their mathematical and scientific acumen.

Our society should commit to building a strong education profession. Public policy should aim to raise the standards for entry into teaching. Teachers should be well-educated and well-prepared for their profession. Principals and superintendents should be experienced educators.

Schools should have the resources they need for the students they enroll.

As a society, we must establish goals, strategies, and programs to reduce poverty and racial segregation. Only by eliminating opportunity gaps can we eliminate achievement gaps. Poor and immigrant children need the same sorts of schools that wealthy children have, only more so. Those who start life with the fewest advantages need even smaller classes, even more art, science, and music to engage them, to spark their creativity, and to fulfill their potential.

There is a solid research base for my recommendations. If you want a society organized to promote the survival of the fittest and the triumph of the most advantaged, then you will prefer the current course of action, where children and teachers and schools are "racing to the top." But if you believe the goal of our society should be equality of opportunity for all children and that we should seek to reduce the alarming inequalities children now experience, then my program should win your support.

My premise is straightforward: you can't do the right things until you stop doing the wrong things. If you insist on driving that train right over the cliff, you will never reach your hoped-for destination of excellence for all. Instead, you will inflict harm on millions of children and reduce the quality of their educations. You will squander billions of dollars on failed schemes that should have been spent on realistic, evidence-based ways of improving our public schools, our society, and the lives of children.

Stop doing the wrong things. Stop promoting competition and choice as answers to the very inequality that was created by competition and choice. Stop the mindless attacks on the education profession. A good society requires both a vibrant private sector and a responsible public sector. We must not permit the public sector to be privatized and eviscerated. In a democracy, important social goals require social collaboration. We must work to establish programs that improve the lives of children and families. To build a strong educational system, we need to build a strong and respected education profession. The federal government and states must develop policies to recruit, support, and retain career educators, both in the classroom and in positions of leadership. If we mean to conquer educational inequity, we must recognize that the root causes of poor academic performance are segregation and poverty, along with inequitably resourced schools. We must act decisively to reduce the causes of inequity. We know what good schools look like, we know what great education consists of. We must bring good schools to every district and neighborhood in our nation. Public education is a basic public responsibility: we must not be persuaded by a false crisis narrative to privatize it. It is time for parents, educators, and other concerned citizens to join together to strengthen our public schools and preserve them for future generations. The future of our democracy depends on it.

CHAPTER 2

The Context for Corporate Reform

Federal law and policy turned the education reform movement of the twenty-first century into a powerful force that no school or district dared to ignore.

Since the publication in 1983 of a report called *A Nation at Risk,* federal and state policy makers have searched for policy levers with which to raise academic performance. That report was the product of a commission—called the National Commission on Excellence in Education—appointed by Secretary of Education Terrel H. Bell, during the administration of President Ronald Reagan. The commission warned that the nation was endangered by "a rising tide of mediocrity" in the schools; it pointed to the poor standing of American students on international tests, a recurring phenomenon since the first international test was offered in the mid-1960s. Its basic claim was that the American standard of living was threatened by the loss of major manufacturing industries—such as automobiles, machine tools, and steel mills—to other nations, which the commission attributed to the mediocre quality of our public educational system; this claim shifted the blame from shortsighted corporate leadership to the public schools. The commission called for better curriculum standards, higher graduation requirements, better teacher training, higher teacher pay, and other customary improvements. The commission said very little about testing, accountability, and choice.

The first Bush administration, in which I served, had little appetite for an expanded federal role in education. It announced a program called America 2000, which relied mainly on voluntarism since a Democratic Congress would not consider any education bills sponsored by President George H. W. Bush. Congressional Democrats in the early

1990s wanted greater resources and greater equity in public schools, not standards and tests. The Clinton administration liked the idea of national standards and national testing, but when Republicans took control of Congress in 1995, that idea died. The administration settled for a program called Goals 2000, which offered money to states to set their own standards and tests.

Along came the George W. Bush administration in 2001, which proposed sweeping federal legislation called No Child Left Behind (NCLB). On the campaign trail, Bush spoke of "the Texas miracle," claiming that testing and accountability had led to startling improvements in student performance. He said that test scores and graduation rates were up, and the achievement gap was narrowing, thanks to the Texas reforms. We now know that there was no such miracle; Texas made some increases on federal tests, like many other states, but its students register at the national average, nowhere near the top. In 2001, no one listened to those who warned that the "Texas miracle" was an illusion.[1] Congress swiftly passed the law, which dramatically changed the federal role in education.

The law declared that all states must test every child annually in grades 3 through 8 in reading and mathematics and report test scores by race, ethnicity, low-income status, disability status, and limited-English proficiency. By the year 2014, all students were supposed to achieve proficiency on state tests. The states were required to monitor every school to see if every group was on track to reach proficiency. Any school that persistently failed to meet its annual target would be labeled a school in need of improvement (in the eyes of the media and thus the public, that means a "failing" school). With each year that the school failed to meet its target, the sanctions became increasingly more punitive. Eventually, if the school kept failing, it was at risk of having its staff fired or having the school closed, handed over to state control or private management, or turned into a charter school or "any other major restructuring." Many schools "failed" year after year, and as 2014 approached, the majority of public schools in the nation had been declared failures, including some excellent, highly regarded schools (typically, the group that was not making sufficient progress toward 100 percent proficiency was students with disabilities, and the schools that were likeliest to be labeled as failing enrolled high proportions of poor and minority students). In Massachusetts, for example, the state with the nation's highest-performing students as judged by federal tests, 80 percent of the state's public schools were "failing" by NCLB standards in 2012.

Let's be clear: 100 percent proficiency is an impossible goal; no nation in the world has ever achieved this, nor has any other nation ever passed legislation to punish its schools for not reaching an unattainable goal. It was as though Congress had passed a law saying that every city in America should be crime-free. Who could disapprove of such a laudable goal? What city would not want to be crime-free? But imagine if the law set a deadline twelve years off and said that any city that did not meet the goal would be punished; its police stations would be closed and privatized; its police officers would lose their badges. The first to close would be the police stations in the poorest neighborhoods, where crime rates were highest. Eventually, the scythe would swing even in affluent neighborhoods, because no city is completely crime-free. Wishing that it might be so, or passing laws to require that it be so, does not make it so.

NCLB opened the door to huge entrepreneurial opportunities. Federal funds were set aside for after-school tutoring, and thousands of tutoring companies sprang up overnight to claim a share. Many new ventures opened to advise schools on how to meet NCLB testing targets, how to analyze NCLB data, how to "turn around" failing schools, and how to meet other goals embedded in the legislation.

NCLB encouraged the growth of the charter sector by proposing that charter schools were a remedy for failing public schools. When NCLB was passed, charters were a new and untested idea. The original idea for charters was first suggested in 1988, not to promote competition, but to allow teachers to try out new ideas. One of its originators, Ray Budde, was a professor at the University of Massachusetts who envisioned charters run by teachers, free to teach without interference by the local district bureaucracy. The other originator was Albert Shanker, president of the American Federation of Teachers, who envisioned charters where teachers sought out the lowest-performing students, the dropouts, and the disengaged, then figured out innovative ways to ignite their interest in education. Both these men, unknown to each other, saw charters as schools empowered to devise innovative practices and ready to collaborate and share what they had learned with their colleagues and existing schools. Certainly, neither imagined a charter sector that was nearly

90 percent non-union or one that in some states presented profit-making opportunities for entrepreneurs.

Minnesota passed the first charter law in 1991, and the first charter school opened in 1992. Only nine years later, Congress passed the No Child Left Behind law, recommending conversion of a low-performing school to a charter as a remedy. At the time, there was no evidence that charters would succeed where the local public school had failed. Nonetheless, the congressional endorsement was valuable publicity for charters, which gained public recognition and new opportunities to expand and compete with neighborhood public schools for higher test scores. In addition, it paved the way for federal appropriations and federal tax breaks for charter school construction.

As 2014 neared, states were spending hundreds of millions of dollars each year on testing and on test preparation materials; the schools in some districts and states were allocating 20 percent of the school year to preparing for state tests. This misallocation of scarce resources was hardly surprising, because schools lived or died depending on their test scores. Educators and parents raised their voices against the incessant testing, but no one seemed to know how to stop it. Some states not only tested children in grades 3 through 8, as NCLB required, but started testing children in the early grades and in prekindergarten to ready them for the testing that began in the third grade. And the number of tests administered to high school students increased as well, both as a measure of progress and as a condition for graduation. Texas, the epicenter of the testing fetish, insisted that students needed to pass fifteen different tests to get a high school diploma.

The thirst for data became unquenchable. Policy makers in Washington and the state capitals apparently assumed that more testing would produce more learning. They were certain that they needed accountability and could not imagine any way to hold schools "accountable" without test scores. This unnatural focus on testing produced perverse but predictable results: it narrowed the curriculum; many districts scaled back time for the arts, history, civics, physical education, science, foreign language, and whatever was not tested. Cheating scandals occurred in Atlanta, Washington, D.C., and other districts. States like New York manipulated the passing score on state tests to inflate the results and bring them closer to Washington's unrealistic goal. Teaching to the test, once considered unprofessional and unethical, became common practice in the age of NCLB. Districts invested many millions of dollars in test preparation materials to help teachers do it better. Under pressure to get higher scores to save their jobs and their schools, teachers drilled students in how to take tests and taught them the types of questions that had been used on previous tests and were likely to appear again.

NCLB remained on the books year after year, long after it was due to be revised, reauthorized, or scrapped in 2007. Congress was deadlocked and unable to escape a trap of its own devising. No one seemed able to imagine a federal education policy that did not rely on testing, that did not demand measures to hold schools "accountable" for failure to produce quantifiable results. No one seemed to remember that this had not been the federal role before 2002, when NCLB was signed into law. Even though the "Texas miracle" was long ago forgotten, the federal law that mimicked the Texas model remained in force.

With the election of Barack Obama in 2008, many educators expected a change in federal education policy. Their hopes were dashed, however, by Obama's education policies, specifically his Race to the Top competition. At the beginning of the new president's term, Congress passed economic stimulus funding in response to the financial collapse of 2008. Congress set aside $100 billion for education. Of the total, $95 billion was allocated to keep teachers employed, to offset the shrinkage of state and local budgets. The remaining $5 billion was used to fund a competition among the states, called Race to the Top. Secretary Arne Duncan set the conditions. To be eligible, states had to agree to adopt new common standards and tests (the Common Core State Standards); expand the number of charter schools; evaluate the effectiveness of teachers in significant part by the test scores of their students (and remove any statutory barriers to doing so); and agree to "turn around" their lowest-performing schools by taking such dramatic steps as firing staff and closing the schools.

Eleven states and the District of Columbia won Race to the Top funding. Dozens of states competed for the funds, all of them accepting the premises of the competition so they could be eligible to win the millions of federal dollars at a time of deep fiscal distress. By dangling the chance to win millions of dollars before hard-pressed states, the Obama administration leveraged changes across the nation, aligning state education policies with the requirements of Race to the Top.

Among the premises of Race to the Top was that charter schools and school choice were necessary reforms; that standardized testing was the best way to measure the progress of students and the quality of their teachers, principals, and schools; and that competition among schools would improve them. It also gave a bipartisan stamp of approval to the idea that a low-performing school could be improved by firing the staff, closing the school, and starting over with a new name and a new staff.

All of these ideas were highly contested; not one has a strong body of evidence or research to support it or to justify the imposition of so many different and untested changes at the same time. But with the joint imprimatur of No Child Left Behind and Race to the Top, advocates of standardized testing, school choice, merit pay, and tough accountability measures like school closings heralded these measures as "reforms." Race to the Top was only marginally different from No Child Left Behind. In fact, it was worse, because it gave full-throated Democratic endorsement to the long-standing Republican agenda of testing, accountability, and choice.

Race to the Top abandoned equity as the driving principle of federal aid. From the initiation of federal aid to local school districts in 1965, Democratic administrations had insisted on formula grants, which distributed federal money to schools and districts based on the proportion of students who were poor, not on a competition among states. The Obama administration shifted gears and took the position that competition was a better way to award federal funding. This change worked in favor of advantaged states and districts that could hire professional grant writers to compete for federal funding. In many cases, the Bill & Melinda Gates Foundation gave grants to hire professionals to develop applications for specific states, which tilted the field toward the applicants favored by Gates. By picking a few winners, the Race to the Top competition abandoned the traditional idea of equality of educational opportunity, where federal aid favored districts and schools that enrolled students with the highest needs.

The new billions of federal funding encouraged entrepreneurs to enter the education market. Almost overnight, consultants and vendors offered their services to advise districts and states on how to design teacher evaluation systems, how to train teachers, how to train principals, how to turn around failing schools, how to use new technologies, how to engage in data-driven decision making, on and on. With the adoption of the Common Core standards by almost every state, education publishers hurried to align their products with the new standards, entrepreneurs began developing technology to support the Common Core standards, and even more consultants hung out their shingles to sell their services to districts and states about how to implement the Common Core and how to engage in data collection, data management, and data analysis. *The Denver Post* determined that 35 percent of the federal funds allocated to that city in a School Improvement Grant was spent for consultants, not for students or teachers or schools.[2]

The U.S. Department of Education awarded $350 million to two consortia to develop national assessments to measure the new national standards. States and districts will have to make large investments in technology, because the new national assessments will be delivered online. By some estimates, the states will be required to spend as much as $16 billion to implement the Common Core standards. Unfortunately, neither the Obama administration nor the developers of the Common Core standards thought it necessary to field-test the new standards. They have no idea whether the adoption of the new standards and tests will improve education or how they will affect students who are now performing poorly. State education departments warned that the enhanced rigor of the Common Core would cause test scores to plummet by as much as 30 percent, even in successful districts. Should this occur, the sharp decline in passing rates will reinforce the reformers' claims about our nation's "broken" education system. This, in turn, will create a burgeoning market for new products and technologies. Some reformers hoped that the poor results of the new tests would persuade even suburban parents to lose faith in their community schools and demand not only new products but school closings, charters, and vouchers.[3]

This burst of entrepreneurial activity was planned. Joanne Weiss, Secretary Duncan's chief of staff, formerly the director of Duncan's Race to the Top competition, wrote an article in which she described the imperative to match entrepreneurs with school systems. Weiss had previously been the chief operating officer at the NewSchools Venture Fund, which invests in new charter schools and new technology ventures. Race to the Top, she wrote, was designed to scale up entrepreneurial activity, to encourage the creation of new markets for both for-profit and nonprofit investors. The new standards were a linchpin to match "smart capital" to educational innovation:

The development of common standards and shared assessments radi-
cally alters the market for innovation in curriculum development, professional development, and formative assessments. Previously, these
markets operated on a state-by-state basis, and often on a district-
by-district basis. But the adoption of common standards and shared
assessments means that education entrepreneurs will enjoy national
markets where the best products can be taken to scale.[4]

And indeed the investment opportunities seemed to grow by leaps
and bounds after the Obama administration launched its Race to the
Top. There were not only high-priced consultants and experts to assist
in complying with new federal demands but additional ways to invest
in new technologies and the growth industry of charter schools. Equity
investors held conferences to discuss the expanded opportunities for
making a profit in the public education sector.[5] The tennis star Andre
Agassi formed a partnership with an equity investing firm to raise
$750 million in capital to build at least seventy-five charter schools for
forty thousand or more students. This was not philanthropy; it was a
profit-making venture.[6] Investors quickly figured out that there was
money to be made in the purchase, leasing, and rental of space to charter schools, and an aggressive for-profit charter sector emerged wherever
it was permitted by state law; in states where for-profit charters were
not allowed, nonprofit charters hired for-profit operators to run their
schools. Technology companies competed to develop new applications
for the new Common Core State Standards, and there appeared to
be many exciting opportunities to make money in the emerging education marketplace.[7] This was the first time in history that the U.S.
Department of Education designed programs with the intent of stimu-
lating private sector investors to create for-profit ventures in American
education.

The combination of No Child Left Behind and Race to the Top
redefined the meaning of education reform. In this new environment,
education reformers support testing, accountability, and choice. Education reformers rely on data derived from standardized testing. Education
reformers insist that all children be proficient (NCLB) or increase their
test scores every year (Race to the Top), or their schools and teachers are
failures. Education reformers accept "no excuses." Education reformers
believe that schools improve if they are forced to compete. Education
reformers believe that teachers will produce higher test scores if they

are "incentivized" by merit pay. Education reformers use testing data to fire principals and teachers and to close schools. Education reformers applaud private management of public schools. Education reformers support the proliferation of for-profit organizations into school management. Education reformers don't care about teacher credentials or experience, because some economists say they don't raise test scores. Education reformers in the early twenty-first century believe that school quality and teacher quality may best be measured by test scores.

Once upon a time, education reformers thought deeply about the relationship between school and society. They thought about child development as the starting point for education. In those days, education reformers recognized the important role of the family in the education of children. Many years ago, education reformers demanded desegregation. They debated how to improve curriculum and instruction and what the content of the curriculum should be.

But that was long ago. Those concerns were no longer au courant. Now there was bipartisan consensus around the new definition of education reform. Those who held the levers of power at the U.S. Department of Education, in the big foundations, on Wall Street, and in the major corporations agreed on how to reform American education. The debates about the role of schooling in a democratic society, the lives of children and families, and the relationship between schools and society were relegated to the margins as no longer relevant to the business plan to reinvent American education.

CHAPTER 3

Who Are the Corporate Reformers?

The education reform movement must be defined in terms of its ideology, its strategies, and its leading members.

The "reformers" say they want excellent education for all; they want great teachers; they want to "close the achievement gap"; they want innovation and effectiveness; they want the best of everything for everyone. They pursue these universally admired goals by privatizing education, lowering the qualifications for future teachers, replacing teachers with technology, increasing class sizes, endorsing for-profit organizations to manage schools, using carrots and sticks to motivate teachers, and elevating standardized test scores as the ultimate measure of education quality.

"Reform" is really a misnomer, because the advocates for this cause seek not to reform public education but to transform it into an entrepreneurial sector of the economy. The groups and individuals that constitute today's reform movement have appropriated the word "reform" because it has such positive connotations in American political discourse and American history. But the roots of this so-called reform movement may be traced to a radical ideology with a fundamental distrust of public education and hostility to the public sector in general.

The "reform" movement is really a "corporate reform" movement, funded to a large degree by major foundations, Wall Street hedge fund managers, entrepreneurs, and the U.S. Department of Education. The movement is determined to cut costs and maximize competition among schools and among teachers. It seeks to eliminate the geographically based system of public education as we have known it for the past 150 years and replace it with a competitive market-based system of school choice—one that includes traditional public schools, privately managed charter schools, religious schools, voucher schools, for-profit schools, virtual schools, and for-profit vendors of instruction. Lacking any geographic boundaries, these schools would compete for customers. The customers would choose to send their children and their public funding wherever they wish, based on personal preference or on information such as the schools' test scores and a letter grade conferred by the state (based largely on test scores).

Some in the reform movement, believing that American education is obsolete and failing, think they are promoting a necessary but painful redesign of the nation's ailing schools. Some sincerely believe they are helping poor black and brown children escape from failing public schools. Some think they are on the side of modernization and innovation. But others see an opportunity to make money in a large, risk-free, government-funded sector or an opportunity for personal advancement and power. Some—a small but important number—believe they are acting rationally by treating the public education sector as an investment opportunity.

The corporate reform movement has its roots in an ideology that is antagonistic to public education. Partisans on the far right long ago turned against public schools, which they call "government schools." As a matter of ideology, they do not believe that government can do anything right. From the time that the University of Chicago economist Milton Friedman introduced the idea of vouchers in 1955, his supporters embraced vouchers as the best school reform ever, because it would enable parents to take government money to a school of their choice, including private and religious schools. Voucher advocates have long argued that the money should follow the child to whatever institution the family chooses, be it public, private, or religious. For years, they made the seductive pitch that parents should be "free to choose" (as Friedman put it) and that government should supply each family its share of the money and get out of the way. But for many years after the *Brown v. Board of Education* decision of 1954, the idea of school choice was tainted because segregationists used it to evade desegregation in districts facing court-ordered desegregation.

President Ronald Reagan, an admirer of Milton Friedman's, supported vouchers but was never able to persuade Congress to go along. In state referenda, the public has consistently opposed vouchers. Every time vouchers were put to a public vote, they were defeated by large margins. As recently as 2012, voters in Florida decisively rejected a constitutional amendment to permit vouchers. Voucher proponents complain that the public doesn't understand its own best interest and is misled by teachers' unions, who are just protecting their jobs and power. The election results in state after state show that the public does not want to subsidize religious schools with its tax dollars. Voucher advocates do not accept that the public likes and supports its community public schools, free from any religious teachings, with doors open to all. So choice supporters continually parrot or manufacture a steady stream of bad news about public education to shake the public's faith in public schools. However, even when polls show that people have a low opinion of American education, they nonetheless continue to have a high opinion of their own neighborhood schools.

Today's reformers assert that "the money should follow the child," and they herald this as a bold new reform idea. But it is not new. It is the same idea that was behind vouchers more than half a century ago. Today, the same arguments are made by Governor Bobby Jindal in Louisiana, who wants the money to follow the child to any school (even schools that teach creationism as science), any online corporation, any for-profit vendor of educational services, regardless of experience, quality, or qualifications. As public money is dispersed, so is public oversight and accountability for the spending of public money. Governor Rick Snyder of Michigan, eager to dismantle public education, proposed a formula for education funding based on this principle: "Any time, any place, any way, any pace." Conservative governors in other states make the same arguments.[1] But there is nothing conservative about replacing a beloved and traditional community institution—the public school—with a marketplace of privately run schools and for-profit vendors. This is a radical project, not conservative at all.

The organizations that advocate for "reform" have names that are appealing and innocuous, like the American Federation for Children, the American Legislative Exchange Council (ALEC), Better Education for Kids (B4K), Black Alliance for Educational Options, the education program at the Brookings Institution, the Center for Education Reform, Chiefs for Change, ConnCAN (and its spin-off, 50CAN, as well as state-specific groups like MinnCAN, NYCAN, and RI-CAN), Democrats for Education Reform, the Education Equality Project, Education Reform Now, Educators 4 Excellence, EdVoice, the Foundation for Excellence in Education, the National Council on Teacher Quality, New Leaders for New Schools, NewSchools Venture Fund, Parent Revolution, Stand for Children, Students for Education Reform, StudentsFirst, Teach for America, Teach Plus, and a host of others. Many of these groups have overlapping membership on their boards and are funded by the same foundations. They exist in a giant echo chamber, listening and talking only to one another, dismissing the concerns of parents, teachers, and communities.

The reformers are Republicans and Democrats. They include not only far-right Republican governors but some Democratic governors as well. They include President Barack Obama and Secretary Arne Duncan, as well as Democratic mayors in such cities as Newark, Chicago, and Los Angeles. Elected officials of both parties have signed on to an agenda that threatens the future of public education.

The aims of the corporate reform movement are supported by a broad array of think tanks, some purportedly liberal, some centrist, some on the right, and some on the far right. These include the American Enterprise Institute, the Center for American Progress, the Center on Reinventing Public Education, Education Sector, the Thomas B. Fordham Institute, the Friedman Foundation for Educational Choice, the Goldwater Institute, the Heartland Institute, the Heritage Foundation, the Koret Task Force at the Hoover Institution, and Policy Innovators in Education Network, as well as a bevy of state-level public policy think tanks that support privatization. Many of these think tanks—both liberal and conservative—work closely together, co-sponsoring conferences and publications to advance their shared agenda. Major foundations handsomely fund the think tanks that promote the corporate reform ideology.

The corporate reform movement has co-opted progressive themes and language in the service of radical purposes. Advocating the privatization of public education is deeply reactionary. Disabling or eliminating teachers' unions removes the strongest voice in each state to advocate for public education and to fight crippling budget cuts. In every state, classroom teachers are experts in education; they know what their students need, and their collective voice should be part of any public decision about school improvement. Stripping teachers of their job protections limits academic freedom. Evaluating teachers by the test scores of their students undermines professionalism and encourages teaching to the test. Claiming to be in the forefront of a civil rights movement while ignoring poverty and segregation is reactionary and duplicitous.

The leading funders of the reform movement are the Bill & Melinda Gates Foundation, which supports charter schools and test-based teacher evaluation; the Eli and Edythe Broad Foundation, which supports charter schools and trains urban superintendents in its managerial philosophy; and the Walton Family Foundation, which funds vouchers and charters. These powerful and wealthy foundations have overlapping interests. They subsidize many organizations in common, such as Teach for America (which recruits young college graduates to teach for two years in low-income schools), the KIPP charter schools, and Parent Revolution (the chief advocates of the "parent trigger" idea). They jointly funded the digital learning policy statement issued by Jeb Bush, former governor of Florida, and Bob Wise, former governor of West Virginia, which promotes the proliferation of low-quality virtual charter schools. Many other wealthy foundations support the corporate reform agenda, including the Laura and John Arnold Foundation, the Michael & Susan Dell Foundation, the Bradley Foundation, the Robertson Foundation, the Fisher Foundation, and the Anschutz Foundation, as well as fabulously rich individuals, including the Bezos family (Amazon.com), Reed Hastings (Netflix), and Rupert Murdoch (News Corporation).

The Gates Foundation is by far the largest foundation in the United States and possibly the world. It awards hundreds of millions of dollars in education grants every year. In addition to underwriting the expansion of charter schools, it invests heavily in test-based evaluation of teachers and merit pay. It has made grants to the biggest teachers' unions, the American Federation of Teachers and the National Education Association, and also made grants to start groups of young teachers to challenge the teachers' unions. It is difficult to find education organizations that have not been funded by the Gates Foundation. It underwrites "advocacy," by subsidizing almost every major think tank in Washington, D.C. It supported the creation, evaluation, and promotion of the Common Core State Standards, which have been adopted in almost every state. In addition, the Gates Foundation has joined in a partnership with the British publisher Pearson to develop online curriculum for teaching the Common Core standards. And the Gates Foundation underwrote the creation of a large database project to collect confidential student data with Wireless Generation, a subsidiary of Rupert Murdoch's News Corporation; critics fear that this information will be disclosed to vendors to market new products to schools and students.[2]

The corporate reform movement has a well-honed message: We are the reformers. We have solutions. The public schools are failing. The public schools are in decline. The public schools don't work. The public schools are obsolete and broken. We want to innovate. We know how to fix schools. We know how to close the achievement gap. We are leading the civil rights movement of our era. We want a great teacher in every classroom. Class size doesn't matter. Teachers should be paid more if their students get higher scores. They should be fired if their students don't get higher scores. Teachers should have their seniority and tenure stripped from them because those things protect bad teachers. Bad teachers cause the achievement gap. Great teachers close the achievement gap. Teachers' unions are greedy and don't care about children. People who draw attention to poverty are just making excuses for bad teachers and failing public schools. Those who don't agree with our strategies are defenders of the status quo. They have no solutions. We have solutions. We know what works. Testing works. Accountability works. Privately managed charter schools work. Closing schools with low test scores works. Paying bonuses to teachers to get higher scores works. Online instruction works. Replacing teachers with online instruction not only works but cuts costs while providing profits to edu-entrepreneurs who will spur further innovation.

It is a seductive message because it offers hope that someone knows how to fix difficult problems. They claim they not only know how to do it but *are* doing it. They express their message with clarity and certainty. Their message resonates with the major media and with the most powerful people in our society: billionaires, corporate executives, the leaders of major foundations, the president of the United States, the U.S. secretary of education, Wall Street hedge fund managers, pundits, and think tank opinion makers.

The corporate reformers don't like local school boards, because they sometimes defer to the views of teachers and they squabble too much; school boards, they say, slow down decision making with public hearings, and sometimes they make the wrong decisions. That is always a risk in a democracy; deliberative bodies are slow and sometimes make mistakes.

Corporate reformers want education decisions in the hands of a powerful executive who is immune to public opinion. They like the idea of a governor who appoints a commission to override the decisions of local school boards that resist charter schools. They like the idea of a superintendent at the state level who has unlimited power to impose his (their) policies, especially closing public schools and opening charter schools. In urban districts, their preferred mode of governance is a mayor or superintendent who controls the schools and answers to no one. At the school level, they want principals who can hire and fire at will, without due process. Corporate reformers don't like checks and balances. They want executives who can ignore the protests of parents, students, teachers, and community leaders, no matter how loudly they complain and no matter how many show up at public hearings or protest at rallies.

It pays to be on the reform team, certainly much more than it does to be a public school teacher. When Chicago's teachers went on strike in September 2012, the national media thought it shocking that the average Chicago teacher was paid $75,000 a year; they ignored the fact that Chicago teachers are compelled by law to live in Chicago and that this is not an outrageous salary for an educated, experienced professional who lives in a major city. Yet the media are indifferent when charter executives receive salaries of $300,000, $400,000, $500,000, to oversee a single school or a chain of small schools. The reformers are flush with cash from foundations and corporations. The Walton Family Foundation alone made school-reform grants of $159 million in 2011. Reformers often complain about the power and influence of the teachers' unions, but the unions cannot match the resources of the Gates Foundation and the Walton Family Foundation, as well as the many other foundations that march in lockstep with them, plus individual billionaires and millionaires who support candidates for state and local school board races. (The Gates and Walton foundations alone spend more than $500 million annually on education projects, which is more than ten times what unions spend to support civil rights groups and other allies.) When you combine the wealth of the big foundations with the financial and political clout of the U.S. Department of Education, they are a mighty force.[3] The "reformers" *are* the status quo.

For an ambitious person, being part of the corporate reform movement offers not only access to money but an accelerated route to professional success. Graduates of the Broad Superintendents Academy, an unaccredited program created by the Broad Foundation to teach Eli

Broad's management style of corporate reform, are on a fast track to become superintendents of urban districts—and the Broad Foundation may enhance their salaries. Some of the graduates of this short-term program are now state superintendents. Many are in charge of urban districts.

The young person who joins up with Teach for America or one of the big charter chains becomes part of a powerful network. These organizations provide an escalator to the top that no ordinary teaching career can match. Teachers without these connections may work for years in their classrooms before they are even considered for department chair or assistant principal. Those who rise in the corporate reform movement are soon managing their own charter schools or assuming leadership roles in large urban districts or state education departments, some before they reach the age of thirty.

Wall Street hedge fund managers have their own organization, called Democrats for Education Reform (DFER). DFER raises money for candidates and elected officials whom it likes, and it doesn't like them unless they agree to the corporate reform agenda, especially the expansion of charter schools and the imposition of teacher evaluation systems based on test scores (though not for teachers in the charter schools it supports). At the inaugural meeting of DFER in 2005, the speaker for the event was a promising young senator from Illinois, Barack Obama. When Obama ran for president in 2008, his chief education spokesperson was Linda Darling-Hammond of Stanford University. But when Obama was elected, he chose Arne Duncan as secretary of education. Duncan not only was his friend but was recommended by DFER.[4]

Arne Duncan is one of the recognized leaders of the corporate reform movement who implemented many of its ideas when he was superintendent of schools in Chicago. Jeb Bush, former governor of Florida, is another national leader. He created an organization called the Foundation for Excellence in Education, which actively promotes vouchers, charter schools, for-profit charter schools, virtual learning, and for-profit online corporations, as well as testing and accountability tied to test scores. In states with a Republican governor and a Republican supermajority in the legislature, the measures to privatize education advanced rapidly. In Michigan, Governor Rick Snyder promoted legislation to allow emergency managers to take over fiscally troubled districts; in two small school districts, the emergency managers closed the public schools and gave the students to a for-profit charter school chain (the law was repealed in 2012 by Michigan voters, but Snyder left the emergency managers and their decisions in place). Governor Mitch Daniels and the Indiana legislature authorized vouchers, for-profit charter schools, for-profit cyber-charters, and a test-based teacher accountability system. Governor Bobby Jindal of Louisiana pushed through sweeping legislation in 2012 that offered vouchers to more than half the students in the state and authorized the opening of many new charter schools; in addition, students will be able to take their state money and spend it in almost any place that calls itself a vendor of educational services. The money to support the alternatives to public education was to be taken out of the budget for public schools, until state courts ruled it unconstitutional to do so. The Louisiana reform legislation ties teachers' evaluations to the test scores of their students, but teachers in charter schools and voucher schools do not need to be certified or subject to the same requirements, as is the case in many other states and districts.

When the Louisiana legislation was hurriedly passed, it was hailed by a group of state superintendents called Chiefs for Change as "student-centered reforms" that "will completely transform Louisiana and its students."[5] Chiefs for Change is affiliated with Jeb Bush's Foundation for Excellence in Education. It describes itself as a coalition of state leaders who share a "zeal for education reform." Its members include the state superintendents in Rhode Island, Indiana, Louisiana, Oklahoma, Tennessee, Florida, Maine, New Jersey, and New Mexico.

Much of the legislation for the education reform movement in states with conservative governors or legislatures comes from a shadowy group called ALEC (the American Legislative Exchange Council). ALEC stayed out of the public eye until 2012, when a shooting in Florida brought it unwanted national attention. A black teenager named Trayvon Martin was killed by a man who said he was defending himself in accordance with Florida's "stand your ground" law, which was based on model legislation written by ALEC. ALEC was founded in 1973 to advance privatization and free-market principles. Its membership includes some two thousand state legislators. Funded by scores of major corporations and philanthropists, ALEC writes model legislation, which its members bring to their state legislatures. Many states have adopted ALEC model laws, simply inserting the name of the state into the proposed legislative language. ALEC does not like public

schools or unions. ALEC likes vouchers and charter schools. It wants
to eliminate tenure and seniority and to encourage paths into teaching
that don't involve getting a license or pedagogical training. ALEC likes
for-profit schools, especially cyber-charters. It promotes "parent trigger"
laws to enable privatizers to convince parents to sign petitions that will
turn their schools over to charter managers.[6]

The most unexpected supporter of corporate reform was President
Barack Obama. Educators enthusiastically supported Obama, expecting that he would eliminate the noxious policies of President Bush's No
Child Left Behind. They assumed, given his history as a community
organizer and his sympathy for society's least fortunate, that his administration would adopt policies that responded to the needs of children,
rather than concentrating on testing and accountability.

The first big surprise for educators occurred when President Obama
abandoned Linda Darling-Hammond and selected Arne Duncan, who
had run the low-performing schools of Chicago, as secretary of education. The second big surprise—shock, actually—happened when the
Obama administration released the details of Race to the Top, its major
initiative, which was designed in Secretary Duncan's office with the
help of consultants from the Gates Foundation, the Broad Foundation,
and other advocates of high-stakes testing and charter schools.

There was very little difference between Race to the Top and NCLB.
The Obama program preserved testing, accountability, and choice at
the center of the federal agenda. Race to the Top was even more punitive than NCLB. It insisted that states evaluate teachers in relation
to the test scores of their students, which made standardized testing
even more important than it was under NCLB. It encouraged states
to authorize more privately managed charter schools, an initiative that
President George W. Bush would never have been able to get through a
Democratic-controlled Congress. It endorsed competition and choice,
which were traditional themes of the Republican Party. The very concept of a "race to the top" repudiates the traditional Democratic Party
commitment to equity; it suggests that the winner will "race to the
top," leaving the losers far behind. But a commitment to equity means
that federal resources should be allocated based on need, not on a competition between the swift and the slow.

Because Race to the Top was handsomely funded, states eagerly competed for a share of its $5 billion. President Obama spoke out of both sides of his mouth about this signature program. He said in his State of the Union address in 2011 that Race to the Top was not a top-down mandate (after all, states had volunteered to accept its mandates) but "the work of local teachers and principals; school boards and communities" (which was not true in any sense).

Even though Race to the Top made standardized testing more important than ever, President Obama spoke out against testing. In 2011, he said he was strongly opposed to teaching to the test. He said,

One thing I never want to see happen is schools that are just teaching to the test. Because then you're not learning about the world; you're not learning about different cultures, you're not learning about science, you're not learning about math. All you're learning about is how to fill out a little bubble on an exam and the little tricks that you need to do in order to take a test. And that's not going to make education interesting to you. And young people do well in stuff that they're interested in. They're not going to do as well if it's boring.

His critics agreed with him. The California teacher and blogger Anthony Cody wondered if the president knew that Race to the Top required states to tie teacher evaluations to test scores, that Secretary Duncan wanted to evaluate teacher preparation programs by the test scores of the students of the teachers they produced, and that Obama's Department of Education "is proposing greatly expanding both the number of subjects tested, and the frequency of tests, to enable us to measure the 'value' each teacher adds to their students." At the same time that the president was lamenting "teaching to the test," his own policies made it necessary to teach to the test or be fired.[7]

In his 2012 State of the Union, the president's message was even more inconsistent. He said that he wanted schools to encourage teachers to "teach with creativity and passion; to stop teaching to the test," but at the same time he wanted schools to "reward the best ones" and "replace teachers who just aren't helping kids learn." He didn't acknowledge that the rewards and the punishments he approved would be tied, at his administration's insistence, to test scores.

In response to Race to the Top, the number of charter schools grew rapidly. For-profit charter schools expanded, as did virtual charter schools. Neither President Obama nor Secretary Duncan expressed any concern about the risks of deregulating public money to private corporations, nor did they oppose the entry of for-profit entrepreneurs into the charter school market. By advocating for school choice rather than public schools, Race to the Top implicitly encouraged not only charters but the other form of school choice: vouchers.

The 2010 elections brought a new crop of far-right governors into office, and these governors warmly embraced charter schools and advocated for vouchers. The Obama administration was silent; after a brief attempt to defund the Washington, D.C., voucher program, the administration gave in to Republican protests and permitted it to continue. As state after state adopted vouchers, the Obama administration raised no protest against the advance of privatization. Nor did Obama strongly object when the governors of Republican states attacked the collective bargaining rights of public-sector unions. In the spring of 2011, Wisconsin's right-wing governor, Scott Walker, proposed to strip away the collective bargaining rights of most public sector workers, including teachers, and they organized massive protests in Madison. They surrounded the state capitol and mounted daily protests. President Obama said he sided with the workers but didn't show up in Madison to demonstrate his support. Instead, he and Secretary Duncan flew to Miami in the middle of the Wisconsin protests to praise the former Florida governor Jeb Bush as "a champion of education reform" and to celebrate the successful "turnaround" of Miami Central High School. The national media recognized that President Obama was bestowing important support on Jeb Bush's policies of testing, accountability, and grading of schools. The national media did not pay attention, however, when the Florida Department of Education announced plans to shutter Miami Central because of its low performance only four months after the meeting between President Obama and Governor Bush. The state granted the school a waiver to avoid closure. Despite some gains, it was still one of the state's lowest-performing high schools.[8]

In his support for charter schools, high-stakes testing, merit pay, and evaluating teachers by test scores, President Obama forged a bipartisan consensus. But he had strange bedfellows, at least for a Democrat. When I blogged about ALEC and its right-wing agenda for privatization and lowering standards for entry into teaching, the organization's research director responded that President Obama shared credit with ALEC for promoting charter schools and "teaching-profession reforms." During the 2012 election campaign, the only difference between Obama and Mitt Romney in relation to their K–12 policy was that Romney supported vouchers (which he called "opportunity scholarships") and Obama did not.[9]

Neither candidate in the 2012 election supported public education. Both agreed that it was in crisis and that it needed radical change. In their debates, the subject of poverty never came up. Indeed, the subject of education was barely mentioned aside from the candidates' agreement that Race to the Top was a great success.

The public is only dimly aware of the reform movement's privatization agenda. The deceptive rhetoric of the privatization movement masks its underlying goal to replace public education with a system in which public funds are withdrawn from public oversight to subsidize privately managed charter schools, voucher schools, online academies, for-profit schools, and other private vendors.

No matter how many Hollywood movies the corporate reformers produce, no matter how many television specials sing the glories of privatization, no matter how often the reformers belittle the public schools and their teachers, the public is not yet ready to relinquish its public schools to speculators, entrepreneurs, ideologues, snake-oil salesmen, profit-making businesses, and Wall Street hedge fund managers.

CHAPTER 4

The Language of Corporate Reform

As long as anyone can remember, critics have been saying that the schools are in decline. They used to be the best in the world, they say, but no longer. They used to have real standards, but no longer. They used to have discipline, but no longer. What the critics seldom acknowledge is that our schools have changed as our society has changed. Some who look longingly to a golden age in the past remember a time when the schools educated only a small fraction of the population. But the students in the college-bound track of fifty years ago did not get the high quality of education that is now typical in public schools with Advanced Placement courses or International Baccalaureate programs or even in the regular courses offered in our top city and suburban schools. There are more remedial classes today, but there are also more public school students with special needs, more students who don't read English, more students from troubled families, and fewer students dropping out. As for discipline, it bears remembering a 1955 film called *Blackboard Jungle,* about an unruly, violent inner-city school where students bullied other students. The students in this school were all white. Today, public schools are often the safest places for children in tough neighborhoods.

The claim that the public schools are in decline is not new. In his Pulitzer Prize–winning book *Anti-intellectualism in American Life,* Richard Hofstadter characterized writing on education in the United States as "a literature of acid criticism and bitter complaint . . . The educational jeremiad is as much a feature of our literature as the jeremiad in the Puritan sermons." From the 1820s to our own time, reformers have complained about low standards, ignorant teachers, and incompetent school boards. He noted that anyone longing for the "good old days" would have difficulty finding a time when critics were not bemoaning the quality of the public schools.

There is a tendency nowadays to hark back with nostalgia to the mythical good old days, usually imagined as about forty or fifty years ago. But few people seem to realize there never was a time when everyone succeeded in school. When present-day critics refer to what they assume was a better past, they look back to a time when a large proportion of American youths did not complete high school and only a small minority completed four years of college. In those supposedly halcyon days, the schools in many states were racially segregated, as were most colleges and universities. Children with disabilities did not have a right to a free public education until after the passage of federal legislation in 1975 and were often excluded from public schools. Nor did schools enroll significant numbers of non-English-speaking students in the 1940s and 1950s or even the 1960s. Immigration laws restricted the admission of foreigners to the United States from the early 1920s until the mid-1960s. After the laws were changed, the schools began to enroll students from Latin America, Asia, the Middle East, Russia, Africa, and other parts of the world who had previously arrived in small numbers.

Thus, those who now sharply criticize the public schools speak fondly of an era when most schools were racially segregated; when public schools were not required to accept children with physical, mental, and emotional handicaps; when there were relatively few students who did not speak or read English; and when few graduated from high school and went to college.

Indifferent to history, today's corporate reformers insist that the public schools are in an unprecedented crisis. They tell us that children must be able to "escape" their "failing public schools." They claim they are "for the children," unlike their teachers, who are not for the children. They would have the public believe that children and their teachers are in warring camps. They put "children first" or "students first." Their policies, they say, will make us competitive and give us "great teachers" and "great schools" in every community. They say they know how to "close the achievement gap," and they claim to be leading "the civil rights issue of our time." Their policies, they say, will make our children into "global competitors." They will protect our national security. They will make America strong again. The corporate reformers play to our anxieties, even rekindling dormant Cold War fears that we may be in jeopardy as a nation if we don't buy what they are selling.

The critics want the public to believe that our public schools are a clear and present danger to our society. Unless there is radical change, they say, our society will fall apart. Our economy will collapse. Our national security is in danger. The message is clear: public education threatens all that we hold dear.

Recognizing that most Americans have a strong attachment to their community schools, the corporate reformers have taken care to describe their aims in pseudo-populist terms. While trying to scare us with warnings of dire peril, they mask their agenda with rhetoric that is soothing and deceptive. Though they speak of "reform," what they really mean is deregulation and privatization. When they speak of "accountability," what they really mean is a rigid reliance on standardized testing as both the means and the end of education. When they speak of "effective teachers," what they mean is teachers whose students produce higher scores on standardized tests every year, not teachers who inspire their students to love learning. When they speak of "innovation," they mean replacing teachers with technology to cut staffing costs. When they speak of "no excuses," they mean a boot-camp culture where students must obey orders and rules without question. When they speak of "personalized instruction," they mean putting children in front of computers with algorithms that supposedly adjust content and test questions to the ability level of the student but actually sacrifice human contact with a real teacher. When they speak of "achievement" or "performance," they mean higher scores on standardized tests. When they speak of "data-driven instruction," they mean that test scores and graduation rates should be the primary determinant of what is best for children and schools. When they speak of "competition," they mean deregulated charters and deregulated private schools competing with highly regulated public schools. When they speak of "a successful school," they refer only to its test scores, not to a school that is the center of its community, with a great orchestra, an enthusiastic chorus, a hardworking chess team, a thriving robotics program, or teachers who have dedicated their lives to helping the students with the highest needs (and often the lowest scores).

The reformers define the purpose of education as preparation for global competitiveness, higher education, or the workforce. They view students as "human capital" or "assets." One seldom sees any reference in their literature or public declarations to the importance of developing full persons to assume the responsibilities of citizenship.

Of equal importance are the topics that corporate reformers don't talk about. Seldom do they protest budget cuts, no matter how massive they may be. They do not complain when governors and legislatures cut billions from the public schools while claiming to be reformers. They do not protest rising rates of child poverty. They do not complain about racial segregation. They see no harm in devoting more time and resources to standardized testing. They are not heard from when districts cut the arts, libraries, and physical education while spending more on testing. They do not complain when federal or state or city officials announce plans to test children in kindergarten or even prekindergarten. They do not complain about increased class size. They do not object to scripted curricula or teachers' loss of professional autonomy. They do not object when experienced teachers are replaced by recruits who have only a few weeks of training. They close their eyes to evidence that charters enroll disproportionately small numbers of children with disabilities, or those from troubled homes, or English-language learners (in fact, they typically deny any such disparities, even when documented by state and federal data). They do not complain when for-profit corporations run charter schools or when educational services are outsourced to for-profit businesses. Indeed, they welcome entrepreneurs into the reform community as investors and partners.

If the American public understood that reformers want to privatize their public schools and divert their taxes to pay profits to investors, it would be hard to sell the corporate idea of reform. If parents understood that the reformers want to close down their community schools and require them to go shopping for schools, some far from home, that may or may not accept their children, it would be hard to sell the corporate idea of reform. If the American public understood that the very concept of education was being disfigured into a mechanism to apply standardized testing and sort their children into data points on a normal curve, it would be hard to sell the corporate idea of reform. If the American public understood that their children's teachers will be judged by the same test scores that label their children as worthy or unworthy, it would be hard to sell the corporate idea of reform. If the American public knew how inaccurate and unreliable these methods are, both for children and for teachers, it would be hard to sell the corporate idea of reform. And that is why the reform message must be rebranded to make it palatable to the public.

The leaders of the privatization movement call themselves reformers, but their premises are strikingly different from those of reformers in the past. In earlier eras, reformers wanted such things as a better curriculum, better-prepared teachers, better funding, more equitable funding, smaller classes, and desegregation, which they believed would lead to better public schools. By contrast, today's reformers insist that public education is a failed enterprise and that all these strategies have been tried and failed. They assert that the best way to save education is to hand it over to private management and let the market sort out the winners and the losers. They wish to substitute private choices for the public's responsibility to provide good schools for all children. They lack any understanding of the crucial role of public schools in a democracy.

The central premise of this movement is that our public schools are in decline. But this is not true. The public schools are working very well for most students. Contrary to popular myth, the scores on the no-stakes federal tests—the National Assessment of Educational Progress (NAEP)—are at an all-time high for students who are white, black, Hispanic, and Asian. Graduation rates are also at an all-time high. More young people than ever are entering college. Even more would go to college if the costs were not so high.

Of course some schools and districts have very low test scores and low graduation rates, and this has always been true. Most of these schools and districts have two features in common: poverty and high concentrations of racial minorities. The combination of these two factors is associated with low test scores. Children whose parents are poor and have low educational attainment tend to have lower test scores. Children who are poor receive less medical attention and less nutrition and experience more stress, disruption, and crises in their lives. These factors have an ongoing and profound effect on academic performance. That is why poor children need even more stability, more support, smaller class sizes, and more attention from their teachers and others in their schools, but often receive far less, due to underfunding.

Unfortunately, many people are unwilling to address the root causes of poor school outcomes, because doing so is either too politically difficult or too costly. They believe it is faster, simpler, and less expensive to privatize the public schools than do anything substantive to reduce poverty and racial isolation or to provide the nurturing environments and well-rounded education that children from prosperous families receive. Instead, the privatization movement nonchalantly closes the schools attended by poor children and destabilizes their lives. The privatization agenda excites the interest of edu-entrepreneurs, who see it as a golden opportunity to make money. But it is bad for our society. It undermines the sense of collective responsibility for collective needs. It hurts public education not only by attacking its effectiveness and legitimacy but by laying claim to its revenues. The money allocated to privately managed charters and vouchers represents a transfer of critical public resources to the private sector, causing the public schools to suffer budget cuts and loss of staffing and services as the private sector grows, without providing better education or better outcomes for the students who transfer to the private-sector schools.

Reformers in every era have used the schools as punching bags. In one era, progressives complained that the schools were obsolete, backward, mindless, rigid, and out of step with the demands of the modern age. Then, in their turn, came anti-progressives or "essentialists" who complained that the schools had grown soft, standards and curriculum had collapsed, and students were not learning as much as they once did.

At the beginning of the twentieth century, reformers lambasted the schools, saying they were too academic and ignored the economy's need for trained workers. In 1914, Congress passed the first federal legislation to encourage industrial and vocational education so that schools could prepare young people for jobs on the nation's farms and factories. In the 1930s, with millions of people out of work, reformers blamed the schools for their inability to keep students enrolled and out of the ranks of the unemployed. Reformers called on the schools to be more attentive to the needs of adolescents so as to entice them to stay in school longer. The New Deal created the Civilian Conservation Corps and the National Youth Administration to provide education and training for young people during the Depression.

In the 1940s, reformers complained that the schools were obsolete and were failing to give students the skills they needed for life and work; "life adjustment education" became the reformers' battle cry. In the 1950s, reformers said that the schools had forgotten the basics and

needed to raise academic standards and return to time-honored subject matter disciplines. In the 1960s, reformers said that the schools
were too academic and that students were stifled by routine and dreary
assignments; the reformers wanted more spontaneity, more freedom,
and fewer requirements for students. At the same time, the civil rights
movement achieved major gains, and the schools became the focus of
national legislation and Supreme Court rulings that required desegregation. In the late 1970s, a backlash against the reform ideas of the
1960s and early 1970s led to the rise of minimum competency testing
and, once again, a return to the basics. Despite the pendulum swings,
despite the critics and reform movements, the American public continued to be grateful for public education and to admire its community
schools.

Then came the 1980s, with a stern warning in 1983 from the National
Commission on Excellence in Education that we were "a nation at risk"
because of the low standards and low expectations in our schools. Our
national slippage was caused, said the commission, by "a rising tide of
mediocrity that threatens our very future as a Nation and a people."
This mediocre educational performance was nothing less than "an
act of unthinking, unilateral educational disarmament." The alarmist
rhetoric was excessive, but it was enough to generate media attention
and caused many states to raise their graduation requirements.

In response to the dire warnings in the 1983 report, standards, testing, and accountability became the national agenda for school reform.
Many policy makers agreed: set higher standards; test to see if students
have mastered them; hold back students or prevent them from graduating if they don't pass. There was no research to support these strategies,
but they were widely accepted anyway, as were proposals to reward
the schools that succeeded on state tests and penalize those that did
not. The first Bush administration embraced these ideas, as did the
Clinton administration. The second Bush administration made testing
and accountability the federal agenda with passage of its No Child Left
Behind legislation.

Somehow, in the midst of all this nonstop controversy and criticism,
the public schools continued teaching generations of students. And
somehow, despite the endless complaints and policy churn, the American economy continued to be the largest in the world. And somehow,
American culture continued to be a creative and vibrant force, reshap-

ing the cultures of other nations (for better or worse). Our democracy survived, and American technological innovations changed the way people live around the globe. Despite the alleged failures of the schools that educated the vast majority of them, American workers are among the most productive in the world.

After the publication of *A Nation at Risk,* public discourse about the nation's educational system settled on the unfounded belief that America's public schools were locked into an arc of decline. Report after report was issued by commissions, task forces, and study groups, purporting to document the "crisis" in American education, the "crisis" of student achievement, the "crisis" of high school dropouts, the "crisis" of bad teachers.

News magazines like *Time* and *Newsweek* published stories about the crisis, television networks ran specials about the crisis, editorialists opined about the causes of the crisis. The steady drumbeat of negative journalism had its effect: Public opinion about the quality of American public education dropped from 1973 to 2012. In 1973, 58 percent of Americans felt confident about the public schools, but by 2012 their approval rating had dropped to only 29 percent (which still was higher than public confidence in banks and big business, which stood at 21 percent, or Congress at 13 percent).[1]

In striking contrast, Americans whose children attended public schools continued to have a very high opinion of their own schools. In another Gallup poll in 2012, only 19 percent of the public gave an A or a B to the nation's public schools, but 77 percent of parents awarded high marks to their own public school, the one they knew best. Two-thirds of respondents said they read mostly "bad stories" in the media about public schools. So, the parents who had the most direct experience with the schools thought well of them, but the relentless negative coverage by the media very likely drove down the general public's estimation of American public education.[2]

More recently, the Bill & Melinda Gates Foundation dedicated its considerable energies to persuading the public and policy makers that the nation's public schools are failing. In 2005, Bill Gates told the nation's governors that the nation's high schools were "obsolete" and "broken." At that time, he wanted to redesign the American high school by making schools smaller, with the goal that every student would be prepared to enter college.[3] Three years later, his foundation abandoned its small-school initiative, having spent $2 billion to persuade districts to replace their comprehensive high schools with schools too small to offer a balanced curriculum. Despite this setback, Gates remained certain that the public school system was obsolete and broken. The solution, his foundation now believed, was to develop new evaluation systems that could identify ineffective teachers so that there would be an effective teacher in every classroom.

In 2012, Melinda Gates was interviewed on the *PBS NewsHour.* When the interviewer asked her what was "working and what can scale up," she responded:

If you look back a decade ago, when we started into this work, there wasn't even a conversation across the nation about the fact that our schools were broken, fundamentally broken. And I think that dialogue has changed. I think the American public has woken up to the fact now that schools are broken. We're not serving our kids well. They're not being educated for the—for technology society.[4]

The Gates Foundation and others financed a lavish, well-coordinated media campaign to spread the word about our broken public schools; its leading edge was a documentary film called *Waiting for "Superman."* The film, which included interviews with Michelle Rhee, Bill Gates, and the economist Eric Hanushek, among others, made the central points that public education was failing, that resources don't matter, and that the best ways to fix the national crisis of low test scores were to expand the number of privately managed charters, fire ineffective teachers, and weaken the unions that protected them. It was released in September 2010 with an unprecedented publicity campaign, funded in large part by the Gates Foundation, and was featured on the cover of *Time* magazine. The film was also the centerpiece of a week of programming on NBC, which the network called "Education Nation," as well as the subject of two programs on Oprah Winfrey's popular television show.

The film told the story of five children who were desperate to enroll in privately managed charter schools and whose hopes depended on winning the lottery to gain admission. Each child was adorable, and the viewers' emotions became engaged with their plights and their dreams of escaping from awful public schools (and in one case a Catholic school). The film painted public schools as failures whose teachers were self-centered, uncaring, and incompetent. The statistics in the film about poor educational performance were misleading and erroneous, as was its idyllic portrait of charter schools. Yet the producers and promoters of the film made sure it was viewed as widely as possible, giving free screenings throughout the country to parent groups, state legislatures, even to the national conference of the PTA.[5]

Waiting for "Superman" provided the charter school movement with a degree of public visibility it had never had. It also gave the movement a populist patina, making it seem that if you were concerned about the plight of poor inner-city children, you would certainly support the creation of many more charter schools. The film burnished the claim by charter advocates that they were involved in "the civil rights issue of our time," because they were leading the battle to provide more choice to poor and disadvantaged children trapped in low-performing public schools.

The film's narrative, as well as the larger public discussion, was directed away from the controversial issue of privatization to the ideologically appealing concept of choice. Reformers don't like to mention the word "privatization," although this is indeed the driving ideological force behind the movement. "Choice" remains the preferred word, since it suggests that parents should be seen as consumers with the ability to exercise their freedom to leave one school and select another. The new movement for privatization has enabled school choice to transcend its tarnished history as an escape route for southern whites who sought to avoid court-ordered desegregation in the 1950s and 1960s.

To advance the privatization agenda, it was necessary never to mention the *P* word and to keep repeating the *C* word. After all, the public had no reason to be enthusiastic about the takeover of one of its essential public institutions by private financiers and entrepreneurs. Privatization of libraries, hospitals, prisons, and other basic services had long been hailed by those on the political right, but how could one persuade entire communities to hand over their children and their public schools to private sector corporations, some of which hoped to turn a profit off their children, in order to reward their shareholders? The only way to accomplish this sleight of hand was to pursue a skillful public relations campaign that drummed in the message, over and over, that our public schools are failures, that these failures harm our children and threaten our nation's future prosperity. Repeat it often enough, and people would come to believe that any alternative would be better than the current system.

Once that message sank in, Americans would be ready for the antidote: eliminating the public schools they had long known and cherished as the centers of their communities.

The prestigious Council on Foreign Relations issued a report in 2012 intended to provoke fears that the public schools not only were failing but endangered the future survival of our nation. Joel I. Klein, former chancellor of the New York City public schools, and Condoleezza Rice, former secretary of state in the administration of President George W. Bush, were co-chairs of the task force that produced the report. The report warned that the nation's public schools were a very grave threat to national security. It recited doleful statistics showing that students in the United States were not leading the world on international assessments but scoring only in the middle (but not mentioning that this was the same complaint that had been expressed in *A Nation at Risk* thirty years earlier). It asserted that employers could not find qualified workers and that the schools were not preparing people to serve in the military, the intelligence service, or other jobs critical to national defense. On and on went the bill of indictment against the public schools.[6]

The task force offered three recommendations. One was that the states should adopt the Common Core standards in mathematics and reading, already endorsed by forty-six states. Since the Common Core standards have never been field-tested, no one knows whether they will raise test scores or cause the achievement gap among different racial, ethnic, and income groups to narrow or to widen. One study, by Tom Loveless of the Brookings Institution, predicted that the standards would have little or no effect on academic achievement; he noted that "from 2003 to 2009, states with terrific standards raised their National Assessment of Educational Progress scores by roughly the same margin as states with awful ones." Loveless reported that there was as much variation within states, even those with excellent standards, as between states.[7]

The task force's second recommendation was that the schools of the nation should have a "national security readiness audit" to see if they were doing their job in preparing students to meet the nation's economic and military needs. This seemed like a hollow attempt to revive

Cold War fears, given that there was no military adversary comparable to the Soviet Union. The report did not suggest what agency should conduct this audit, what it would cost, and what would happen to those schools that failed it.

The key recommendation of the task force, whose members included leading figures in the corporate reform movement, was that more school choice was needed, specifically the expansion of privately managed charter schools and vouchers.

If it were true that the nation faced a very grave security threat, this was not much of a call to arms to combat it, since most states had already adopted the Common Core standards and were increasing school choice in response to the Obama administration's Race to the Top program.

Perhaps the most curious development over the three decades from *A Nation at Risk* to the 2012 report of the Council on Foreign Relations was this: what was originally seen in 1983 as the agenda of the most libertarian Republicans—school choice—had now become the agenda of the establishment, both Republicans and Democrats. Though there was no new evidence to support this agenda and a growing body of evidence against it, the realignment of political forces on the right and the left presented the most serious challenge to the legitimacy and future of public education in our nation's history.

CHAPTER 5

The Facts About Test Scores

CLAIM *Test scores are falling, and the educational system is broken and obsolete.*

REALITY *Test scores are at their highest point ever recorded.*

Critics have complained for many years that American students are not learning as much as they used to or that academic performance is flat. But neither of these complaints is accurate.

We have only one authoritative measure of academic performance over time, and that is the National Assessment of Educational Progress, known as NAEP (pronounced "nape"). NAEP is part of the U.S. Department of Education. It has an independent governing board, called the National Assessment Governing Board. By statute, the governing board is bipartisan and consists of teachers, administrators, state legislators, governors, businesspeople, and members of the general public.

President Clinton appointed me to that board, and I served on it for seven years. I know that the questions asked on its examinations are challenging. I am willing to bet that most elected officials and journalists today would have a hard time scoring well on the NAEP tests administered across the nation to our students. Every time I hear elected officials or pundits complain about test scores, I want to ask them to take the same tests and publish their scores. I don't expect that any of them would accept the challenge.

Critics may find this hard to believe, but students in American public schools today are studying and mastering far more difficult topics in science and mathematics than their peers forty or fifty years ago. People who doubt this should review the textbooks in common use then and now or look at the tests then and now. If they are still in doubt, I invite them to go to the NAEP Web site and review the questions in math and science for eighth-grade students. The questions range from easy to very difficult. Surely an adult should be able to answer them all, right? You are likely to learn, if you try this experiment, that the difficulty and complexity of what is taught today far exceed anything the average student encountered in school decades ago.

NAEP is central to any discussion of whether American students and the public schools they attend are doing well or badly. It has measured reading and math and other subjects over time. It is administered to samples of students; no one knows who will take it, no one can prepare to take it, no one takes the whole test. There are no stakes attached to NAEP; no student ever gets a test score. NAEP reports the results of its assessments in two different ways.

- One is by scale scores, ranging from 0 to 500. Scale scores reflect what students know and can do. It is like a scale that tells you how much you weigh but offers no judgment about what you *should* weigh.
- The other is achievement levels, in which the highest level is "advanced," then "proficient," then "basic," and last "below basic." Achievement levels are judgments set by external panels that determine what students *should* know and be able to do.

To see how these two measures work, consider the reporting of scores for fourth-grade mathematics. If we were looking at the scale scores, we would learn that the scale score in the year 2000 was 226; by 2011, it was 241. The score is higher, but there is no qualitative judgment about what it ought to be. The maximum on the scale is 500, but there is no expectation that the nation will one day score 500 or that a score of 241 can be translated to mean $241/500$. It is not a grade of 48 percent. It is not a passing grade or a failing grade. It is a trend line, period.

If you take the same fourth-grade mathematics report and look at the achievement levels, you will learn that 65 percent scored at basic or above in 2000, and 82 percent were at basic or above in 2011. Unlike the scale score, which shows only the direction of the trend, the achievement levels represent a judgment about how well students are performing.

1. Trend in Fourth-Grade NAEP Mathematics Average Scores

Scale score

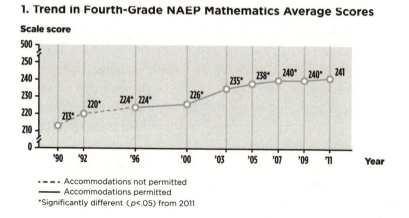

- - - - Accommodations not permitted
——— Accommodations permitted
*Significantly different (*p*<.05) from 2011

2. Trend in Fourth-Grade NAEP Mathematics Achievement-Level Results

Percent

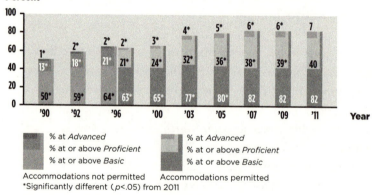

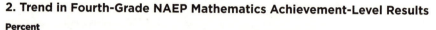

	% at *Advanced*			% at *Advanced*
	% at or above *Proficient*			% at or above *Proficient*
	% at or above *Basic*			% at or above *Basic*

Accommodations not permitted   Accommodations permitted
*Significantly different (*p*<.05) from 2011

The NAEP governing board authorized the establishment of achievement levels in the early 1990s with the hope that the public would have a better understanding of student performance, as compared with scale scores. Critics of the achievement levels complained at the time that the process was rushed and that the standards might be flawed and unreasonably high. But a member of the governing board, Chester E. Finn Jr., said it was necessary to move forward promptly and not to let the perfect become the "enemy of the good" for fear of sacrificing "the sense of urgency for national improvement."[1]

The critics were right. The achievement levels have not led to better understanding. Instead, the public is confused about what expectations are appropriate. The achievement levels present a bleak portrait of what students know and can do and, like No Child Left Behind, create the expectation that all students ought to be proficient.

All definitions of education standards are subjective. People who set standards use their own judgment to decide what students ought to know and how well they should know it. People use their own judgment to decide the passing mark on a test. None of this is science. It is human judgment, subject to error and bias; the passing mark may go up or down, and the decision about what students should know in which grades may change, depending on who is making the decisions and whether they want the test to be hard or easy or just right. All of these are judgmental decisions, not science.

Here are definitions of NAEP's achievement levels:

"Advanced" represents a superior level of academic performance. In most subjects and grades, only 3–8 percent of students reach that level. I think of it as A+. Very few students in any grade or subject score "advanced."

"Proficient" represents solid achievement. The National Assessment Governing Board (NAGB) defines it as "solid academic performance for each grade assessed. This is a very high level of academic achievement. Students reaching this level have demonstrated competency over challenging subject matter, including subject matter knowledge, application of such knowledge to real-world situations, and analytical skills appropriate to the subject matter." From what I observed as a member of the NAGB who reviewed questions and results over a seven-year period, a student who is "proficient" earns a solid A and not less than a strong B+.

"Basic," as defined by the NAGB, is "partial mastery of prerequisite knowledge and skills that are fundamental for proficient work at each grade." In my view, the student who scores "basic" is probably a B or C student.

"Below basic" connotes students who have a weak grasp of the knowledge and skills that are being assessed. This student, again in my understanding, would be a D or below.

The film *Waiting for "Superman"* misinterpreted the NAEP achievement levels. Davis Guggenheim, the film's director and narrator, used the NAEP achievement levels to argue that American students were woefully undereducated. The film claimed that 70 percent of eighth-grade students could not read at grade level. That would be dreadful if it were true, but it is not. NAEP does not report grade levels (grade level describes a midpoint on the grading scale where half are above and half are below). Guggenheim assumed that students who were not "proficient" on the NAEP were "below grade level." That is wrong. Actually, 76 percent on NAEP are basic or above, and 24 percent are below basic. It would be good to reduce the proportion who are "below basic," but it is 24 percent, not the 70 percent that Guggenheim claimed.[2]

Michelle Rhee, the former chancellor of the District of Columbia public schools, makes the same error in her promotional materials for her advocacy group called StudentsFirst. She created this organization after the mayor of Washington, D.C., was defeated and she resigned her post. StudentsFirst raised millions of dollars, which Rhee dedicated to a campaign to weaken teachers' unions, to eliminate teachers' due process rights, to promote charter schools and vouchers, and to fund candidates who agreed with her views. Her central assertion is that the nation's public schools are failing and in desperate shape. Her new organization claimed, "Every morning in America, as we send eager fourth graders off to school, ready to learn with their backpacks and lunch boxes, we are entrusting them to an education system that accepts the fact that only one in three of them can read at grade level." Like Guggenheim, she confuses "grade level" with "proficiency." The same page has a statement that is more accurate, saying, "Of all the 4th graders in the U.S., only ⅓ of them are able to read this page proficiently." That's closer to the NAEP definition, yet it is still a distortion, akin to saying it is disappointing that only ⅓ of the class earned an A. But to deepen the confusion, the clarifying statement is followed by "Let me repeat that. Only one in three U.S. fourth-graders can read at grade level. This is not okay." So, two out of three times, Rhee confuses "proficiency" (which is a solid A or B+ performance) with "grade level" (which means average performance).[3]

What are the facts? Two-thirds of American fourth graders were reading at or above basic in 2011; one-third were reading below basic. Thirty-four percent achieved "proficiency," which is solid academic performance, equivalent to an A. Three-quarters of American eighth graders were reading at or above basic in 2011; a quarter were reading below basic. Thirty-four percent achieved "proficiency," equivalent to a solid A. (See graph 5; graphs 5–41 appear in the appendix.)

Unfortunately, you can't generate a crisis atmosphere by telling the

American public that there are large numbers of students who don't earn an A. They know that. That is common sense. Ideally, no one would be "below basic," but that lowest rating includes children who are English-language learners and children with a range of disabilities that might affect their scores. Only in the dreams of policy makers and legislators is there a world where all students reach "proficiency" and score an A. If everyone scored an A or not less than a B+, the reformers would be complaining about rampant grade inflation—and they would be right.

In recent years, reformers complained that student achievement has been flat for the past twenty years. They make this claim to justify their demand for radical, unproven strategies like privatization. After all, if we have spent more and more and achievement has declined or barely moved for two decades, then surely the public educational system is "broken" and "obsolete," and we must be ready to try anything at all.

This is the foundational claim of the corporate reform movement.

But it is not true.

Let's look at the evidence.

NAEP has tested samples of students in the states and in the nation every other year since 1992 in reading and mathematics.

Here is what we know from NAEP data. There have been significant increases in both reading and mathematics, more in mathematics than in reading. The sharpest increases were registered in the years preceding the implementation of NCLB, from 2000 to 2003.[4]

Reading scores in fourth grade have improved slowly, steadily, and significantly since 1992 for almost every group of students. (See graph 6.)

- The scale scores in reading show a flat line, but this is misleading. Every group of students saw gains, but the overall line looks flat because of an increase in the proportion of low-scoring students. This is known to statisticians as Simpson's paradox.[5]
- The proportion of fourth-grade students who were proficient or advanced *increased* from 1992 to 2011. In 1992, 29 percent of students were proficient or above; in 2011, it was 34 percent.
- The proportion of fourth-grade students who were "below basic" *declined* from 38 percent in 1992 to 33 percent in 2011.
- The scores of white students, black students, Hispanic students, and Asian students in fourth grade were *higher* in 2011 than in 1992. The only group that saw a decline was American Indian

students.[6] (See graphs 7, 8, 9, and 10, which show rising scores for whites, blacks, Hispanics, Asians, but not for American Indians.)

Reading scores in eighth grade have improved slowly, steadily, and significantly since 1992 for every group of students.

- The proportion of eighth-grade students who were proficient or advanced *increased* from 1992 to 2011. In 1992, 29 percent of students were proficient or above; in 2011, it was 34 percent. (See graph 11.)
- The proportion of eighth-grade students who were "below basic" *declined* from 31 percent in 1992 to 24 percent in 2011.
- The scores of white students, black students, Hispanic students, Asian students, and American Indian students in eighth grade were *higher* in 2011 than in 1992. (See graphs 12, 13, 14, and 15.)

Don't believe anyone who claims that reading has not improved over the past twenty years. It isn't true. NAEP is the only gauge of change over time, and it shows slow, steady, and significant increases. Students of all racial and ethnic groups are reading better now than they were in 1992. And that's a fact.

Mathematics scores in fourth grade have improved dramatically from 1992 to 2011.

- The proportion of fourth-grade students who were proficient or advanced *increased* from 1990 to 2011. In 1990, 13 percent of students were proficient or above; in 2011, it was 40 percent. (See graph 2.)
- The proportion of fourth-grade students who were "below basic" *declined* from 50 percent in 1990 to an astonishingly low 18 percent in 2011.
- The scores of white students, black students, Hispanic students, Asian students, and American Indian students in fourth grade were *higher* in 2011 than in 1992. (See graphs 16, 17, 18, 19, and 20.)

Mathematics scores in eighth grade have improved dramatically from 1992 to 2011. (See graph 21.)

- The proportion of eighth-grade students who were proficient or advanced *increased* from 1990 to 2011. In 1990, 15 percent were proficient or above; in 2011, it was 35 percent. (See graph 22.)
- The proportion of eighth-grade students who were "below basic" *declined* from 48 percent in 1990 to 27 percent in 2011. (See graph 22.)
- The scores of white students, black students, Hispanic students, Asian students, and American Indian students in eighth grade were *higher* in 2011 than in 1992. (See graphs 23, 24, 25, 26, and 27.)

As it happens, there is another version of NAEP that the federal government has administered since the early 1970s. The one I described before is known as the "main NAEP." It tests students in grades 4 and 8; scores on the main NAEP reach back to 1990 or 1992, depending on the subject. It is periodically revised and updated.

The alternative form of NAEP is called the "long-term trend assessment." It dates back to the early 1970s and tests students who are ages nine, thirteen, and seventeen (which roughly corresponds to grades 4, 8, and 12). The long-term trend NAEP contains large numbers of questions that have been used consistently for more than forty years. Unlike the main NAEP, the content of the long-term trend NAEP seldom changes, other than to remove obsolete terms like "S&H Green Stamps." The long-term trend NAEP is administered to scientific samples of students every four years.

Both the main NAEP and the long-term trend NAEP show steady increases in reading and mathematics. Neither shows declines. The long-term tests hardly ever change, so they provide a consistent yardstick over the past four decades.

Here are the changes in the long-term trend data in mathematics, from 1973 to 2008:[7]

3. Mathematics: Changes from 1973 to 2008

AGE GROUP	WHITE	BLACK	HISPANIC
Age 9	⬆ 25 points	⬆ 34 points	⬆ 32 points
Age 13	⬆ 16 points	⬆ 34 points	⬆ 29 points
Age 17	⬆ 4 points	⬆ 17 points	⬆ 16 points

The overall score does not reflect the large gains that were made over the past four decades, again because of Simpson's paradox. Each of the four major groups of students saw significant gains. (See graphs 28 and 29).

White students over the past forty years show impressive gains: age nine, up 25 points; age thirteen, up 16 points; age seventeen, up 4 points.

Black students over the past forty years show remarkable gains: age nine, up 34 points; age thirteen, up 34 points; age seventeen, up 17 points.

Hispanic students also show remarkable gains: age nine, up 32 points; age thirteen, up 29 points; age seventeen, up 16 points.

On the main NAEP, from 1990 to 2011, here are the data for mathematics:

White students: fourth grade, up 29 points; eighth grade, up 23
    points. (See graphs 16 and 23.)
Black students: fourth grade, up 36 points; eighth grade, up 25
    points. (See graphs 16 and 23.)
Hispanic students: fourth grade, up 29 points; eighth grade, up 24
    points. (See graphs 17 and 24.)
Asian students: fourth grade, up 31 points; eighth grade, up 28
    points. (See graphs 18 and 25.)

In reading, the changes are less dramatic, but they are steady and significant.

On the long-term trend assessments, these were the changes in reading from 1971 to 2008:

4. Reading: Changes from 1973 to 2008

AGE GROUP	WHITE	BLACK	HISPANIC
Age 9	↑ 14 points	↑ 34 points	↑ 25 points
Age 13	↑ 7 points	↑ 25 points	↑ 10 points
Age 17	↑ 4 points	↑ 28 points	↑ 17 points

White students: age nine, up 14 points; age thirteen, up 7 points; age
    seventeen, up 4 points.

Black students: age nine, up 34 points; age thirteen, up 25 points; age seventeen, up 28 points.

Hispanic students: age nine, up 25 points; age thirteen, up 10 points; age seventeen, up 17 points.

Compare this with gains on the main NAEP reading from 1992 to 2011:

White students: fourth grade, up 7 points; eighth grade, up 7 points. (See graphs 7 and 12.)

Black students: fourth grade, up 13 points; eighth grade, up 12 points. (See graphs 7 and 12.)

Hispanic students: fourth grade, up 9 points; eighth grade, up 11 points. (See graphs 8 and 13.)

Asian students: fourth grade, up 19 points; eighth grade, up 7 points. (See graphs 9 and 14.)

NAEP data show beyond question that test scores in reading and math have improved for almost every group of students over the past two decades: slowly and steadily in the case of reading, dramatically in the case of mathematics. Students know more and can do more in these two basic skills subjects now than they could twenty or forty years ago.

Why the difference between the two subjects? Reading is influenced to a larger extent by differences in home conditions than mathematics. Put another way, students learn language and vocabulary at home and in school; they learn mathematics in school. Students can improve their vocabulary and background knowledge by reading literature and history at school, but their starting point in reading is influenced more by home and family than in mathematics.

So the next time you hear someone say that the system is "broken," that American students aren't as well educated as they used to be, that our schools are failing, tell that person the facts. Test scores are rising. Of course, test scores are not the only way to measure education, but to the extent that they matter, they are improving. Our students have higher test scores in reading and mathematics than they did in the early 1970s or the early 1990s. Of course, we can do better. Students should be writing more and reading more and doing more science projects and more historical research papers and should have more opportunities to engage in the arts.

But let's recognize the progress that our educators and students have made, give credit where credit is due, and offer educators the encouragement and support to continue their important work.

CHAPTER 6

The Facts About the Achievement Gap

CLAIM *The achievement gaps are large and getting worse.*

REALITY *We have made genuine progress in narrowing the achievement gaps, but they will remain large if we do nothing about the causes of the gaps.*

One of the persistent claims of the corporate reform movement is that the reformers are leading the "civil rights issue of our time." Reformers point to the disparity between the test scores of white students and students of color as proof that the public schools are failing and that black and Hispanic students must be liberated from public schools to attend privately managed charter schools or to use vouchers to enroll in private and religious schools.

It defies reason to believe that Martin Luther King Jr. would march arm in arm with Wall Street hedge fund managers and members of ALEC to lead a struggle for the privatization of public education, the crippling of unions, and the establishment of for-profit schools. Privatization inevitably means deregulation, greater segregation, and less equity, with minimal oversight by public authorities. Privatization has typically not been a friend to powerless groups.

Reformers make the case for privatization by insisting that black and Hispanic students are failing in the public schools and that they must be "saved."

Reformers often say that African American and Hispanic students have made no progress for decades. But this is not true. The scores of black students in fourth-grade math increased dramatically in the two decades after 1990, when the federal tests were first offered; black student achievement was higher in 2009 than white student achievement in 1990. In addition, over this past generation there has been a remarkable decline in the proportion of African American and Hispanic students who register "below basic," the lowest possible academic rating on the NAEP tests.

If white achievement had stood still, the achievement gap would be closed by now, but of course white achievement has also improved, so the gap remains large.

In mathematics, over the past two decades, all students made dramatic progress. In 1990, 83 percent of black students in fourth grade scored "below basic," but that number fell to 34 percent in 2011. In eighth grade, 78 percent of black students were below basic in 1990, but by 2011 the proportion had dropped to 49 percent. Among Hispanic students, the proportion below basic in fourth grade fell from 67 percent to 28 percent; in eighth grade, that proportion declined from 66 percent to 39 percent. Among white students in fourth grade, the proportion below basic dropped in that time period from 41 percent to only 9 percent; in eighth grade, it declined from 40 percent to 16 percent. The proportion of fourth-grade Asian students below basic dropped from 38 percent in 1990 to 9 percent in 2011; in eighth grade, Asian students who were below basic declined from 36 percent to 14 percent. (See graphs 20 and 27.)

This is truly remarkable progress.

The changes in reading scores were not as dramatic as in math, but they nonetheless are impressive. In fourth-grade reading, the proportion of black students who were below basic in 1992 was 68 percent; by 2011, it was down to 51 percent. In eighth grade, the proportion of black students who were reading below basic was 55 percent; that had declined to 41 percent by 2011. Among fourth-grade white students, the proportion below basic declined from 29 percent to 22 percent in the same twenty-year period. Among fourth-grade Hispanic students, the proportion reading below basic dropped from 62 percent to 49 percent. Among eighth-grade Hispanic students, the proportion reading below basic declined from 51 percent to 36 percent. Among fourth-grade Asian students, the proportion below basic fell from 40 percent to 20 percent. In the eighth grade, it declined from 24 percent to 17 percent. (See graphs 30 and 31 for all racial, ethnic groups.)

Clearly, performance on NAEP is not flat. The gains in reading have been slow, steady, and significant. The gains in mathematics in both tested grades have been remarkable for whites, blacks, Hispanics, and Asians.

Despite these increases, the achievement gaps remain between white and black students and between white and Hispanic students because all groups are improving their scores. Asian students perform as well as white students in reading and better than white students in math. Reformers ignore these gains and castigate the public schools for the persistence of the gap.

Closing the racial achievement gap has been a major policy goal of education policy makers for at least the past decade. There has been some progress, but it has been slow and uneven. This is not surprising: it is hard to narrow or close the gap if all groups are improving.

There is nothing new about achievement gaps between different racial and ethnic groups and between children from families at different ends of the income distribution. Such gaps exist wherever there is inequality, not only in this country, but internationally. In every country, the students from the most advantaged families have higher test scores on average than students from the least advantaged families.[1]

One of the major reasons for the passage of the No Child Left Behind law was the expectation that it would narrow, perhaps even close, the black-white and also the Hispanic-white achievement gaps. Policy makers and legislators believed in 2001, when NCLB was debated, that testing and accountability would suffice to close the gaps. Lawmakers believed that the combination of test-based accountability and transparency would produce the desired results.

The very act of publishing the disparate results, they expected, would compel teachers to spend more time teaching the students who had low scores, especially if there were punitive consequences for not raising those scores. President George W. Bush staked his claim to being a "compassionate conservative" because, as he put it, he opposed "the soft bigotry of low expectations." If teachers were required by law to have high expectations for all students, the theory went, then all students would learn and meet high standards.

Now we know that, despite some gains, NCLB did not close the gaps. Paul Barton and Richard Coley of the Educational Testing Service wrote an overview of the black-white achievement gap over the course of the twentieth century and concluded that the period in which that gap narrowed most was the 1970s and 1980s, in response to such things as desegregation, class size reduction, early childhood education, the addition of federal resources to schools enrolling poor children, and wider economic opportunities for black families. From that time forward, the gap has wavered up and down without resuming the sharp narrowing of the earlier period.[2]

What was impressive about the 1970s and 1980s was that black students gained so much more ground than white students. In the years since then, both white and black students improved their test scores, which made it hard to narrow the gap. So, for example, the black-white gap in fourth-grade reading was 30 points in 2002, but narrowed to 25 by 2011. White student scores increased by 2 points, while black scores increased by 6 points. The gap narrowed by a few points. It is still a sizable gap of 25 points, but there was improvement, not stasis or decline.[3] (See graph 7; also graph 40.)

In mathematics, where both white and black students made large test score gains, the gap in fourth grade narrowed from 31 points in 2000 to 25 points in 2011. That's a narrowing of 6 points. Two-thirds of that improvement occurred before the implementation of No Child Left Behind. The scores of black students rose from 203 on the NAEP scale to 224. At the same time, the scores of white students increased from 234 to 249, and two-thirds of that gain happened before the implementation of NCLB. Both groups recorded strong gains.[4] (See graph 16.)

The black-white achievement gap has existed as long as records have been kept. The source of the gap is no secret. African Americans have been subject to a long history of social and economic oppression and disadvantage; they have experienced higher levels of poverty and lower levels of education than white Americans. After the *Brown* decision of 1954, the federal government and many states adopted policies to redress past inequities, but those policies were insufficient to overcome generations of racism, which limited access to jobs and education. Despite significant progress in expanding educational access, educational attainment, and economic opportunities for black citizens in the past half century, blacks continue to be disproportionately poor, to attend racially segregated schools, to experience high rates of incarceration, and to live in racially isolated communities where children are likely to be exposed to violence, gangs, and drug use.

Today's reformers often imply that schools alone can close the achievement gaps among different groups. They like to point to exemplary charter schools with high test scores to prove their point. They say that teachers with high expectations can close the achievement gap. To date, no charter operator has taken responsibility for an entire school district and demonstrated that his or her pedagogical methods were powerful enough to overcome the disadvantages of poverty.

The impressive academic gains of the past two decades demonstrate that schools can significantly reduce the proportion of students who are poorly educated in reading and math. This is hugely important for students and for our society. But most people who study the achievement gap recognize that it cannot be sharply narrowed or closed without addressing the social and economic conditions that cause systemic disadvantages.

Achievement gaps begin long before children start kindergarten. On the first day of school, some children have had better medical care than others; are better nourished than others; are likelier to have a larger vocabulary because of having a parent who is college educated; are likelier to have books and computers in the home; and are likelier to live in sound housing in a safe neighborhood. The children at the wrong end of the gap are likelier to attend schools in overcrowded classrooms with inadequate resources and inexperienced teachers, as compared with the children at the advantaged end of the gap, whose schools are likelier to have small classes, experienced teachers, a full curriculum, laptops, libraries, playing fields, and a full staff. Schools that have large numbers of inexperienced teachers and inadequate resources are ill-prepared to reduce the achievement gap. If we were serious about narrowing the gap, the schools attended by African American and Hispanic children would have a stable, experienced staff, a rich curriculum, social services, after-school programs, and abundant resources to meet the needs of their students.

The black-white achievement gap is now smaller than the achievement gap between the poorest and the most affluent students, according to the sociologist Sean Reardon of Stanford University.

Strikingly, he found that "the achievement gap between children from high- and low-income families is roughly 30 to 40 percent larger among children born in 2001 than among those born twenty-five years earlier. In fact, it appears that the income achievement gap has been growing for at least fifty years, though the data are less certain for cohorts of children born before 1970." In contrast to the racial achieve-

ment gap, which has narrowed, the income achievement gap is growing. In fact, he found that the income achievement gap was nearly
twice as large as the black-white achievement gap; the reverse was true
fifty years earlier. The income achievement gap is already large when
children start school, and according to the work of other researchers it
"does not appear to grow (or narrow) appreciably as children progress
through school." Reardon suggests that the income-based gap is growing in part because affluent families invest in their children's cognitive development, with tutoring, summer camp, computers, and other
enriching experiences. He concludes that "family income is now nearly
as strong as parental education in predicting children's achievement."[5]

Thomas B. Timar of the University of California reviewed the efforts to close the black-white achievement gap and the Hispanic-white
achievement gap and concluded that while there had been progress, the
overall situation was discouraging. Why was there so little progress? He
wrote: "One reason is that although schools can be held accountable for
some of the disadvantage these students experience, *they have been given
the entire responsibility for closing the achievement gap* [emphasis mine].
Yet the gap is the symptom of larger social, economic and political
problems that go far beyond the reach of the school . . . While schools
are part of the solution, they alone cannot solve the problem of educational disparities."[6]

Another reason for the persistence of the gaps, Timar writes, is that
policy makers have invested in strategies for thirty years that are "misdirected and ineffectual," managing to keep urban schools in a state of
"policy spin," bouncing from one idea to another but never attaining
the learning conditions or social capital that might make a difference.

Schools can't solve the problem alone, Timar acknowledges, as long
as society ignores the high levels of poverty and racial isolation in which
many of these youngsters live. He writes of children growing up in
neighborhoods that experience high rates of crime and incarceration,
violence, and stress-related disorders. In the current version of reform,
fixing schools means more legislation, more mandates, and more regulations. What is missing from reform, he says, is an appreciation for the
value of local and regional efforts, the small-scale programs that rely
on local initiative for implementation. Without local initiative, reforms
cannot succeed.

Of great importance in creating lasting change is social capital,
Timar notes. This is the capital that grows because of relationships

within the school and between the school and the community. Social capital is a necessary ingredient of reform, and it is built on a sense of community, organizational stability, and trust. Successful schools in distressed communities have stable leadership and a shared vision for change. They have "a sense of purpose, a coherent plan, and individuals with responsibility to coordinate and implement the plan. Teachers worked collaboratively to improve teaching and learning across the entire school curriculum . . . School improvement wasn't something done to them (like some sort of medical procedure), but a collaborative undertaking. Students also realized that the school's engagement in school improvement activities was meant for them, for their benefit."[7]

If we are serious about significantly narrowing the achievement gaps between black and white students, Hispanic and white students, and poor and affluent students, then we need to think in terms of long-term, comprehensive strategies. Those strategies must address the problems of poverty, unemployment, racial isolation, and mass incarceration. Income inequality in the United States, he points out, cannot be ignored, since it is greater now than at any time since the 1920s and more extreme than in any other advanced nation. But American politics has grown so politically conservative and unwilling to address structural issues that the chances of this happening are slim.

So we are left with the short-term strategies. Timar says that the strategies of "bureaucratizing the process of school improvement and turning it into a chase for higher test scores" have not worked. They have not made schools more stable, more coherent, and more professional. NCLB plus the Obama administration's Race to the Top have made schools less stable, encouraged staff turnover, promoted policy churn, and undermined professionalism.

Timar believes that the best hope for a school-based strategy for reducing the gaps lies in a grassroots model of change. He points to approaches like the Comer Process, developed by Dr. James Comer of Yale University, which engages the school community in meeting the emotional, psychological, social, and academic needs of students. What works best is not regulation and mandates but professional collaboration, community building, and cooperation. Such a scenario can happen only when those in the school have the authority to design their own improvement plans and act without waiting for instructions or permission from Washington or the state capital.

What we know from these scholars makes sense. The achievement gaps are rooted in social, political, and economic structures. If we are unwilling to change the root causes, we are unlikely ever to close the gaps. What we call achievement gaps are in fact opportunity gaps.

Our corporate reformers insist that we must "fix" schools first, not poverty. But the weight of evidence is against them. No serious social scientist believes that rearranging the organization or control or curriculum of schools will suffice to create income equality or to end poverty. The schools did not cause the achievement gaps, and the schools alone are not powerful enough to close them. So long as our society is indifferent to poverty, so long as we are willing to look the other way rather than act vigorously to improve the conditions of families and communities, there will always be achievement gaps.

CHAPTER 7

The Facts About the International Test Scores

CLAIM *We are falling behind other nations, putting our economy and our national security at risk.*

REALITY *An old lament, not true then, not true now.*

Critics say that the nation is more at risk than ever because American students are getting mediocre scores on international tests and falling behind other nations. If we don't have top scores soon, our nation will suffer grievously, our national security will falter, our economy will founder, and our future will be in jeopardy.

By now, this is a timeworn bugbear, but it still works, so the critics continue to employ it to alarm the public. In 1957, critics blamed the public schools when the Soviets were first to launch a space satellite, even though this feat was the work of a tiny scientific and technological elite. In 1983, critics blamed the public schools for the success of the Japanese automobile industry (overlooking the lack of foresight by leaders of the American automobile industry) and said the nation was "at risk." In 2012, critics asserted that the nation's public schools are "a very grave national security crisis," even though the nation has no significant international enemies.[1]

Today, critics use data from international assessments to generate a crisis mentality, not to improve public schools but to undermine public confidence in them. To the extent that they accomplish this, the public will be more tolerant of efforts to dismantle public education and divert public funding to privately managed schools and for-profit vendors of instruction.

In 2010, the release of the international assessments called PISA (Program for International Student Assessment) provided a new occasion for lamenting the mediocre performance of American students. Sixty countries, including thirty-four members of the OECD (Organization for Economic Cooperation and Development), participated in the international assessment of fifteen-year-olds in reading, mathematics, and science. Students in Shanghai ranked first in all three subjects (Shanghai is not representative of China, which did not participate in the assessments). Of the OECD nations, the United States ranked fourteenth in reading, seventeenth in science, and twenty-fifth in mathematics (these rankings are overstated because the United States was in a statistical tie with several other nations on each test).

The media, elected officials, and think tank pundits reacted with shock and alarm. President Obama said it was "our generation's Sputnik moment" and warned that we were losing ground to economic competitors in India and China (neither of which participated in the international tests). Secretary of Education Arne Duncan said the results were "a wake-up call" to the nation.[2] Editorialists were alarmed that Shanghai had scored at the top, which seemed to symbolize a new era of Chinese supremacy. The front-page story in *The New York Times* carried the headline "Top Test Scores from Shanghai Stun Educators." The Chinese-born educator Yong Zhao, now a professor at the University of Oregon, cautioned Americans that China had long ago perfected the art of test taking, and Chinese parents were not happy with this practice, but his voice did not reach as many people as did the major media.[3]

Examined closely, the scores reveal two salient points.

First, the scores of American fifteen-year-olds had not declined. In reading and mathematics, the U.S. scores were not measurably different from earlier PISA assessments in 2000, 2003, and 2006. In science, U.S. students improved their scores over an earlier assessment in 2006.[4]

Second, American students in schools with low poverty—the schools where less than 10 percent of the students were poor—had scores that were equal to those of Shanghai and significantly better than those of high-scoring Finland, the Republic of Korea, Canada, New Zealand, Japan, and Australia. In U.S. schools where less than a quarter of the students were eligible for free or reduced-price lunch (the federal definition of poverty), the reading scores were similar to those of students in high-performing nations. Technically, the comparison is not valid, because it involves comparing students in low-poverty schools in the United States with the average score for entire nations. But it is important to recognize that the scores of students in low-poverty schools in the United States are far higher than the international average, higher even than the average for top-performing nations, and the scores decline as poverty levels increase, as they do in all nations. Two scholars, Martin Carnoy and Richard Rothstein, asserted that the international testing agency had made a sampling error, assuming far higher levels of poverty in American schools than was the case; when the scores were readjusted appropriately, they argued, the United States was actually fourth in the world in reading and tenth in the world in mathematics.[5]

But what do these international scores really mean? Do they predict the economic future? Do average scores mean that our nation is trapped in a cycle of decline? Will top-scoring nations rule the world in twenty years?

Fact: American students have never scored especially well on international assessments.

The first such assessment, called the First International Mathematics Study, was offered in the mid-1960s. It tested thirteen-year-olds and seniors in twelve countries. American thirteen-year-olds scored significantly lower than students in nine other educational systems and ahead of only one. On the test given only to seniors enrolled in a mathematics course, U.S. students scored last. On the test given to seniors not enrolled in a mathematics course, U.S. students also scored last. In brief, our scores were dreadful.[6]

The First International Science Study was administered in the late 1960s and early 1970s to ten-year-olds from sixteen educational systems, to fourteen-year-olds, and to students in the last year of secondary school from eighteen educational systems. Among the youngest group, only Japanese students scored higher than those in the United States. Among fourteen-year-olds, five systems scored higher than the United States, and three were lower. Among students in their last year of high school, Americans scored last.[7]

When mathematics was tested again in the early 1980s, American thirteen-year-olds tested at or near the median. American seniors placed at or near the bottom on most subjects, and the scores of our top students in algebra (the top 1 percent) were lower than those of the same group in every other country. Science was tested again in the mid-1980s, and U.S. students did not excel: ten-year-olds scored at the median, fourteen-year-olds were in the bottom quarter, and seniors scored at or near the bottom in biology, chemistry, and physics.[8]

Why have American students scored poorly over the years on international tests? No one can say for certain, but I recall that when I worked in the U.S. Department of Education in the early 1990s, we were briefed on the latest dismal results. The representative from the testing agency described how Korean students in eighth grade were excited about doing well on the test, on behalf of their nation, while American students didn't seem to care about the tests because they knew their scores didn't "count," didn't matter, wouldn't affect their grades or their chances of getting into college. Later, when I was a member of the National Assessment Governing Board, we held discussions about the problem of motivating high school seniors; they didn't take the NAEP seriously, because they knew it had no stakes for them. Some doodled on the exam; some made patterns on their answer sheet.

Given the current emphasis on testing and the ongoing pressure to raise scores, students have learned to pay more attention to tests, even when they don't count toward grades or graduation.

In 2012, the results of the TIMSS (Trends in International Mathematics and Science Study), the major international assessments of mathematics and science, were released. American students have participated in TIMSS since 1995. The major American media presented the 2012 results in a negative light, reflecting the reformers' gloomy narrative. The headline in *The New York Times* read, "U.S. Students Still Lag Globally in Math and Science, Tests Show." *The Washington Post* ran the headline "U.S. Students Continue to Trail Asian Students in Math, Reading, Science."[9]

But the media were wrong. American students performed surprisingly well in mathematics and science, well above the international average in both subjects in grades 4 and 8. Two American states (Florida and North Carolina) volunteered to take the TIMSS tests in fourth grade, and another seven states took the tests in eighth grade, to gauge how they were doing by international standards.[10]

In fourth-grade mathematics, U.S. students outperformed most of the fifty-seven educational systems that participated. American students were tied with their peers in Finland, Denmark, the Netherlands,

England, and Russia. South Korea, Singapore, and Japan were the only nations that outperformed fourth-grade students in the United States (as did certain regions, like Hong Kong and Chinese Taipei). American students outperformed their peers in such nations as Germany, Norway, Hungary, Australia, and New Zealand. North Carolina ranked as one of the top-performing entities in the world.

In eighth-grade mathematics, U.S. students also did very well. They were tied with their peers in Israel, Finland, Australia, Hungary, Slovenia, Lithuania, and England. The only nations that outperformed the United States were Singapore, Japan, South Korea, and Russia (along with the two Chinese regions noted above). Students in four American states that offered to take the tests ranked among the world's highest-performing entities: Massachusetts, Minnesota, Indiana, and North Carolina. Black students in Massachusetts received the same scores as students in Israel and Finland. Imagine that! It should have been a front-page story across the nation, but it was not.

In fourth-grade science, American students ranked in the top ten systems of the fifty-seven that took the test. Only South Korea, Japan, Finland, Russia, and Singapore ranked higher (along with Chinese Taipei).

In eighth-grade science, American students were outperformed by only six nations (Singapore, Japan, South Korea, Russia, Finland, and Slovenia, along with Hong Kong and Chinese Taipei) and tied with those in England, Hungary, Israel, and Australia. The states of Massachusetts, Minnesota, and Colorado, which volunteered to participate in TIMSS, ranked among the top-performing nations in the world. Massachusetts, had it been an independent nation, would have been ranked second in the world, behind Singapore.

Four dozen nations participated in the latest international reading assessment called PIRLS (Progress in International Reading Literacy Study). Fourth-grade students in the United States were among the top performers in the world, ranked behind only Hong Kong, Russia, Finland, and Singapore. The only U.S. state to participate, Florida, scored behind Hong Kong; if it were a nation, Florida would have been tied for second in the world with Russia, Finland, and Singapore.[11]

So, contrary to the loud complaints of the reform chorus, American students are doing quite well in comparison to those of other advanced nations. Are the test scores of American students falling? No. Between

1995 and 2011, the mathematics scores of our students in fourth grade and eighth grade increased significantly. In science, the scores did not fall; they were about the same in both years. In reading, the scores increased from 2001 to 2011.[12]

Although the media did not report the improvement, some reformers may recover from the shock of seeing American students performing well on international assessments by claiming credit. See, they might say, all that testing has raised our standing on the international tests. Perhaps the constant drilling in reading and mathematics did have some effect on test performance—as Yong Zhao points out, Chinese educators long ago perfected the art of test taking—but it would be ludicrous to give credit to the reformers' other strategies. The number of students enrolled in charters and holding vouchers (perhaps 4 percent of American students) was too small to matter, and test-based evaluation of teachers was too new to affect student performance on tests taken in 2011. To what must certainly be the chagrin of our reformers, American public schools produced these strong results.

What we can say with reasonable assurance is that American students have never been number one on the international assessments and—over the past half century—more typically scored either about average or even in the bottom quartile. It should thus be a source of satisfaction that in the latest international assessments of mathematics, science, and reading American students performed very well, and their performance is not declining.

But what do these tests mean, and do they matter?

Recall that *A Nation at Risk* warned that if we didn't change course, our nation was in deep trouble. We stood to lose our global leadership, our economy, and even our identity as a people. A very stern warning. But thirty years after that warning was issued, the American economy was the largest in the world, and the nation did not seem to be in danger of losing its identity or its standing in the world. How could this be?

Some of our policy makers look longingly at the test scores of Singapore, Japan, and South Korea even as those nations look to us and try to figure out how to make their schools more attentive to creativity and inquiry-based learning. Others look to Finland as a model, ignoring the fact that educators in Finland do not share our national obsession with testing. Finnish educators profess not to care about their standing on the international tests, other than to note that doing well protects their schools from demands for testing and accountability. Unlike us, the Finns place a high premium on creativity, the arts, and problem solving and still manage to do well on international tests, without subjecting their students to a steady diet of standardized testing.

Yong Zhao sees the decentralization and absence of standardization in American education as one of its strengths. He writes, "American education has many problems, but to paraphrase Sir Winston Churchill, it is the worst form of education except for all others that have been tried. The decentralized system with local governance is a fundamentally sound framework that has evolved within the American context, that has led to America's economic prosperity and scientific preeminence so far, and that is being studied and copied by others." He worries that in our eagerness to copy nations with higher test scores, we may sacrifice the qualities of individualism and creativity that have been the source of our nation's economic, social, and technological success.[13]

Yong Zhao writes that China wants to transform itself from "a labor-intensive, low-level manufacturing economy into an innovation-driven knowledge society." Innovative people, he says, create an innovation-driven society. "Innovative people cannot come from schools that force students to memorize correct answers on standardized tests or reward students who excel at regurgitating spoon-fed knowledge." He asks the obvious questions: "If China, a developing country aspiring to move into an innovative society, has been working to emulate U.S. education, why does America want to abandon it?" Why would Americans "allow the government to dictate what their children should learn, when they should learn it, and how they are evaluated"? Continuing to pursue this course of action, he warns, can do serious damage to American education because it demoralizes educators and at the same time "denies the real cause of education inequality—poverty, funding gaps, and psychological damages caused by racial discrimination—by placing all responsibilities on schools and teachers."[14]

The Chinese public "seems eager to embrace what is viewed as a more liberal and creative system." Zhao quotes a Chinese journalist who was a visiting scholar in Arizona in the 1990s. The journalist admired American education because it had "no uniform textbooks, no standardized tests, no ranking of students, this is American education." The journalist's ten-year-old son attended an American school, and the father was impressed:

American classrooms don't impart a massive amount of knowledge into their children, but they try every way to draw children's eyes to the boundless ocean of knowledge outside the school; they do not force their children to memorize all the formulae and theorems, but they work tirelessly to teach children how to think and ways to seek answers to new questions; they never rank students according to test scores, but they try every way to affirm children's efforts, praise their thoughts, and protect and encourage children's desire and effort.[15]

Zhao observed that "what the Chinese found valuable in American education is the result of a decentralized, autonomous system that does not have standards, uses multiple criteria for judging the value of talents, and celebrates individual differences."

Vivek Wadhwa, an Indian American technology entrepreneur and academic, challenged the popular perception that U.S. schools are failing and that we are doing poorly in comparison to those in China and India. It is true, he said, that the schools of those nations are "fiercely competitive," and that children spend most of their childhood "memorizing books on advanced subjects." This kind of education has been a hindrance, he wrote, and that is why so many engineers trained in their schools and universities must spend two or three years unlearning the habits instilled by years of rote memorization. By contrast, American students learn independence and social skills. "They learn to experiment, challenge norms, and take risks. They can think for themselves, and they can innovate. This is why America remains the world leader in innovation."[16]

The attitudes and skills that Wadhwa admires are the very ones that are sacrificed by the intensive focus on standardized testing that has been foisted on American schools by federal policies like No Child Left Behind and Race to the Top.

Keith Baker, who worked for many years as an analyst at the U.S. Department of Education, asked, "Are international tests worth anything?" Do they predict the future of a nation's economy? He reviewed the evidence and concluded that for the United States and about a dozen of the world's most advanced nations, "standings in the league tables of international tests are worthless. There is no association between test scores and national success, and, contrary to one of the major beliefs driving U.S. education policy for nearly half a century, international test scores are nothing to be concerned about. America's schools are doing just fine on the world scene."[17]

Baker argued that the purveyors of doom and gloom were committing the "ecological correlation fallacy." It is a fallacy to generalize that what is good for an individual (a higher test score, for example) must be right for the nation as a whole. Maybe it is, maybe it isn't, he said, but evidence, not just an assumption, is required to make the case. To test the predictive value of the international assessments, he used the results of the First International Mathematics Study, given in 1964 to thirteen-year-olds in twelve nations. Students in the United States placed next to last, ahead of Sweden.

Baker looked at per capita gross domestic product of the nations whose students competed in 1964. He found that "the higher a nation's test score 40 years ago, the worse its economic performance on this measure of national wealth—the opposite of what the Chicken Littles raising the alarm over the poor test scores of U.S. children claimed would happen." The rate of economic growth improved, he held, as test scores dropped. There was no relationship between a nation's productivity and its test scores. Nor did high test scores bear any relationship to quality of life or livability, and the lower-scoring nations in the assessment were more successful at achieving democracy than those with higher scores.

But what about creativity? On this measure, the United States "clobbered the world," wrote Baker, with more patents per million people than any other nation. A certain level of educational achievement may be considered "a platform for launching national success, but once that platform is reached, other factors become more important than further gains in test scores. Indeed, once the platform is reached, it may be bad policy to pursue further gains in test scores because focusing on the scores diverts attention, effort, and resources away from other factors that are more important determinants of national success."

The United States has been a successful nation, Baker argues, because its schools cultivate a certain "spirit," which he defines as "ambition, inquisitiveness, independence, and perhaps most important, the absence of a fixation on testing and test scores."

Baker has a message for the reformers, foundation executives, journalists, policy makers, and government officials who have foisted an unhealthy obsession with testing and test scores on our nation's schools:

For more than a quarter of a century, the American public has been barraged by politicians and pundits claiming that America's schools are disaster zones because we are not at or near the top of the league standings in test scores. This claim is flat out wrong. It is wrong in fact, and it is wrong in theory. For almost 40 years, those who believe this fallacious theory have been leading the nation down the wrong path in education policy. It turns out that the elementary teachers who have said all along that there is more to education than what is reflected in test scores were right and the "experts" were wrong.

Trying to raise America's test scores in comparison to those of other nations is worse than pointless. It looks to be harmful, for the only way to do it is to divert time, energy, skill, and resources away from those other factors that propel the U.S. to the top of the heap on everything that matters: life, liberty, and the pursuit of happiness.

The fixation with test scores also harms the nation by diverting time, attention, and resources away from America's real educational problems, such as too few minorities graduating from college, the run-down schools in the nation's inner cities, misdirected parental interference in schools, and the lack of parental and administrative support for teachers. There are more, of course, but nowhere on the list of our educational problems should we ever again find worries over our performance on tests compared to that of other nations.

As Yong Zhao has pointed out, it is bizarre for the world's leader in science and technology, the nation with the most powerful economy in the world, to be on a perpetual hunt for another nation to emulate. Of course, nations should learn from one another, but why would we want to copy the rote systems that nations like China and India are trying to shed? Why would we abandon the intellectual freedom and professional autonomy that have produced a spirit of inquiry and a love of tinkering and innovation? Why would we kill the seed corn of entrepreneurship by squeezing all of our children into a uniform mold? Why would we insist on judging their individual worth by their ability to guess the right answer to prescribed questions? Why do we not appreciate what we have that works and focus instead on solving our genuine problems?

More testing does not make children smarter. More testing does not reduce achievement gaps. More testing does nothing to address poverty and racial isolation, which are the root causes of low academic achievement. More testing will, however, undermine the creative spirit, the innovative spirit, the entrepreneurial spirit that have made our economy and our society successful. Used wisely, to identify student learning problems, testing can be useful to teachers. But testing should be used diagnostically, not to hand out rewards or punishments.

Surely, there is value in structured, disciplined learning, whether in history, literature, mathematics, or science; students need to learn to study and to think; they need the skills and knowledge that are patiently acquired over time. Just as surely, there is value in the activities and projects that encourage innovation. The incessant demand for more testing and standardization advances neither.

CHAPTER 8

The Facts About High School Graduation Rates

CLAIM *The nation has a dropout crisis, and high school graduation rates are falling.*

REALITY *High school dropouts are at an all-time low, and high school graduation rates are at an all-time high.*

"Everyone knows" that there is a dropout crisis in America and that huge numbers of young people never get a high school diploma. We read it in the newspapers, we see it in television documentaries, we hear annual reports on "the dropout crisis." The conventional wisdom tells us that things are bad and getting worse.

But it is not true.

The nation does not have a dropout crisis, and high school graduation rates are not falling. Those students who do not complete high school are certainly disadvantaged in their ability to earn a living, and a disproportionate number of them are African American and Hispanic students who drop out of highly segregated schools. Being poorly educated is a handicap in life, and we should strive to educate everyone well. But let us direct our efforts to improve the situation by relying on accurate information.

Having a high school diploma is crucial for entry into almost any line of work these days, so it is important that everyone have one. This may be a mark of credential inflation, as there are many jobs where a diploma is required but not really necessary, such as truck driving, housekeeping, retail sales, and home health care. A high school diploma signifies, if nothing else, the ability to persist and complete high school. Certainly, all people should have the literacy and numeracy to survive in life, as well as the historical and civic knowledge to carry out their political and civic responsibilities. Unfortunately, the pressure to raise graduation rates—like the pressure to raise test scores—often leads to meaningless degrees, not better education.

As a nation, we should continue to strive to raise the graduation rate and to reduce the dropout rate, but we should do so based on real facts, not based on fear-driven and inaccurate assertions.

Not until 1940 did the high school graduation rate reach 50 percent. The graduation rate dropped during World War II, as young men went into the armed forces, but rose to 70 percent by 1970. By 1990, the four-year graduation rate reached 74 percent and remained virtually flat until 2010. (See graph 32.) In 2012, the Department of Education announced that the four-year graduation rate had reached 78.2 percent in 2010, the first significant increase in three decades. Nevada and the District of Columbia had the lowest graduation rates, while Wisconsin and Vermont had the highest. Headlines about the high school graduation "crisis" refer to the apparent long-term stagnation of the four-year graduation rate. This is the figure often cited by the secretary of education, other government officials, and many academics to raise alarms about the condition of American education.[1]

The crisis talk that has been so common in recent years has fastened on dropout rates and graduation rates as sure signs of the low quality of American education, but the picture is more complicated. The persistent four-year rate of 75 to 78 percent may signify that nearly a quarter of our young people, for whatever reasons, are unable or unwilling to complete their studies in the traditional four years. Or it may signify that many high schools are maintaining standards for graduation and not granting degrees to those who are not qualified to graduate.

The U.S. Department of Education uses the four-year completion rate as the gold standard; this method produces the lowest possible graduation rate. It does not account for students who take more time to graduate or who earn a GED.

The four-year graduation rate is one way to measure graduation rates, but it is not the only way. Many young people take longer than four years to earn a high school diploma. Some graduate in August, not May or June. Some take five or six years. Others earn a GED. When their numbers are added to the four-year graduates, the high school graduation rate is 90 percent.[2] (See graph 33.)

Thus, it is accurate to say that only about three-quarters of American students get a high school diploma in four years. And it is accurate to say that the graduation rate of 2010 (which was 78 percent) is only a few points higher than it was in 1970, when it was 70 percent. But it is also accurate to say that 90 percent of those between the ages of eighteen and twenty-four have a high school diploma.

In contrast to the current rhetoric of crisis, Lawrence Mishel and Joydeep Roy of the Economic Policy Institute analyzed census data for the past four decades, not four-year graduation rates, and concluded that "there has been remarkable progress in raising both high school completion rates and in closing racial/ethnic gaps in high school completion." In reviewing the debate among scholars, Mishel and Roy offer a valuable guide to the different ways of calculating graduation rates.[3]

Mishel and Roy recognize that some students take longer than four years to get their high school diplomas. Some get a GED instead of a four-year diploma. By the time the census counts high school graduates in the eighteen- to twenty-four-year-old cohort, 90 percent have a high school diploma. It's true that a GED does not carry the same prestige as a four-year diploma, and economists say that holders of the GED do not earn as much as those with a four-year high school diploma. But most colleges accept a GED as evidence of graduation, and those with a GED have a chance to get postsecondary education and are likely to earn more than high school dropouts. Whatever its drawbacks, the GED is nonetheless a high school diploma, and for many young people whose high school education was interrupted, for whatever reason, it is a lifeline.

Federal data show that the proportion of people between the ages of eighteen and twenty-four who are not presently enrolled in high school and who have earned either a high school diploma or an alternative credential, including a GED, is 90 percent. This rate includes people who may have earned their high school degrees in another country, but it does not include those who are in the military (almost all of whom have high school degrees) and those who are incarcerated (who are less likely than their peers to have high school diplomas).[4] Unlike the four-year graduation rate, which has increased slowly, the completion rate for this age group has trended steadily upward for the past thirty years.

Looked at this way, the narrative is transformed from a story of stag-nation and crisis to a story of incremental progress.

Most of these additional diplomas were earned by the age of eigh-teen or nineteen. Among that age group, 89 percent had a high school diploma. In other words, within one year after the traditional four-year program, the graduation rate went from 75 percent (or 78 percent) to 89 percent.

Among young people between the ages of eighteen and twenty-four who were Asian/Pacific Islanders, the completion rate was 96 percent. Among white youths, it was 94 percent. Among black youths, it was 87 percent. Among American Indians/Alaska Natives, it was 82 per-cent. Among Hispanics, it was 77 percent.[5] (See graph 34.)

The lowest graduation rate (63 percent) was found among Hispanic youths aged eighteen to twenty-four who were born outside the conti-nental United States. Many of the Hispanic youths in this age group are recent immigrants who never attended American high schools.

As with the graduation rate, there are different ways of calculating the dropout rate. One is called the "event dropout rate." It measures the percentage of youths from age fifteen through twenty-four who dropped out of grades 10–12 in a twelve-month period, from October to October. The other is called the "status rate," which includes all dropouts between the ages of sixteen and twenty-four who lack a high school diploma, regardless of when or where they left school (some in this group may be immigrants who never attended school in the United States). The status rate is always higher than the event rate because the status rate includes all dropouts.

Let's look at the event dropout rate. Federal data say this about the event dropout rate: "On average, 3.4 percent of students who were enrolled in public or private high schools in October 2008 left school before October 2009 without completing a high school program . . . Since 1972, event dropout rates have trended downward, from 6.1 per-cent in 1972 to 3.4 percent in 2009."[6] Another federal report in 2013 broke down the dropout rate by race and ethnic group as follows: for whites, it was 2.3 percent; for blacks, 5.5 percent; for Hispanics, 5.0 percent; for Asians, 1.9 percent; for American Indians/Alaska Natives, 6.7 percent.[7] (See graph 35.)

So far, no dropout crisis. Let's look at the status rate, which casts a wider net than the event rate. In October 2009, three million people between the ages of sixteen and twenty-four were not in high school and did not have high school diplomas (this number does not include incarcerated youths). They accounted for 8 percent of all those in this age group. Some undoubtedly were recent immigrants who never attended high school in the United States. To be sure, it is terrible that three million young men and women do not have high school diplomas, because their life chances and their future income will be reduced for lack of the diploma.

But it is important to know whether the situation with dropouts is getting worse. After all, the definition of a "crisis" is that matters are getting worse than they were and are reaching a critical point.

Here is what the federal data show: "Among all individuals in this age group, status dropout rates trended downward between 1972 and 2009, from 15 percent to 8 percent." Asian/Pacific Islanders have the lowest dropout rate at 3 percent. Among whites, the dropout rate was 5 percent. The black dropout rate was 9 percent. The Hispanic dropout rate was 18 percent.[8] (See graphs 36 and 37.)

And look at the trend over time in the status dropout rate.

Among whites, the dropout rate in 1972 was 12 percent. That is the proportion of whites between the ages of sixteen and twenty-four who were not enrolled in school and did not have high school diplomas. By 2009, the dropout rate for whites was down to 5 percent.

Among blacks, the dropout rate in 1972 was 21 percent in this age group. By 2009, the dropout rate for blacks was down to 9 percent. That is impressive progress.

Among Hispanics, the dropout rate in 1972 was 34 percent. By 2009, it was down to 18 percent. That is impressive progress, too.

We can't keep crying wolf when we are making progress. The progress has been slow and steady. But it is progress. We are moving in the right direction.

It would be best if no one dropped out. It would be best if everyone earned a high school diploma, but the crucial fact to note is that the data contradict the narrative of crisis. The dropout rate is trending downward. We are moving forward. We are making progress. The dropout rate has actually been cut by about 40 percent overall between 1972 and 2009 and reduced even more for blacks and Hispanics, the groups that are most at risk for dropping out.

Another criticism leveled at the schools is that the high school graduation rate is not rising as fast as it is in other countries. The United

States used to have the highest high school graduation rate in the world, but other nations have overtaken us and are now producing more high school graduates than we are. This is true. As we have seen, the four-year high school graduation rate has been relatively flat for many years, hovering at about 75 percent and only recently rising to 78 percent. At the same time, other nations were increasing their high school graduation rates. Nations such as the Republic of Korea, the Slovak Republic, the Czech Republic, Poland, Slovenia, Canada, Sweden, the Russian Federation, and Finland have boosted their high school completion rates, while we have not.[9] (See graph 38.)

Of course, with all international comparisons like this, it is never certain that all these nations are describing the same institutions or the same level of academic demand. That is also true even in a nation like ours where the rigor of a high school diploma varies considerably from place to place.

Furthermore, the data may be interpreted in various ways, because so many variables are involved. And the data may be presented in a negative or a positive light. When the U.S. Department of Education described the international data (drawing on the same sources as the previously cited report from OECD), it showed impressive growth for the twenty-seven OECD nations but a flat line for the United States. In the OECD as a whole, the proportion of the population from age twenty-five to sixty-four with a high school degree rose from 65 percent to 72 percent between 2001 and 2008, while it remained steady in the United States, going from 88 percent to 89 percent.

Most OECD nations saw large growth in the high school graduation rate among the youngest group (ages twenty-five to thirty-four), as compared with those who were fifty-five to sixty-four. "The United States was the only country in 2008 where the percentage of 25- to 34-year-olds who had completed high school did not exceed the percentage of 55- to 64-year-olds who had completed high school." At both ends of the age spectrum, the high school graduation rate in the United States was 88–89 percent.[10] *Our growth is flat because our rate is so high.*

The United States had a higher graduation rate in 2009 than the average for the OECD nations, whether looking at the population from twenty-five to sixty-four or looking only at the youngest group, from twenty-five to thirty-four. The other nations are gaining while we remain stuck at 89 percent.

Can we raise our high school graduation rate above the 90 percent range? There are two ways to do that. One is to make sure that every student gets the necessary preparation and support in the early grades so that he or she is well prepared for high school. The other is to lower standards to meet an artificial target, which is pointless.

This is a dilemma. If we focus solely on producing a higher graduation rate—as many U.S. school districts are doing now—then the value of the high school diploma might be weakened by lowering standards and awarding diplomas to poorly prepared students. Many districts are reaching to meet the goal by putting low-performing students into "credit recovery" courses, where they earn lost credits in a few days of low-level studies. Or the students make up credits by taking an online course, where they can easily pass undemanding tests, tests where they may be allowed to guess the answer until they get it right or where they are able to get the right answer by searching for it online. Just getting the graduation rate up is not a sufficient goal. More time and energy must be spent preparing students in the early grades so that they are academically ready to meet the expectations of a high school diploma. Perhaps our current graduation rate numbers are inflated; the more we concentrate on raising the graduation rate instead of raising the quality of education, the more likely it is that we will have high school graduates who are not well prepared for work or postsecondary education or being a good citizen.

One recent proposal to end "the dropout crisis" noted that the current emphasis on "college for all" was discouraging students who were at risk of dropping out. The author, Russell W. Rumberger, leads the California Dropout Research Project. What discouraged students need most, Rumberger argued, is not a college-preparatory curriculum (since they are not college bound) but an education that promotes their motivation, perseverance, and self-esteem. They need an education that develops their academic and vocational interests. Most job openings for the foreseeable future don't require any postsecondary education, he noted, and these students could qualify for many jobs. But these students need a high school diploma just to get in the door. They need support and encouragement to stay in school, and they need high school courses that will prepare them to enter the job market. If we are serious about reducing the dropout rate, Rumberger suggested, we would desegregate schools because concentrated racial segregation and poverty contribute to dropping out. He pointed out that "two-thirds of all high schools in the United States in 2002 with more than 90 percent minority enroll-ments had fewer than six in 10 students remain in school from 9th to 12th grade." If we really want to make a difference, we would take action to strengthen families and communities by reducing poverty and racial segregation.[11]

Black and Hispanic youths who attend high-poverty, racially iso-lated schools have serious problems. Large numbers are not completing high school. Our efforts should focus on reducing the causes of their disengagement from school, part of which has to do with being unpre-pared for high school work and part of which results from the circum-stances in which they live.

The constant talk about "crisis" can be debilitating since it is based on distortions. It can make people feel that all their efforts are in vain. It can make them cast aside the necessary but difficult courses of action and grab at any proposal that offers a quick fix, no matter how illusory. That way lies wasted time and resources. It is better to know the facts and to have a realistic understanding of the problem than to be driven by a sense of panic.

People tend to work harder if they know that their hard work is pro-ductive. If we recognize the good work that so many principals, teach-ers, parents, youth counselors, school psychologists, and social workers have done over the years, they—and we—wouldn't feel hopeless about conquering problems. Could we do better? Certainly. We should not despair. We have made progress and can make even more progress if we persist and have a realistic grasp of the problems.

CHAPTER 9

The Facts About College Graduation Rates

CLAIM *Our economy will suffer unless we have the highest college graduation rate in the world.*

REALITY *There is no evidence for this claim.*

Since World War II, the United States has steadily expanded access to higher education on the assumption that an educated populace would benefit individuals, society, and the economy. Widespread higher education, it was generally believed, would elevate the knowledge and wisdom of the populace and spur technological innovation. Investing in education was, most policy makers believed, a good bet for the nation.

These days, our policy makers tend to see investment in higher education strictly as preparation for the workforce, for career readiness and global competition. If another nation has more college graduates, they fear, then it might beat us in the global competition for markets and technological innovation. But we should not lose sight of other ways of thinking about higher education. Going to a college or university is about more than acquiring job skills. It is a time to study different subjects and fields in depth; to explore one's interests and to give full range to one's curiosity about ideas; to study under the tutelage of scholars who have devoted their lives to their field. It is a time to develop one's intellectual and cultural life. It is a time in which to gain the political, historical, and economic understanding that was not contained in high school textbooks, to explore issues that were once thought settled, to acquire and exercise the critical perspective that prepares people to become actively involved in civic life and democratic politics.

In recent decades, the utilitarian argument for higher education has nearly supplanted understanding of the role of higher education in developing intellectual, cultural, political, and aesthetic judgments. Yet even those who go to college to study business may find time in their schedule to read literature and history, to learn about philosophy, music, and art. They may, for the first time in their lives, have the opportunity to think critically about society. These are the fruits of higher education, as distinct from vocational education. It may be a vain hope, but we should continue to urge our policy makers not to lose sight of the intangible values of higher education as they promote higher college graduation rates.

The great expansion of higher education began when veterans of World War II returned home. As a reward for their service, Congress passed the GI Bill of Rights. Among its many benefits were subsidies for tuition, books, and fees of those who wanted more education. More than two million veterans took advantage of the offer and enrolled in institutions of higher education. Unfortunately, the GI Bill occurred in the context of racial segregation, and most African American veterans were unable to gain admission to most institutions of higher education; instead, they used their benefits for trade schools. While the GI Bill did nothing to end racial segregation, it largely severed the connection between income and higher education by providing access to many who otherwise would not have been able to afford it, and American higher education was transformed. Higher education was no longer seen as a privilege of the privileged. State universities expanded, and community colleges opened and grew to meet a variety of needs, not only academic, but technical and vocational as well.

The college-going rate has increased at a phenomenal pace over the past century. In 1900, only 2 percent of those in the eighteen- to twenty-four-year-old group were enrolled in college. By 1930, it was 7 percent. By 1949, it was 15 percent. By 1969, the college-going rate among that age group was 35 percent. The increased availability of public higher education made college more affordable and accessible to large numbers of students. To bolster enrollments, many states made a point of underwriting the cost of public higher education.[1]

At present, higher education is the pathway to every profession and to technical careers that require at least two years of postsecondary study. College graduates on average earn more money than high school graduates, and high school graduates earn more money than high school dropouts. College graduates have a lower unemployment rate than those with less education. Thus, it is reasonable to encourage more individuals to acquire more education to improve their knowledge and skills. Unfortunately, many states have increasingly shifted the cost of higher education to students, raising tuition and making higher education an expensive investment. Many students leave college burdened by debt and spend years paying off their student loans. As public subsidies are replaced by student loans, college and university education becomes too expensive and out of reach for many students. Many decide to take their degrees online, hoping that they can get a degree faster and at less cost. For those who want a four-year degree, this is not a good decision. For-profit online universities have extremely low graduation rates.[2]

Reformers complain that students in the United States are falling behind those in other nations because the college completion rate in this country is flat, while it is rising elsewhere. The college completion rate for older Americans (fifty-five to sixty-four) is the same as for younger Americans (twenty-five to thirty-four). Reformers cite an OECD chart showing that the United States ranked sixteenth in the world in its graduation rate, as compared with other OECD nations. The implication is that our nation is losing the international race to create brainpower and educated talent and is therefore careening into economic decline. President Obama is convinced that the United States must increase the number of college graduates and has pledged that by the year 2020 "America will once again have the highest proportion of college graduates in the world."

Should we aspire to have the highest college graduation rate in the world? What will happen if we don't?

These are issues that need to be deconstructed.

The OECD chart shows fifteen nations with a higher postsecondary graduation rate than ours. Nations are ranked by the percent of their population aged twenty-five to thirty-four that completed either an associate's degree or a higher degree by 2009. The completion rate for the United States is 41 percent. The nation with the highest completion rate is South Korea, where 63 percent of the age group has earned a postsecondary degree. About 55 percent of the cohort has received degrees in Canada, Japan, and the Russian Federation. The rates are in the mid-to-high 40s in Ireland, Norway, New Zealand, Luxembourg, the U.K., Australia, and Denmark. Such nations as France, Israel, Belgium, Sweden, the Netherlands, Switzerland, and Finland have rates within a point or two of the United States.[3] (See graphs 38 and 39.)

On the surface, this appears to be a terrible indictment of American education.

However, there is one curious fact about the OECD rankings: while the United States is in the middle of the pack, only a few points above the average for the OECD nations as a whole, Germany is near the bottom. This is odd; it doesn't fit the conventional wisdom of our time. Germany has a degree completion rate of 26 percent among the younger cohort, yet Germany is the dominant economic engine of Europe. The degree completion rate of its older population is the same as that of the youngest cohort, just like in the United States, but at a much lower level. Germany is renowned for its high technology, its sophisticated industries, and its productivity. Yet only 26 percent of its population aged twenty-five to thirty-four received a degree from a postsecondary institution. Germany has succeeded economically by having a strong educational system and a strong apprenticeship system. It has also taken care not to outsource its major industries to low-wage nations.

The bearers of doom and gloom try to convince the public that there has been stagnation in the college-degree completion rate of Americans, but this is not true. Consider the changes over time in the proportion of those in the age group from twenty-five to twenty-nine who have earned a bachelor's degree. Among those in this age group, 22 percent had earned a BA in 1980; by 2011, it was up to 32 percent. Among whites, the proportion grew from 25 percent to 39 percent. Among blacks, it nearly doubled, from 11 percent to 20 percent. Among Hispanics, it grew from 8 percent to 13 percent. Among Asian Americans, it increased from 42 percent (in 1990) to 56 percent.[4]

Be that as it may, our leaders agree that we must aim for a higher degree completion rate. The College Board gathered a commission of education leaders, who declared this goal: "Increase the proportion of 25- to 34-year-olds who hold an associate degree or higher to 55 percent by the year 2025 in order to make America the leader in educational attainment in the world."[5]

So now there are two goals: President Obama says we must be first in the world by 2020, and the College Board commission says we must raise the completion rate to 55 percent by 2025 to become "the leader in educational attainment in the world." The unasked question is this: Will the degrees obtained under pressure to reach a target represent real learning, or will they be reached by credential inflation, credit recovery, and other schemes that devalue the meaning of the diploma?

The commission made some impressive recommendations about improving preschool education, reducing dropouts, and making college more affordable. Taking these steps will surely raise the proportion of students who are ready and able to complete a college degree.

But America won't be the world leader by raising degree completion to 55 percent. South Korea was the world leader in 2009 with a rate of 63 percent and is not standing still. The question is whether we can increase degree completion from 41 percent to more than 65 percent by 2025, and even that may not be enough to pass South Korea.

Is it possible? Could we become the world leader? The College Board's commission thought so, but getting there would require significant new investments in precollegiate education, and that is not happening. Instead, we are seeing budget cuts in many states, increased class sizes, and reductions in funding for everything the College Board commission recommended. Without additional investments in preschool education, dropout prevention, counseling, and other strategies to keep students on track to high school graduation, it is unlikely that more students will stay in school and enroll in postsecondary education. Unless the federal government or states help students pay for college, we are not likely to see big increases in the number of those enrolling in postsecondary institutions.

As we saw in an earlier chapter, high school graduation rates are now about 90 percent—not in four years, but in five or six years after students start high school. And more high school graduates enroll in college right after graduation. In 1975, about half of all high school graduates enrolled in college right after graduation. By 2009, the rate had increased to 70 percent. For students from high-income families, 84 percent entered college right after high school; from middle-income families, it was 67 percent; from low-income families, it was 55 percent. Two-thirds of males and three-quarters of females enroll in college after finishing high school. In terms of access, we have made impressive progress since 1975. But to push it even higher would mean concentrating new resources on low-income students and students of color. Those investments are not being made.[6]

Perhaps we should feel ashamed that the youngest group in the United States is earning about the same number of bachelor's degrees as the oldest group and that we are not producing more and more bachelor's degrees. We like to think that we are number one in everything, so why are we not producing more and more bachelor's degrees?

Here are the likely reasons: People won't spend the time and money to get a college degree—either two-year or four-year—unless they think it will help them get a better job or career; and people won't pursue more education unless they can afford it. As I noted earlier, college graduates earn more on average than those with only a high school diploma, and those with a high school diploma earn more than those who never finished high school. But the job prospects for everyone are uncertain in a rapidly changing economy, and everyone has heard stories of college graduates working as retail clerks or in other jobs that pay low wages.

How do people know what they need in the future? One clue is to see what is happening right now. The advance of technology and globalization has led to the outsourcing of many kinds of jobs, not only factory jobs, but white-collar jobs. As the economist Paul Krugman points out, "Since 1990 or so the U.S. job market has been characterized not by a general rise in the demand for skill, but by 'hollowing out': both high-wage and low-wage employment has grown rapidly, but medium-wage jobs—the kinds of jobs we count on to support a strong middle class—have lagged behind. And the hole in the middle has been getting wider: many of the high-wage occupations that grew rapidly in the 1990s have seen much slower growth recently, even as growth in low-wage employment has accelerated." The jobs that are growing are those that can't be outsourced, such as truck drivers and janitors. High-wage jobs performed by highly educated workers are even easier to outsource to other nations, he wrote, than low-wage jobs. Yes, Krugman argues, we should remove the inequalities in American education, but we should stop pretending that "putting more kids through college can restore the middle-class society we used to have." Having a college degree is no longer a guarantee of getting a good job, and it will be even less true in the future. Many of the jobs that cannot be outsourced do not require so much as a high school diploma, other than as an entry-level credential providing evidence of persistence.[7]

Krugman concludes: "So if we want a society of broadly shared prosperity, education isn't the answer—we'll have to go about building that society directly. We need to restore the bargaining power that labor has lost over the last 30 years, so that ordinary workers as well as superstars have the power to bargain for good wages. We need to guarantee the essentials, above all health care, to every citizen." College degrees won't take us where we want to go; they may be "no more than tickets to jobs that don't exist or don't pay middle-class wages." The political prospects for Krugman's vision—which requires shared sacrifice and higher tax rates—seem to be as remote as the likelihood of boosting the college graduation rate to first in the world by 2020.

Krugman's analysis was supported by a report that large numbers of recent college graduates were unemployed or underemployed. A 2012 study of census data by researchers at Northeastern University, Drexel University, and the Economic Policy Institute found that about 1.5 million, or 53.6 percent, of people under the age of twenty-five with a bachelor's degree were jobless or underemployed. "Broken down by occupation, young college graduates were heavily represented in jobs that require a high school diploma or less. In the last year, they were more likely to be employed as waiters, waitresses, bartenders and food-service helpers than as engineers, physicists, chemists and mathematicians combined (100,000 versus 90,000)." Some economists suggested that most of the jobs lost in the recession of 2008 were middle-class jobs, like bank tellers, that were automated and would never return. More college graduates were working in "office-related jobs such as receptionist or payroll clerk than in all computer professional jobs (163,000 versus 100,000). More also were employed as cashiers, retail clerks and customer representatives than engineers (125,000 versus 80,000)." Further, only three of the thirty occupations (teachers, college professors, and accountants) with the largest projected number of job openings by 2020 would require a bachelor's degree or higher. "Most job openings are in professions such as retail sales, fast food and truck driving, jobs which aren't easily replaced by computers."[8]

The Bureau of Labor Statistics forecast that two-thirds of the jobs available between 2008 and 2018 would not need any postsecondary education. Most would require on-the-job training. Jobs will open for 175,000 computer engineers and 600,000 nurses, which require post-secondary degrees. But the economy is likely to offer jobs for 460,000 home health aides, 400,000 customer service agents, 400,000 fast-food workers, 375,000 retail salesclerks, 255,000 construction workers, and other occupations that require on-the-job training, not degrees. Unless there are unexpected changes in the economic outlook, many of the young people who graduate from two- and four-year colleges will not find jobs that require the education they have purchased at a high price. But the demand for college degrees will continue because many employers will hire only college graduates, even for jobs that don't require a college education.[9]

What is painfully obvious is that the policy makers' discussion of college completion rates hinges completely on the economic gains of getting a college degree. The purpose of going to college, they constantly reiterate, is to get a better job and to make more money. Many who accept this as their goal will be disappointed. They will not get the job or the income that they hoped for. They will get a degree and be burdened by debt without getting a job commensurate with their time or investment or aspirations. We would do well to think of college not as an economic activity (which it may or may not be, depending on the individual and the economy) but as an opportunity to develop one's knowledge, to encounter new ideas, to deepen one's appreciation of the arts, and to emerge with a wider understanding of the world. Perhaps our policy makers have oversold the economic returns of higher education and lost sight of the value of education for personal, civic, aesthetic, and social purposes.

If we expect to increase the rate of degree completion, we must invest in early childhood education and enhance the quality of precollegiate education, especially for students who are African American, Hispanic, and low income. These are the groups with the lowest degree completion rates. We should do this on grounds of equity, not international competition. If we are serious about increasing the number of students who complete postsecondary education, then states and the federal government must reduce the cost of public higher education so that it is affordable to more students. Students should not leave college burdened by tens of thousands of dollars of debt.[10]

If college completion is important as an investment in the knowledge and skills of our population (and not just as a credential), then we must encourage and enable students to persist. If we treated education as both an economic good for the ongoing development of our nation and a basic human right, then public higher education would be subsidized by the state and freely available to all who choose to pursue a degree. That's about as likely to happen as becoming first in the world in degree completion by 2020, but it would move us closer to the latter goal.

It would be a good idea if elected officials stopped selling the goal of college completion as a form of international competition. Because postsecondary education is not compulsory, the decision to pursue it is up to the individual. Individuals must determine for themselves that a commitment of two or four or more years of their lives and a great deal of money is a worthy investment in their future.

Even if a college degree does not necessarily lead to a high-paying job or career or profession, it is still worth pursuing. A better-educated populace is a wise investment in the future of our society. We should cultivate an educated citizenry who are informed and knowledgeable about mathematics, science, history, technology, and world cultures. We should recognize the importance of preparing more people with the skills and knowledge to be leaders in science, technology, and the arts. We should willingly invest in the growth of the historical, civic, political, and economic knowledge of our people, as well as their readiness to earn a living.

Learning is never finished and complete. It does not end with the attainment of a degree, not at age eighteen or age twenty-one or any other age. The opportunity to enlarge one's education should be available at reasonable cost for people of all ages, whether on campus, online, or elsewhere. Knowledge continues to grow, and our ability to understand it and use it well should grow too.

CHAPTER 10

How Poverty Affects
Academic Achievement

CLAIM *Poverty is an excuse for ineffective teaching and failing schools.*

REALITY *Poverty is highly correlated with low academic achievement.*

Reformers often say that poverty is an excuse for "bad teachers." If all teachers were great, then all children would score well on tests, and there would be no achievement gaps between children of different groups. If test scores went up every year for all children, eventually all children would graduate from high school and go to college. If all students went to college, then eventually there would be less poverty because college graduates make more money than high school graduates or high school dropouts.

Those who speak on behalf of the current reform movement—like Michelle Rhee, the former chancellor of the District of Columbia public schools; Joel Klein, the former chancellor of the New York City public schools; Bill Gates, the head of the Bill & Melinda Gates Foundation; Wendy Kopp, the chief executive officer of Teach for America; and Arne Duncan, the Obama administration's secretary of education—all agree that poverty can be overcome by effective teachers. In articles, interviews, and speeches, they assert that all poor children would reach the same high level of achievement as affluent children if they had effective teachers. Thus, if impoverished children are not achieving at high levels, it is because their teachers have low expectations and are not effective teachers. Some charter schools use the slogan "no excuses" to assert that every child, no matter how poor she is, no matter what her home circumstances, can succeed.

In 2009, Joel Klein, then the chancellor of the New York City public schools, stated the reformers' views with precision:

> No single impediment to closing the nation's shameful achievement gap looms larger than the culture of excuse that now permeates our schools. Too many educators today excuse teachers, principals, and school superintendents who fail to substantially raise the performance of low-income minority students by claiming that schools cannot really be held accountable for student achievement because disadvantaged students bear multiple burdens of poverty. The favored solution du jour to minority underachievement is to reduce the handicap of being poor by establishing full-service health clinics at schools, dispensing more housing vouchers, expanding preschool programs, and offering after-school services like mental health counseling for students and parents. America will never fix education until it first fixes poverty—or so the argument goes.
>
> In fact, the skeptics of urban schools have got the diagnosis exactly backward. The truth is that America will never fix poverty until it fixes its urban schools.[1]

In a similar vein, but somewhat more diplomatically, Bill Gates spoke to the National Urban League in the summer of 2011 and said, "We know you can have a good school in a poor neighborhood, so let's end the myth that we have to solve poverty before we improve education. I say it's more the other way around: Improving education is the best way to solve poverty."[2]

In her book *A Chance to Make History,* Wendy Kopp maintained that "we don't need to wait to fix poverty in order to ensure that all children receive an excellent education."[3]

Some prominent reformers don't agree. Geoffrey Canada's organization, Harlem Children's Zone, provides a full range of social services, health care, tutoring, preschool education, family support, and whatever else seems necessary to help improve the lives of children and their families.

Still, the question remains: Should we "fix" poverty first or "fix" schools first? It is a false choice. I have never heard anyone say that our society should "fix" poverty before fixing the schools. Most thoughtful people who want to help children and families speak of doing both at the same time, or at least trying. Yet here are all these powerful people saying we should "fix" the schools first, then, someday, turn our attention to poverty. Or maybe they mean that fixing schools will take care of poverty.

The reformers' case is superficially appealing. It ought to be easier to "fix" schools than to "fix" poverty, because poverty seems so intractable. Our society has grown to accept poverty as an inevitable fact of life, and there seems to be little or no political will to do anything about it. It should also be cheaper to fix schools instead of poverty, because no matter how much it costs to fix schools, it will surely be less than the cost of significantly reducing poverty in a society with great economic inequality like our own. The problem is that if you don't really know how to fix schools, if none of your solutions actually improve education, then society ends up neither fixing schools nor doing anything about poverty.

The reformers' big idea is to establish a free market of schools, with many privately managed charter schools, and assumes that the resultant competition will improve all schools. Some reformers, like Jeb Bush and Bobby Jindal, think the answer is to offer vouchers so that children in low-performing public schools can go to private and religious schools. The reformers can point to isolated examples of charter schools in which poor children got higher test scores or achieved a higher graduation rate or a higher college acceptance rate than their peers in public schools. But after twenty years of charter school experience, the number of these exemplars remains small. The evidence for vouchers is even weaker. As yet, no entire district has been transformed by private management. We would know more if the reformers took over an entire low-performing district, like Newark or Detroit, leaving no children out. But that has not happened.

Meanwhile, they rest their claim to be reformers on the belief that schools can be fixed now and that student outcomes (test scores) will reach high levels without doing anything about poverty.

But this makes no sense.

Poverty matters. Poverty affects children's health and well-being. It affects their emotional lives and their attention spans, their attendance and their academic performance. Poverty affects their motivation and their ability to concentrate on anything other than day-to-day survival. In a society of abundance, poverty is degrading and humiliating.

Some children are able to rise above all the burdens imposed upon them by poverty. Some are able to focus on their schoolwork and to master whatever assignments they receive. They become excellent students and get high test scores. Some graduate from high school. Some go to college. A few will become highly successful professionals.

Most don't. Most are dragged down by the circumstances into which they were born, through no fault of their own. Our most endangered children are raised by single parents who struggle to feed and clothe their children. Some are raised by two parents who face similar obstacles. Some are raised by grandparents. Some are raised by a parent who is addicted to drugs or mentally ill or emotionally incapacitated. Some are homeless or in foster care. Some do not know who their parents are.

It is easy for people who enjoy lives of economic ease to say that poverty doesn't matter. It doesn't matter to *them*. It is an abstraction. For them, it is a hurdle to be overcome, like having a bad day or a headache or an ill-fitting jacket.

But for those who live in a violent neighborhood, in dingy surroundings, it is a way of life, not an inconvenience. Children who have seen a friend or relative murdered cope with emotional burdens that are unimaginable to the corporate leaders who want to reform their schools or close them.

The rate of childhood poverty in the United States is higher than in any other advanced nation. Nearly a quarter of American children live in poverty. The latest report from UNICEF says that it is 23 percent. No other advanced nation tolerates this level of poverty. In Finland, which has an excellent school system, 5 percent of the nation's children live in poverty. The U.S. rate for child poverty is about double the rate found in such countries as the United Kingdom, Canada, New Zealand, and Australia. It is triple the rate of child poverty in Germany, Austria, and France. And it is quadruple the rate of child poverty in such nations as Denmark, Slovenia, Norway, the Netherlands, Cyprus, Finland, and Iceland.[4]

The UNICEF report says that the only "economically advanced" nation with a higher child poverty rate than the United States is Romania. But having visited that nation and seen how it was impoverished by decades of misrule and dictatorship during the Cold War, I would not place it in the same category as the United States and Western

European nations. Romania aside, it is clear that the United States has the dubious distinction of having the highest rate of child poverty of any of the economically advanced nations in the Western Hemisphere.

Poverty matters before children are born. According to the Centers for Disease Control, poverty is "one of the most important predictors of insufficient prenatal care. Women with incomes below the federal poverty level consistently show higher rates of late or no prenatal care and lower rates of early care than women with larger incomes." The United States has an especially high rate of women who do not receive prenatal care until relatively late in their pregnancies. A delay in obtaining prenatal care or not getting any prenatal care is associated with "increased risks of low birth-weight babies, premature births, neonatal mortality, infant mortality, and maternal mortality."[5]

Preterm births pose risks to both mother and child, and the proportion of such births increased by 20 percent between 1990 and 2006, according to the American Congress of Obstetricians and Gynecologists. At present, one of every eight live births is preterm. Two-thirds of all infant deaths are preterm babies. Those who survive may have "lifetime health complications, including breathing problems, cerebral palsy and intellectual disabilities. Late-preterm infants (babies born between 34 and 37 weeks gestation) are 4 times more likely than term infants to have at least 1 medical condition and 3.5 times more likely to have 2 or more conditions. Approximately 8 percent of preterm babies have a major birth defect. Preterm birth is a leading cause of neurological disability, including cerebral palsy in children."[6]

Preterm births are associated with a greater likelihood of learning disabilities: "Infants born early have higher rates of hospitalization and illness than full-term babies. Growth and development in the last part of pregnancy are vital to the baby's health. The earlier the baby is born, the greater the chance he or she will have health problems. Preterm babies tend to grow more slowly than term babies. They also may have problems with their eyes, ears, breathing, and nervous system. Learning and behavioral problems are more common in children who were born before 39 weeks."

Whatever it might cost to assure that every pregnant woman gets the prenatal care she needs at the earliest possible date, the cost of the status quo is far larger: "Medical costs for a premature baby are much greater than for a healthy newborn. A 2006 report by the Institute of Medicine found the economic burden associated with preterm birth in the United States was at least $26.2 billion annually, or $51,600 per infant born preterm."[7]

Given these facts, how can anyone reasonably claim that poverty is just an excuse? How can people ignore the fact that poverty is the most reliable predictor of which women will receive adequate prenatal care to assure the health of their babies? Think of the improvement in the physical health of children and their mothers if our nation's philanthropists determined to solve this one very finite problem: the lack of adequate prenatal care. Other nations have figured it out. Why can't we?

There are many significant differences between children of the poor and children of the nonpoor. As Richard Rothstein wrote in his major study of the causes of the black-white achievement gap, "Demography is not destiny, but students' social and economic family characteristics are a powerful influence on their relative average achievement."[8] Very poor children can succeed in school, and middle-class children may do very badly despite their advantages. But on average, the advantages and disadvantages into which children are born make a difference. As the singer Sophie Tucker used to say, "I've been rich and I've been poor, and rich is definitely better."

Children born to poor mothers are less likely to receive regular medical care. They are less likely to see a dentist. They are less likely to have educated parents. They are less likely to have books and magazines in their home. They are less likely to be read to each day by a parent or guardian. They are less likely to be enrolled in a prekindergarten program. They are less likely to have their own bedroom and a quiet place to study. They are less likely to hear a large and complex vocabulary at home, as compared with children in professional families. They are less likely to get three nutritious meals every day. They are less likely to live in sound housing. They are less likely to live in a safe neighborhood. They are less likely to take family trips to the local library or museum. They are less likely to participate in organized activities after school, such as sports, dramatics, art or dance or music classes. They are less likely to take a family vacation or go to summer camp.[9]

Children of the poor are more likely to be born preterm or with low birth weight and consequently to suffer cognitive impairments, learning disabilities, and attention deficits. They are more likely to suffer "fetal alcohol syndrome," a collection of severe cognitive, physical, and behavioral problems that occurs ten times more often among low-income black children than among middle-class white children. They are more likely to live in a dwelling infested with rats and roaches. They are more likely to have a parent or guardian who is incarcerated or unemployed. They are more likely to be homeless. They are more likely to move frequently and change schools frequently because their parents or guardians couldn't pay the rent. They are more likely to have asthma ("the disease is provoked in part from breathing fumes from low-grade home heating oil and from diesel trucks and buses . . . as well as from excessive dust and allergic reactions to mold, cockroaches, and secondhand smoke"). Children who suffer from asthma are likely to wake up during the night wheezing and to be drowsy and inattentive the next day in school. Poor children are more likely to be ill without getting treated by a doctor. They are more likely to be hungry or to suffer anemia because of a poor diet. They are more likely to have undetected vision problems. They are more likely to have undetected hearing problems. They are more likely to have toothaches and cavities. They are more likely to be exposed to lead in the paint on their walls. Lead poisoning may cause cognitive deficiencies, which obviously affect academic performance.[10]

Children of poor families are more likely to be chronically absent from school, missing as much as a month of the school year. This sustained absence from daily instruction widens the achievement gap.[11]

The burdens imposed on children by poverty are physical, emotional, cognitive, and psychological. Because of poverty, the achievement gap begins before the first day of kindergarten. The advantage is definitely with children who have good health, regular checkups, good nutrition, educated parents, a literate environment, basic economic security, and an array of after-school and summer activities.

When one considers the difference in life circumstances of children who are poor and children who are not poor, it is inconceivable how any responsible person could claim that poverty doesn't matter or that poverty is an "excuse." What such a person is really saying is that we don't need to do anything about the health issues of poor children. We need not concern ourselves with their inability to see well or hear well, with their toothaches or their asthma or anemia. We need not fuss about the conditions in which they live. The reformers seem to think that the burdens of poverty, no matter how oppressive, can be overcome by effective teachers and by a regime of strict discipline. "Great" teachers, they assert, will enable the success not just of a small number of determined children but of *all* children in their classes. They reason that if children afflicted with all these burdens are taught by someone with high expectations, if they learn to sit quietly and walk in silence, if they learn to follow instructions without questioning, if they learn proper manners, then they will succeed in school, they will get high test scores, they will go to college, and they will succeed in life.

But the weight of social science evidence says they are wrong.

The economist Helen F. Ladd, in her presidential address to the Association for Public Policy Analysis and Management, reviewed the evidence and found a clear linkage between poverty and academic performance in state and national assessments, as well as international assessments. In every nation, even in high-performing nations such as Finland, South Korea, and Canada, the achievement levels of students from low socioeconomic backgrounds fall short of their more advantaged peers. The gap between poor and advantaged students is greatest, she found, where income inequality is greatest.[12]

The gaps are smallest in those countries like Finland and the Netherlands that do the most to support the health and well-being of their children. Ladd found that "the low average test scores of U.S. students largely reflect our extremely high poverty rate and our relative lack of attention to the overall well-being of our children." She concluded that "it would be difficult, if not impossible, for the U.S. to replicate the success of higher scoring countries such as Finland, Canada and the Netherlands by focusing on school reform alone, and that is especially true for school reform that pays little attention to meeting the social needs of disadvantaged children."

If no other nation has managed to eliminate the achievement gap between children of the haves and children of the have-nots, why expect that the United States can do it without a major investment in reducing the causes of low achievement, which exist before the first day of school? If nations that devote significant resources to ensuring that their children are healthy have not closed the gaps, why expect that the United States can do so without improving the material condition of children's lives?

Other countries demonstrate that the gap can be narrowed, but narrowing it requires a willingness to protect children and families.

The reformers' belief that fixing schools will fix poverty has no basis in reality, experience, or evidence. It delays the steps necessary to heal our society and help children. And at the same time, it castigates and demoralizes teachers for conditions they did not cause and do not control.

CHAPTER 11

The Facts About Teachers and Test Scores

CLAIM *Teachers determine student test scores, and test scores may be used to identify and reward effective teachers and to fire those who are not effective.*

REALITY *Tests scores are not the best way to identify the best teachers.*

Many educators hoped that No Child Left Behind's emphasis on high-stakes testing would diminish when Barack Obama was elected. Unfortunately, President Obama's Race to the Top adopted the same test-based accountability as NCLB. The two programs differed in one important respect: where NCLB held schools accountable for low scores, Race to the Top held both schools and teachers accountable. States were encouraged to create data systems to link the test scores of individual students to individual teachers. If the students' scores went up, the teacher was an "effective" teacher; if the students' scores did not go up, the teacher was an "ineffective" teacher. If schools persistently had low scores, the school was a "failing" school, and its staff should be punished. No excuses for failure, said the corporate reformers; we can't wait, children have only one chance. We must close their schools and fire their teachers now, for the sake of the children.

Educators say that every child can learn, but they understand that children learn at different rates and that some inevitably learn more than others. Educators recognize that some children have more advantages and a faster start than others. Some have disabilities that interfere with their learning. Not all children start at the same place and not all children end at the same place, and test scores are not the only way to determine whether children are learning. Even the Obama administration's use of "growth scores," which measure increases in test scores from year to year, places far too much emphasis on standardized tests.

In the corporate reform mythology, every child can learn, and there can be no excuses for those who don't. If they don't get higher test scores every year, it is the fault of their teachers, whose expectations are low. Anyone who suggests that students' family life or poverty might have anything to do with their test scores is just making excuses for bad teachers. Reformers believe that "highly effective" teachers can cause their students' scores to go up every year. Lesser teachers cannot; those who can't produce, they believe, must be found and fired without delay. Reformers say that an effective teacher can bring about three times as much learning in a year as a hapless, ineffective teacher. Or they say that three effective teachers in a row will change the life chances of their students, but a run of ineffective teachers will ruin students' lives forever.

By the spring of 2010, the narrative of the corporate reformers was fully formed. In Central Falls, Rhode Island, a tiny and impoverished district, the local superintendent threatened to fire every teacher in the high school because its test scores were low. The state superintendent of schools supported the idea; so did Secretary of Education Arne Duncan and President Obama. None of the teachers received individual evaluations, but our nation's leaders agreed they should all be fired. A cover story in *Newsweek* spelled out the reform narrative. On the cover was emblazoned the headline "The Key to Fixing American Education," and behind it, written again and again, as if on a blackboard, was the solution: "We must fire bad teachers, we must fire bad teachers."[1]

Where did these ideas come from? One important source is the work of the statistician William Sanders in Tennessee, who began his career advising agricultural and manufacturing industries. Sanders claimed that his statistical modeling could determine how much "value" a teacher added to her students' testing performance. By monitoring students' progress on standardized tests from year to year, Sanders figured, he could isolate the "value added" by the teacher of that child. By comparing prior test scores, Sanders reasoned that the racial and socioeconomic characteristics of that student became unimportant. In effect, Sanders treated student learning as a finite quantity, with the teacher as the variable. The students' test score increases or losses could be attributed to the teacher. In his studies, an effective teacher was one who produced large test score gains year after year. Based on Sanders's work, reformers concluded that three effective teachers in a row could close the achievement gap.[2]

Other economists said it might take four great teachers in a row, or even five great teachers in a row, to close the gaps, but the reformers usually preferred to stay with the claim of three years. (Of course, if all children have a great teacher, and all children are making the same gains, the achievement gap won't close, but that's another issue.) The reformers often repeat the claim that three "great" or "effective" teachers in a row would close the test score gap between black and white children, between rich and poor children, between Hispanic and white children. Michelle Rhee cited this supposed finding many times; she said, for example, at the University of Southern California in 2011: "We know for poor minority children, if they have three highly effective teachers in a row, versus three ineffective teachers in a row, it can literally change their life trajectory."[3]

Arne Duncan often said something similar: "Three great teachers in a row, and the average child will be a year and a half to two grade levels ahead. Three bad teachers in a row, and that average child might be so far behind they might never catch up."[4]

A variation on the same theme is that a great teacher produces three times as much learning in a year as a poor teacher. Or, put another way, the students of the great teacher get a test score gain of eighteen months in a year, while the students of the poor teacher learn only six months' worth of whatever they studied in a year. The Stanford economist Eric Hanushek wrote in 2010 that the difference in effectiveness among teachers "is truly large, with some teachers producing 1½ years of gain in achievement in an academic year while others with equivalent students produce only ½ year of gain. In other words, two students starting at the same level of achievement can know vastly different amounts at the end of a single academic year due solely to the teacher to which they are assigned. If a bad year is compounded by other bad years, it may not be possible for the student to recover."[5] Perhaps such "great" teachers exist, but there is no evidence that they exist in great numbers or that they can produce the same feats year after year for every student.[6]

In the fall of 2010, the documentary film *Waiting for "Superman"*

popularized the idea in the national media that American public education was in desperate condition because there were so many bad teachers in the schools. At the same time, a group of urban superintendents
led by Joel Klein and Michelle Rhee published a "manifesto" about
how to fix the schools, which asserted: "So, where do we start? With
the basics. As President Obama has emphasized, the single most important factor determining whether students succeed in school is not the
color of their skin or their ZIP code or even their parents' income—it
is the quality of their teacher."[7] Their manifesto asserted that teachers'
credentials, experience, and education were irrelevant in judging their
quality. The only thing that matters, they argued, is "performance,"
meaning the test scores of their students.

Klein and Rhee misquoted President Obama. President Obama had
said that "the biggest ingredient in school performance is the teacher.
That's the biggest ingredient within a school. But the single biggest
ingredient is the parent."[8] Richard Rothstein described the Klein-Rhee
manifesto as a "caricature" and added:

> Decades of social science research have demonstrated that differences
> in the quality of schools can explain about one-third of the variation in
> student achievement. But the other two-thirds is attributable to non-
> school factors . . . What President Obama means is that if a child's
> parents are poorly educated themselves and don't read frequently to
> their young children, or don't use complex language in speaking to
> their children, or are under such great economic stress that they can't
> provide a stable and secure home environment or proper preventive
> health care to their children, or are in poor health themselves and
> can't properly nurture their children, or are unable to travel with their
> children or take them to museums and zoos and expose them to other
> cultural experiences that stimulate the motivation to learn, or indeed
> live in a zip code where there are no educated adult role models and
> where other adults can't share in the supervision of neighborhood
> youth, then children of such parents will be impeded in their ability
> to take advantage of teaching, no matter how high quality that teach-
> ing may be.[9]

Social scientists generally agree that students' families (especially
family income, which determines advantages and opportunity) have
an even bigger impact on student performance than their school or

teachers. According to some economists, family accounts for about 60 percent of the variation in test scores; the school (its leadership, its staff, its resources, its programs, and such matters as the presence or absence of peer effects, that is, the presence or absence of willing students) is responsible for about 20–25 percent of the variation. Within the 20–25 percent attributable to the school, teachers are the biggest component affecting how students perform on tests, possibly as much as 15 percent. President Obama accurately said that the teacher matters most within the school, but "the biggest ingredient" in students' academic performance is their family.[10] (Personally, I am skeptical about these precise statistical calculations about large and complex human activities, but I am not an economist, so what do I know?)

Yet the myth persists that the teacher is primarily responsible for student scores and that great teachers can overcome the influence of family, poverty, disability status, language proficiency, and students' own levels of interest and ability. Certainly, there are many people whose lives were changed by one teacher, but their stories typically describe teachers who were unusually inspiring, not "the teacher who raised my test scores to the top." Teachers do have the power to change lives. But after more than a decade of No Child Left Behind, researchers are still searching for a nonselective school or a district where every student, regardless of his or her starting point, has achieved proficiency on state tests because that school or that district has only effective teachers.

Despite the absence of evidence, the claims persist. On its Web site, Michelle Rhee's organization StudentsFirst says, "Research shows that a highly effective teacher generates 50% more learning than an average teacher. Conversely, an ineffective teacher generates 50% less learning than an average teacher. This means that kids learn three times more in a highly effective teacher's classroom than in an ineffective teacher's classroom."[11] Presumably, if a school hired and retained only those highly effective teachers, there would be dramatic gains in student test scores for all students. But Rhee doesn't seem to understand that very few teachers get the same high test score gains year after year. In 2012, Melinda Gates said in a television interview, "An effective teacher in front of a student, that student will make three times the gains in a school year that another student will make."[12] She said that the job of the Gates Foundation is "to make sure we create a system where we can have an effective teacher in every single classroom across the United States."

Given the reformers' conviction that the teacher is the key to raising test scores dramatically for every student, they had to find a strategy to identify those highly effective teachers and get rid of those who didn't have the right stuff.

In his academic studies and in *Waiting for "Superman,"* Eric Hanushek proposed that public schools should fire 5–10 percent of the teachers whose students got the lowest scores. If that happened, he said, the United States would rise nearly to the top of international test rankings. Moreover, he argued, replacing those bottom-of-the-barrel teachers with average teachers would add trillions of dollars to the nation's gross national product. He wrote:

> U.S. achievement could reach that in Canada and Finland if we replaced with average teachers the least effective 5 to 7 percent of teachers, respectively. Assuming the lower-bound estimate of teachers' impact, U.S. achievement could reach that in Canada and Finland if we replaced with average teachers the least effective 8 to 12 percent of teachers, respectively . . .
>
> Closing the achievement gap with Finland would, according to historical experience, have astounding benefits, increasing the annual growth rate of the United States by 1 percent of GDP. Accumulated over the lifetime of somebody born today, this improvement in achievement would amount to nothing less than an increase in total U.S. economic output of $112 trillion in present value. (That was not a typo—$112 trillion, not billion.)[13]

Hanushek suggested that there were three ways to get this dramatic improvement in teacher quality. One was to recruit higher-caliber teachers; another was to improve the skills of current teachers. But he maintained that both these methods had been tried and found inadequate. Instead, he recommended "deselection" of the bottom teachers based on their performance, defined as the test scores of their students. But school districts and states would need to change their policies, he believed, to attract and retain the kinds of teachers who could produce amazing test scores:

> They would need recruitment, pay, and retention policies that allow for the identification and compensation of teachers on the basis of their effectiveness with students. At a minimum, the current dys-

functional teacher-evaluation systems would need to be overhauled so that effectiveness in the classroom is clearly identified. This is not an impossible task. The teachers who are excellent would have to be paid much more, both to compensate for the new riskiness of the profession and to increase the chances of retaining these individuals in teaching. Those who are ineffective would have to be identified and replaced. Both steps would be politically challenging in a heavily unionized environment such as the one in place today.

Although Hanushek is associated with the Hoover Institution at Stanford, his views were embraced by the Obama administration's Race to the Top program and lauded by Republican governors across the nation, such as Scott Walker in Wisconsin, John Kasich in Ohio, Mitch Daniels in Indiana, Jeb Bush and his successor, Rick Scott, in Florida, and Chris Christie in New Jersey. Even Democratic governors like Dannel Malloy in Connecticut and Andrew Cuomo in New York endorsed the belief that low test scores were caused by "bad" or "ineffective" teachers, not by poverty and not by the relationship between resources and student needs.

Hanushek's theory that test scores will improve by "deselecting" teachers whose students receive low test scores got a huge boost in 2012 with the highly publicized release of a study by the economists Raj Chetty and John N. Friedman of Yale University and Jonah E. Rockoff of Columbia University. The Chetty study reviewed the records of students and teachers in the 1990s, before the advent of high-stakes testing, and concluded that students who had an effective teacher for a single year would have higher lifetime earnings and other benefits. The study was announced on the front page of *The New York Times,* where one of the authors said, "The message is to fire people sooner rather than later." The study said that replacing a poor teacher with an average teacher would raise a single classroom's lifetime earnings by $266,000.[14] President Obama was so impressed by the Chetty study that he referred to it a few weeks later in his State of the Union address, saying, "We know a good teacher can increase the lifetime income of a classroom by over $250,000."

However, critics were quick to raise questions about the study. They said that the authors may have confused correlation with causation (a class that gets higher test scores is also likelier to go to college and earn more) and that a large-scale study cannot pinpoint the effects of individual teachers. More than one critic pointed out that a lifetime gain of $266,000 for a class of twenty-six children, engaged in the labor force for forty years, translated to about $250 a year, or $5 a week. It would be even less for a larger class. As Bruce Baker observed, "What this boils down to is that a student can get a lifetime boost of $5 a week if we now spend billions of dollars on value-added rating systems. Maybe. Or maybe not."[15]

None of the enthusiasts of value-added assessment recognized that nations at the top of the international league tables did not get there by "deselecting" teachers whose students got low test scores. Nations such as Finland, Canada, Japan, and South Korea spend time and resources improving the skills of their teachers, not selectively firing them in relation to student test scores.

Nonetheless, what entered the reform lexicon was a fixed belief that bad teachers must be found out and fired.

But then came the knotty problem: How can a school district measure teacher quality? How can district leaders know which teachers should get bonuses and which should be fired? The only way to answer these questions, reformers believe, is to collect test scores every year and then see which teachers got those big gains and which ones didn't. Then rank the teachers from top to bottom. Once the ranking is done, according to reform theory, the teachers whose students got the big gains get bonuses and the ones whose students got no gains get fired. Eventually, if this is done consistently, the district ends up with only great teachers.

Some districts and states have already collected enough data to rank teachers by the test score gains of their students. Whether the rankings are accurate or not, some teachers have gotten bonuses and some have been fired. But no district has yet demonstrated the reformers' thesis that firing teachers based on student test scores will bring about great increases for the district. Despite the oft-repeated claims by reformers that three years in a row of great teachers will close the gap, no school district has ever done it, not even districts with a superintendent and school board fully supportive of the corporate reform faith and without a teachers' union to stand in the way. It remains a theory based on speculation, not evidence.

One reason it is hard to prove the theory is that the ratings are unstable from year to year. A teacher may be rated effective one year but ineffective the next. And the fact that the top-rated teachers produce gains large enough to close the achievement gap in three to five years doesn't necessarily matter much if you cannot identify the teachers who have this impact year after year. Only a small proportion of teachers gets big test score gains year after year, so it may be difficult to find enough of them to staff an entire school, let alone an entire school district. As Matthew Di Carlo of the Shanker Institute has pointed out, "Because of the imprecision of these growth models, various sources of bias, and year-to-year variation in students and conditions, very few teachers manage to be 'top' teachers for three, four or five consecutive years. A huge chunk of the 'top' teachers in year one are average—or even below average—in year two. Even more of them fall out of the 'top' bracket in the third, fourth, and fifth years."[16]

Another reason it is hard to prove the theory is that teachers are not factory workers who can be shifted from spot to spot as if they were on an assembly line. The teacher who is highly effective in one school may not be equally effective in another. But we can't know for sure, because no one has tried to move teachers around to prove the theory that three great teachers in a row will close the achievement gap for an entire school or district. Not yet, anyway.

While it seems certain that some teachers are excellent and others are not, the theory is based on some wobbly claims. The very concept of value-added assessment reflects the mind-set of statisticians and economists who measure productivity gains. A farmer plants corn of a certain variety in a certain type of soil, treats it with certain conditions, and then measures the growth of the crop to determine the worthiness of the treatment. In the context of value-added assessment, the teacher is the treatment. If the teacher is effective, the corn grows to a certain height. If the teacher is not, the corn does not grow or grows very little.

But children are not corn. They are not seeds or plants with fixed characteristics. Children's lives are not static. They have crises and ups and downs in their home lives and their personal lives. Maybe their parents got divorced. Maybe a parent lost her job. Maybe a student broke up with her boyfriend or totaled the family car. Maybe a family member died. Maybe the family moved to a new home. Maybe they were evicted from their home. These changes affect motivation, attention, and school performance. Children are not crops. They are not empty vessels waiting to be filled by a teacher.

In addition, the conditions for the teacher do not remain static. There may be more or fewer high-scoring students assigned to the teacher's class. Class size may increase because of state budget cuts. The curriculum and instructional materials may be better or worse this year. The school leader may change and be more or less supportive. Valued colleagues may retire. The school climate may be tranquil or disruptive. Any number of changes in the school may affect the teacher's classroom, the availability of resources and support, and ultimately the test scores of students.

The problems with value-added assessment are legion. Students are not randomly assigned, so teachers face different challenges every year. An excellent teacher may have a highly motivated group of students one year, while an equally effective teacher may be assigned a class with two or three troublemakers, who disrupt the class. Some teachers are deliberately assigned high-performing or low-performing students, or choose to teach one group or the other. One teacher gets great results, the other does not, but they faced different challenges, and the comparison is unfair.

The American Educational Research Association (AERA) and the National Academy of Education (NAE) prepared a joint statement about the problems with value-added assessment. They found that students' test scores are influenced by far more than their teacher, and the various statistical models don't account for all these factors. The other factors include:

- school factors such as class sizes, curriculum materials, instructional time, availability of specialists and tutors, and resources for learning (books, computers, science labs, and more)
- home and community supports or challenges
- individual student needs and abilities, health, and attendance
- peer culture and achievement
- prior teachers and schooling, as well as other current teachers
- differential summer learning loss, which especially affects low-income children
- the specific tests used, which emphasize some kinds of learning and not others, and which rarely measure achievement that is well above or below grade level[17]

Value-added ratings, they emphasized, are not stable. They vary from class to class, from year to year, and from one way of measuring to another. There are different ways to calculate value added, and the results will vary depending on which method is used. Different applications of value-added methodology produce different teacher ratings. When students take a different test, the teacher ratings also change.

The report by these two professional associations found that "teachers' value-added ratings are significantly affected by differences in the students who are assigned to them." Students are not randomly assigned. Those who teach students who are English-language learners or who have disabilities or who are homeless or who have poor attendance might have lower value-added ratings. Also, teachers of the gifted are likely to see small value added, because their students begin with high scores. "Even when the model includes controls for prior achievement and student demographic variables, teachers are advantaged or disadvantaged based on the students they teach." Thus, to the extent that teachers' job evaluations and compensation are tied to value-added measures, they may feel encouraged to avoid the neediest students, the students who are going to jeopardize their reputations, their careers, and their salaries.

Advocates of value-added assessment claim that they want to improve education for the neediest students by identifying the most effective teachers. They presume over time, as the weakest teachers are fired, only effective teachers would remain. But given the instability of the measures, and the threat to teachers' livelihoods, value-added assessment may well harm the most vulnerable students. Current levels of inequality will deepen if teachers are incentivized to shun the students with the highest needs. Schools in high-poverty districts already have difficulty retaining staff and replacing them. Who will want to teach in schools that are at risk of closing because of the students they enroll?

The very concept of "value added" assumes that it is possible to isolate the effects of a single teacher on student achievement. But, says the joint AERA-NAE panel, this is overly simplistic:

No single teacher accounts for all of a student's learning. Prior teachers have lasting effects, for good or ill, on students' later learning, and current teachers also interact to produce students' knowledge and skills. For example, the essay writing a student learns through his history teacher may be credited to his English teacher, even if she assigns no writing; the math he learns in his physics class may be credited to his math teacher. Specific skills and topics taught in one year may not be tested until later, if at all. Some students receive tutoring, as well as help from well-educated parents. A teacher who works in a well-resourced school with specialist supports may appear to be more effective than one whose students don't receive these supports.

Children are not corn or tomatoes, and no statistical methodology can successfully control for all the factors that influence changes in students' test scores. When analyzing the growth of cornstalks, we take into account the quality of the seeds, soil, water, wind, sunlight, weather, nutrients, pests, and perhaps other factors as well as the skill of the farmer. Measuring learning is far more complex than measuring agricultural production and involves many more factors because human beings are even less predictable than plants.

The champions of value-added assessment could learn from Harvey Schmidt and Tom Jones, whose musical *The Fantasticks* got it right:

Plant a radish.
Get a radish.
Never any doubt.
That's why I love vegetables;
You know what you're about!

Plant a turnip.
Get a turnip.
Maybe you'll get two.
That's why I love vegetables;
You know that they'll come through!

They're dependable!
They're befriendable!
They're the best pal a parent's ever known!
While with children,
It's bewilderin'.

You don't know until the seed is nearly grown
Just what you've sown.

Another complicating factor in the creation of value-added rankings is that they are based completely on standardized tests. But are the tests robust enough to serve as a proxy for teacher quality? The tests are not barometers or yardsticks. They are designed and constructed by humans and subject to error. Testing experts warn about measurement error, statistical error, human error, and random error. Given all the problems with standardized tests, and given the limited range of knowledge and skills that they test, can we be sure that they are truly an adequate or appropriate measure of student learning or teacher effectiveness? One can easily imagine a teacher who spends most of the year drilling her students to take the state tests. That teacher may get a high value-added rating yet be an uninspiring teacher. Do we want to honor and reward only those teachers who excel at teaching to the test? Or do we want to honor those teachers who are best at getting their students to think and ask good questions?

The cardinal rule of psychometrics is this: a test should be used only for the purpose for which it is designed. The tests are designed to measure student performance in comparison to a norm; they are not designed to measure teacher quality or teacher "performance." Teaching is multifaceted and complex. Good teachers want students to participate in discussion and debate in the classroom; they want students to be active and engaged learners and to take the initiative in exploring more than what was assigned. Can standardized, multiple-choice tests accurately reflect teacher quality? What students have learned may be gauged more accurately by their classroom work and by their independent projects—their essays, their research papers, and other demonstrations of their learning—than by their test scores.

Certainly teachers should be evaluated, but evaluating them by the rise or fall of their students' test scores is fraught with perverse consequences. It encourages teaching to multiple-choice tests; narrowing the curriculum only to the tested subjects; gaming the system by states and districts to inflate their scores; and cheating by desperate educators who don't want to lose their jobs or who hope to earn a bonus. When the tests become more important than instruction, something fundamental is amiss in our thinking.

Some districts and states are trying to avoid narrowing the curriculum by expanding testing beyond reading and mathematics; they intend to test the arts, physical education, science, and everything else that is taught. They are doing this to create the data to evaluate all teachers. Students will be tested more so their teachers' can be evaluated more. As the current national obsession with testing intensifies, we can expect to see more testing, more narrowing of the curriculum, more narrowing of instruction to only what is tested, more cheating, and less attention to teaching students to think, to discuss, to consider different ways to solve problems, and to be creative.

Linda Darling-Hammond, a Stanford University professor who is one of the nation's leading experts on the subject of preparing and evaluating teachers, lost her enthusiasm for evaluation by test scores as she saw the confusing and misleading results in such places as Tennessee, Houston, the District of Columbia, and New York City.[18]

Darling-Hammond concluded that the teacher ratings "largely reflect whom a teacher teaches, not how well they teach. In particular, teachers show lower gains when they have large numbers of new English-learners and students with disabilities than when they teach other students. This is true even when statistical methods are used to 'control' for student characteristics."

Why punish teachers for choosing to teach the students with the greatest needs or for being assigned to a class with such students?

If the goal of teacher evaluation is to help teachers improve, this method doesn't work. It doesn't provide useful information to teachers or show them how to improve their practice. It just labels and ranks them in ways that teachers find demeaning and humiliating. Darling-Hammond noted that Houston used a value-added method to fire a veteran who had been the district's teacher of the year. Another teacher in Houston said: "I teach the same way every year. [My] first year got me pats on the back. [My] second year got me kicked in the backside. And for year three, my scores were off the charts. I got a huge bonus. What did I do differently? I have no clue."

In 2010, the *Los Angeles Times* commissioned its own value-added analysis, based on nothing but test scores, and published the rankings of thousands of teachers. This initiated a national controversy about the ethics of publishing teachers' job ratings. No one claimed that instruction improved as a result.[19] The flaws of value-added analysis set off another heated debate in early 2012, when the New York City Department of Education publicly released the names and ratings of thousands of teachers. Rupert Murdoch's *New York Post* filed a freedom-of-information request for the ratings, which the teachers' union opposed, citing the ratings' inaccuracy. Mayor Michael Bloomberg contended that parents and the public had a right to know the teacher ratings. After the newspaper won the court battle with the union, the scores were released and widely published. The Department of Education warned the public about a large margin of error: On a 100-point scale, the margin of error in mathematics was 35 percentage points; the margin of error in reading was 53 points. In other words, a teacher of mathematics might be ranked as a 50 but might in fact be anywhere from the 15th percentile to the 85th percentile. In reading, the same teacher might improbably be at the -3rd percentile or the +103rd percentile, which demonstrates how useless the rankings were.[20]

The *New York Post* printed a story and photograph of the city's "best" teacher and its "worst" teacher. The teacher who was allegedly the worst was hounded by reporters at her home, as was her father. A few days later, it was revealed that she was a teacher of new immigrant students, who left her class as they learned English. She worked in a good school, and the principal said she was an excellent teacher. What was gained by giving her a low rating and putting her name and photograph in the newspaper? She suffered public humiliation because she taught English-language learners.[21]

Stated as politely as possible, value-added assessment is bad science. It may even be junk science. It is inaccurate, unstable, and unreliable. It may penalize those teachers who are assigned to teach weak students and those who choose to teach children with disabilities, English-language learners, and students with behavioral problems, as well as teachers of gifted students who are already at the top.

So, we circle back to the assertion that is common among reformers: Will three great teachers in a row close the achievement gap? It is possible, but there is no statistical method today that can accurately predict or identify which teachers are "great" teachers. If by great, we mean teachers who awaken students' desire to learn, who kindle in their students a sense of excitement about learning, scores on standardized tests do not identify those teachers. Nothing about a multiple-choice test is suited to finding the most inspiring and the most dedicated teachers in every school. In every school, students, teachers, and supervisors know who those teachers are. We need more of them. We will not get them by continuing to turn teachers into testing technicians or judging teachers by inappropriate statistical models.

If by great, we mean the ability to get students to produce higher scores every time they are tested, the current value-added assessments may identify some teachers who can do this. But, to my knowledge, there is no school in which every teacher achieves this target. Claiming, as reformers do, that one day every classroom will have a teacher who can produce extraordinary test score gains for every student, no matter what his or her circumstances, is simply not leveling with the American public. No nation in the world has achieved 100 percent proficiency. And no other nation in the world evaluates its teachers by the rise or fall of their students' test scores.

It is not even clear that this is a worthy goal.

Aside from the absence of evidence for this way of evaluating teachers, there remains the essential question of why scores on standardized tests should displace every other goal and expectation for schools: character, knowledge, citizenship, love of learning, creativity, initiative, and social skills.

CHAPTER 12

Why Merit Pay Fails

CLAIM *Merit pay will improve achievement.*

REALITY *Merit pay has never improved achievement.*

The reformers at the big foundations and the U.S. Department of Education decided that they could raise test scores and change the nature of the teaching profession by offering a type of financial incentive known as merit pay.

Like other corporate reformers, they believed that American public education is failing because of its teachers. They believed that the wrong kinds of people entered teaching, the kinds who did not graduate from elite colleges and universities and did not rank in the top third of their graduating classes. The reformers thought that the chance to earn performance pay would attract recruits with strong academic backgrounds. This, they thought, would solve the teacher-quality problem.

Reformers want education to become more like business, governed by the same principles of competition, with compensation tied to results. They see teacher tenure and teacher seniority as obstacles to achieving the flexible, results-oriented workforce that they believe is needed. They see teachers' unions as an obstacle, because the unions defend job protections for teachers and demand a salary scale with increases related to experience and education. In the reformers' ideal scenario, teachers would serve at the pleasure of their supervisors, as do employees in the business world. If they produce results, they win bonuses. If they do not produce results, their jobs will be on the line. Two or three years of lackluster results, and they will be fired. In some districts, such as the District of Columbia, a teacher may be fired based on a single year of poor results.

Teachers usually find this line of argument objectionable. They see themselves as professionals, not just employees. They don't like the idea that non-educators (and most of the reformers are non-educators or have taught for only a few years) are redesigning the rules of their workplace and profession. They don't like merit pay, because they know it will destroy the collaboration that is necessary for a healthy school climate. They are dumbfounded that the public discourse about education is fixated on blaming teachers for the ills of society. They don't understand why so much political energy is now being expended to remove their job security and put their careers in jeopardy.

Teachers are right to feel aggrieved. The remedies now promoted as cures for the teaching profession are unlikely to have a beneficial effect; they are almost certain to make the profession less attractive to those who want to make a career of teaching. The constant criticism that has dominated reform discourse for the past few years has discouraged and demoralized teachers.

Many teachers were disheartened by No Child Left Behind, which overemphasized standardized testing. Obama's Race to the Top proved even more discouraging than NCLB because it directly targets teachers as the source of student success or failure. Race to the Top offers incentives for school districts to fire the teachers in schools with low test scores as a remedy. The U.S. Department of Education set aside $1 billion for merit pay in the Teacher Incentive Fund.

Merit pay is not an innovative idea. It has been tried in school districts across the nation for the past century. Richard J. Murnane and David K. Cohen surveyed the history of merit pay in the mid-1980s and concluded that it "does not provide a solution to the problem of how to motivate teachers." In 1918, they reported, 48 percent of the school districts in the United States had some kind of merit pay plan, but few of them survived. By 1923, the proportion of districts with a merit pay plan had fallen to 33 percent, and in 1928 it was down to 18 percent. During the 1940s and 1950s, interest in merit pay declined, and by 1953 only 4 percent of cities with a population over thirty thousand offered merit pay. This could not have been because of the power of teachers' unions, because there were few unionized teachers at the time, and where unions existed, they were poorly organized and weak. After

Sputnik in 1957, there was again a flurry of interest in merit pay, and 10 percent of districts offered it. But many of these programs disappeared, and by the mid-1980s, when Murnane and Cohen wrote their article, 99 percent of the nation's teachers were in districts that had a uniform salary schedule, based on education and experience.[1]

Murnane and Cohen found two types of merit pay plans. One offered bonuses to teachers if their students got higher test scores. The other offered bonuses to teachers who got superior evaluations from their principals. They described efforts to tie teachers' pay to student test scores as the "new style" of merit pay; they called it a "piece-rate compensation system." This method avoids the subjectivity of the "old style," which depends on principal judgment, but the "new style" does not fit the nature of teachers' work. Piece-rate work, they noted, is better suited to manufacturing jobs, where it is relatively easy to measure the true contribution of the individual worker to the firm's output at low cost. So, for example, a commercial laundry can pay workers based on how many shirts they iron in an hour or a day. Quality can be determined by customer complaints.

But piece-rate compensation doesn't work with teachers, said Murnane and Cohen. First, it encourages teachers to spend more time with the students who will respond to their coaching and to spend less time with those who will not. This problem was observed in the 1970s, when the U.S. government offered performance contracts to private firms to manage schools; evaluations revealed that the firms overlooked the students at the top, who could manage on their own, and the students at the bottom, who were the toughest challenge. Most of their efforts were concentrated on the students in the middle, who would show the biggest improvement.

Another problem with piece-rate evaluation had been noted in similar evaluation schemes in mid-nineteenth-century England: when judged by test scores, teachers were likely to ignore the subjects that were not tested, meaning there was a narrowing of the curriculum, and important skills were ignored because they were hard to test.

The most significant obstacle to performance pay based on test scores, the authors argued, is the nature of teachers' work. Very few private schools engage in the practice, even though it would be easy for them to do so. They don't do it because schools have multiple goals, not just raising test scores. Even if you could isolate the teachers' contribution to test scores, you would simultaneously destroy the teamwork that is necessary to accomplish other important goals, such as encouraging good behavior or reducing drug use. School principals recognize the multiplicity of goals and the importance of teamwork; they also understand the perverse incentives introduced by piece-rate compensation. That may explain, said Murnane and Cohen, why "paying teachers on the basis of their students' test scores is extraordinarily rare in American education." Even if the quality of standardized tests were far better, even if they perfectly matched what students were supposed to learn, they argued, the negative consequences of piece-rate compensation would still make it objectionable.

The authors also found fault with the "old style" of merit pay, where the principal decides who gets a bonus. Most of these experiments failed too. The problem is fairness and the perception of fairness. The supervisor must be able to answer two questions: One, why did worker X get merit pay and I didn't? Two, what can I do to get merit pay? The task of unloading boxes from a truck is an activity for which it is easy to answer these questions. Worker X unloads more boxes than you; if you unload more boxes, you too can get merit pay. That makes sense to the worker. It is defensible. But when a principal awards merit pay to teacher X and not to teacher Y, he needs an explanation better than "I know good teaching when I see it." Did the teacher get merit pay because she was outstanding or because she was a favorite of the principal's? Will teachers know what to do to improve their chances of getting merit pay? And will they hide their problems from the principal instead of asking for help? Thus, it is the nature of the teaching activity itself that causes "old style" merit pay to fail repeatedly.

When Murnane and Cohen interviewed teachers and administrators, they learned that when teachers got poor ratings, they didn't work harder; they "responded by working less hard." If teachers felt their evaluation was unfair, they reacted angrily. Some of the principals who were interviewed said that before the introduction of merit pay, they often gave higher ratings than the teachers deserved because teachers would try to live up to their praise. With a higher rating (even if undeserved), teachers not only worked harder but were more open about seeking help for their problems.

Once merit pay was introduced, the principals no longer had the freedom to give so many high ratings because it would cost too much in bonuses. They came under pressure from budget-conscious superintendents to limit the number of high ratings, so they had to make choices. As one principal said to the authors, "Merit pay turns my job from being a coach into being a referee." As the principal became a judge rather than a coach, teachers viewed him differently, with less trust. Merit pay changed the role of the principal in some respects by removing one of his motivational tools. He has to rely on his teachers to do their best and be highly motivated, but every time the principal gives a rating that is less than the teacher expected, he undermines the teacher's morale. The primary reasons that school districts decided to eliminate merit pay were the demoralization of teachers and the problems of administering the program fairly.

The authors looked for districts where merit pay had survived. They found only a few. Not one of them was an urban district. Not one was a once-troubled district that successfully used merit pay to improve its performance. Most were small homogeneous districts that offered very small amounts of money. The few districts where merit pay had survived were notable for high salaries and good working conditions. But of greater importance was that the merit pay *was extra pay for extra work,* not bonuses for higher test scores or for something indefinable that the principal liked. The districts with merit pay also pursued a strategy of "make everyone feel special," because almost every teacher received some monetary award, and the differences among them were not large. That eased tensions among teachers.

In other districts with long-lasting merit pay plans, the conditions for winning merit pay were so onerous and the rewards so small that no one cared much who got it. In all of the districts with merit pay, it was understood that no one would find out who won the extra money or how much they won. Another reason for the longevity of the merit pay plans is that all of them were designed by teachers to make them acceptable, non-divisive, and relatively unobtrusive.

I have delved into the Murnane and Cohen paper in detail because I think it sheds light on the dilemmas of merit pay today. When they were writing, in the mid-1980s, there was very little interest in the idea of pay for performance and very few districts where any form of merit pay existed.

What they learned then remains pertinent.

Although many districts had tried test-based performance pay in the past, not a single school district in the United States at that time awarded bonuses based on student test scores.

Merit pay turned out not to motivate teachers. In fact, it typically caused resentment and dissension among teachers who did not get merit pay.

Merit pay was not associated with improved student performance.

Where merit pay survived, it was connected to the extra work that teachers do, it was inconspicuous, and the awards were kept secret to avoid causing bad feelings.

Certainly, there are lessons for us today in this not-so-distant history. Only a generation ago, educators, school board members, and the general public abandoned the idea that bonuses might motivate teachers, yet today we have a reform movement that demands what has never worked in the past. Not only has the U.S. Department of Education committed to spend $1 billion of taxpayer money to support test-based bonuses ("piece-rate compensation," to use Murnane and Cohen's term), but many states have passed programs committing hundreds of millions of dollars for state-based merit pay programs at a time of budget cuts.

The goal of current merit pay plans is simple: the lure of a bonus is supposed to motivate teachers to work harder and therefore to get students to produce higher test scores. The goal is also to get the "effective" teachers to remain in the classroom and to attract new teachers who are motivated by the chance to make more money than a standard teacher's salary.

It is not clear what the connection is between teachers working harder and students getting higher test scores. I recall hearing the late Albert Shanker say at a public meeting many years ago, "Let me get this clear. If you offer teachers more money, the students will work harder and get better grades?"

But that is in fact the main theory of action today behind merit pay. Offer bonuses to teachers, they will be motivated to get the money, they will teach more and better, and students will get higher test scores. Of course teachers want to be paid more, but they don't want to compete with one another for bonuses tied to test scores. Some reformers believe that merit pay will lead to a restructuring of the teaching profession, making it more attractive to people who were in the top third of their graduating class at university; they will be attracted to teaching because of the opportunity to make more money. But frankly, anyone who becomes a teacher with the expectation of making big money is not making a wise career choice. He or she would be better off in another field.

The National Center on Performance Incentives at Vanderbilt University carried out the most definitive study of merit pay. Some economists speculated that the reason merit pay had never gotten good results in the past was that the reward was so small. So the Vanderbilt study offered a bonus of $15,000 for teachers whose students got higher math scores. Over three years, the researchers closely observed the performance of teachers in a control group and an experimental group in the Nashville public schools. In 2010, the results were released: the study found no significant difference in the test scores of the students taught by teachers in the two groups. Presumably, both groups of teachers were doing the best they could.[2]

Within days of the release of the Vanderbilt study, the U.S. Department of Education released the first $500 million for the Teacher Incentive Fund to encourage more districts to try merit pay.

At the same time that the Nashville experiment was initiated, New York City embarked on its version of merit pay. After negotiation with the teachers' union, the city's Department of Education announced that two hundred schools would receive school-wide bonuses if test scores went up. A committee at each school would decide how to divide the bonus and whether to split it up among teachers only or among the entire school staff. The city paid out $56 million in bonuses but at the end of three years abandoned the experiment. A study by the Rand Corporation documented the failure of the New York City plan. It did not raise test scores in reading or mathematics. It did not increase teacher satisfaction. It was a waste of public money.[3]

Undaunted by the failure of the school-wide bonus plan, Mayor Michael Bloomberg announced in 2011 that he wanted to initiate a new merit pay plan, offering $20,000 to individual teachers who were able to raise test scores.[4] This plan closely paralleled the one that failed in Nashville.

Meanwhile, a four-year study of the Teacher Advancement Program in Chicago concluded that the schools offering merit pay showed a somewhat higher retention rate of teachers but no significant impact on student test scores.[5] Merit pay didn't work in Texas, either. There the program got poor results in a pilot test, but the state legislature responded to this failure by expanding the program to $200 million a year (the funding was slashed in 2011 when the state legislature cut $5.4 billion from the public schools' budget). In sum, all contemporary evidence on merit pay plans in American schools shows that they have had no effect on student test scores.[6]

The business expert W. Edwards Deming strongly opposed performance pay. Speaking of corporations, not schools, Deming warned against the corrosive effect of performance pay in the workplace. He said that it promotes rivalry and destroys teamwork. It ruins morale. It gets workers focused on themselves, not on what is good for the organization. It promotes short-term thinking and undermines long-term goals. He saw no value in using money to encourage employees to compete with one another. Deming contended that if management is doing its job, hiring the right employees, supporting them in their work, and keeping the system stable, most employees will perform well. As one biographer, Andrea Gabor, put it, "Deming believes that ranking employees is a cop-out for inadequate leadership."[7]

The paradox of merit pay in education is that even if it did work, it would still fail. The more that teachers and schools are compelled to focus on raising test scores, the more they are likely to narrow the curriculum; the more likely that districts and schools will game the system to inflate scores; the more likely that there will be cheating; the more likely that teachers will seek to avoid low-scoring students. So, to the extent that schools are promised rewards for raising test scores (and punishments for not raising test scores), the quality of education will suffer. Schools will reduce the time for the arts, history, science, foreign languages, physical education, and anything else that is not tested. Or test everything, which would reduce instructional time even more than testing only basic skills. That way lies bad education, whether it is a narrow curriculum or a school that expends disproportionate amounts of time testing and preparing for testing.

Economists discount the importance of experience and education on grounds that they have no effect on test scores. They should also discount merit pay—for the same reason.

Merit pay is the idea that never works and never dies. Merit pay is faith-based policy. No matter how many times it fails, its advocates never give up. They are true believers. Next time it will work, they say. Next time we will get it right. No matter how many hundreds of millions of dollars are squandered with no benefit to anyone, there is always next time. Their belief in the magical power of money is unbounded. Their belief in the importance of evidence is not.

CHAPTER 13

Do Teachers Need Tenure and Seniority?

CLAIM *Schools will improve if tenure and seniority are abolished.*

REALITY *There is no evidence for this claim.*

One of the cardinal rules of the corporate reformist dogma is that teachers should have no job protections. Reformers believe that schools will be more successful if teachers serve at the will of their supervisors, who may dismiss them at any time for any reason. Reformers say that the business world works this way, and it is wrong for educators to have tenure or seniority. They say that these job protections make it impossible to fire bad teachers. Since they believe that firing bad teachers is the key to improving education, it follows that teachers should have no job protections. Reformers assume that if teachers can be easily fired, schools can quickly get rid of the low performers, and those who remain will work harder and produce higher test scores.

Reformers want to retain only effective teachers. The effective teacher is the one whose students get higher scores every year. If a first-year teacher can get students to produce higher test scores, then she is a better teacher than the teacher with fifteen years of experience. The reformers are convinced that experience, credentials, and degrees don't matter. Bill Gates told the nation's governors in 2010 that teachers should not be paid more for master's degrees or years of experience because they do not increase test scores. Only "effectiveness," that is, the ability to raise test scores, matters. The most effective teachers, he proposed, should be paid more to teach larger class sizes and work in the neediest schools.[1]

Thus, the traditional way of paying teachers is completely wrong, in the eyes of the reformers, because it rewards additional education and experience, not effectiveness.

Not only are ineffective teachers retained and promoted, the reformers say, but it is impossible to fire them because of tenure and seniority.

The reformers' mission has therefore been to tie compensation to test scores (which they refer to as either "effectiveness" or "performance") and to abolish tenure and seniority, thus making it easier to get rid of the deadbeat teachers, the incompetents who hang on forever, the ones who (as some governors charged) are paid "just for breathing" or "just for showing up."

Michelle Rhee, Michael Bloomberg, and Joel Klein, among others, declared war on tenure and seniority in articles, public testimony before legislative bodies, and political advertisements. Michelle Rhee campaigned in state after state against tenure and seniority, and her organization StudentsFirst funded politicians who agreed. Their arguments received a warm reception in conservative states in the South, the West, and the Midwest. The Gates Foundation helped establish new organizations of young teachers with names like Teach Plus and Educators 4 Excellence, who publicly opposed tenure and seniority in legislative hearings. Other reform groups like Democrats for Education Reform, Education Reform Now, and Stand for Children have lobbied against job protections for teachers and against the seniority principle that they call LIFO (or "last in, first out").

The reformers believe that scores will go up if it is easy to fire teachers and if unions are weakened.

But is this true?

No. The only test scores that can be used comparatively are those of the National Assessment of Educational Progress, because it is a no-stakes test. No one knows who will take it, no one knows what will be on the test, no student takes the full test, and the results are not reported for individuals or for schools. There is no way to prepare for NAEP, so there is no test prep. There are no rewards or punishments attached to it, so there is no reason to cheat, to teach to the test, or to game the system.

So, let's examine the issues at hand using NAEP scores as a measure. The states that consistently have the highest test scores are Massachusetts, New Jersey, and Connecticut. Consistently ranking at the bottom are states in the South and the District of Columbia. The highest-ranking states have strong teachers' unions and until recently had strong tenure protections for teachers. The lowest-ranking states do not have strong teachers' unions, and their teachers have few or no job protections. There seems to be no correlation between having a strong union and having low test scores; if anything, it appears that the states with the strongest unions have the highest test scores. The lowest-performing states have one thing in common, and that is high poverty. The District of Columbia has a strong union and high poverty; it also has intense racial isolation in its schools. It has very low test scores. Most of the cities that rank at the very bottom on NAEP have teachers' unions, and they have two things in common: high poverty and racial isolation.

Having unionized teachers does not get in the way of high academic achievement, nor, in the case of the District of Columbia (and other high-poverty urban districts), does it guarantee high achievement. Conversely, the states where unions are weak or nonexistent have low achievement. Eliminating unions does not produce higher achievement, better teachers, or even higher test scores. Eliminating unions silences the most powerful advocate for public education in every state. It assures that there will be no one at the table to object when the governor or legislature wants to cut the budget for public schools. The union's main role is to advocate for better working conditions and better compensation for its members. Better working conditions translate into better learning conditions for students, such as reduced class size and more resources for the schools. Better compensation attracts and retains teachers, which reduces teacher attrition. That too benefits students.[2]

What about tenure? Does it prevent schools from getting rid of bad teachers? Is it an obstacle to high student performance?

The first thing to realize about tenure is that teachers demanded and got tenure long before there were unions. In the nineteenth and early twentieth centuries, teachers could be fired for arbitrary or capricious reasons. No explanation was required when supervisors and school boards decided to fire teachers. They could be fired because of their color, their ethnic background, their accent, their religion, their looks, or for any other reason. They could be fired because someone on the school board wanted to give their job to his nephew or his friend's wife. Women could be fired if they got married; when they fought and won the right to get married, they could be fired if they became pregnant. If they were active as teacher leaders, they could be fired for their activism. Teachers fought for tenure—and won it—long before they had collective bargaining and unions. Until the 1960s, teachers had no political power and their unions were disorganized and weak, but they agreed on one principle: they needed to be protected from unjust firing. And they won these concessions from courts and by making persistent demands on their employers. The fact that they won anything at all is even more remarkable when you consider that most teachers were women and most women did not have the right to vote until 1920 and lacked political power.

It is important to bear in mind that tenure in K–12 education does not mean the same thing as it does in higher education. A professor in higher education who has tenure can seldom, if ever, be fired. Only the most egregious behavior would be grounds for dismissing a tenured professor. Tenure in higher education is close to ironclad.

In the public schools, however, tenure means due process. There is no ironclad tenure for teachers. A teacher who has tenure is entitled to a hearing before an impartial arbitrator, where the teacher has the right to see the evidence and the grounds for the charges against him or her and to offer a defense. Critics say that the dismissal process is too cumbersome and too costly; they say it takes too long to remove an incompetent teacher. In some states and districts, that is true. It is the job of the state and the district to negotiate a fair and expeditious process to handle charges and hearings. The hearings should be resolved in months, not years. After a fair hearing, teachers found to be incompetent or guilty of moral turpitude should be removed without delay.

Critics like to cite the small number of teachers who have been fired for incompetence as proof that more should be fired. What they never admit, however, is that many teachers are asked to leave (that is, terminated) without ever winning tenure. About 40 percent of those who enter teaching leave the profession within the first five years. In some urban districts, where class sizes are larger and teaching conditions are more difficult than in suburban schools, the attrition rate is even higher. Some leave because they are asked to leave. Some leave for easier jobs in the suburbs; some quit because the job was too hard for them, they didn't like their assignments, or they didn't get the resources and help they needed.[3]

After a teacher has been on the job for three or four years, depending on state law, the principal decides whether he or she qualifies for tenure. By that time, the principal and her assistants or department chairs are supposed to have observed the teacher repeatedly, seen the conduct of the classroom, reviewed the kinds of assignments the teacher's classes were turning in. By that time, the teacher should have gotten support and help to improve at the job. Only after observation and positive evaluation by supervisors—and sometimes peers—do teachers receive tenure. When the principal awards tenure, he or she has determined that the teacher is well qualified to teach and deserves the protection of due process. If the award of tenure is made without careful deliberation, then the principal and the central administration should be held accountable for failing to fulfill their responsibilities.

Once the teacher has tenure, he has a measure of job security. He knows that he won't be fired except for just cause and that he will have a chance to defend himself if accused of misconduct. For many who enter the teaching profession, the prospect of having job security is part of what makes the profession attractive. Many are willing to work for less money because they have the possibility of job security. The job security is a form of real income to teachers. It signals to them that they are part of a team and a profession. Once the teacher has tenure, he has professional autonomy; a new supervisor can't compel him to adopt the latest fad. With tenure, the teacher is free to exercise his best professional judgment in the classroom without fear of political reprisals; with tenure, he can take the risk of being a whistle-blower if he sees administrators or other teachers abusing children or changing test scores or doing something else that is wrong.

What does it mean if teachers don't have tenure? At the very least it means they will be insecure in their jobs. Without tenure, experienced teachers might be laid off to cut costs and replaced by inexperienced and less costly teachers. Without tenure, teachers will worry about running afoul of the principal or their other supervisors. If the principal is zealous about a particular method of teaching—say, phonics or whole language—teachers had better comply and not risk the principal's displeasure. They will worry about offending parents, such as the parent who thinks her child should have gotten a higher grade and who might complain to the principal. If they see wrongdoing or cheating, they will be reluctant to report it for fear of getting into trouble. They might hesitate to teach evolution or global warming for fear that someone in the community might object. They will think twice before assigning a novel that any parent might find offensive, such as Mark Twain's *Huckleberry Finn* or Aldous Huxley's *Brave New World* or the Harry Potter books (fundamentalist groups do not approve of magic and witchcraft) or a novel by John Steinbeck or some other classic author. Just take a look at the American Library Association's list of the hundred most frequently censored books to see how easy it would be for a teacher to arouse the ire of a disgruntled parent or pressure group. Without tenure, teachers would be wise to stick to the blandest, least controversial books and topics, or to the textbooks, which have already been carefully screened by review panels to eliminate anything remotely controversial.

So, if reformers succeed in eliminating tenure, they will eliminate teachers' academic freedom as well. This is not a wise trade-off. Teachers are being asked to assume more risk (lack of job security) without any assurance of additional compensation; this is not even good market economics. A veteran superintendent recently said to me, "The reformers want to get rid of a few rats by burning down the whole barn." Indeed, the reformers are moving from state to state, attacking tenure even in the high-performing states of Massachusetts, New Jersey, and Connecticut. They claim that eliminating tenure will make it easier to fire teachers and thus to close the achievement gap. Yet they cannot show any connection between tenure and academic performance. Teachers in the highest-performing schools have it, and teachers in the lowest-performing schools have it. Tenure does not cause low academic performance; taking it away won't cause academic performance to rise. But one thing is sure: teachers see the attack on their job security as an economic and psychological loss, a betrayal, a punishment inflicted on them for being teachers. The removal of tenure, now advancing from state to state, is profoundly demoralizing. It is impossible to say what the benefits are or might be.

The other prong of this two-pronged attack is the effort to remove any seniority rights. Reformers demean the importance of experience. They point to studies by Eric Hanushek and Robert Gordon as evidence that experience does not produce higher test scores. This is one of those instances where the findings of economists do not concur with the wisdom of teachers. I have never met a teacher, other than the handful paid by foundations to advocate otherwise, who discounted the importance of experience in teaching. All the teachers I know say that they are constantly learning, constantly working at improving their lessons and strategies. And young teachers express gratitude toward the experienced teachers who helped them learn the ropes. Teaching is such a labor-intensive and demanding job that it is impossible to imagine that experience doesn't matter. Not every veteran teacher is first-rate, but that is no reason to discount the importance of experience.

Many experienced teachers were educated in a different era, before No Child Left Behind, and they remember a time when standardized tests were not the measure of everything. Many came into teaching with the expectation that it would be their career and their profession, not a way station while they decided on a different career. Veteran educators do not like to be lectured to by non-educators or by those with only two years in the classroom. Call it human nature.

Some history might be helpful here. In the absence of any tenure protections, teachers in the late nineteenth century created their own informal seniority system. In the big cities, there was an informal understanding among teachers that the oldest had the most stature. The longer a teacher stayed in a school, the higher her rank on the staff. Where such systems arose, as they did in New York City, teachers would not transfer to another school, because they would lose their seniority and their status.

In some districts, seniority was taken to absurd lengths. The date a teacher was appointed governed how much seniority she had, and those with the most seniority got choice appointments. Even the difference of a day or a week could affect the teacher's place in line to get an assignment. Seniority as such had nothing to do with competence; there was no way of ascertaining that a teacher with twenty-two years of experience was better than a teacher with fifteen years of experience. And then there is the problem of the teacher who clings to the job long after she has lost her sharpness and even her wits.

So unlike tenure, which protects academic freedom and professional autonomy, seniority should be restructured. Experience matters, but beyond a certain point it's not possible to weigh and calibrate the value of more or fewer years of experience. Gray hair in and of itself is not a virtue.

Seniority becomes a major issue when there are budget cuts and teachers are laid off. Traditionally, teachers are laid off based on seniority: the teacher with the least seniority gets the first pink slip. There should be a better way to do it, but it's not obvious what the better way is. There ought to be a way of gauging the need for a specialized teacher—for example, a teacher of mathematics or science or a teacher of special education or bilingual education, all of which are fields with shortages—and finding a reasonable weight for a teacher's contribution to the school as a student adviser, teacher mentor, or in a position with other responsibilities. Consideration must also be given to a teacher's contribution in supporting the culture of the school, the teamwork and collaboration that schools need to function effectively.

Such issues require human judgment, professional judgment. Seniority became prevalent as a supposedly objective way to decide who gets the first pink slips and who gets the best assignments. Teachers don't like principals to be able to pick and choose their favorites. And they are fearful that the most experienced teachers may be laid off not because they are bad teachers but because they have the highest salaries and are expensive.

The reformers' answer to this dilemma is to use student test scores as the definition of "effectiveness." But teachers know that this measure will favor those who teach the "easiest" students and will punish those who choose to teach or are assigned to teach the most challenging students. They know that only a minority of teachers teach in subjects and grades that are regularly tested. They also know that the variability in test scores is not necessarily of their making. And they understand that putting so much emphasis on the tests will lead to negative consequences, like teaching to the test.

No teacher should win tenure automatically. Even tenured teachers should be regularly evaluated by their supervisors. The principal and the assistant principal should regularly observe teachers, not to judge them, but to provide them with useful feedback about how to improve their lessons. To do this, the principal and the assistant principal must be master teachers themselves. If they are not master teachers, they cannot give advice to other teachers. The primary job of the principal is to be "head teacher." That means he or she should be an excellent teacher and an excellent teacher of teachers.

The evaluation process should include peer review. The school should have a team of excellent teachers available to visit classrooms and provide feedback and support. Teachers who are new or who are struggling should get help promptly. The administrators and the peer reviewers should be responsible for providing help in a timely fashion. I recall sitting next to John Jackson, the president of the Schott Foundation for Public Education, at a conference in New Orleans. When the discussion turned to teacher evaluation, Jackson said he had recently concluded visits to several other nations to meet with their ministries of education. At each stop, he asked the question: "What do you do about bad teachers?" And each time, he got the same reply: "We help them." And then he asked, "What do you do if you help them and they don't improve?" And the answer was everywhere the same: "We help them more."

In the present climate, there is hardly any public official in the United States who would give the second answer. At this point, I would be happy if they were willing to give the first answer. "We help them."

The current reform narrative emphasizes the importance of firing "bad" teachers. But the reality is that our current system is hemorrhaging teachers. Since the adoption of No Child Left Behind, teacher retirements have accelerated. Federal data reveal alarming facts: In 1988, there were more teachers with fifteen years of experience than any other group. By 2008, "the modal teacher was not a gray-haired veteran; he or she was a beginner in the first year of teaching. In 1987–88, there were about 65,000 first-year teachers; by 2007–8, this number had grown to 200,000. By that year, a quarter of the teaching force had five years or less of experience."[4]

Can a nation expect to have a good educational system without a stable workforce of experienced professional educators? The greatest imperative we face as a nation with regard to teacher quality is not to find and fire teachers but to find and develop a highly skilled professional teacher corps. We must improve the recruitment of good candidates into teaching, prepare them well for the challenges of the classroom, support them as they begin their teaching careers, provide good working conditions, give them the public respect they deserve for the important work they do, ensure them the professional autonomy they deserve in their classrooms, and treat them as professionals.

CHAPTER 14

The Problem with Teach for America

CLAIM *Teach for America recruits teachers and leaders whose high expectations will one day ensure that every child has an excellent education.*

REALITY *Teach for America sends bright young people into tough classrooms where they get about the same results as other bright young people in similar classrooms but leave the profession sooner.*

It's hard to be critical of Teach for America (TFA) because the idea is so positive and the young people it attracts are so terrific. Who could possibly object to an organization that recruits thousands of smart young college graduates to teach for two years in some of our nation's most distressed urban and rural schools? Who could question the sincerity and idealism of these young men and women?

It is necessary, however, to distinguish between the young people who join TFA and the organization itself.

Wendy Kopp conceived the idea of Teach for America as her undergraduate thesis at Princeton University in 1989. This organization, she proposed, would attract the nation's top college graduates into teaching for a two-year stint. It was akin to the Peace Corps in that it would enlist the idealism of young people and give them an opportunity to serve the less fortunate members of society. Even before a single new teacher had entered a single classroom, major publications such as *The New York Times, Newsweek,* and *Time* lauded TFA, and corporations offered millions of dollars to launch the new program. College students responded enthusiastically. The two-year commitment gave them time to think about what they wanted to do next, whether to go to graduate school or enter business or even stay in education.

The earliest cohort had 500 recruits; the next year's had 750. As TFA became established, the number of applicants grew, and it had more applicants than places available. It screened applicants and tapped those it considered the best. TFA developed a reputation among college students as a highly selective organization, as indeed it was. TFA became its own brand. Not only was it a feather in your cap to be accepted as a corps member, but having TFA on your résumé was like getting a gold star, a signal to future employers in the corporate, legal, and financial sectors and to graduate school admissions committees that you were one of "the best and brightest."

Kopp proved to be a genius at marketing, organization, and fund-raising. She built a high-powered board made up of superstars from the corporate, financial, and media sectors, and she established partnerships with leaders in each field, both for fund-raising and as valuable connections for TFA corps members. TFA provided entrée for its alumni to a powerful and influential network and a path to professional success. When TFA convened a party in 2011 to celebrate its twentieth anniversary, its corps members of the previous twenty years rubbed shoulders with corporate titans, education leaders, well-known journalists, major financial figures, think tank intellectuals, and top government officials.

Each year, TFA selected and sent out newly minted young teachers. Each year, it reached agreements with school districts and states to hire them. As of 2012, in its twenty-first year, TFA counted about thirty thousand alumni. Typically, TFA trains its corps members for five weeks before school opens, and the district agrees to pay $2,000–$5,000 as a fee to the organization for each TFA teacher, plus a full salary to the teacher. Some districts underwrite the cost of courses that TFA members must take to win state certification as they teach.

If this were the beginning and the end of the TFA story, it would be rightly hailed as a wonderful social innovation, a much-needed help for distressed districts that are unable to find enough qualified teachers for high-poverty schools with shortages of teachers of science and mathematics. For sure, having a hardworking and well-educated young graduate of a fine university is far better than having no teacher at all or having a coach teach science, even though he has no degree in science.

But then the story changes from the original idea to a different narrative: the story of TFA's grand ambition. TFA is not content to send out young people to do useful work in the schools. Flush with media acclaim and corporate largesse, TFA sells its brand as the best means of changing American education and ending educational inequity. It maintains that its teachers are singularly equipped to save children's lives, because TFA teachers have high expectations, clear goals, and a sense of purpose. It portrays itself as a prominent actor in the new civil rights movement, a force to abolish inequality and establish social justice. It is as though the Peace Corps claimed that its young volunteers are more successful than seasoned diplomats, know how to bring about world peace, and should be making foreign policy.

On the face of it, such claims should have been laughable. No first-year teacher, especially one with only five weeks of training, is fully prepared for the challenges of a classroom filled with boisterous students in the nation's poorest communities. How can these young people expect to close the achievement gap and establish equality across the land when they agree to remain for only two years? Even though some stay for three or four years and a few decide to become career teachers or move into administrative roles, this makes no sense.

It seems even more improbable to say that TFA is leading the new civil rights movement when Wendy Kopp often says that we don't have to fix poverty, we have to fix schools. What civil rights leader would say that? What civil rights leader would assert that we can "fix" the schools instead of improving jobs, health care, and housing?

In her book *A Chance to Make History,* Kopp writes that when she started, "many assumed that fixing education would require fixing poverty first." She is now convinced, however, that TFA teachers, "even in their first and second years of teaching, are proving it is possible for economically disadvantaged children to compete academically with their higher-income peers." This actually isn't true, but no matter. She asserts there is "hard evidence that we can ensure all of our children in urban and rural communities have the opportunity to attain an excellent education." She maintains that "over the last twenty years we in the United States have discovered that we don't have to wait to fix poverty to dramatically improve educational outcomes for underprivileged students." When she appeared at Harvard in 2012, *Harvard Magazine* summed up her presentation: "Two decades ago, many educators thought urban schools could improve only if progress was made against poverty. Wendy Kopp thought there was another way to make a difference."[1]

But Kopp was wrong. The educators who thought we could improve schools by making progress against poverty were right. We must work *both* to improve schools and to reduce poverty, not to prioritize one over the other or say that schools come first, poverty later. Children are more likely to do well in school if they arrive in school healthy and ready to learn. TFA teachers are no substitute for jobs, nutrition, good housing, and health care. Poverty rises or falls in response to the economy, not in response to smart young people who teach for two or three years in poor communities or work in the state department of education, even as state commissioner.

In *A Chance to Make History*, Kopp acknowledges that there are no "silver bullets," that Teach for America does not have all the answers, and that the work of education is hard and complex. Yet she does not retreat from her claim that TFA recruits are as good as or better than veteran teachers and that the education leaders trained by TFA are transforming American education in fundamental and positive ways. The Teach for America Web site says that the problem of low academic performance in high-poverty neighborhoods is "a solvable problem": "We can provide an excellent education for kids in low-income communities. Although 16 million American children face the extra challenges of poverty, an increasing body of evidence shows they can achieve at the highest levels."[2] Nothing is said on the Web site about addressing or reducing poverty, leaving the implication that "the problem" (low test scores of students who are poor) is "solvable" by TFA.

We live in an age of public relations and perception. And the TFA brand is a winner. The organization from the start was a fund-raising colossus. Its board of directors contains some of America's most powerful figures from Wall Street and the corporate sector. At the same time that it raises millions from its sponsors and allies, TFA appeals to the public to contribute its nickels and dimes. Giving to TFA is pitched as equivalent to giving to the Girl Scouts, as a noble act of charity.

When the U.S. Department of Education ran a competition in 2010 for the most innovative programs in education, with four top prizes of $50 million, TFA was one of the winners (the KIPP charter chain, headed by Wendy Kopp's husband, Richard Barth, also won $50 million). In 2011, a group of foundations led by the Broad Foundation made a gift of $100 million to TFA. In the same year, the Walton Family Foundation—one of the nation's most conservative foundations—pitched in $49.5 million, the largest single education grant made that year by a foundation committed to privatization. TFA also received federal funding through AmeriCorps grants and an annual congressional earmark of about $20 million. In the five years from 2006 to 2010, TFA raised an astonishing $907 million in foundation grants, corporate gifts, and government funding.[3]

Wendy Kopp says that "one day, all children in our nation will have the opportunity to attain an excellent education."[4] This will happen, she says, for two reasons.

First, she claims that TFA's recruits, fresh out of college and with only five weeks of training, get better results than new teachers who spent a year or more in teacher education programs, and that "a significant body of rigorous research" shows that they are "on average, equally or more effective than veteran teachers."[5]

Second, she claims that TFA alumni will take their places in the halls of power and become advocates for education. She wrote: "In the long run, we build a force of leaders who, with the insight and added conviction that comes from teaching in a low-income community, influence civic consciousness from inside education and other professions. Our alumni are a powerful leadership force working to effect the fundamental, systemic changes necessary to ensure educational opportunity for all."[6]

Do TFA members get their students to produce higher test scores than other teachers, both new ones and veterans, as Kopp and TFA often claim?

Careful reviews of research have concluded that TFA corps members get about the same test score results as other new and uncertified teachers. Some studies show that TFA teachers get small but significant gains in math but not in reading. One of the most positive studies found that the students taught by TFA teachers increased their math scores from the 14th percentile to the 17th percentile, which was significant but very far from closing the achievement gap between low-income students and their high-income peers.[7]

Julian Vasquez Heilig and Su Jin Jez reviewed the research about Teach for America and concluded that when compared to other new and uncredentialed teachers in the same schools, "novice TFA teachers perform equivalently, and experienced TFA teachers perform comparably in raising reading scores and a bit better in raising math scores." When compared to beginning teachers who are credentialed, said Heilig and Sun, "the students of novice TFA teachers perform significantly less well in reading and mathematics." Furthermore,

> the relatively few TFA teachers who stay long enough to become fully credentialed (typically after two years) appear to do about as well as other similarly experienced credentialed teachers in teaching reading; they do as well as, and sometimes better than, that comparison group in teaching mathematics. However, since more than 50% of TFA teachers leave after two years, and more than 80% leave after three years, it is impossible to know whether these more positive findings for experienced recruits result from additional training and experience or from attrition of TFA teachers who may be less effective.

The reviewers found that the high attrition of TFA teachers presented a problem for schools and districts: "From a school-wide perspective, the high turnover of TFA teachers is costly. Recruiting and training replacements for teachers who leave involves financial costs, and the higher achievement gains associated with experienced teachers and lower turnover may be lost as well."[8]

TFA contends that the high turnover rate of its recruits doesn't matter because its long-term goal is to increase the number of influential people who care about education and who become transformative education leaders. To some extent, it has succeeded. Of the thirty thousand or so TFA alumni, many are successful in politics, Wall Street, the media, business, and other walks of life. Since they were carefully culled from top universities, this is not surprising. But it is debatable whether those who have achieved eminence in education are advancing the cause of public education.

Many of the most prominent alumni have taken leading roles in the corporate reform movement. They have created charter schools, they lead charter school chains, and they actively advance the cause of privatization. The best-known graduate of TFA is Michelle Rhee, who is a prominent opponent of teachers' unions and teachers' tenure and an outspoken advocate of high-stakes testing and privatization. John White, the state superintendent of education in Louisiana, is another graduate of TFA. His dual credentials as a graduate of TFA and the Broad Superintendents Academy propelled him to his leadership role in Louisiana at the age of thirty-five, a feat that would be almost unimaginable for someone who had risen through the traditional route of teaching and administration. White was not just any state superintendent. He served governor Bobby Jindal of Louisiana, who launched a radical effort to privatize education by diverting money dedicated by the state constitution to the support of public elementary and secondary schools, not only to charters and vouchers, but to for-profit online businesses and private vendors of every kind.

Many of the TFA alumni who became leading figures in education are strong proponents of test-based accountability. In Tennessee, the TFA alumnus Kevin Huffman was appointed by a conservative Republican governor to push through an agenda of evaluating teachers by the test scores of their students and expanding school choice; like Rhee and White, he supports vouchers and for-profit virtual schools. In Colorado, the TFA alumnus Michael Johnston was elected to the state legislature and wrote legislation to make student test scores count for 50 percent of every teacher's and principal's evaluation, despite the absence of any evidence for doing so. When you consider that many TFA alumni are graduates of our nation's finest liberal arts colleges, you must wonder about their devotion to these narrow testing instruments that are used for ranking students, teachers, and schools. Perhaps because they were students who always excelled at test taking, they believe that these measures are truly meritocratic and should be applied universally.

To be sure, not every graduate of TFA supports the privatization agenda. Some of TFA's most articulate critics are former corps members, like Gary Rubinstein, who did his TFA stint in Houston in the early 1990s. There were 750 members of his cohort. At the time, he writes, there were massive shortages of teachers:

> We knew that we weren't going to be great teachers. It was unrealistic to believe otherwise. But we also knew that the jobs we were taking were jobs that nobody else wanted. Principals who were hiring these "Teachers For America" or other paraphrasings of this unknown organization, were completely desperate. If not for us, our students, most likely, would be taught by a different substitute each day. Even if we were bad permanent teachers, we WERE permanent teachers and for

kids who had little in life they can call permanent, it was something. The motto for TFA back then could have been "Hey, we're better than nothing."

Rubinstein eventually became a career teacher of mathematics in a New York City public high school. He has written searing criticism of the TFA alumni who are now taking control of states and districts:

> These leaders are some of the most destructive forces in public education. They seem to love nothing more than labeling schools as "failing," shutting them down, and blaming the supposed failure on the veteran teachers. The buildings of the closed schools are taken over by charter networks, often with leaders who were TFA alums and who get salaries of $200,000 or more to run a few schools.
>
> Rather than be honest about both their successes and their failures, they deny any failures, and charge forward with an agenda that has not worked and will never work. Their "proof" consists of a few high-performing charters. These charters are unwilling to release the data that proves that they succeed by booting the "worst" kids—the ones that bring down their test scores.[9]

Today TFA is at the center of the corporate reform movement, supplying young teachers to staff the growing number of non-union, privately managed charter schools across the nation. These inexperienced young men and women will work incredibly hard, as much as seventy or eighty hours a week, trying to perform a job for which they are ill-prepared, with no expectation of a pension or benefits, then move on. TFA is not just a beneficiary of the privatization movement but one of the central drivers of the movement.

Those who have the power and resources to change the nature of the teaching profession—the U.S. Department of Education and the major foundations—are mistakenly pouring resources into TFA instead of devoting their attention to improving the teaching profession. TFA is no substitute for thoughtful, long-term federal and state policies to transform the recruitment, preparation, and retention of career teachers.

The teaching profession needs to be strengthened and improved. The standards for entry into teaching should be far higher than they are today. Five weeks of training is insufficient. Many teachers are now getting their degrees online from "universities" of dubious quality. The biggest producers of master's degrees in education are online universities.[10] This is wrong. Teachers should have a year of study, research, and practice teaching before they are allowed to teach. They should be masters of their subject, even better, two subjects. They should have a strong liberal arts education, as young recruits into TFA do. But a strong liberal arts education is not enough. In addition to knowing their subject, they should learn how to teach, how to manage the classroom, how to deal with disruptive behavior, how to educate students with special needs, and how to engage parents to help their children. There is much more they should learn—about the history, philosophy, and politics of education, about cognitive psychology, and about the sociology of education—and there is much more that they will learn on the job. They should pass tests to demonstrate their mastery of what they intend to teach. Once in the classroom, they should have mentors who help them improve their teaching. Teaching is complex, and it should be a career, not a springboard to bigger and better things.

Where is TFA in this scene? By its exaggerated claims, TFA reinforces the public perception that teachers need very little training. This was the dominant sentiment that characterized public views of teachers in the nineteenth century, when it was believed that "anyone can teach," and teaching was a stopgap before moving on to something better. One of the great achievements of education reformers in the nineteenth and twentieth centuries was to insist—and to persuade state legislatures—that education is a profession and that professionals need professional education, not just a few weeks of training or none at all. TFA uses its powerful platform in the national media to insist that those they select need no professional preparation. This idea turns the clock back on the teaching profession to the early nineteenth century.

There is a synergy here. As the reform movement insists that bad teachers are destroying children's lives, TFA puts itself forward as the source of "great" teachers, "transformative" teachers, and "effective" teachers who are "changing the trajectory" of children's lives. As we have seen, the research does not support these claims. TFA teachers are no better or worse than other new teachers. Wendy Kopp points to New Orleans and Washington, D.C., as the sites where TFA has made a significant difference.

But the examples don't hold up to scrutiny. About 80 percent or more of the students in New Orleans are in charter schools, which are staffed with large numbers of hardworking, dedicated TFA teachers. The proportion of students passing state tests has increased since 2005, when Hurricane Katrina leveled large parts of the city, but comparisons before and after the hurricane are meaningless because the students are not the same; many of the district's students never returned. By the state's own measures, New Orleans is a very low-performing district in a low-performing state. The state gave a grade of D or F to two-thirds of the charters in New Orleans. Only nine percent received an A and 14 percent earned a B.[11] There are vast disparities among the charters: some are high performing, but most are low performing. Even if the news from this unusual district were far better, it could hardly be a model for the nation. Some reformers might think it wise to wipe out public education, turn the schools over to private management, eliminate the teachers' unions, and rely on energetic and inexperienced youngsters who work hard and leave every two or three years. But such a model is unsustainable for a single large district, let alone an entire nation. Even if it were possible, there is no reason to believe that a system of privately managed schools with a corps of nonprofessional teachers would produce a high-quality education for most or all students. No high-performing nation in the world has such a system.

Nor is Washington, D.C., an exemplar for the nation. Since 2007, it has been controlled by TFA alumni, starting with Michelle Rhee. It was a low-performing district when she arrived, and it was still a low-performing district after she turned the reins of power over to her deputy and fellow TFA alumna, Kaya Henderson.

Critics do not have the national platform that TFA has. But they have raised important questions. The investigative journalist Barbara Miner decided to "follow the money." She drew a line between the extraordinary corporate contributions to TFA and TFA's support for privatization and its claim that poverty can be set aside for now.

The organization is, without a doubt, a fundraising mega-star. In one day in June 2008, for instance, TFA raised $5.5 million. The event, TFA's annual dinner, "brought so many corporate executives to the Waldorf-Astoria Hotel in New York that stretch limousines jammed Park Avenue for blocks," the *New York Times* reported.

. . . TFA has no public criticism of pro-market reforms such as privatization and for-profit charters. Nor does it ask hard questions about the relationship between the achievement gap and problems of segregation, poverty, and an unemployment rate among African American men that hovers around 50 percent in some urban communities.[12]

Barbara Torre Veltri trains Teach for America teachers at Northern Arizona University. She helped mentor the young, inexperienced teachers through crises as they brought their problems to her. In her book, *Learning on Other People's Kids,* she tells their stories as they struggle to meet the needs of the children in their classrooms. One TFA corps member says, "My students need experienced teachers who know what works and can implement it effectively. Instead, they have me, and though I am learning quickly, I am still learning on them, experimenting on them, working on their time." Another: "Seven students (out of 28) speak limited English. Two students speak no English, two are resource (special education) students. Kids range in skills from K–6. Help!"[13]

The claims made by Teach for America distract the nation from the hard work of truly reforming the education profession. Instead of building a profession that attracts well-qualified candidates to make a career of working in the nation's classrooms, our leaders are pouring large sums of money into a richly endowed organization that supplies temporary teachers. If we were serious about improving teacher quality, we would encourage all future teachers to get a solid education and preparation for teaching, and we would expect districts and states to construct a support system to help them get better every year. Instead of expending so much energy on whom to fire, we would focus energy on making teaching a prestigious profession in which classroom teachers have considerable professional autonomy over what and how they teach.

By its design, TFA exacerbates teacher turnover, or "churn." No other profession would admire and reward a program that replenished its ranks with untrained people who expected to move on to a new career in a few years. Our schools already have too much churn. Too many teachers leave the classroom within the first five years, especially in high-poverty schools. These schools need stability and experience, not churn. Few members of TFA stay in the classroom as long as five years. Researchers have found that experience matters; the weakest teachers are in their first two years of teaching, which is understandable because they are learning how to teach and manage their classes. Researchers have also found that staff stability matters. The more that teachers come and go, the worse it is for the schools and their students. One recent study determined that teacher turnover depressed achievement in both mathematics and reading, especially in schools with more low-performing and black students. The disruption was harmful to students whose teachers left, as well as to other students in the school. Turnover itself is harmful, possibly because it undermines the cohesion and collegiality of the community of educators.[14]

Anthony Cody, a science teacher in Oakland, California, and a prominent spokesman for the teaching profession, engaged in an online debate with Heather Harding, the research director for TFA. Based on research and on his own work as a mentor to TFA recruits, Cody emphasized that "the positive effect of a teacher with three or more years of experience is much greater than the effect of any entry program on student learning. Thus, programs that keep teachers in the profession have long-term effects on student achievement."[15] TFA rejects the idea that its recruits should sign up for longer than two years or that they need more than five weeks of training.

In 2009, a surgeon in Texas was so excited by Teach for America that he wrote an article for *The Wall Street Journal* in which he proposed a program in health care that he called Heal for America (HFA). He imagined a program to train enthusiastic young college graduates to teach patients how to comply with a physician's orders. The members of HFA would improve "cleanliness in homes" and help patients with personal hygiene. They could teach patients "tasks as simple as hand washing" and convey to them the importance of sleep and exercise. The program, he explained, would follow the example of TFA and cut down on the cost of health care by making patients better informed. He added, "Of course, the members of this program would not try to be amateur physicians, physician's assistants or substitute registered nurses."[16] The work of medical professionals was far too important to permit these eager and enthusiastic amateurs to do more than assist those with the appropriate expertise.

The medical profession would never permit a fresh college graduate to substitute for a doctor or even a nurse. Why, then, do American schools entrust vulnerable children to brand-new teachers with only five weeks of training?

CHAPTER 15

The Mystery of Michelle Rhee

More than anyone else, Michelle Rhee is the face of the corporate reform movement. She is the leading spokesperson for its strategies: evaluating teachers by test scores; awarding merit bonuses; firing teachers and principals who don't get higher scores; opposing tenure and seniority; attacking collective bargaining; closing public schools; and encouraging privatization by opening charters, both nonprofit and for profit, and by increasing the availability of vouchers.

Adrian Fenty, the newly elected mayor of the District of Columbia, appointed her chancellor of the district's public schools in June 2007, and she led the D.C. school system until October 2010, resigning after Fenty ran for reelection and lost the Democratic primary. She was a major factor in the mayor's defeat because her policies of firing teachers and closing schools had alienated many black voters. After she left her position in D.C., she created an organization called StudentsFirst with the intention of raising $1 billion and enlisting one million members. Its purpose was to eliminate tenure and seniority so that "great" teachers could be rewarded with bonuses and bad teachers fired. It was also a staunch advocate for privatization of public schools. As StudentsFirst became active in political campaigns, Rhee worked closely with conservative Republican governors and endorsed candidates who shared her views about teachers, charters, and vouchers.

When she was appointed to run the D.C. public school system, Michelle Rhee had never run a school system or even a school. In the early 1990s, as a member of Teach for America, she taught for three years in a Baltimore elementary school that was part of a for-profit experiment in privatization, which was terminated by the district after four years.[1] After her teaching stint, she ran a program to recruit teachers for urban schools called the New Teacher Project. When Adrian Fenty selected her to lead the D.C. public schools, she was thirty-seven years old. Joel Klein, chancellor of the New York City public schools, recommended her to Fenty; Klein, too, had come to his position without education credentials.

From the moment she was appointed, Rhee became renowned for her candor and toughness. She minced no words in castigating the culture of complacency, inefficiency, and incompetence that she encountered. The D.C. school system, whose students were overwhelmingly black and poor, had a long history of abysmal test scores. Rhee blamed their low academic performance on lazy and indifferent teachers; she often complained about the "crappy education" that students in the D.C. schools were getting. She pledged to get rid of ineffective teachers and hire only great teachers. She said that teachers and their union were greedy and self-interested; she, unlike the teachers, cared about the children. With Fenty's support, she pledged to make D.C. the highest-performing urban district in the nation. She said she would close the district's yawning achievement gaps. And she made clear that she was there to fire people.

Why the public fascination with Rhee? Part of it was due to the perception that she, unlike other education leaders, was willing to act tough in a field where professionals stress that they are caring and nurturing people. Every instance of her abrasive, confrontational style cemented her image as someone who would crush anyone who got in her way. She alone was "for the children." The media loved her decisiveness, her lack of compassion, her hardness. So did the big foundations and corporations. She was the quintessential corporate reformer.

Her tough talk brought her instant notoriety. During the presidential debates in 2008, both Barack Obama and John McCain praised her, even though she had been on the job for only a year and a few months. Right after the election, she was featured on the cover of *Time*. The cover said, "How to Fix America's Schools," implying that Rhee knew precisely what to do. The cover photograph portrayed an unsmiling Rhee in a classroom, dressed in black, broom in hand, looking defiant and determined. To her admirers, she was the new broom, ready to sweep the schools clean of lazy teachers and incompetent bureaucrats. To her detractors, she was a mean witch with a broom. She was a star of the film *Waiting for "Superman,"* which opened in D.C. the day after Fenty lost his reelection bid.

Rhee did what she said she would do. She closed schools, fired half the central office staff, fired hundreds of teachers, fired dozens of principals, and established a performance-based teacher evaluation system after a public battle with the Washington Teachers Union and Randi Weingarten, the president of the American Federation of Teachers. By the time Rhee left, she had replaced nearly half the district's teachers and about a third of its principals, according to her biographer Richard Whitmire.[2]

By the summer of 2008, she had attracted an "army of believers." She selected dozens of new principals, who agreed to do whatever was necessary to disrupt the culture and raise scores.[3] She met with every principal and got a promise of test score gains. Those whose schools met their target won a bonus; those who failed to meet their target were at risk of losing their jobs. Overnight, she became the national hero of the brassy new reform movement. A profile in *The Atlantic* captured some of the excitement that reformers felt:

> "People are coming from across the country to work for her," says Andrew Rotherham, the co-director of Education Sector, a Washington think tank. "It's the thing to do." Rhee had Stanford and Harvard business-school students on her intern staff this summer, and she has received blank checks from reform-minded philanthropists at the Gates and Broad foundations to fund experimental programs. Businesses have flooded her with offers to help—providing supplies, mentoring, or just giving cash.[4]

With her brusque and unapologetic style, Rhee gleefully burned bridges. She alienated veteran educators and parents who opposed school closings. She mocked the idea of collaboration. She said in the fall of 2008 (and often repeated, in one form or another): "I think if there is one thing I have learned over the last 15 months, it's that cooperation, collaboration and consensus-building are way overrated."[5] She felt that if she listened to people who disagreed with her, it would slow her down, and she had no intention of slowing down. She gloried in being an intimidating and glowering superstar who fired people and closed schools, because she was doing it "for the kids."

Rhee believed that the key to raising test scores was to find and reward great teachers and great principals and to find and fire bad ones. She believed in test scores as the ultimate measure of schooling, and

she scorned those who didn't share her devotion to standardized testing. She felt certain that she could close the achievement gaps between
black and white students if she could get the teachers and principals she
wanted. Rhee believed that three great teachers in a row would close
the achievement gap, and she often recited that claim. She felt sure that
she could staff the entire school system with great teachers. To reach
her goals, she needed to change the evaluation system and the salary
structure. She expended much of her time negotiating a deal with the
Washington Teachers Union to install her teacher evaluation system,
called IMPACT, in 2009. She raised $80 million from several founda-
tions to fund the new salary scale, one that offered significantly higher
salaries to teachers willing to give up their tenure. (Many of the teachers who were eligible for big bonuses turned them down, preferring to
keep their tenure.)[6]

Rhee enjoyed stepping on toes and kicking people out, but there
was a price to be paid for her hard-charging style. She became a major
issue in the mayoral election of 2010, and her boss, Adrian Fenty, lost
to the city council president, Vincent Gray. Gray won the black vote by
a large margin, while Fenty won the white vote by a large margin. Gray
was elected, and Rhee resigned. But Gray had no appetite for changing
what Rhee started; he did not want to alienate the powerful people in
the business and philanthropic communities who supported Rhee. To
guarantee continuity, he appointed her deputy, Kaya Henderson, also a
TFA alumna, to replace Rhee.

What did Michelle Rhee accomplish? A review of her tenure a year
later concluded that she had improved purchasing, textbook delivery,
and food services. Most parents thought that the school system was
improving. And the issue of school reform had been elevated as a major
topic for public concern.[7]

Rhee's relentless pressure to raise the passing rates on tests brought
some early gains, but it produced a major cheating scandal as well. In
the spring of 2011, four months after Rhee left the district, *USA Today*
published a report about widespread cheating at more than half the
district's schools. The investigation focused on the Crosby S. Noyes
Education Campus, where the passing rates in reading had shot up
from 44 percent in 2007 to 84 percent in 2009. The gains were so large
that they should have set off alarm bells, but they did not. Instead, the
school was recognized in 2009 by the U.S. Department of Education

as a National Blue Ribbon School. Michelle Rhee congratulated the principal and "touted the school . . . as an example of how the sweeping changes she championed could transform even the lowest-performing Washington schools. Twice in three years, she rewarded Noyes' staff for boosting scores: In 2008 and again in 2010, each teacher won an $8,000 bonus, and the principal won $10,000."[8]

USA Today reported that the erasure rates on the standardized tests at Noyes were unusually high: "On the 2009 reading test, for example, seventh-graders in one Noyes classroom averaged 12.7 wrong-to-right erasures per student on answer sheets; the average for seventh-graders in all D.C. schools on that test was less than 1. The odds are better for winning the Powerball grand prize than having that many erasures by chance, according to statisticians consulted by *USA Today*."

Rhee honored Wayne Ryan of Noyes as a model principal. The district featured him and the school in recruitment ads and asked, "Are you the next Wayne Ryan?" Rhee promoted Ryan to the position of instructional superintendent, where he supervised other principals. Noyes's great success proved to Rhee that her methods worked. She distributed more than $1.5 million in bonuses to teachers, principals, and support staff in schools that saw big test score gains; in three of those schools, *USA Today* found that "85 percent or more of classrooms were identified as having high erasure rates in 2008." District officials knew of the high erasure rates before the exposé but did not conduct an investigation. Three months after the story was published, Wayne Ryan abruptly resigned.[9]

The cheating scandal was referred to the office of the D.C. inspector general for investigation. That office concluded that there may have been cheating at one school but nowhere else. It saw "insufficient basis" to investigate any other schools. The inspector general of the U.S. Department of Education concurred. Chancellor Kaya Henderson said, "I am pleased that the investigation is complete and that the vast majority of our schools were cleared of any wrongdoing." The *Washington Post* columnist Jay Mathews, who had supported Rhee, was outraged by the cursory investigation and wrote that it looked like a cover-up to him. Meanwhile, the reading proficiency rates at Noyes, which were celebrated when they reached 84 percent in 2009, fell to 32 percent in 2012, and the math proficiency rates were equally low. Similar high-pressure tactics in Atlanta produced another major cheating scandal, which was thoroughly investigated and led to indictments of the superintendent and thirty-four other educators. But no one was held accountable for the mysterious rise and fall of test scores in Washington, D.C.[10]

Other things happened during Rhee's tenure that bolstered her image among the corporate reform crowd while giving ammunition to her critics. Because she enjoyed the adulation of the media, she gave free access to many national reporters. When John Merrow visited, accompanied by a PBS camera crew, Rhee said to him, "I'm going to fire somebody in a little while. Do you want to see that?" That was too good to pass up, and the camera crew shot over the principal's shoulder as Rhee said, "I'm terminating your principalship—*now.*" As she spoke, Rhee's face was impassive; she showed no emotion, no regret, no compassion. The film clip was included in *Waiting for "Superman"* to demonstrate her legendary take-no-prisoners style. Her biographer said that her actions were "thoughtless and reckless," but Rhee said that there was an "upside" to the media attention because it "helped attract foundations willing to commit millions to teacher pay-for-performance bonuses."[11]

Shortly after Rhee left office, critics questioned her account of her years as a TFA teacher in Baltimore. She had described herself to the media as a teacher who was awful in her first year but who then achieved astonishing results in the next two years. Her own success, she said, proved to her that a teacher with high expectations can overcome all obstacles. Her résumé said, "Taught in Harlem Park Community School, one of the lowest-performing elementary schools in Baltimore City, effecting significant measurable gains in student achievement. Over a two-year period, moved students scoring on average at the 13th percentile on national standardized tests to 90% of students scoring at the 90th percentile or higher."[12]

Critics doubted that oft-told claim, but the records could not be found to verify or challenge it. Some of Rhee's critics kept digging and found a report written in 1995 by researchers at the University of Maryland, Baltimore. The report said that the combined scores of all the classes in the grade where Rhee taught had increased significantly, but the gain was not large enough to substantiate the spectacular claim on Rhee's résumé. The blogger G. F. Brandenburg, a retired mathematics teacher, was first to break the news. The *Washington Post* columnist Jay

Mathews concluded that Brandenburg "has proved that Rhee's results weren't nearly as good as she said they were."[13] Rhee's office promptly issued a statement saying that "the attacks" were "unfounded" and that the report covered all the students in the third grade, but not necessarily Michelle's. It concluded, "This episode is further proof of what we're up against."[14]

A few days later, Brandenburg published a comment by the principal investigator for the 1995 report, who told him that even though the scores were not broken out by classroom, Brandenburg's conclusion was correct. With only four third-grade classrooms in the school, if one class had average scores in the range of 90 percent, it would have lifted the average of the entire grade.[15]

Another part of Rhee's legacy was the IMPACT system she devised to evaluate teachers. Fifty percent of the evaluation was based on the value-added test score gains of students. This is a model aligned with the Obama administration's Race to the Top program, which encouraged states to judge teachers by changes in their students' test scores (D.C. won one of the Race to the Top awards). Rhee's system was supposed to identify the "best" and the "worst" teachers, since the best will supposedly produce big test score gains while the worst will not. In 2011, based on both test scores and observations, the district fired 206 teachers.

But were those fired the city's worst teachers? According to *The Washington Post,* one of the fired teachers received a commendation in May 2011 from her supervisor, who said, "It is a pleasure to visit a classroom in which the elements of sound teaching, motivated students and a positive learning environment are so effectively combined." Two months later, this fifth-grade teacher was fired: Her students' scores didn't go up as much as the statistical model predicted based on their previous year's scores. The classroom observation counted for 35 percent and other factors for 15 percent, but the value-added scores doomed her. The teacher suspected her students came from a school that had cheated and inflated their previous year's grades. She appealed her firing but was turned down by the district. No excuses! The school principal gave her a glowing recommendation "without reservation" when she applied to teach in nearby Fairfax County, Virginia. He said she was "enthusiastic, creative, visionary, flexible, motivating and encouraging."[16] She was hired.

The District of Columbia, like other high-poverty districts, had long had a high level of teacher turnover. This teacher churn continued during Rhee's tenure. Hundreds were fired within a few years, while others resigned or left to teach elsewhere. One in every five teachers in the district left in a single year, 2010–11. The New Teacher Project, the advocacy group founded by Rhee, claimed that this was not so significant because the "best" teachers were retained, but somehow the "best" teachers (the report called them "the irreplaceables") were highly concentrated in the district's low-poverty schools. Few were teaching in high-poverty schools. At this rate, the district would lose nearly half its teachers in only two years. One longtime analyst of the D.C. system, the civil rights lawyer Mary Levy, calculated the five-year teacher turnover rate at 75 percent. The principal turnover rate was no less disturbing. In the spring of 2008, Rhee replaced one-third of the district's principals with her choices. By 2012, 60 percent of the forty-six new principals were gone. A few had moved into senior administrative jobs or to other schools, but most had left the D.C. school system.[17]

After Rhee left the D.C. chancellorship, she created StudentsFirst and led a national crusade to abolish teacher tenure and promote charters and vouchers. She quickly attracted millions of dollars from wealthy supporters of school choice and opponents of teachers' unions. She poured large sums of money into political campaigns for candidates and issues that advanced her agenda. Although nominally a Democrat, she backed the political agenda of the nation's most conservative Republican governors, like Rick Scott in Florida, John Kasich in Ohio, Mitch Daniels in Indiana, and Chris Christie in New Jersey. Most of her organization's political contributions in state races went to Republican candidates. In Tennessee, she spent nearly $1 million to enable the Republicans to achieve a supermajority in the legislature.[18]

What did Michelle Rhee accomplish during her three and a half years in charge of the D.C. public schools? Did she accomplish her goal of making it the highest-performing urban district in the nation? Did she make substantial progress? Under the heading "Driving Unprecedented Growth in the D.C. Public Schools," the Web site of StudentsFirst says about her time in D.C., "Under her leadership, the worst performing school district in the country became the only major city system to see double-digit growth in both their state reading and state math scores in seventh, eighth and tenth grades over three years."[19]

Boasting about her accomplishments brought her additional media attention and made her the toast of the reform movement, but it also invited additional scrutiny. Alan Ginsburg, who worked as a policy research director for many years at the U.S. Department of Education under both political parties, analyzed Rhee's record. He reviewed the district's NAEP scores in reading and math from 2000 to 2009 and concluded: "Rhee did not initiate the DC schools' test-score turnaround when she took office in 2007. DC's NAEP scores had already steadily improved under her two predecessors, Superintendents Paul Vance and Clifford Janey. Moreover, the rates of DC score gains under Rhee were no better than the rates achieved under Vance and Janey."[20] Ginsburg did not refer to the D.C. state tests that Rhee cited on her StudentsFirst Web site, because the D.C. tests "were redesigned between 2005 and 2006 and performance levels for 2006 and afterwards are not comparable with those from prior years."

Ginsburg found that the largest gains on NAEP occurred during the Vance administration. He cautioned that U.S. education has a long history of looking for "silver bullet" solutions that fail when tried on a large scale. He found no evidence to support Rhee's policy of teacher removal and urged policy makers to evaluate this approach carefully before adopting it nationally. Other nations, he pointed out, have developed more positive and successful ways to improve teaching, and he urged attention to them.

We can now add to Alan Ginsburg's analysis because we have NAEP scores for 2011.

From 2009 to 2011, the D.C. public schools saw no statistically discernible increases in fourth-grade mathematics scores, but there was a discernible increase in eighth-grade mathematics scores.

In fourth-grade mathematics, the scores of higher-income students, lower-income students, white students, black students, and Hispanic students were flat.

In eighth-grade mathematics, the scores of higher-income students, lower-income students, white students, and Hispanic students were flat, but there was a statistically significant increase in the scores of black students.

From 2009 to 2011, the D.C. public schools saw no significant change in fourth-grade reading scores and no significant increase in eighth-grade reading scores.

In fourth-grade reading, the scores of higher-income students, lower-income students, white students, and Hispanic students were flat. The scores of black students declined by a statistically real margin.

In eighth-grade reading, there was no change in the scores. The scores of higher-income students, lower-income students, white students, and black students were flat. The scores of Hispanic students declined significantly.[21]

Looking at NAEP scores, we know for certain that Rhee did not turn it into the highest-performing urban district in the United States. Its students still have low scores on the no-stakes federal assessment. It remains in the bottom group of urban districts along with Atlanta, Baltimore City, Chicago, Cleveland, Detroit, Fresno, Los Angeles, Milwaukee, and Philadelphia (Atlanta is in the bottom tier in mathematics but not in reading).

Did Rhee reduce the achievement gap between black and white students? No, the achievement gap between black and white students was unchanged from 2007, when she started, to 2011, after she departed.[22] Washington, D.C., continues to have the largest black-white gap of any urban district tested by NAEP, because of the extremes of affluence (mostly white) and poverty (mostly black) in the district. The Hispanic-white gap in D.C. in both reading and math is almost as large as the black-white gap, and here, too, D.C. has the biggest gaps among the nation's urban districts.

Rhee continued to be dogged by persistent suspicions that she had failed to investigate widespread cheating, especially after a confidential memo was leaked to PBS correspondent John Merrow. Merrow considered the memo to be confirmation that Rhee knew about a pattern of cheating but ignored it. Merrow, who filmed Rhee a dozen times when she was chancellor, summarized her tenure: little or no gains on test scores, high turnover of teachers and principals, lowest graduation rate of any big city, largest achievement gap of any big city, a truancy crisis, big increase in spending, a bloated central office staff, and declining enrollments.[23]

At this point, it is impossible to discern a lasting legacy from the Rhee era in the D.C. schools, which continued under the control of her deputy Kaya Henderson. The schools have experienced high levels of instability because of the frequent turnover of teachers and principals. More public schools will close, and more charter schools will open.

Nearly half the students in the district are enrolled in charter schools, more than in any other city except New Orleans. The district's public schools have not been transformed academically. The students in D.C. are still poor and are still low performing on the federal tests. The reform program of privatization, teacher bonuses, and teacher firings was not successful. Rhee did not prove that poverty doesn't matter. She made promises she could not keep. The problems she inherited remain unchanged.

CHAPTER 16

The Contradictions of Charters

CLAIM *Charter schools will revolutionize American education by their freedom to innovate and produce dramatically better results.*

REALITY *Charter schools run the gamut from excellent to awful and are, on average, no more innovative or successful than public schools.*

Albert Shanker, president of the American Federation of Teachers from 1974 to 1997, was a founding father of the charter school movement. It is ironic that one of the nation's leading trade unionists promoted an idea that produced a sector that is privately managed, receives public money, and is overwhelmingly non-union. A 2009–10 survey found that only 12 percent of charter schools were unionized; among the newest schools, the proportion is even smaller.[1]

In 1988, Shanker was trying to figure out what to do about the large number of students who were disengaged, who dropped out of school, or who sat sullenly in their classrooms, apparently indifferent to instruction. His idea was that a group of six or eight teachers in a school might collaborate on designing a new sort of school for these students, then go to their colleagues in the school and ask for their approval. Before they could proceed, they would also need to get the support of their union and the district school board. Then they would recruit those students who were hanging out on street corners and who were likely to drop out. The new school would be free from the usual regulations, and teachers would be free to come up with their own ideas to help these youths. Whatever they learned, they would share with their colleagues. They would collaborate with the public school system, not compete with it.

Borrowing the terminology from a University of Massachusetts professor, Ray Budde, who had a similar idea, Shanker called it a "charter school." The basic concept was that the school would have a charter for a set period of time, would work with the students who were at high risk for failure, and at some point its work would be done. He introduced the concept at a national convention of his union and carried the message to locals. He often wrote about the idea in his weekly paid column in *The New York Times*. He was very enthusiastic until 1993, when he saw what was happening in Baltimore. There, a private, for-profit firm called Education Alternatives Inc. was given a contract to run nine struggling schools. These were not charter schools; they were privately managed schools operating under contract to the district and subject to the rules of the district. (The Baltimore school where Michelle Rhee began her teaching career was part of this privatization experiment.) The company cleaned up the schools, brought in computers, and retrained teachers. But the company and the city quarreled over finances, and scores did not go up, so the city canceled its contract. Initially, the company and the union collaborated. But the company made a fatal error: it fired unionized paraprofessionals, who earned $10 an hour (in 1991 dollars) with benefits, and replaced them with college graduates who were paid $7 an hour without benefits. This was unacceptable to Shanker.[2]

Shanker concluded that management by private corporations was incompatible with public education. The management's decisions would be based on reducing costs, he realized, not improving education. In 1993, he turned decisively against the charter idea when he realized that it would become a vehicle for privatization. In 1994, he learned that the first charter school in Michigan was Noah Webster Academy, which enrolled seven hundred students, mostly Christian homeschoolers, and that instruction was given mainly through computers. The students continued to stay at home but with a state-funded computer and a curriculum that taught creationism. Shanker was aghast. He was even more disturbed to realize that the academy's founder had discovered a tiny, impoverished school district with only twenty-three students that agreed to sponsor the academy and give it a

ninety-nine-year contract, in return for "a kickback of about $40,000."
Meanwhile, the Noah Webster Academy would receive $4 million in
state funding for its at-home pupils. Shanker warned that the real aim
of some advocates of charters was "to smash the public schools." He
began referring to charter schools, vouchers, and privatization as "gimmicks," "magic bullets," and "fads" that would do nothing to change
the essentials of teaching and learning.[3] Shanker was a strong supporter
of national standards, and he recoiled at the idea of a "do-your-own-
thing" curriculum.

Despite this history, some charter advocates continued to cite
Shanker's endorsement of charters long after he renounced his own
idea. It is doubly surprising that they claim Shanker's approval for the
creation of non-union schools.[4]

Charter schools became the hot new idea in American education,
beloved by advocates of school choice on the right. Conservatives at the
Hoover Institution, the Thomas B. Fordham Institute, the Center for
Education Reform, ALEC, the American Enterprise Institute, and the
Heartland Institute realized that charters were the next best thing to
vouchers. NCLB recommended charter schools as an option to replace
low-performing public schools, despite the lack of any evidence for their
efficacy when the law was passed in 2001. Major foundations, including the Walton Family Foundation, the Bill & Melinda Gates Foundation, the Eli and Edythe Broad Foundation, the Fisher Foundation,
the Michael & Susan Dell Foundation, and dozens of others lavished
funding on the expansion of charter schools and charter chains. The
U.S. Department of Education required states to lift their limits on
charter schools if they wanted to be eligible to compete for the billions
of dollars in President Obama's Race to the Top competition. Their
advocates portrayed them as the salvation for poor minority children
trapped in subpar urban and suburban schools. Candidates for state
and local office could count on contributions from wealthy individuals
and organizations across the nation if they promised to support charter
schools.

By 2012, forty-two states had passed legislation authorizing charter
schools.[5] Only twenty years after the charter idea was first proposed,
more than six thousand charter schools enrolled about two million students, about 4 percent of the nation's K–12 students. In big-city districts, charter school enrollments were far larger. About 80 percent or
more of the students in New Orleans were enrolled in charter schools,

as were nearly half the students in the District of Columbia. In six districts, at least 30 percent of students attended charter schools, and another eighteen districts had at least 20 percent of their students in charters. Nearly one hundred districts counted at least 10 percent of their students in charters.[6]

Because the charter sector is by nature composed of thousands of different entities, it is impossible to make a generalization that applies equally to all charters. Some are run like military boot camps, with rigidly applied rules of behavior. Some are progressive in pedagogy and tone. A few are dedicated to the needs of autistic children and others with disabilities. Many exclude children with severe disabilities and accept very few English-language learners. Many have high attrition rates. Charters vary from state to state, and charters vary even within the same district.

Charter schools are deregulated and free from most state laws other than those governing health and safety. This freedom allows charter schools to establish their own disciplinary policies and their own admissions rules. Deregulation also frees charters from the financial oversight that traditional public schools receive. Some states exempt charters from the teacher evaluation schemes that are imposed on public schools. In Louisiana and some other states, charter school teachers do not need to be certified. Charter schools are funded with taxpayer dollars; some receive additional private-sector support and spend more than local public schools.

With encouragement and funding by the federal government, major corporations, and the big foundations, the charter sector has become a bustling enterprise zone for entrepreneurs, consisting of both nonprofit and for-profit organizations. Albert Shanker's idea that charter schools would collaborate with the public schools was obsolete. In the new era, the watchword for charters was competition, not collaboration.

After the enactment of No Child Left Behind, all schools were put on notice that they must raise their proficiency rates or suffer humiliation and possible closure. The law made clear that those rates must rise every year without fail for every designated group of students until all were proficient, without exception. In this climate, any school that enrolled the lowest-performing students was doomed to lose the competition. The harsh consequences of NCLB created incentives for schools to avoid the weakest students, by whatever means necessary.

The convergence of NCLB and the charter school movement was a boon to the latter. Even though charters were new and unproven, the law offered them as a remedy for low-scoring students. At the same time, NCLB pressured charters to prove they could get higher test scores than public schools. This encouraged charters to try to prove their superiority to public schools, not to collaborate and share their strategies. To succeed, many charter schools devised subtle or obvious ways to limit or exclude students with expensive disabilities, students with limited English proficiency, and students with low skill levels. Even the lottery system, while seemingly fair, is a selection mechanism, since the least functional families seldom take the steps necessary to enter.

NCLB's demand for testing and ever-rising scores determined the direction of the charter school movement. With rare exceptions, charters would not seek out and enroll the weakest students, because to do so would endanger their survival and their reputation as panaceas. Charter schools that took the risk of enrolling large numbers of low-performing students might not last long.

But an even more troubling development occurred. Wall Street hedge fund managers became interested in school reform and became devotees of the charter school movement. They believed that charters would provide the educational opportunities to poor children that they assumed the public system could not provide. These are men who like to compete and win and have succeeded in the free market. They judge their own success by metrics (dollars), and they judge the success of their schools by test scores. They want their schools to have higher scores than anyone else's schools. The hedge fund managers created an organization called Democrats for Education Reform (DFER), which gives generously to candidates and elected officials who support the expansion of charter schools and to organizations that open charter schools. Many of the hedge fund managers serve on the board of directors of a charter. In New York City, they sought and received free space for their schools in public school buildings and then crowed that they were far superior to the public school whose space they shared, even though the public school typically had higher proportions of the students with severe disabilities and English-language learners. The spirit of collaboration was extinguished. What mattered most was winning, by getting higher scores than the public school.

Other financiers saw public education as a potentially lucrative opportunity. They looked at the hundreds of billions of taxpayer dollars spent each year on schools and saw a market waiting to be exploited. Their interest was not philanthropy but making money on real estate deals and educational services, taking advantage of federal tax credits and a steady flow of no-risk public funding.

The federal government first created a program to support the creation of charter schools during the Clinton administration. Under the George W. Bush administration, the federal charter school program grew to more than $100 million annually. The Obama administration expanded financial support for privately managed charters still more. In addition to direct funding of charter schools, the federal government provides tax breaks to encourage banks and individuals to invest in charter school construction. The Community Renewal Tax Relief Act of 2000 included the New Markets Tax Credit, which allowed investors in charter school construction to collect a safe and reliable return of 39 percent over seven years.[7] Construction loans to charter schools are also lucrative. In Albany, New York, one charter school saw its rent jump from $170,000 in 2008 to $560,000 only a year later, just to pay debt service to its financiers for construction loans.[8]

Another federal program known as EB-5 enabled foreign investors to get immigration visas (green cards) by investing $500,000 or more to build charter schools. A Reuters reporter found that "wealthy individuals from as far away as China, Nigeria, Russia and Australia are spending tens of millions of dollars to build classrooms, libraries, basketball courts and science labs for American charter schools."[9]

Real estate investment trusts have found it lucrative to buy buildings and lease space to charter schools. One called Entertainment Properties Trust manages over $3 billion in properties, including megaplex movie theaters and charter schools. David Brain, the head of the company, explained that charter schools are "a very stable business, very recession-resistant . . . a very high-demand product . . . [I]f you do business with states with solid treasuries, then it's a very solid business." Brain cited bipartisan support for the charter sector—"it's part of the Republican platform and Arne Duncan, secretary of education in the Obama administration, has been very high on it"—and said that he liked to have charters in his company's portfolio because the sector offers "a great opportunity set with 500 schools starting every year. It's a two and a half billion dollar opportunity set in rough measure annually."[10]

Charter schools satisfied a long-standing ideological drive by libertarians to remove schools from government control and shift public assets into private hands. ALEC—the American Legislative Exchange Council—immediately saw the possibilities. ALEC, an organization of some two thousand state legislators and business leaders, promotes privatization and corporate interests. ALEC's model law for charter schools is called the Next Generation Charter Schools Act. It has several key points: first, it insists that charter schools are public schools, even though they may be controlled by private boards and operate for profit; second, charter schools should be exempt from most state laws and regulations applied to public schools; third, charter schools may be authorized by multiple agencies, such as the state board of education, universities, and charter-friendly organizations, which maximizes the opportunities to open new charters; and fourth, the governor should have the power to appoint a board to authorize charters and override local school boards, which are often reluctant to grant these charters because they drain resources from the school system whose interests they are elected to protect. This legislation encourages the acceleration of privatization and undermines local control of schools. The corporate agenda of privatization and free markets, in this instance, takes precedence over the traditional conservative belief in small government and local control. In that sense, the reform agenda is not really a conservative agenda but a radical attack on local control that serves corporate interests, not Main Street.[11]

Several states have recently adopted the ALEC model law for charters. In Georgia, for example, ALEC members in the legislature introduced a bill to create a state commission to circumvent local objections to charter schools. It passed easily. The language mirrored the ALEC charter model law. When the Georgia Supreme Court declared the law unconstitutional, the legislature passed it again as an amendment to the state constitution, which was submitted to voters in a referendum; the campaign for the measure received heavy financial support from charter operators, the Walton family, who own Walmart, and other out-of-state donors. In New Jersey, education legislation sponsored by Governor Chris Christie mirrored the language of ALEC model legislation, in some places verbatim.[12]

In North Carolina, legislators introduced a bill in 2013 that reflected ALEC priorities. The bill would create a charter commission appointed by the governor and other state leaders. By law, the commission would be composed of charter supporters, of appointees who have "an understanding and commitment to charter schools as a strategy to strengthen public education." Charters would apply for authorization to this commission, bypassing the local board. They would be overseen by this board, not by the local districts or the State Board of Education. Local districts would be required to lease any available space to the charters for $1 a year. The charters would not be required to hire certified teachers. Charter school staff would not be required to pass criminal background checks. The proposed law would not require any checks for conflicts of interest—not for the commission members or for the charter operators. The bill, in effect, would remove all meaningful oversight of charter schools, putting them under the wing of their advocates. Not surprisingly, the bill was warmly endorsed by the chairman of the NC Alliance for Public Charter Schools, who owns an academy that runs two charter schools; this individual "received more than $3 million from the two charter schools for management fees and the cost of renting the buildings," according to the charter schools' tax returns.[13]

But is ALEC right? Are charter schools really public schools? Or is this rhetorical spin, meant to assuage those who instinctively recoil at the notion of public funds going to private schools? Charter operators insist that they are public schools, fully entitled to be treated the same as other public schools and to receive the same funding, even though they are privately managed and are exempt from most of the rules and regulations that public schools must follow. Many call themselves "public charter schools."

Charter operators want to have it both ways. When it is time for funds to be distributed, they want to be considered public schools. But when they are involved in litigation, charter operators insist they are private organizations, not public schools. The courts and regulatory bodies have agreed with the latter point. In 2010, the Ninth Circuit Court of Appeals ruled that a charter school operator in Arizona was a private nonprofit corporation, not an agency of the state, when a teacher who was discharged sued the school. Even though state law says that charters are public schools, the federal court ruling rejected the claim that charters are state actors.[14] Legal scholars, taking note of this decision, warned that "students of color may be unwittingly surrendering protections guaranteed under the Constitution when enrolling in charter schools."[15]

In 2009, the New York Charter Schools Association successfully sued to prevent the state comptroller from auditing the finances of charter schools, even though they receive public funding. The association contended that charter schools are not government agencies but "non-profit educational corporations carrying out a public purpose." The association maintained that charter schools were no different from social service agencies or a "construction contractor." The state court of appeals agreed with the charter association by a vote of 7–0. By contrast, public schools may be audited by the state comptroller and have no grounds on which to object. The year after the court's ruling, the state legislature authorized the state comptroller to audit charter schools.[16]

Labor issues were another front on which charter schools preferred to be treated as private entities. In 2011, when more than 60 percent of the staff at the New Media Technology Charter School in Philadelphia tried to form a union, the school countered that it was not a public school. The school was funded entirely by more than $5 million of public money each year to educate 450 students. Its lawyer maintained that it was not a public employer subject to state labor law, but was governed by the National Labor Relations Board (NLRB) as a private employer. Coincidentally, at the same time, the school's former board president and founder and its former chief executive officer pleaded guilty and were sentenced to prison for stealing over half a million dollars from the school's funds for business and personal expenses.[17]

Two-thirds of the teachers at the Chicago Math and Science Academy sought to form a union in 2011. The charter operator, as in Philadelphia, fought their action by claiming that it was not subject to state law because it was a "private entity." In 2012, the National Labor Relations Board agreed that the charter school was not a public agency, asserting that it was neither a government agency nor administered by officials "who are responsible to public officials or the general electorate." The NLRB concluded that the charter school is a private, non-profit corporation whose board is selected not by government but by the board itself. In effect, it is a private entity operating under contract to the government and is therefore subject to federal laws governing the private sector.[18]

Bruce Baker of Rutgers University analyzed the question of whether charter schools are private, public, or some sort of hybrid. He noted that they are similar to voucher-supported private schools in several ways. They have limited public access in that they can cap enrollment and class size according to their individual preferences; they can admit students only in certain grades and at particular times of the year and are not required to admit students midyear or in any grade; they can adopt their own disciplinary procedures, which are sometimes harsher and more restrictive than those typical in public schools; and "they can set academic, behavioral and cultural standards that promote exclusion of students via attrition." Baker and his colleagues also documented that charters often spend substantially more than public schools. Some charters—for example, those in Washington, D.C.—have been found to have far higher expulsion rates as well. In general, public oversight and control of their financial, academic, disciplinary, and admissions policies are far less than with public schools, which "must accept students at any point during the year" and "cannot shed students who do not meet academic standards, comply with more general behavioral codes or social standards, such as parental obligations."[19]

Reasonable people may reach different conclusions on the question of whether charter schools are truly public schools. Charter school operators have asked the courts and the National Labor Relations Board to rule that they are private entities, private employers, and private contractors. This seems reason enough to conclude that they are private actors and that their expansion represents privatization.

The rapid proliferation of charter legislation and the growth of the charter sector produced a new phenomenon in American education: national charter school chains. These are described either as educational management organizations (EMOs) or as charter management organizations (CMOs). The terms are used interchangeably. The development of chain schools is akin to the development of retail chain stores, like Walmart or Target or McDonald's, which provide a central management structure and an economy of scale in some aspects of the operation. The CMO or EMO provides a "brand" and a certain uniformity of administration, curriculum, and policies, as well as financial oversight, back-office operations, human resources, marketing, and public relations. There are currently about two hundred different CMOs or EMOs operating in twenty-eight states. About 35 percent of all charter schools are part of a CMO or EMO; nearly half of all charter school students are enrolled in a charter chain school.[20]

One of the fastest-growing nonprofit charter chains is KIPP, founded in 1994 by two alumni of Teach for America. KIPP managed somewhat more than a hundred charter schools across the nation in 2013 and was poised to add more. KIPP stands for Knowledge Is Power Program. It is nonprofit but has collected many millions of dollars from corporate, foundation, and government sources. KIPP typically spends more per pupil than the public schools in the same district. It boasts a "no excuses" culture, where discipline is strict. The KIPP schools created a behavioral technique called SLANT: Sit up, Listen, Ask questions, Nod, and Track the speaker with your eyes. It has longer school days and longer school years than public schools. With few exceptions, its schools are non-union. Critics maintain that KIPP schools have an unusually high attrition rate, especially among black males, but KIPP denies it.[21]

The largest chain of charters in the nation is not KIPP but the Gulen charter schools. These are charter schools loosely affiliated with a reclusive imam named Fethullah Gulen, who lives in rural Pennsylvania but commands a powerful political organization in Turkey. As of 2013, there were nearly 140 Gulen-associated charter schools, which focus on mathematics and science, in at least twenty-six states. These schools employ many Turkish teachers, and their boards are usually made up entirely of Turkish men. They have names like Harmony Science Academy, Horizon Science Academy, Magnolia Science Academy, and Sonoran Science Academy. Auditors in Texas and Georgia have criticized Gulen schools for steering contracts to vendors affiliated with the movement. *The New York Times* reported that the three dozen Gulen schools in Texas received some $100 million annually in public funding and "had granted millions of dollars in construction and renovation contracts to firms run by Turkish-Americans with ties to the movement, in some cases bypassing lower bids from firms with no connections to the movement. The Texas schools awarded contracts for cafeteria food, after-school programs and teacher training to organizations affiliated with Gulen followers." Three Gulen charters in Georgia defaulted on bonds, and auditors in Fulton County questioned hundreds of thousands of dollars awarded to Gulen-connected vendors.[22]

The first of the for-profit charter chains was the Edison Schools, established in 1992. Although Edison turned out not to be as profitable as its backers expected, there are now many national for-profit charter chains, such as Imagine Schools Inc., National Heritage Academies,

Mosaica, and the Leona Group. Probably the most profitable are the cyber-charter chains. A cyber-charter or virtual school does not have school buildings. It delivers instruction to students at home via computers. The parents of the children are their "learning coaches." These schools may draw students from across an entire state or even across state lines. The largest chains of cyber-charters are K12 Inc. and Connections Academy. Connections is owned by the mega-giant educational testing and publishing firm Pearson. The senior vice president of Connections was co-chair of the ALEC education task force that drafted model legislation promoting virtual schools.

Advocates of charter schools claim they produce better academic results than traditional public schools and cost less because of lower overhead. Neither of these promises has been fulfilled. The academic results of charter schools are inconsistent, which is unsurprising because the sector itself is so variable. Some charter schools get consistently high test scores, and some get low test scores. Even charters within the same network can differ widely in results (like those in the KIPP network or Harlem Children's Zone's Promise Academies). Most studies consistently conclude that on average the academic results of charters are no better than those of traditional public schools serving the same sorts of students.[23] Nor have charter schools produced cost savings.

A 2012 study of charter schools in Michigan concluded that they spend more on administration and less on instruction than traditional public schools. (Other states may have different patterns; Michigan has a very large proportion of charters that operate for profit.) While both groups of schools get similar state funding, charters spend nearly $800 more per pupil per year on administration and $1,140 less on instruction than traditional public schools. "As a share of total expenditures, Michigan's districts devote 60.5 percent to instruction, while charters devote only 47.4 percent." Some of the charters' higher administrative costs were attributed to the EMO's management fees; the charters reduced the cost of instruction by paying lower salaries to those teachers who had credentials similar to those who worked in public schools, while relying primarily on a less experienced teaching force that turned over frequently. The self-managed charters in Michigan spend about $300 less per pupil than EMO charters. The authors concluded that "if one were searching for a contemporary reform to shift resources from classroom instruction to administration, it is hard to

imagine one that could accomplish this as decisively as charter schools
have done in Michigan."[24]

Currently, thirty-three states permit schools to be operated by for-
profit organizations and paid for with taxpayer dollars. The number of
for-profit EMOs grew from five to ninety-nine between 1995 and 2010,
and enrollment grew from 1,000 to nearly 400,000.[25] It is important
to recognize how unusual this is in American history. Aside from an
experimental program here and there, such as Education Alternatives
Inc. and the Edison Project, both launched in the early 1990s, for-profit
public schooling has been virtually unknown across nearly two hundred years of American education. Today, states such as Michigan,
Indiana, Arizona, and Florida welcome for-profit charter schools. Even
in states that do not permit for-profit schools, like Ohio, charter schools
are allowed to contract out their management and/or services to for-
profit operators, and often the boards of the charters are financially
entangled with the operators who make a profit. In Michigan, at least
80 percent of the charter schools operate for profit. Erik Kain, a columnist at *Forbes,* wrote: "Four out of five charter schools in Michigan are
run by for-profit corporations. Let that sink in a minute. This should be
deeply, deeply troubling for anyone thinking about their child's future
education, or the future of this country." Kain somberly observed, "The
corporate takeover of public education is underway."[26]

Charter management corporations make handsome profits in Ohio,
even though state law does not permit for-profit corporations to obtain
a charter. However, state law permits the board of a nonprofit charter
to hire a for-profit entity to manage its school. The Republican legislator who wrote the charter law opened a business to lobby for charters
after she retired from the legislature, and she also works for her daughter's for-profit business, which oversees forty-five charter schools. *The
Toledo Blade* wrote in an editorial, "When charter schools emerged on
the Ohio educational scene more than a decade ago, they were hailed
by many, including this newspaper, as a potentially innovative and
lower-cost alternative to the state's disturbingly mediocre public school
system. What was not envisioned is that charter schools—officially
known as community schools—would become cash repositories to be
siphoned of sponsorship and management fees, in some cases by politically connected individuals."[27]

The Akron businessman David Brennan owns a charter chain called

White Hat Management, which operates some fifty schools in six states, thirty of them in Ohio. Since 1999, White Hat has collected nearly $1 billion in revenues from the state for its charter schools. Brennan and his family members have donated millions of dollars to the state's politicians. Lobbyists for White Hat have played a significant role in writing charter legislation. Like many other states, Ohio gives schools a letter grade, based on test scores and other measures. In 2010–11, no White Hat charter school in Ohio earned a grade higher than C; most received a D or an F. In 2010, the boards of ten White Hat charter schools sued the corporation in an effort to compel it to open its financial books. White Hat collects 96 percent of the state funds, and the boards complained that they did not know how the money was spent. A judge ruled in favor of disclosure, but White Hat appealed the decision, claiming that as a private company it is not obliged to disclose its profits, losses, or revenues. It owns everything in the building, including the furniture, computers, and student files, which were purchased with public funds. Under Ohio charter law, if there is a dispute between the school board and the management company, the management company can fire the school board. A curious arrangement.[28]

In 2012, despite its unimpressive academic record, the state awarded White Hat two additional charter schools.[29]

For-profit charter chains have been subject to criticism because of issues of power, control, and money. *The New York Times* described how Imagine Schools Inc. takes complete control when it is invited to manage a school and that "regulators in some states have found that Imagine has elbowed the charter holders out of virtually all school decision making—hiring and firing principals and staff members, controlling and profiting from school real estate, and retaining fees under contracts that often guarantee Imagine's management in perpetuity." Imagine seeks to dominate the board that hired it and dictate the terms of its engagement. The corporation typically charges a management fee of 12 percent of all revenues, plus additional charges as determined by the company. Imagine's real estate dealings are complex and profitable. It buys school properties, sells them to real estate investment trusts, leases them back, and charges rent to the charter schools it manages. An Imagine-managed charter school in New York City paid the company $10,000 a month more in rent than Imagine paid the owner of the building. In Nevada, an Imagine charter paid 40 percent of its state revenues for rent. In 2012, Missouri closed six Imagine charters in St. Louis for poor performance, abruptly displacing thirty-eight hundred children, about 11 percent of the district's enrollment. When Georgia closed two Imagine schools, the Entertainment Properties Trust lost $72 million, experienced a drop in its stock price, and learned a lesson about the unpredictability of investing in charter schools.[30]

Imagine is not the only for-profit corporation that profits by charging exorbitant rental fees. National Heritage Academies (NHA), a Michigan-based for-profit charter operator, manages two charter schools in Brooklyn, New York. NHA leased a school building for $264,000 a year and bills its client Brooklyn Dreams Charter School a whopping $2.67 million for rent and related expenses. NHA also manages Brooklyn Excelsior Charter School, which was audited by the state comptroller in 2012. NHA leases the building from a company that it owns. The school pays NHA $2.57 million annually in rent, plus additional expenses that bring the cost of occupancy to $3.2 million, which was nearly a third of the school's $10.2 million in annual revenues. The auditor complained that the school was paying $800,000 more in rent each year—a total of $4 million over the life of the five-year lease—than was recommended by independent appraisers.[31]

Investing in charter school construction presents another opportunity for profit. In 2011, the tennis star Andre Agassi entered into a partnership with Los Angeles–based Canyon Capital Realty Advisors to create a fund of $750 million to finance the construction of charter schools across the nation. Investors were assured that they could do good and make a profit at the same time. The model for this venture was Agassi's own charter—the Andre Agassi College Preparatory Academy in Las Vegas—which opened in 2001. Agassi told the media and investors, "I'm interested in seeing this school duplicated and used as a blueprint, a model for how our education system should be in this country." Agassi portrayed the charter as an elite school for the city's neediest students. Its goal is to "prepare all of its students to attend and to compete at the top 100 colleges and universities in the nation." As a celebrity athlete, Agassi had no difficulty raising tens of millions of dollars to construct a state-of-the-art facility with ample resources; one billionaire made a gift of $18 million to Agassi's charter school.[32]

But the reality of the school did not match its image. In its first decade of operation, it had six principals; a local reporter noted that "teachers, principals and staff come and go like visiting teams." Some classes had four or five different teachers in the same year. According to former teachers, "The constant turnover creates a chaotic learning environment." The school's proficiency rates on state tests were about the same as the district, but it served fewer English-language learners and special education students. Students in its first three graduating classes took thirty-seven Advanced Placement tests but passed only four. In 2010, the principal of the middle school was investigated for a cheating scandal, and the state department of education invalidated the scores. The cheerleading coach was arrested on suspicion of running an international prostitution ring. Former teachers and security guards described a school without discipline, where high staff turnover contributed to student misbehavior. The school spent more per pupil than regular public schools. It is not a model or blueprint for any other school.[33]

Typically, nonprofit EMOs manage their schools and charge the state an administrative fee for their services. In some cases, the nonprofit management fee is no different from the fee of a for-profit. In New York City, for example, the Success Academy Charter Schools chain has a board that includes very wealthy Wall Street hedge fund managers. Eva Moskowitz, the CEO and founder of the Success Academy Charter Schools chain, is paid a salary and bonuses of about $400,000 annually. The organization is not-for-profit but charges a management fee of 15 percent, or $2,000 per student, which is comparable to the hefty fees charged by for-profit charter chains.[34]

Arizona has sometimes been called the Wild West of the charter movement, and for good reason. With state encouragement, the charter sector of more than five hundred schools enrolls nearly 15 percent of Arizona's school-age children, a far larger proportion than any other state. Under Arizona law, charters receive public money with minimal oversight. The result is not pretty. *The Arizona Republic* investigated the tax returns and audits of the state's fifty largest nonprofit charters and found that more than a dozen engaged in questionable self-dealing. It discovered some $70 million in contracts that schools had awarded to board members and administrators. The investigation did not include any for-profit charter operators, which are not required by law to disclose their spending or revenues.[35]

Nearly 90 percent of the state's charters have sought and obtained permanent exemption from state laws that require them to seek competitive bids for goods and services. In some instances, a nonprofit charter outsourced its management to a for-profit corporation owned by a board member of the charter. Because the for-profit companies are not required to disclose their spending, that part of the operation cannot be investigated.

Nothing in Arizona state law prohibits a charter from doing business with board members or staff members. In one nonprofit charter chain called Great Hearts, the newspaper reported, the schools purchased nearly $1 million in books from a textbook company owned by a board member.

In 1998, Michael and Olga Block founded Arizona's Basis charter schools, which are known for their rigorous curriculum and outstanding results. In 2009, the Blocks established a for-profit corporation to supply the six Basis charters with "most everything they need to operate: school directors, teachers, accounting, technology, human resources, public relations and Michael and Olga Block." The nonprofit corporation signed a ten-year agreement with the for-profit. Michael remained on the board of the nonprofit, while Olga resigned. According to *The Arizona Republic,* "The nonprofit paid the Blocks' company $9.8 million out of $13.7 million in total spending." Under state law, the state may audit the charter school but not the for-profit corporation hired to run the school.

Arizona law does not prohibit a charter from having a board consisting of members of only one family. A school in Peoria, Arizona, has a three-member board: the president and the secretary are married to each other, and the third member is their son. From 2007 to 2011, the school paid nearly half a million dollars to a business owned by the same family to provide curriculum, business consulting, maintenance, and other services. The school also awarded a contract for landscaping to the son and grandson of board members.

Two Arizonans started an online charter school in 2002 as a nonprofit, for which they are both board officers and salaried employees. The same two people created and own a for-profit called the American Virtual Academy that develops curriculum and software. From 2007 to 2011, the nonprofit paid the for-profit $42.3 million for its services.

The Espiritu charter schools, according to *The Arizona Republic,* are "a mesh of relatives." The three schools are situated on one property in

Phoenix. Armando Ruiz is the founder of Espiritu and a board member as well as a member of another nonprofit that Espiritu pays to handle nonacademic functions such as sports, technology, bookkeeping, and parental involvement. The schools pay rent to a third nonprofit that owns the land, whose board consists of Ruiz's brother, sister, and nephew. Nine members of the Ruiz family collect salaries from and serve on the boards of the nonprofits.

Oakland's American Indian Public Charter School became a favorite of corporate reformers and received national publicity for its achievements. It was a middle school that originally served American Indians and had low scores. In 2000, Ben Chavis took over the school and changed its policies and its demographics. Almost all its students were poor, yet the school consistently posted some of the state's highest test scores. Admirers hailed the school as a low-cost, no-frills model for the nation. Governor Arnold Schwarzenegger visited the school to offer his praise. The Bush administration honored it as a National Blue Ribbon School. Conservative foundations sent grants. David Whitman's book, *Sweating the Small Stuff,* singled out Chavis for his politically incorrect paternalism; Whitman described the middle school as "one of the great educational turnaround stories in recent history." (After the book's publication, Whitman became chief speech writer for Secretary of Education Arne Duncan.) The school practiced harsh discipline and no-excuses regimentation. Chavis became known for his public use of abusive language and racial epithets. He sneered at unions and quickly fired teachers who did not measure up to his expectations. Chavis opened two more charter schools in Oakland, including a high school. Skeptics pointed out that the schools' autocratic leader had changed the demographics so that most of the students were Asian Americans, and very few were American Indians. But nothing ended the media adulation of the schools until an audit in 2012 raised questions about $3.8 million that had been diverted to businesses owned by Chavis and his wife, the schools' financial administrator. Chavis stepped away from the schools' leadership but continued to collect hundreds of thousands of dollars annually in rental fees, because he owned the buildings in which the schools were located. As a charter leader, Chavis wanted public funding with no oversight at all, not over admission policies or disciplinary policies or finances.[36]

The great hope of charter entrepreneurs is that they will eventually develop a replicable, inexpensive model that will raise the test scores of poor children and close the achievement gap between poor and affluent students and between racial groups. In a PBS documentary, the correspondent John Merrow asked why America—which had pioneered the mass-produced automobile with the Ford Model T—had not been able to mass-produce high-quality schools. He sought the answer in the Rocketship charter chain, which began its operations in San Jose, California, in 2006 and hoped eventually to enroll one million children. Its business plan was straightforward: cut costs by putting large numbers of children in front of computers for an hour a day, supervised by low-wage, part-time aides. This "blended learning" model is described as "personalized instruction" because the software adjusts the questions to the ability level of each student; the model enables the school to reduce the number of teachers and save $500,000 a year. Three-quarters of the Rocketship teachers are from Teach for America, and half have less than two years of experience. The students, well practiced in point-and-click assessments, get high test scores. The schools offer no music or art. The model is cheap and replicable.[37]

But consider the contrast between the Rocketship charter model and the schools that the high-technology experts choose for their own children. Three-quarters of the students at the Waldorf School of the Peninsula in Los Altos, California, the heart of Silicon Valley, are children of top executives at Google, eBay, Apple, Yahoo!, and other giants of the industry. The Waldorf School has no computers at all; it emphasizes physical activity and creative, hands-on projects.[38]

The connoisseurs of technology know that it has a place in education. But they don't want a Model T education for their children.

To date, charter schools have not fulfilled the hope that they would produce superior academic results. There is wide variation among charter schools just as there is wide variation among public schools. Most studies conclude that on average the scores are no different if charter schools and public schools enroll the same kinds of students. No generalization is true for all charter schools. Some charters are excellent schools by any measure. Some charters have unusually high scores because they accept students only in kindergarten or first grade, or only in fifth grade; over time, the weakest students tend to leave, because

the school's academic or behavioral demands are too high. Some charters with high test scores have a series of admissions hurdles, like the
Philadelphia charter school that "required applicants to complete an
11-page application, write an essay, respond to 20 short-answer questions, provide three recommendations, be interviewed, and provide
records related to their disciplinary history, citizenship and disability
status." Or the Philadelphia charter school that accepted applications
for admission only one day of the year, available only on the premises
of a private golf club in the suburbs.[39]

Some charter schools have disproportionately small numbers of students with disabilities. These students are expensive to educate and,
depending on their disability, may lower a school's test scores. In 2012,
the U.S. Government Accountability Office (GAO) issued a report
concluding that while 11 percent of students in the nation have disabilities, charter schools enroll only 8 percent.[40] The GAO report may
have underestimated the underenrollment of special education students
in charters; most charters are concentrated in urban districts, where
the proportion of students with disabilities is significantly higher than
11 percent. Most charters refuse students with severe disabilities; in
Minneapolis, a Gulen-related charter school took control of an existing
public school and asked forty autistic students to leave. In 2010, civil
rights lawyers representing students with disabilities filed a class action
lawsuit in federal court against education officials in New Orleans and
the state of Louisiana, complaining that charter schools discriminated
against them.[41]

To be sure, there are good community-based charter schools that do
not skim the easiest-to-educate students and do not "counsel out" the
students they don't want. Some are trying to fulfill the original vision
of schools that fill a niche, doing something that public schools can't
do or can't do well. Some are run by teachers or others seeking a refuge
from the overscripted, hyper-regulated, and overtested public schools.
Such schools do not trumpet their superiority over the public schools.
In the current climate of competition for market share, however, the
aggressive and entrepreneurial charter chains are driving the growth of
the charter sector.

Corporate reformers believe that charters are the answer to the problems of urban education. In city after city, corporate leaders and their
allies promote charter schools, promising academic success. As char-

ter schools open, enrollments in public schools decline; then corporate reformers close public schools because of declining enrollments.
In Chicago, dozens of public schools were closed in the first decade of
the twenty-first century and large numbers of charter schools opened.
In 2013, Chicago mayor Rahm Emanuel decided to close another fifty-
four public schools, the largest mass closing of public schools in the
history of the United States. In Cleveland, the mayor devised a plan to
replace many public schools with charter schools, even though charter
schools in Ohio perform worse than public schools. In Philadelphia, a
major local foundation hired a management consulting firm—the Boston Consulting Group—to write a report on the public school system
(which has been under state control for many years); the consultants
recommended privatizing numerous public schools. The report did not
note that Philadelphia had tried a privatization experiment a decade
earlier, which had failed, or that many of the city's charter schools had
been under federal investigation. In Indianapolis, a corporate reform
group called the Mind Trust recommended expanding the charter sector to cure the ills of that city's educational system. In Memphis, where
the public schools were merging with those of the county, a planning
commission recommended swift expansion of the charter sector from
4 percent to 19 percent of the city's pupils. In Michigan, the state put
emergency managers in charge of two small school districts—Highland
Park and Muskegon Heights—that were operating in deficit; both districts are predominantly African American. The emergency managers'
solution was to dissolve the public school system in both districts and
turn the students over to for-profit charter operators. In Detroit, the
city's emergency manager devised a plan to eliminate large numbers of
public schools and open more charters. In city after city, district after
district, the answer to fiscal distress and low academic performance has
been privatization, despite the absence of any evidence that corporate
managers would either produce savings or provide better education.
Rather than making thoughtful and sustained efforts to improve public schools, the corporate reform leadership has responded by closing
public schools and replacing them with charter schools.

The opening of charter schools has had a particularly devastating
effect on urban Catholic schools. Parochial schools were already expe-
riencing financial problems and declining enrollments in response to
the movement of many Catholic families to the suburbs and the loss of

low-wage religious teachers. With the arrival of charters, the collapse of Catholic school enrollments accelerated. As charters open, mimicking Catholic schools with uniforms and strict discipline, many parents remove their children from Catholic schools, which charge tuition, expecting to find the same values at charter schools, which are free. Despite their admirable record of serving the children of poor and immigrant families, Catholic schools are forced to close their doors as families take their chances on charter schools with no track record or history. Some have suggested that Catholic schools could survive if they turned into charters, but to do so, they would have to abandon their religious identity and cease to be Catholic schools.[42]

The charter issue cannot be fully assessed without taking into account the impact of charters on the local public schools. Inglewood, California, was once an iconic district for conservatives, who warmly praised its high test scores despite its high poverty. Inglewood allegedly proved that an ordinary school without extra resources could overcome poverty if it stuck to the basics of phonics and strict discipline. Some wrote about "the Inglewood Miracle." The Heritage Foundation singled out the district's Bennett-Kew Elementary School as one of the nation's very best schools, a school that accepted "no excuses" for low performance. President George W. Bush paid the school a visit. But from 2003 to 2011, the district lost one-third of its eighteen thousand pupils to charter schools, and the model district was a model no longer. Because of the lost enrollment and lost revenue, the district was forced to lay off teachers and custodians and increase class sizes. At the end of 2012, the state took over the Inglewood district, appropriated an emergency loan of $55 million to stave off bankruptcy, and installed an interim administrator to take control of the schools and make deep cuts in spending. Reports on the state takeover of Inglewood noted that "at the heart of the district's financial demise is an exodus of students that refuses to let up. Despite taking active steps to bring students back— such as the January opening of a sparkling new La Tijera K–8 school— the district lost 900 students last year, many of them to nearby charter schools, leaving it with a total enrollment of about 12,000."[43]

In Pennsylvania's Chester Upland School District, a charter school operated by the governor's biggest campaign contributor absorbed half the district's children. The owner of the for-profit corporation that manages the charter school receives nearly $16 million annually in fees for

goods and services. The public schools in the district have lost so much
funding as a result that they are near bankruptcy and may eventually
be forced to close, with their remaining students handed over to private charter corporations. Other districts are in financial trouble. The
conservative-dominated legislature in Pennsylvania seems eager to give
away fiscally stressed districts to charter managers, whether nonprofit
or for-profit, effectively finishing public education in those towns. The
charter operators can then cut costs and increase their profits by firing teachers, slashing salaries and benefits, eliminating programs, and
increasing class sizes.[44]

Albert Shanker's worst fears have been realized. The charter movement has become a vehicle for privatization of large swaths of public
education, ending democratic control of the public schools and trans-
ferring them to private management. The charters seek to compete, not
to collaborate, with public schools.

The charter movement began with high hopes in the early 1990s.
Charter schools were supposed to enroll the neediest students. But in
the era of NCLB, it was dangerous to enroll the students who had a
hard time sitting still, those with disabilities, and those who couldn't
speak or read English. They might pull down the school's test scores.
Few charters want the students for whom charters were first invented.

Charters were supposed to be laboratories for bold innovations, but
the most successful charters follow a formula of "no excuses": strict discipline, eyes on the teacher, walk in a straight line, no deviation from
rigid rules and routines. Some of the most successful charters seem
determined to reinvent the schoolhouse of a century ago.

As the charter movement continues to grow, with the unwavering
support of the U.S. Department of Education, major foundations, Wall
Street, big corporations, think tanks, school choice advocates, and politicians in both parties, important questions are unasked: What is the
endgame? Will charter schools contribute to the increasing segregation
of American society along lines of race and class? Will the motivated
students congregate in charter schools while the unmotivated cluster in
what remains of the public schools? Will the concentration of charter
schools in urban districts sound a death knell for urban public education? Why do the elites support the increased stratification of American
society? If charter schools are not more successful on average than the
public schools they replace, what is accomplished by demolishing pub-

lic education? What is the rationale for authorizing for-profit charters or charter management organizations with high-paid executives, since their profits and high salaries are paid by taxpayers' dollars?

The developments of the past two decades have brought about massive changes in the governance of public education, especially in urban districts. Some children have gained; most have not. And the public schools, an essential element in our democracy for many generations, have suffered damage that may be irreparable.

CHAPTER 17

Trouble in E-land

CLAIM *Virtual schools will bring the promise of personalized, customized learning to every student and usher in an age of educational excellence for all.*

REALITY *Virtual schools are cash cows for their owners but poor substitutes for real teachers and real schools.*

New technologies appear almost daily, and schools are rightly expected to help young people learn to use them. Computers and access to the Internet are nearly ubiquitous, and no one doubts that if used appropriately, these are valuable tools for teaching and learning. Ingenious teachers integrate technology into their lessons and engage young people in science experiments, historical research, and projects of all kinds. Students today can vicariously visit other lands, not just read about them in a textbook. They can see and hear presidents giving their major speeches. They can watch the historical events that changed the world with their own eyes, as if they were there. The possibilities for making learning interactive and lively are limitless, and a new age of teaching and learning is within reach, one where students can learn at their own pace and explore topics far beyond the assignment.

Yet with all its great potential, technology can never substitute for inspired teaching. Students will respond with greater enthusiasm to a gifted teacher than to a computer with the world's best software. Electronic technology has its charms, but it can't compete with the lively interchange of ideas that happens when students discuss a book they read or a math problem they wrestled with or a play they saw or an unsolved mystery in history or the most recent elections. Ultimately, it is imagination, joy, and disciplined inquiry that make education valuable, that distinguish real education from seat time, that constitute the difference between learning and a credential.

Faced with tightened budgets and the incessant demand for more high-stakes testing, our policy makers have been all too willing to sacrifice such nebulous concepts as imagination, joy, and disciplined inquiry. After all, they can't be measured, so why should they matter?

Entrepreneurs look at declining budgets and see an opportunity, not a problem. The biggest cost in education is teachers' salaries, so they devise online programs, new devices, and new kinds of schools to cut costs by replacing teaching with technology. They see public education as a new business opportunity, an emerging market. For years, equity firms have circled what they call the "education industry" with interest, uncertain how to break in or how to find a niche. After the passage of No Child Left Behind, many entrepreneurs started businesses to offer tutoring and consulting services to districts. Many of these businesses, however, were small-time, able to obtain only a small chunk of the federal revenues for after-school activities or for professional development in one or several districts.

After the launch of Race to the Top, however, equity investors saw new possibilities for major returns on a statewide or national scale. Now that the federal government was firmly planted on the side of privately managed charter schools, many investors poured millions into the expansion of charter chains. Others saw possibilities in the development of technological resources, hardware, and online curricula for the new national Common Core State Standards. National standards and national assessments created a national marketplace for products. A journalist attended a conference of private equity investors in Manhattan where a consultant predicted that if the Common Core tests turn out to be as rigorous as advertised, "a huge number of schools will suddenly look really bad, their students testing way behind in reading and math. They'll want help, quick. And private, for-profit vendors selling lesson plans, educational software and student assessments will be right there to provide it." He added, "You start to see entire ecosystems of investment opportunity lining up . . . It could get really, really big." Some reformers hoped that the Common Core standards would cause suburban parents to lose faith in their public schools and demand charters, perhaps even vouchers.[1]

The biggest pot of gold for business-minded reformers was the for-profit online charter school market. The first to see this opportunity, and to act on it, were the founders of a new company called K12 Inc. The brothers Lowell and Michael Milken and their associate Ron Packard started the company in 2000. Michael Milken was known as the 1980s junk bond king. Since his release from prison, he had become a philanthropist with a particular interest in education. Packard had worked at McKinsey and Goldman Sachs. The founders invited the former secretary of education Bill Bennett to serve as chairman of the K12 board. At the time, Bennett was a skeptic about electronic learning; he was co-author of the book *The Educated Child,* published in 1999, which asserted there was "no good evidence that most uses of computers significantly improve learning." Given the opportunity to join the Milkens and Packard in this new venture, however, he changed his mind. The investors thought he would be a magnet for conservative Christians and parents who were schooling their children at home.[2]

In 2007, K12 went public and was listed on the New York Stock Exchange. K12 soon became the leader of the for-profit online school industry. By 2012, there were more than 200,000 full-time students enrolled in virtual charter schools in the United States. K12 claimed at least 100,000 in twenty-nine states plus the District of Columbia. The next in size was Connections Academy, established in 2001, which enrolled about 40,000 students (it was acquired by the testing publisher Pearson in 2011). Others soon joined the lucrative marketplace. The online charter schools were cash cows. Once they got permission from the state legislature to open an online charter school, they could enroll students from anywhere in the state. They recruited students through the Internet, radio, television, billboards, vans, meetings, and telemarketing. According to an analysis by *The New York Times,* K12 spent $26.5 million on advertising in 2010, funded with public dollars.[3] Some students were homeschoolers who previously received no tuition money from the state. Some were homebound for health or other reasons. Whatever their reason for enrolling in a virtual charter school, the school welcomes them because its revenues rely on growing enrollments.

The virtual charters receive tuition payments from the state that far exceed their costs. Even though they receive less funding per student than brick-and-mortar schools, they still make handsome profits. Because they have no school buildings, their costs are minimal.

They have no custodians, no heating or cooling costs, no libraries, no gyms, no cafeterias, no social workers, no guidance counselors, no playgrounds, no after-school activities, and no transportation costs. In addition, they are able to have a larger "class size," because one teacher can monitor forty, fifty, a hundred, or more computer screens. And the teachers may or may not be certified. The cost savings are enormous, and the savings go to the schools, not the taxpayers. Even when the virtual school gets less money than the local public school, the business is profitable.

Conservatives waxed rhapsodic about online charter schools and about selling online programs to the public schools as a way to reduce the number of teachers needed. They recognized the online charters' potential to disrupt traditional schooling and to destroy the influence of teachers' unions. It was the very force for "creative destruction" that proponents of the free market admired. Terry Moe of Stanford University and John Chubb of the Edison Project, both critics of the unions and advocates of school choice, embraced online learning as a revolutionary force that would transform learning, reduce costs, and bypass the unions. Rupert Murdoch of News Corporation hired Joel Klein to promote online learning and paid $360 million to buy a company called Wireless Generation to generate electronic content. Murdoch saw a multibillion-dollar industry ready to be mined for vast profits.

Jeb Bush campaigned tirelessly to popularize the promise of online learning. In 2010, he and Bob Wise, the former governor of West Virginia, and their respective organizations—the Foundation for Excellence in Education and the Alliance for Excellent Education—released a joint statement called "10 Elements of High Quality Digital Learning," which contained glowing promises of high-quality instruction delivered online, personalized and customized to meet the needs of every learner.

The ten elements were (1) student eligibility—all students are eligible; (2) student access—all students should have access to online education; (3) "personalized learning"—all students can get a customized online education from an approved provider; (4) advancement—students progress based on demonstrated competency, not by age or grade or seat time; (5) content—all courses are high quality; (6) instruction—digital instruction and teachers are high quality; (7) providers—all students have access to multiple high-quality providers of digital

instruction; (8) assessment and accountability—student learning
is the metric for evaluating the quality of content and instruction;
(9) funding—funding creates incentives for performance, options, and
innovation; and (10) delivery—infrastructure supports digital learning.
The "10 Elements" supported online courses and online assessments
in regular schools—a boon for the marketplace—and virtual schools,
operating with minimal state regulation.

Its sponsors said this proposal would bring excellent education to
every student in America and claimed that it would prepare everyone
for college and a career, close the achievement gap, and narrow the
income divide in American society. Free and easy and universal access
to digital learning, they said, would transform American education
and American society. Embedded in the "10 Elements of High Quality Digital Learning" was a recommendation that states should treat
all education providers equally, whether they were "public, chartered,
not-for-profit, or private." This would make cyber-charters equally
deserving of public dollars as public schools. The "10 Elements" urged
lawmakers not to set any limits on how much, how often, or in what
manner online instruction was delivered, while encouraging alternative certification for teachers. States should not permit school districts
to restrict access to online schools, and states should require students
to take online courses to graduate from high school. What a boon this
was for providers.

The underlying theme of the "10 Elements" was deregulation: removing any obstacles to digital providers, such as requirements that teachers be certified (which would "stifle innovation and diminish quality"),
that class sizes be limited, or that providers have a brick-and-mortar
office in the district or state where they sell their products. Such an
administrative requirement, they cautioned, might create "obstacles"
that "prevent high quality providers from participating." The "10 Elements" was truly a bill of rights for online providers, giving them free
access to a state's students without any quality controls for teachers
or programming. One wonders how many providers of virtual schools
would find it burdensome to have a physical office located in a state
where they intend to collect millions of dollars of taxpayers' money.[4]

The statement confidently asserted, "Digital learning is a proven
method." It is successful in the military, in industry, and in higher education, it asserts, so it will surely succeed in the schools, where it will be

the "great equalizer" and "students will learn more." The only research cited to support this claim was a U.S. Department of Education report. The authors of that report said they could find only five recent studies comparing online instruction with face-to-face instruction in the schools and that much more research was needed. It contained no support for the extravagant claims of the "10 Elements" about the benefits of digital learning in elementary and secondary schools.[5]

The preparation of the "10 Elements" statement was funded by the Gates Foundation, the Broad Foundation, and the Walton Family Foundation, as well as by many online providers who stood to benefit by its recommendations, including K12 Inc., Pearson, Houghton Mifflin Harcourt, Apex Learning, McGraw-Hill, and other big technology companies.

ALEC, the conservative organization of state legislators committed to privatization of public education, is a major promoter of online learning. The co-chair of ALEC's education task force was Mickey Revenaugh, the senior vice president of Connections Academy, for-profit online school provider. The two thousand state legislators who belong to ALEC could be counted on to bring ALEC's model laws back to their home states. ALEC's Virtual Public Schools Act authorized for-profit virtual academies and declared that they would be recognized as public schools, treated equitably, and allocated the same resources as other "public schools." Connections Academy quit ALEC after the shooter of an unarmed teenager in Florida said he was acting in accord with the ALEC-devised "stand your ground" law. Some other corporations that sponsored ALEC were also embarrassed and withdrew their support.[6]

A state legislator in Tennessee introduced ALEC's model legislation for virtual schools without even bothering to disguise its origin: "Asked by the Knoxville *News Sentinel*'s Tom Humphrey where he got the idea for the bill, [Representative Harry] Brooks readily admitted that a K12 Inc. lobbyist helped him draft it. Governor Bill Haslam signed Brooks's bill into law in May [2011]. The statute allows parents to apply nearly every dollar the state typically spends per pupil, almost $6,000 in most areas, to virtual charter schools that are authorized by the state."[7]

State after state passed legislation opening the door to virtual charter schools and for-profit virtual charters. At least twenty-nine states had one or more virtual charter schools for full-time students in 2012, and the number seemed likely to grow. A report issued by the National Education Policy Center said, "In league with the home schooling and charter school movements, virtual schooling has become the fastest growing alternative to traditional K–12 education in the United States." The virtual charters merged the three disparate movements—charter schools, homeschooling, and online learning—into a single for-profit format.[8]

It was not a love of innovation that opened doors in many states for the for-profit virtual charter industry but adroit lobbying and campaign contributions. The industry gives generously to politicians and lobbyists to facilitate legislation authorizing them to open virtual schools in the state and obtain public funding. That is part of the cost of doing business. In Pennsylvania, which provides about 10 percent of K12's revenues, the corporation spent nearly $700,000 on lobbying between 2007 and 2011. The corporations contribute to family organizations that support cyber-schools, and the family groups in turn use these resources to lobby legislators, make campaign gifts, and send large delegations of parents and children in matching T-shirts to legislative hearings and other public meetings on behalf of the industry.[9]

Jeb Bush's Foundation for Excellence in Education actively lobbies and advocates for the benefits of online schooling. At a conference in San Francisco, Stephen Bowen, the state commissioner of Maine, got very excited when Bush's top education adviser, Patricia Levesque, offered to help "suggest policies, write laws and gubernatorial decrees, and develop strategies to ensure they were implemented." An investigative report by the *Maine Sunday Telegram* uncovered "a partnership between Maine's top education official and a foundation entangled with the very companies that stand to make millions of dollars from the policies it advocates." The newspaper obtained more than a thousand pages of e-mails documenting how Maine's digital education agenda was guided by the companies likely to benefit financially from the state's policies, especially K12 Inc. and Pearson's Connections Academy. "At stake," said the report, "is the future of thousands of Maine schoolchildren who would enroll in the full-time virtual schools and, if the companies had their way, the future of tens of thousands more who would be legally required to take online courses at their public high school in order to receive their diplomas."[10]

Colin Woodard, the Maine reporter, revealed that Stephen Bowen was a member of ALEC when he was chosen to be commissioner of education for the state of Maine, as were K12 Inc. and Connections Academy. K12 Inc. contributed $19,000 to Paul LePage's campaign to become governor of Maine. Patricia Levesque was a lobbyist for many of the online companies, as well as the College Board. One of the bills proposed to Bowen was a requirement that all students take at least one Advanced Placement test online (that would benefit the College Board and the online companies). When Governor LePage proclaimed "the first ever National Digital Learning Day," said the investigative report, the language of his executive order was largely written by the lobbyists representing the online companies. Woodard's exposé of the profit motive behind the demand for online schools in Maine won a 2012 George Polk Award, one of the most prestigious in journalism.

When K12 Inc. decided to open an online charter in Massachusetts, it created a partnership with the rural Greenfield school district. According to *The Washington Post,* the state's education officials vetoed the plan to start a statewide school. K12 then spent about $200,000 to lobby legislators. A Boston Democrat sponsored legislation allowing the Greenfield district to launch the Massachusetts Virtual Academy. She acknowledged to the *Post* that "the language was imperfect and didn't address issues of funding or oversight but said she couldn't wait to craft a comprehensive plan." According to the *Post,* she received "at least $2,600 in campaign contributions from K12, its executives or its lobbyists."[11]

When K12 wanted to open a statewide online school in Virginia, it followed a politically savvy path. It made generous campaign contributions of $55,000 to the Republican governor, Robert F. McDonnell, a staunch advocate of school choice. McDonnell pushed legislation to authorize full-time virtual schools in 2010. K12 created a partnership with rural Carroll County, taking advantage of the fact that state aid is linked to the district's affluence or poverty. Carroll County receives some $5,400 per student in state aid, and K12 is reimbursed for that amount for every student who enrolls, regardless of where he or she lives. Had K12 located in affluent Fairfax County, *The Washington Post* pointed out, the state aid would have been about half that amount. For its part, Carroll County gets a handsome reward: a $500 registration fee for every out-of-district student, plus a management fee of 6.5 percent of K12's taxpayer dollars for the school. That's a plum for Carroll County but a loss for every district whose students enroll in K12's online school.[12]

Education technology companies, Wall Street equity funds, and school choice advocates combined to promote online schooling. It was a win-win situation for all three sectors. The technology companies won market share as states required every student to take at least one online course and authorized virtual charter schools. Wall Street investors got a piece of an exciting new industry. The school choice advocates saw technology as the wedge that would undermine the preferred status of public schooling. At conference after conference, lobbyists for education technology, hedge fund managers, equity investors, and school choice advocates met to celebrate their victories and to plan for the next round of expansion. Lee Fang of *The Nation* described one of these conferences:

> Standing at the lectern of Arizona State University's SkySong conference center in April [2011], investment banker Michael Moe exuded confidence as he kicked off his second annual confab of education startup companies and venture capitalists. A press packet cited reports that rapid changes in education could unlock "immense potential for entrepreneurs." "This education issue," Moe declared, "there's not a bigger problem or bigger opportunity in my estimation."
>
> Moe has worked for almost fifteen years at converting the K–12 education system into a cash cow for Wall Street. A veteran of Lehman Brothers and Merrill Lynch, he now leads an investment group that specializes in raising money for businesses looking to tap into more than $1 trillion in taxpayer money spent annually on primary education. His consortium of wealth management and consulting firms, called Global Silicon Valley Partners, helped K12 Inc. go public and has advised a number of other education companies in finding capital.
>
> Moe's conference marked a watershed moment in school privatization. His first "Education Innovation Summit," held last year, attracted about 370 people and fifty-five presenting companies. This year, his conference hosted more than 560 people and 100 companies, and featured luminaries like former DC Mayor Adrian Fenty and former New York City schools chancellor Joel Klein, now an education executive at News Corporation, a recent high-powered entrant into the for-profit education field.[13]

As the industry prospered, it came under increased scrutiny. Journalists and researchers began to question the cost and value of the education it provided, and educators awakened to the fact that every student who left a district school for a charter, whether bricks-and-mortar or virtual, diminished the district's enrollment and budget.

In an article in *Bloomberg Businessweek,* John Hechinger pointed out that K12 schools had worse academic results than brick-and-mortar schools. The company's response was that it was enrolling high numbers of poor students, a rationale that would be scorned by reformers as an "excuse" if offered in defense of a regular public school. Critics, including the auditor general for Pennsylvania, complained that the state's cyber-schools—which receive nearly $11,000 per student—were overcharging for their services. When K12 enrolled special education students, its charges far exceeded those of the local school district. Hechinger reported that a parent had two boys who received one hour a week of speech therapy via headset, microphone, and Web conferencing; for this service, the state paid the cyber-charter nearly $22,000 annually for each boy. The same once-a-week speech service from the local school district would have been about $1,500 each. And the money for these services comes out of the state's limited budget for public education.[14]

Unlike most educators, people in the corporate sector believed that education would be transformed by those who have a profit motive. Michael Milken was serenely confident in the education program he initiated. To address education and other major problems, he said, "In each case, the solution is the same: Unleash the energies of entrepreneurial people, and they will change the world." According to Ron Packard, the possibilities for expansion were limitless: "There's no reason why eventually you can't be educating a billion kids online."[15]

The New York Times launched an in-depth investigation into the claim that "corporate efficiencies combined with the Internet can revolutionize public education, offering high quality at reduced cost." The *Times* focused on K12, the industry leader, to explore these issues. What it found was "a company that tries to squeeze profits from public school dollars by raising enrollment, increasing teacher workload, and lowering standards." To bolster profits, the company recruits students

who are ill-suited for online education, which requires "strong parental commitment and self-motivated students." Consequently, K12 and
other for-profit online schools experience "high rates of withdrawal."
Teachers complained of low pay and heavy workloads, with some managing more than 250 students; many said they felt pressured to pass
students who did little work. Students who were inactive remained on
the roster, enabling the company to collect tuition for them. According
to the story, state auditors in Colorado identified 120 students in K12's
Colorado Virtual Academy who could not be verified or never logged
in or did not meet state residency requirements.[16]

Students who enroll in K12 online schools receive a computer, an
Internet connection, materials, and workbooks. Their parents are their
"learning coaches." Teachers work from their homes or other remote
locations. Teacher pay is low, starting in the low $30,000s, less than
their counterparts in traditional schools. Some elementary-level teachers manage online classes of 75 children, while some high school teachers
may be responsible for more than 250. The most significant cost to any
school is teachers' salaries, and the most significant saving is increased
class size, although that means less time and attention for individual
students. Teachers are available on the Internet or by telephone, and
some schedule meetings with students when it is physically possible.

The online industry zealously protects its financial and legal status,
said the *Times*. When Stephen Dyer, a state legislator in Ohio, began
questioning the state's formula for financing charter schools and online
schools, he was picketed by protesters carrying signs that said, "Why
won't Rep. Stephen Dyer let parents choose the best education for their
kids?" The protesters said they were parents, children, and employees of schools who belonged to an organization called My School, My
Choice. But when Dyer's wife questioned them, she learned that they
were "paid temp agency workers."[17] The *Times*'s reporter tracked down
the group's connection to a Republican lawyer in Columbus and from
there to the board president of the Ohio Virtual Academy, which is
managed by K12 and receives $60 million annually from the state.

The K12 corporation boasted to investors about the solid test score
gains of students at its Agora school in Pennsylvania. But the *Times*
learned that students in that school scored far below students in the
state: only 42 percent were at grade level or better in math, compared
with 75 percent of students statewide, and in reading only 52 percent

were at grade level, compared with 72 percent in the state. Said the *Times:* "The school was losing ground, not gaining it."

Within three days of the publication of the *Times*'s investigation, K12's stock price plummeted by 34 percent, from $28.79 a share to $18.90.[18]

The evangelists for online learning made mighty claims for the power of their medium. They said it would put excellence within the reach of every child, it would close achievement gaps, it would narrow the income divide, it would enable every student to have high-quality instruction that met the highest standards.

But there was no evidence for these claims. Bill Bennett, we now know, was right when he wrote in 1999 that there was "no good evidence that most uses of computers significantly improve learning." In fact, as more virtual charter schools were opened, evidence accumulated that online homeschooling did not significantly improve learning and that many students lost ground when they were in full-time cyberschools. Students who enrolled in online schools had lower test scores than those in traditional schools, lower graduation rates, and higher attrition rates.

K12's Colorado Virtual Academy, which enrolls more than five thousand students, had an on-time graduation rate of 12 percent, compared with a statewide graduation rate of 72 percent. K12's Ohio Virtual Academy, which enrolls more than nine thousand students, had a 30 percent on-time graduation rate, compared with a statewide average of 78 percent.[19] Less than a third of online charter schools met the federal law's requirement of adequate yearly progress, compared with 52 percent of the nation's public schools. A review of K12 schools by the National Education Policy Center found the following: "Thirty-six of the 48 full-time virtual schools operated by K12 were assigned school performance ratings by state education authorities in 2010–11, and just seven schools (19.4% of those rated) had ratings that indicated satisfactory progress status." The report said that students in K12 virtual schools consistently scored below students in brick-and-mortar schools in reading and math in every state. Gary Miron, the senior author of the study, said, "Our findings are clear. Children who enroll in a K12 Inc. cyberschool, who receive full-time instruction in front of a computer instead of in a classroom with a live teacher and other students, are more likely to fall behind in reading and math. These children are also more likely to move between schools or leave school altogether—and the cyberschool is less likely to meet federal education standards."[20]

An investigation of online learning in Colorado determined that the state was spending $100 million a year for full-time virtual charter schools. But the results were dismal: half the students who enrolled in the virtual schools dropped out and returned to their public schools within the same year. However, their tuition money stayed with the online schools. When they returned to their local public schools, many were further behind academically than when they started. Thirty-nine students left the Florence School District to enroll in online schools, costing the district a quarter million dollars, the equivalent of four or five teachers' salaries. When thirteen of them returned to their public schools midyear, the online schools kept the money, and the public schools had to scramble to find money to educate them. The analysis also found that the "online schools produce three times as many dropouts as they do graduates. One of every eight online students drops out of school permanently—a rate four times the state average." In addition, the virtual schools were collecting millions of dollars each year for students who were no longer enrolled.[21]

Officials at the online schools offered a familiar excuse: they attributed the high attrition rate to the large proportion of high-risk students they served. However, the journalists reviewed the schools' records and determined that only four hundred of ten thousand students could be considered "at risk" and that most were not struggling academically when they entered the online school.

Brandon Shaffer, the president of the state senate, told the journalists, "We are bleeding money to a program that doesn't work." He noted, "We spend over $100 million a year on online schools now—in an environment where we're cutting $200 to $270 million a year from brick-and-mortar schools."

The Denver Post professed to be alarmed by the statistics about the online schools and urged greater scrutiny but warned, "We hope the scrutiny doesn't morph into a plan to drive these valuable alternative education options out of existence."[22] *The Denver Post* consistently supported corporate-style reform. The editorial didn't say what part of the online school experience or financing or academic results was valuable.

The states with the biggest online charter sector were Pennsylvania and Ohio.

In 2011, the Center for Research on Education Outcomes (CREDO) at Stanford University published its analysis of charter school performance in Pennsylvania, based on four years of data about academic growth on state achievement tests. The CREDO report showed discouraging results for charters in general but devastating results for cyber-charters. The typical student in brick-and-mortar charter schools is black and poor; the typical student in a cyber-charter is white and not poor. The starting scores for cyber-students are significantly higher than those of the brick-and-mortar charter students. But cyber-students are more likely to be repeating a grade. In reading, the students in the brick-and-mortar charters got the same academic gains as their peers in public schools, but in math they learned significantly less. The students in the cyber-charters learned significantly less than their traditional public school peers in both reading and math. They did especially poorly in math.[23]

The study examined test scores in eight different cyber-charters and found that all eight performed significantly worse than their peers in traditional public schools. Thirty-five percent of the brick-and-mortar charters outperformed traditional public schools in reading, as did 27 percent in math.

The following types of students got significantly lower scores in reading and math when they enrolled in charter schools, whether brick-and-mortar or cyber: black students, Hispanic students, poor students, special education students, and grade repeaters.

The CREDO study found that 100 percent of cyber-charters performed significantly worse than traditional public schools in both reading and math. This study, authored by charter-friendly academics at Stanford and the Hoover Institution, was bad news for cyber-charters in Pennsylvania. These are the very schools, according to Jeb Bush and Bob Wise and their "10 Elements of High Quality Digital Learning," that are supposed to give every student an excellent education and close the achievement gaps.

But there was worse news to come.

Pennsylvania's biggest cyber-charter is the Pennsylvania Cyber Charter School. It opened in Midland in 2000 as a replacement for the local high school, which closed when the area lost its steel mill and the population declined.[24] Superintendent Nick Trombetta founded the new online school as a nonprofit intended for the district's fifty students, but it enrolled five hundred students in its first year. It currently enrolls more than eleven thousand students from across the state; the school has revenues of more than $100 million annually. The future appeared to be one of unlimited success until July 2012, when the FBI raided the offices of Pennsylvania Cyber Charter, and of several for-profit and nonprofit businesses in Pennsylvania and Ohio connected to the corporation. Journalists noted that the school pays tens of millions of dollars to a network of companies run by former executives of Pennsylvania Cyber Charter School. The administration of the former governor Ed Rendell had asked the school for better accounting of these relationships, but Governor Tom Corbett's Department of Education "opted early on to let the relationships continue without heightened accountability."[25]

The multiple embarrassments to cyber-schools in Pennsylvania did not affect the decisions of policy makers in the state. In 2012, they voted to approve four more cyber-charters, bringing the total in the state to sixteen. It can't have been because the existing cyber-charters got good academic results; they didn't. For cyber-charters, results and accountability don't matter.

In Oregon, a pair of entrepreneurs opened at least ten online charter schools in 2007, authorized by various school districts. The state gave each school a start-up grant of $450,000 plus $6,000 for each student it enrolled. Five years later, Oregon's Department of Justice accused the founders of inflating their enrollment figures and of racketeering and fraud. The state demanded repayment of $17 million in taxpayer funds, plus another $2.7 million in damages and costs to the state. In Pennsylvania, the FBI indicted the founder of two online charter schools, along with three other executives, for defrauding the schools of $6.5 million. Such instances of misbehavior are not typical of the charter sector, but the opportunities for malfeasance are many, and financial oversight is lax or nonexistent.[26]

In Ohio, the first cyber-charter was the Electronic Classroom of Tomorrow (ECOT), which opened in 2000–2001 with twenty-two hundred students. In 2005, the state imposed a moratorium on creating any new cyber-schools until accountability standards were developed, but Governor John Kasich ignored the moratorium, and it was full speed ahead for cyber-charters with no standards or accountability.[27]

In 2009–10, the Ohio Department of Education issued its school ratings. Of twenty-three cyber-charters in the state, only three were rated "effective" or better. Only 8 percent of the children enrolled in cyber-charters attended schools that the state rated at least a B. In its report on cyber-schools, the public policy center Innovation Ohio wrote, "By contrast, more than 75 percent of traditional public school students attend school in buildings rated B or better. In short, children are nearly 10 times more likely to receive an 'effective' education in traditional public school than they are in E-schools." Worse, only two of the seven statewide cyber-schools had higher graduation rates than the Cleveland public school district, which had the lowest graduation rate of any district in the state. As Innovation Ohio put it, "A child has a better chance of graduating if he or she attends school in the Cleveland Municipal school district (whose poor performance has long served as a punching bag for conservative school choice advocates)—than in an Ohio E-school."

The state reimburses cyber-schools about $6,000 per pupil, as if they had the same costs for teachers and facilities and transportation as traditional public schools. This amount is deducted from the budget of the state's public schools. But the average salary for teachers in public schools was about $56,000, compared with an average of just $36,000 for teachers in cyber-charters. The cyber-schools not only have lower teachers' salaries but larger classes and none of the costs associated with brick-and-mortar schools. Thus, every cyber-school has a cushion of millions of dollars of taxpayer funding, extracted from local school districts but not necessary for its operations.

The state of Ohio originally set minimum amounts that the cyber-charters were required to spend on instruction, to be sure that the funds were used appropriately. But in 2011, Governor Kasich and the legislature removed the minimum requirements, so the cyber-charters could cut costs and increase their profits.

Why was the state sending so many millions of dollars to schools that get such poor results? Innovation Ohio suggested that the answer was to be found in the campaign contributions of the two biggest E-school operators, David Brennan and William Lager.

Brennan's private corporation controls the largest chain of charter schools in the state, as well as a cyber-charter called the Ohio Distance and Electronic Learning Academy (OHDELA). According to Innovation Ohio, he collects about $100 million annually from the state.

From 2001 to 2010, he donated nearly $3 million to mostly Republican candidates. OHDELA graduates 35.9 percent of its students, which is lower than Cleveland. Brennan's corporation receives $11.7 million annually to operate OHDELA.

William Lager is the founder of ECOT (the Electronic Classroom of Tomorrow). He has made nearly $1 million in political contributions since 2001. ECOT obtains $64 million each year in state funding but graduates only 35 percent of its students. On the state's ratings, it is near the very bottom of 613 districts.

The findings of Innovation Ohio's report were replicated in 2012 by a Cincinnati journalist who reviewed state data for the cyber-schools and determined that they spend 15 percent of their state funding on teachers' salaries as compared with 75 percent at traditional public schools. Furthermore, under Governor John Kasich's reform plan, "all statewide e-schools reviewed by Innovation Ohio would have been given F's under the proposed overall grading system." That is, if the cyber-schools were traditional public schools, the state would have closed them down for poor performance—and would have done so long ago. But given their political connections, they could count on a secure future—without accountability for their spending or their performance.[28]

Those who believe that online learning is the key to bringing excellent education to every child and that it would close achievement gaps and lift up the nation to new heights of academic performance, as Jeb Bush and Bob Wise predicted in 2010, were unfazed. They never stopped to wonder whether homeschooling on the Internet was appropriate for some children but not for others. Perhaps it is just right for pregnant teenagers, or for athletes training for the Olympics, or for child actors hoping to make it to Broadway, or for seriously ill children who can't travel to school, or for other students in unusual situations. But once the profit motive entered the equation, all such qualifications were dismissed, and the goal was more enrollment. Greater numbers mean greater revenues. Greater revenues require cost cutting: lower salaries and larger classes for teachers. This is not a formula for educational improvement.

Surely every student should learn to use computers and the Internet in school. The possibilities for imaginative teaching and learning and research are boundless. But that is quite different from inviting the private sector to make money by enrolling students in virtual academies.

As we have seen, the incentives to grow enrollments are much larger than the incentives to provide high-quality education. And very little thought was given to the developmental needs of children of all ages and what it meant to isolate them during their formative years.

In the rush to boost enrollments, no one paused to wonder whether it was appropriate for young children to be placed in front of a home computer for their education. Nor to question what children were missing when they had so little interaction with peers or adults. Nor to judge the value of the content that was delivered or the point-and-click assessments. Nor to gauge what was lost when students are not engaged in face-to-face discussions with other students to exchange ideas. Online learning may work well in the military and in industry and in higher education for highly motivated students, but there is no reason to assume that it is right as a full-time means of educating children in kindergarten or third grade or eighth grade or high school. There is no evidence to support this belief, and many reasons to question it based on children's need for wholesome personal and social development.

Online technology surely holds immense potential to enliven the classroom. But the story of cyber-charters warns us that the profit motive operates in conflict with the imperative for high-quality education. Given the nature of the political process, the question today is whether education technology can be recaptured by educators to benefit students, not investors and stockholders.

CHAPTER 18

Parent Trigger, Parent Tricker

CLAIM *If parents seize control of their school, they can make it better.*

REALITY *There is no evidence for this claim.*

California's Republican governor Arnold Schwarzenegger favored charter schools. While slashing billions of dollars from the budgets of the public schools, he made sure that his cash-strapped state had ample funding for charter facilities and construction. More important, he appointed charter school advocates to a majority of seats on the state board of education, even though charter schools enrolled only 5 percent of the state's children. Ted Mitchell, president of the New-Schools Venture Fund, which develops new charter schools and charter school chains, was president of the state board of education from 2008 to 2010. By 2012, California had more than a thousand charter schools, far more than any other state, with 484,000 students (about 8 percent of the state's six million public school students).[1]

One of Governor Schwarzenegger's appointees to the state board in 2010 was Ben Austin, executive director of an organization created only a year earlier called Parent Revolution. Austin, a lawyer, had previously worked for the Green Dot charter school organization in Los Angeles, which had been launched with $10.5 million from the Broad Foundation. Austin's Parent Revolution was funded by the Gates Foundation, the Walton Family Foundation, and the Broad Foundation, among others. It advocates for school choice. It achieved its first big victory, months after its founding, when the Los Angeles Unified School District passed a school choice program to allow charter operators to compete to run fifty new schools and two hundred existing schools. Parent Revolution worked closely with other pro-charter organizations like the California Charter Schools Association and Families That Can to win that battle.

Parent Revolution's biggest coup, however, was the passage of the "parent trigger" law by the California legislature in January 2010. According to its Web site, Parent Revolution "invented" the idea of the "parent trigger" and persuaded the state senator Gloria Romero to include it in her education reform legislation. If 51 percent of the parents in a low-performing school sign a petition, the law says, the parents may take control of the school, its staff, and its budget, fire some or all of the staff, or turn the school over to a charter management organization. The law assumes that parents know best what is needed to reform their children's schools and should be empowered to turn them over to a private corporation to manage.[2]

The demands of NCLB provided grist for advocates of the parent trigger. In communities with high numbers of students who had limited English skills or were impoverished, many schools were not on track to meet NCLB's impossible target of 100 percent proficiency by 2014. Because of No Child Left Behind, thousands of schools across the state had been labeled low performing. Thus, large numbers of schools were ripe for a parent revolution.

But even though the law was passed early in 2010, no groups of parents stepped up to pull the parent trigger. In the fall of 2010, Parent Revolution sent organizers to McKinley Elementary, a low-performing school in Compton, California, to solicit parent signatures. According to the Web site, "Parent Revolution organizers spent three months talking to McKinley parents, educating them about the academic situation at their school, training them in community organizing and leadership techniques, and gathering signatures." The Parent Revolution organizers, not the parents, gathered the signatures of 61 percent of the parents in the school, demanding that their public school be handed over to the Celerity charter chain (Parent Revolution chose the charter operator). The petition was presented to the local school board in December 2010. The school board questioned the legitimacy of the signatures, each side accused the other of intimidation, and the battle ended up in court. Celerity opened a charter school nearby, but only about one-third of the 61 percent who signed the petition, sent their children there. The *Los Angeles Times* noted that the results of the "parent trigger" legislation were modest: "A dozen or so parent groups have formed throughout the state to consider reforms, and only a couple of those are interested in abandoning their traditional public schools for charters. Some merely want a new principal; others seek to make it easier to get rid of teachers who consistently let their students down. Some yearn for basic, common-sense services such as regular communication from teachers."[3]

The next candidate for the parent trigger was Desert Trails Elementary School in the Adelanto School District, about eighty miles from Los Angeles. Parent Revolution worked with dissatisfied parents, and in January 2012 parent leaders presented a petition with the signatures of nearly 70 percent of the parents. The Parent Revolution community organizers had circulated two petitions, one demanding changes in the school, the other calling for a charter school takeover. But only the latter petition was presented to the school board. Some parents sought to withdraw their names from the petition, and the school board invalidated their signatures, dropping support to 37 percent. The matter went to court, and a county judge ruled that parents were not allowed to rescind their names once they signed the petition. Victorious, the parent leaders—with Parent Revolution's help—invited charter operators to apply to run the school. When it came time to choose between two charters that stepped forward, parents who did not sign the original petition were not allowed to vote. Only fifty-three parents in a school with more than six hundred students chose the new charter operator. Ironically, only a year earlier, the district had closed down a charter school in Adelanto, because the charter operator had formed a for-profit company to sell goods and services to the school, apparently at inflated prices.[4]

Although Parent Revolution described itself as a progressive organization, its ideas found immediate resonance on the right end of the political spectrum. Inspired by the California law, two deeply conservative states—Mississippi and Texas—promptly passed similar laws. Another deeply conservative state, Louisiana, passed a parent trigger law in 2012, and others soon followed.

The conservative Heartland Institute, a free-market think tank in Chicago, wrote its own version of the parent trigger law, which would allow parents in the bottom 20 percent of schools (that is, the schools where the proportion of students who pass state tests is lowest) to take control and included the option that they could demand a voucher for private and religious schools. Heartland took its ideas to ALEC, the secretive national group of corporations and state legislators who favor free-market ideology. ALEC was so impressed by the parent trigger concept that it created its own model legislation and sent it out to states across the nation. Legislators in nearly twenty states introduced parent trigger laws. Gloria Romero, the state senator who championed the parent trigger legislation in California, ran for state superintendent and came in third; after her defeat, she went to work for Democrats for Education Reform, the organization created by Wall Street hedge fund managers to promote charters and other corporate-style reforms. DFER embraced the parent trigger idea, which enlisted parents as the agents of charter school expansion.[5]

Not all parents warmed to the idea of a parent trigger. Parents Across America (PAA) condemned the parent trigger and said that it "creates potential for abuse, turmoil, and massive divisiveness within school communities. It undermines the democratic process by privatizing public space and strips control from School Boards whom we've elected to represent us." PAA saw no value in pitting parents against teachers, parents against principals, and parents against parents. It warned that the underlying goal of the trigger was to hand public schools over to private charter operators and corporations.[6]

The next battleground for the parent trigger was Florida. There, the idea was strongly supported by the former governor Jeb Bush and the gadfly Michelle Rhee. The adoption of a parent trigger law seemed to be a foregone conclusion since the state was controlled by conservative Republicans, who paid close heed to Jeb Bush's advice. But when the legislature took up the issue in 2012 and again in 2013, something surprising happened. Parent groups from across the state opposed it. Here was a seeming paradox. The act was called the Parent Empowerment Act (as it was in California), yet no Florida parent organizations endorsed it. On the contrary, they descended on Tallahassee and told their legislators they didn't want it. Such groups as the Florida PTA, Save Duval Schools, 50th No More, Fund Education Now, and Testing Is Not Teaching objected to the bill. Parent leaders saw the parent trigger as an "underhanded ploy" by well-funded groups to hand public schools over to private charter operators. Parent Revolution flew parents in from California to testify on behalf of the legislation. Five Republican senators joined Democrats to oppose the bill. When the senators deadlocked 20–20 on the bill, it died. Only the week before, they had joined forces to defeat a proposal to privatize state prisons. They were, according to *The Miami Herald,* "a band of renegade senators" who "argued that public education, like public safety, is a core mission of government that shouldn't be outsourced to private vendors."[7]

The *Orlando Sentinel,* which supports charter schools, was glad to see the parent trigger bill die: "Touted as a way to give parents at failing schools a stronger voice in picking turnaround plans, this bad bill would have cued the stampede of for-profit charter school companies looking to sweet talk frustrated parents and turn a fast buck." The newspaper noted that the legislature was busily creating double standards for charter schools and public schools. Another bill promised $55 million for charter school construction but nothing for public schools. And the "accountability-preaching lawmakers" wanted to exempt charters from the tough teacher evaluation measures they imposed on public schools in 2011. The editorial insightfully recognized that the legislature was creating an "uneven playing field," showing favoritism toward charter schools and setting up public schools to fail. The point of the uneven playing field, the editorial noted, was to open the door "for charter schools—which play by different rules—to play savior."[8]

Undeterred, the conservative mayors Kevin Johnson of Sacramento (Michelle Rhee's husband) and Cory Booker of Newark (a member of the board of the hedge fund managers' DFER) brought the parent trigger idea to the U.S. Conference of Mayors in June 2012. The conference passed the proposal unanimously as part of a long laundry list of resolutions covering various issues connected to economic development, the arts, transportation, infrastructure needs, tourism, energy, consumer affairs, crime, federal relations, and others. Like all reform proposals, the parent trigger idea was couched in uplifting rhetoric about improving the prospects of minority students trapped in "dropout factories" and giving their parents the power "to ensure that no child is trapped in a failing school."[9]

It was impossible to know whether the mayors gave a moment's thought to what they were endorsing. Another prime sponsor, Mayor Antonio Villaraigosa of Los Angeles, whose constituents already had access to the parent trigger, told a reporter from Reuters, "Mayors understand at a local level that most parents lack the tools they need to turn their schools around." According to the news report, "Hundreds of mayors from across the United States this weekend called for new laws letting parents seize control of low-performing public schools and fire the teachers, oust the administrators or turn the schools over to private management."[10]

Did the mayors really want parents to "seize control" of the lowest-performing schools in their cities? Did they really think through whether this made any sense? Were they truly convinced that the best way to improve schools was through a process of parent takeovers? Did they believe that parents in the nation's poorest communities were best suited to fire the staffs and run the schools themselves? And did they really approve of the idea that parents should take charge of public property and hand it over to a private operator of their choosing?

Would they feel equally enthusiastic about encouraging the tenants in public housing projects to seize control and privatize their buildings? How would they react if riders on a public bus decided to seize control and give the bus to a private company? What about the patrons who use a public park and are organized by a private park-concession corporation to demand control so they can turn it over to the concessionaire? Or the patrons of a public library? Would the mayors support them too?

A public school belongs to the public whose taxes built it and maintain it. It does not belong to the parents whose children are enrolled this year. Parents whose children are enrolled this year should not be given ownership of a school that belongs to the entire community and to future students and parents. Those who sign a petition this year may not even be parents in the school next year. Giving them the power to privatize public property is irresponsible. If the students in a public school have low test scores, it is the responsibility of those in charge of the district to evaluate the school and bring whatever changes are necessary to improve student performance. The district leadership is responsible for guaranteeing that every school has the resources and personnel it needs to provide a sound education.

The theory of parent empowerment makes no sense. If the cure rate in a hospital were low, one would not expect the patients to seize control and fire the staff. The very idea of the parent trigger is an insult to the education profession and a pretense that turning the schools over to parents will solve problems that are not only educational but social and economic as well. There is a sort of Occupy Wall Street tone to the parent trigger idea, but we know how the mayors responded to the protesters who filled public parks in the summer of 2011. Occupy Wall Street was a ragtag group of demonstrators who demanded the kinds of redistributive policies that the parent trigger pretends to offer. The mayors closed down their tent cities with as much force as they thought necessary. Yet less than a year later, the mayors encouraged parents to "occupy" the public schools, an action likely to result in a transfer of public property to private charter chains.

The *Los Angeles Times* opined that the parent trigger idea was a disappointment. More than two years after it passed, it noted, there had not exactly been a race by parents to take control of their schools. The editorial noted that Parent Revolution had been started and funded by charter school supporters, but now even they had doubts about taking over low-performing schools. Charter schools, it said, prefer to start a new school with a lottery that attracts motivated parents. "But under the parent trigger, charter schools have to accept all students within the low-performing school's attendance boundaries, just as regular public schools do. Few charter operators have been willing to work under that scenario, which tends to result in less dramatic test results for them. Furthermore, the current woeful state of school funding makes it difficult if not impossible for charter schools to provide needed resources—just as it's difficult for traditional public schools. And turning around a deeply troubled school is harder than starting a new school with its own campus culture." The newspaper concluded that other states should "look for evidence that it is making schools better" before enacting a similar law.[11]

In their eagerness to build public support for the parent trigger, corporate reformers trumpeted the release of a Hollywood movie dramatizing the idea called *Won't Back Down*, with big-name stars and a national opening in twenty-five hundred theaters. Michelle Rhee held screenings of the film at both the Democratic and the Republican National Conventions in 2012. It was featured on NBC's annual "Education Nation" broadcast. Its stars appeared on national television programs. In the background was its producer, Walden Media, which was also a producer of the documentary *Waiting for "Superman."* The owner of Walden Media is Philip Anschutz, a billionaire libertarian who funds conservative think tanks and conservative causes, such as the anti-gay Proposition 8 in California, hydrofracking, and the Discovery Institute, which promotes "intelligent design."[12] He also owns the nation's largest chain of theaters.

But none of the publicity was enough to sell the movie. It received bad reviews, and ticket sales were abysmal. Within a month of its opening in September 2012, it had almost completely disappeared from the nation's theaters. The public was not interested in paying to see another movie bashing public schools, teachers, and unions.

Somehow the public got it, even if the politicians did not. There is no evidence that schools will improve if parents seize control, fire the staff, and turn the school over to privately managed charter corporations. It seems odd to legislate a remedy that not only has no evidence behind it but that has never actually been put into practice anywhere before the legislation was passed. Florida parents were justified in concluding that the parent trigger was a ruse intended to trick parents into privatizing their schools and losing any say in how they are run.

As Parents Across America warned, the parent trigger mirrors the federal government's punitive approach of firing staff and closing a school or privatizing it. PAA thought that parents should have positive choices about improving their school. It advised that parents should be involved in developing school improvement strategies in conjunction with professional educators. It urged the implementation of research-based approaches to improvement, tailored to the needs of the students, the school, and the community.[13]

Seen within the context of the larger corporate reform movement, the parent trigger was initially advanced by charter supporters and then quickly embraced by the most conservative legislators and states. Whatever its original intention, the parent trigger became a tool to advance privatization and promote the interests not of parents but of charter organizations.

CHAPTER 19

The Failure of Vouchers

CLAIM *Students who receive vouchers for private and religious schools will experience dramatic success.*

REALITY *There is no evidence for this claim.*

The idea of vouchers has been on the fringes of education debates since 1955. That was when the University of Chicago economist Milton Friedman proposed vouchers as a way to end the squabbling over Catholic schools. Catholics had long complained that they paid taxes for schools but were barred from receiving any public funding. Friedman maintained that if every family got a voucher, then every family could send their children to the school of their choice, whether it was public, private, or religious. That was a solution, he thought, that would satisfy everyone. His essay appeared as the country was reacting to the Supreme Court's *Brown v. Board of Education* decision of 1954, which overturned laws permitting racially segregated schools. States that wanted to preserve racial segregation immediately turned to school choice as their first line of defense, and for many years school choice was widely understood by the courts and the public as a strategy to preserve school segregation.[1]

Those events occurred long ago, and the nation seems now to have accepted that a high degree of actual segregation is tolerable so long as it is not mandated explicitly by law. When big-city districts have schools with few, if any, white students, it is not newsworthy. When school districts open schools intended only for black students, it is not newsworthy. When charter schools appeal to one racial or ethnic or cultural group, it is not newsworthy. Long forgotten is the Supreme Court's 1954 finding that "in the field of public education, the doctrine of 'separate but equal' has no place. Separate educational facilities are inherently unequal." Because students and families are not compelled by law to attend racially separate schools, the new form of segregation is now ignored, accepted, and treated as unremarkable.

Also forgotten is that public schools were created by communities and states for a civic purpose. In the nineteenth century, they were often called "common schools." They were a project of the public commons, the community. They were created to build and sustain democracy, to teach young people how to live and work together with others, and to teach the skills and knowledge needed to participate fully in society. Inherent in the idea of public education was a clear understanding that educating the younger generation was a public responsibility, shared by all, whether or not they had children in the public schools, whether or not they even had children.

For many years, the voucher idea didn't go far, because most Americans were unwilling to see their tax dollars fund religious or private schools. Whenever a voucher proposal was put to a vote, it was rejected by the public at the polls. However, the advocates for vouchers never gave up the hope of prevailing. In 1990, John Chubb and Terry Moe described school choice as "a panacea" that "has the capacity *all by itself* to bring about the kind of transformation that, for years, reformers have been seeking to engineer in myriad other ways." The federal courts had once been vigilant in opposition to school choice, which might be used to evade school desegregation. However, as the Supreme Court became more conservative, it abandoned its close scrutiny of school segregation and its demand for racial integration. Additionally, the idea of choice lost whatever negative connotation it had as many urban districts created magnet schools to hold or attract white families.[2]

In 1990, Milwaukee launched a voucher program for low-income students. In 1995, Cleveland was permitted to offer vouchers, also for low-income students. In 2003, Republicans in Congress created a voucher program for low-income students in the District of Columbia. All of these voucher programs were initiated by legislators, not by voters. Conservative think tanks, like the Center for Education Reform, the Heritage Foundation, the Friedman Foundation, the Heartland Institute, and others at the state level, kept up a steady drumbeat of advocacy for vouchers as the answer to the problems of low-achieving, low-income students. They hoped that once the public accepted vouchers for low-income students, eventually middle-income parents would demand vouchers for their children too. Over time, they expected, the voucher idea would take on a momentum of its own, and the public school system would wither away as all students got vouchers to attend the schools of their choice. In this competitive environment, schools would get better and better, and scores would go higher and higher, and the problems that now beset the schools would be resolved by the simple mechanism of choice and a free market.

Before any city or state offered vouchers with public money, it was easy to speculate on what they might achieve and to predict amazing transformation for the children lucky enough to get them. But over time, the results of the nation's three publicly funded voucher programs became clear. They didn't make any difference in terms of test scores. Competition between voucher schools, charter schools, and public schools did not cause the public schools to get better. Instead, the competing programs drained the public schools of both students and funding and weakened them.

The Milwaukee voucher program started in 1990. In 1998, the courts allowed religious schools to accept voucher students, and the voucher program expanded. For years, the program was closely studied to determine whether voucher students made greater gains than their peers who remained in the public schools. On average, they did not. On Wisconsin state tests, students in Milwaukee's voucher schools performed no better—and sometimes worse—than students in the district's public schools.[3]

Nor did the competition with voucher schools and charter schools bring about improvement in the Milwaukee public schools. In 2009, Milwaukee public schools participated in the National Assessment of Educational Progress for the first time. In reading and mathematics, Milwaukee was found to be one of the lowest-performing cities in the nation. Black students, who were supposed to be the beneficiaries of the city's school voucher program, scored among the lowest-performing students in the nation in both fourth and eighth grades, in English and mathematics. The same poor performance was recorded by Milwaukee again in 2011 on the NAEP test. Twenty-two years after the start of the voucher program, black students in the Milwaukee public schools were performing poorly, and their peers in the Milwaukee voucher schools and charter schools were doing no better.[4]

A comprehensive evaluation of the Milwaukee voucher program by researchers at the University of Arkansas concluded that students in the program showed gains in reading but not in mathematics. More consequentially, the evaluation showed, students in the voucher program were 4 percent likelier to graduate from high school and 7 percent more likely to enroll in a four-year college than their peers in the public schools. However, an independent reviewer questioned the evaluator's claims about higher graduation rates, noting that "roughly 75 percent of the original sample of 801 MPCP [Milwaukee Parental Choice Program] 9th graders were not still enrolled in a MPCP high school in 12th grade. The inferences drawn about the effects of the MPCP on graduation rates compared with those in the MPS are severely clouded by substantial sample attrition." The evaluators at the University of Arkansas later changed the attrition rate from 75 percent to 56 percent. Even at 56 percent, this very high rate of attrition very likely left the most motivated students in the voucher schools and certainly raised questions about whether the voucher program had any effect on the graduation rate or the college enrollment rate.[5]

After twenty-two years of vouchers, there was no evidence that vouchers were a panacea, nor that they were saving poor children who had been in public schools. On average, the voucher schools were not outperforming the public schools; some of them were simply bad schools, not only producing low levels of achievement but absorbing large amounts of taxpayer dollars without any accountability. Veteran Milwaukee journalist Alan J. Borsuk described voucher schools in which less than 5 percent of the students were proficient and staff turnover was high, but the schools had collected $40–50 million in the past decade through the voucher program.[6]

Despite the poor results of the voucher program in Milwaukee, the enthusiasm of voucher advocates was undiminished, and if anything, grew stronger. In 2011, Wisconsin governor Scott Walker expanded the voucher program to Racine and lifted the income eligibility requirement in Milwaukee, extending vouchers to more students in a larger geographic area. Vouchers were a priority for ALEC, the far-right organization of state legislators, including many from Wisconsin.[7] Vouchers were also a priority for the American Federation for Children, an organization founded by a wealthy Michigan activist, Betsy DeVos, to advance school choice, which honored Governor Walker in 2011 for his advocacy for vouchers.

The voucher program in Cleveland began in 1995. The results there were no different from those in Milwaukee. The students in the voucher schools did not perform better than those in the public schools. The students in public schools typically did better on state tests than those in the voucher schools. Competition with voucher schools and charter schools did not improve the Cleveland public schools. Cleveland's schools, populated almost entirely by low-income students, performed very poorly on national tests, and Cleveland was one of the lowest-scoring districts in the nation, along with Detroit, Milwaukee, and the District of Columbia. From 2003 to 2011, when the federal tests were offered, students in the Cleveland public schools not only had low scores but showed no improvement for any group: not for black students, white students, Hispanic students, or low-income students. And students in voucher schools performed below those in public schools on state tests. Despite the absence of evidence for the success of the Cleveland voucher program, the state of Ohio expanded vouchers statewide to students in low-rated schools and to students with autism (the legislature decided to make this kind of voucher available to all students with disabilities in 2012–13). By 2011, the state was spending $103 million on vouchers. With choice advocates in control of the legislature, the voucher program was certain to grow, regardless of evidence about its effects.[8]

In the District of Columbia, a Republican-controlled Congress passed a voucher program in early 2004. It was called the D.C. Opportunity Scholarship Program (OSP). Knowing the American public's distaste for vouchers, Republicans referred to vouchers as "opportunity scholarships." The final, congressionally mandated evaluation of the program concluded, "***There is no conclusive evidence that the OSP affected student achievement.*** [Italics and boldface in the original.] On average, after at least four years students who were offered (or used) scholarships had reading and math test scores that were statistically similar to those who were not offered scholarships. The same pattern of results holds for students who applied from schools in need of improvement (SINI), the group Congress designated as the highest priority for the Program." The evaluation determined that students who participated in the program were likelier to graduate from high school, based on parental reports (82 percent who received vouchers versus 70 percent who did not).[9] Based on this self-reported evidence of improvement, Congress extended the life of the voucher program.

Florida established two voucher programs, one for students in F-rated schools, the other for students with disabilities. The vouchers for students in low-rated schools were called "opportunity scholarships," as in the federal program. Since the American public had repeatedly voted down voucher programs, "opportunity scholarships" was the euphemism preferred by voucher advocates. In 2006, the Florida Supreme Court held the "opportunity scholarship program" unconstitutional. The chief justice of the court said in the opinion that the program "diverts public dollars into separate, private systems . . . parallel to and in competition with the free public schools." Only 720 students were enrolled in the voucher program that was struck down by the court. At the time, the far larger program in Florida, known as McKay Scholarships, enrolled 14,000 students with disabilities. In 2012, there were 24,000 students using a McKay Scholarship to attend a private school.[10]

But the McKay Scholarship program was riddled with problems, due to the state's lack of oversight. Gus Garcia-Roberts of the *Miami New Times* conducted an investigation in 2011 and found that many students were attending substandard schools. The state failed to regulate key aspects of these schools, such as the curriculum, creating what the newspaper called "a cottage industry of fraud and chaos." Schools could qualify to accept voucher students even though the schools had no accreditation and no curriculum. Some administrators, the investigation reported, had criminal records. In one school, the students watched old videos and summarized the plot; the head of the school administered corporal punishment—banned by local law—as he saw fit. The state overlooked practices that would be unacceptable in a public school. No one cared "if students are discovered to be spending their days filling out workbooks, watching B-movies, or frolicking in the park. In one 'business management' class, students shook cans for coins on street corners." Nor was there a systematic effort to pursue fraud and padded enrollments. As the reporter put it, "It's like a perverse science experiment, using disabled school kids as lab rats and funded by nine figures in taxpayer cash: Dole out millions to anybody calling himself an educator. Don't regulate curriculum or even visit campuses to see where the money is going." And he added, "For optimal results, do this in Florida, America's fraud capital." Regular public schools were all too willing to dump their special education students, who might pull down their all-important school grades. The Republican legislature, unconcerned by the problems related to the vouchers, voted to expand the program so that students who were allergic to peanuts or bee stings would qualify.[11]

For his exposé of the underside of the McKay Scholarship program, Gus Garcia-Roberts was honored by the Society of Professional Journalists, which selected him as first-place winner of the Sigma Delta Chi Award for public service journalism at a non-daily newspaper.[12]

After Republicans captured statehouses and legislatures in the 2010 election cycle, the voucher movement picked up steam. Governor Mitch Daniels passed voucher legislation in Indiana, and Governor John Kasich increased the number of vouchers available in Ohio.

Governor Bobby Jindal of Louisiana pushed through the most audacious voucher program in the nation. In the spring of 2012, with Republicans in control of both houses of the legislature, Louisiana passed an education reform act that authorized vouchers for every student in a school graded C, D, or F by the state. That covered over 400,000, more than half the students in the state. These vouchers could be used in any sort of educational institution, whether public, private, religious, online, or operated by a business for profit. About 10,000 students requested vouchers, and about 120 schools offered seats. Most of the schools willing to accept vouchers were religious, and 19 were known to teach creationism, not evolution, and to use textbooks that taught science, history, and other subjects from a biblical point of view. Some of the schools lacked facilities or teachers to accept additional students but promised to expand in time for the opening of school. Unlike the public schools, the Louisiana voucher schools would be allowed to hire uncertified teachers.[13] In May 2013, the state's highest court struck down the funding of vouchers from public school monies as unconstitutional.

Why were so many Republican governors intent on implementing voucher programs, in light of the meager results from Milwaukee, Cleveland, and the District of Columbia?

Conservatives with a fervent belief in free-market solutions cling tenaciously to vouchers. They believe in choice as a matter of principle. The results of vouchers don't matter to them. They cling to any tidbit of data to argue on behalf of vouchers. If there is evidence of parental satisfaction, that's good enough for them. But even if there were no evidence of success, they would still promote vouchers. They want to create a free market in schooling, with multiple providers and competition. The true reward of vouchers is that they will end government control, supervision, and regulation of schooling. They let parents decide where their children should enroll in school, without regard to the quality of the school. Those schools that enroll the most students will thrive; those that do not attract enough students will not survive. Let the market decide.

If the market were always right, the best products would always be the most successful, but that is not necessarily the case. If the market were always right, only the highest-quality books, movies, and television programs would top the charts, but that is not necessarily the case.

Would the free market produce better education? Should the state subsidize schools where teachers are not certified and meet no particular standard of professionalism? Should taxpayers fund religious schools whose beliefs do not accord with modern science or history?

Are vouchers the wave of the future? The public has not embraced the idea. Republicans still insist on calling them "opportunity scholarships," taking pains to avoid the word "voucher." No state has ever passed an initiative or referendum supporting vouchers. To date, as judged by state referenda, most Americans place a high value on keeping public education public. Vouchers represent a major step toward privatization. There is no evidence that the American public is prepared to continue down this path as its ultimate destination become clear.

CHAPTER 20

Schools Don't Improve
if They Are Closed

CLAIM *Schools can be dramatically improved by firing the principal, firing half or all of the teachers, or closing the school and starting fresh.*

REALITY *There is no evidence for this claim.*

School reform in the early twenty-first century followed a pattern. First came high-stakes testing. Test students every year, and grade everyone involved. Grade the students; grade the teachers; grade the schools.

Then came accountability. Use the test scores and grades to hand out rewards and punishments. Give bonuses to those who got higher test scores every year. Punish those who were unable to improve test scores year after year: fire the principal, fire some or all of the teachers, close the school.

Then came reform: hire new staff, turn the school into a charter, or give it to private management.

President George W. Bush's No Child Left Behind law created the template for testing, accountability, and punishment. President Barack Obama's Race to the Top program accepted the template and added to it the concept of "turning around" five thousand of the nation's lowest-performing schools. The Obama administration awarded $5 billion to states and districts that agreed to "turn around" their lowest-performing schools. There were four models offered: turnaround, closure, restart, and transformation. All began with firing the principal. The school could be closed down altogether. Half the staff might be fired, or the entire staff might be fired. The basic approach was to shake up the school, disrupt its culture, and launch a new beginning, with new faces, new leadership, and perhaps even private management.

The disruption was expected to produce innovation. More typically, it produced turmoil and demoralization.

Two major surveys released in the spring of 2012 reported growing levels of demoralization among American teachers. The annual MetLife Survey of the American Teacher said that nearly one-third of teachers were thinking about quitting. The Scholastic-Gates survey did not report numbers that high, but found that teachers did not like the direction of school reform. They did not trust standardized testing. They did not want merit pay or rewards for test scores. They did not want a longer day or a longer year; many were already working eleven-hour days. What did they want? They wanted families to be more involved; they wanted higher expectations; they wanted smaller classes; they wanted better leadership in their schools. The MetLife survey of teachers and principals in 2013 found that both groups were feeling stressed and demoralized. Most principals reported that their jobs had become more difficult in the past five years, and a third said they were likely to leave their job or change occupations.[1]

It is not surprising that morale was low and educators were feeling disheartened. Federal policy constantly bombarded them with the message that they were failing, as did the corporate reformers' media campaign with its negative and demonstrably false claims. With NCLB's unrealistic requirement that all students be proficient by 2014, the number of "failing" schools escalated every year in every district and state. The requirement was guaranteed to produce failure and demoralization. Thousands of schools could not meet the impossible goal. Many failed year after year. Most of the lowest-performing schools enrolled large numbers of African American and Hispanic students and had high levels of students who qualified for free or reduced-price lunch, which is the federal measure of poverty.

The turnaround idea had its origins in Chicago when Arne Duncan was superintendent of schools. In June 2004, Duncan and Mayor Richard M. Daley announced an initiative called Renaissance 2010, which involved the eventual closure of some sixty neighborhood schools and their replacement by a hundred new schools. The Gates Foundation and the city's business leadership enthusiastically supported the program. In 2009, Duncan left Chicago to become Obama's secretary of education, but by then the pattern had been set: reform would proceed by closing low-performing schools and opening new schools that would presumably be better. This turned out to be the model that Duncan applied to the nation with billions of federal dollars to encourage states and districts to participate.

Did the turnaround approach work in Chicago?

Two reports reached diametrically different conclusions in 2012, two years beyond the target date of Renaissance 2010.

One report was prepared by two respected and independent research groups: the Consortium on Chicago School Research and the American Institutes for Research (AIR). Their report found significant improvement in low-performing elementary schools that had been subject to turnaround treatment. After four years, it said, these schools had narrowed the gap with the school system average by "almost half in reading and two-thirds in math." High schools subject to turnaround, however, "did not show significant improvements in absences or ninth grade on-track-to-graduate rates over matched comparison schools."[2]

The second report, released at the same time, asserted that "Chicago's democratically-led elementary schools far out-perform Chicago's 'turnaround schools.'" The report was prepared by Designs for Change (DFC), a Chicago-based research organization. The DFC report said that thirty-three high-poverty public schools had significantly outperformed the twelve "turnaround" elementary schools.[3]

The democratically led schools are run by an elected local school council (LSC). This council is equivalent to a school board. It consists of six parents, two teachers, the principal, one nonteaching staff member, and two community members. The LSC selects the principal, evaluates the principal, approves the budget, monitors the school's improvement plan, and builds community partnerships. Unlike the "parent trigger," which sets parent against parent, and parents against teachers, and uses parents to privatize the school, the LSC works within a democratic framework and promotes the principle of collaboration among the school's constituents. It is no panacea to the problems of urban education, but it is certainly valuable to involve parents and enable them to participate in decision making about their children's schooling.

The DFC report made a strong case. At the time, Chicago had 210 neighborhood elementary schools in which at least 95 percent of students were low income. Thirty-three of these high-poverty schools "were above the citywide average for all 480 CPS [Chicago public schools] elementary schools in reading." Fourteen of these 33 high-scoring schools were more than 90 percent African American; 16 of the 33 were more than 85 percent Latino. All 33 of the high-performing schools were led by elected LSCs that were empowered to choose their principals.

But not one of the turnaround schools ranked above the citywide average in reading.

(I hesitate to say whether the Illinois state standards in reading and mathematics are good gauges of school quality, but they are used by the state and the federal government to close schools. As long as the reformers insist that these are the right benchmarks for closing public schools, then the schools they open must be judged by the same measures.)

Unlike the turnaround schools, the thirty-three democratically led schools never received substantial outside funding and "almost never receive public recognition."

DFC presented brief portraits of these unsung, high-performing, high-poverty schools:

Dunne Technology Academy (352 students, 98% low-income, 99% African American). 77% Meet or Exceed ISAT Standards in Reading, 91% Meet or Exceed ISAT Standards in Math. Close collaboration exists among the LSC, principal, and teachers. Dunne focuses on teaching its students sophisticated **video and music production skills.** Dunne educates children in a **wretched school building,** which lacks many basic physical resources that most people regard as essential for a minimally-adequate school building. Dunne's roof leaks; they have no kitchen, lunchroom, or gym; and the walls are crumbling. Repeated attempts by the LSC and school community to obtain a new building have thus far failed . . .

Gallistel Language Academy (**1,444 students in three buildings,** 93% Latino, 96% low income). 70% of students Meet or Exceed ISAT Standards in Reading. 79% Meet or Exceed ISAT Standards in Math (83% following previous state policy about when English Language Learners had to begin taking the ISAT). Gallistel's LSC hired a new principal in spring 2000, who has unified the school. Gallistel is **intensively over-crowded. 400 to 600** Gallistel parents, teachers, and students have testified at school system facilities hearings each year over the past several years, asking for major repairs. The main building is **plagued** by electrical outages, leaks, and widely varying temperatures. Despite these obstacles, 75% of Gallistel teachers have remained at the school for **at least four years.** [Boldface in the original.]

By contrast, the turnaround elementary schools were not led by an LSC. Instead, they were "tightly controlled" by either an independent contractor (a turnaround company called the Academy for Urban School Leadership, or AUSL) or by a department of the school system called the Office of School Improvement. These organizations have "**near-total authority** to select staff, define the school's learning program and oversee other important aspects of students' learning experiences (such as discipline)" (boldface in the original). In contrast to the thirty-three democratically led schools, the turnaround schools get extra staff, extra resources, and renovated facilities, all part of an additional $7 million per school over a five-year period. The turnaround schools were lavishly praised by the media and regularly touted by Mayor Daley and his successor, Mayor Rahm Emanuel.

AUSL took over the first of the turnaround schools, Sherman School of Excellence, in 2006–7. AUSL promised that by year five, 80 percent of the students would meet or exceed state standards in reading, mathematics, and science. At the time, only 31 percent of its 584 students (98–99 percent of whom were low income and African American) met state standards in reading. At the end of five years, promised AUSL, the school would have a new culture and would be "permanently reset," and AUSL could step away from its role.

Sherman did improve, but it fell far short of AUSL's bold promise. After five years, 52 percent of the students met state standards in reading, not the 80 percent that was AUSL's goal. Sherman ranked well below the thirty-three democratically led schools that did not receive extra resources and a new staff. In reading, it was 171st of the 210 high-poverty schools in the city system, far below the democratically controlled, high-performing, high-poverty schools. AUSL returned to the board of education to get an extension of its contract and additional resources for a sixth year in which to exercise total control over the school, despite failing to meet its goals.

Teacher retention presented another contrast between the highly resourced turnaround schools and the unnoticed, high-performing, high-poverty schools. The turnaround schools had a brand-new, carefully selected staff, half of whom were specially trained by AUSL. Only 42 percent of teachers were still teaching in the original turnaround schools four years later, compared with 71 percent in the non-turnaround elementary schools. The DFC report attributed the superior staff retention rate at the non-turnaround schools to strong leadership, teamwork, and good parent-teacher relations.

Actually, both reports were correct. The turnaround schools made progress, and the democratically led schools—relying on collaboration but lacking the extra resources of the turnaround schools—were more successful than the turnaround schools.

It was not mere happenstance that the two dueling reports were released in February 2012. At the end of the month, the board of education was poised to decide whether to turn around and close more schools. The Consortium-AIR report said the turnarounds were successful, at least in the elementary schools; the DFC report said the turnarounds had not met their goals, were expensive, and had lower test scores and higher teacher turnover compared with the democratically led schools.

On February 22, 2012, the Chicago Board of Education faced a raucous and angry crowd of parents, teachers, and community members who opposed the threat to close their local schools. The board ignored the protests and approved the closure or overhaul of an additional seventeen schools. It awarded six schools to AUSL and four schools to the board's own Office of School Improvement to manage and announced the closure or phaseout of seven other schools. The decision was not surprising. The board was appointed by Mayor Rahm Emanuel and carried out his wishes. As a teacher from one of the affected schools remarked, "The outcomes were already decided beforehand." Regardless of the evidence supplied by the DFC report, regardless of the protests of parents and teachers, the Board never considered anything other than more closures and turnarounds. That was the definition of reform in Chicago.[4]

A year later, Mayor Emanuel and his board announced their intention to close fifty-four public schools, including schools that Arne Duncan closed and "turned around" in 2002. They said the schools were underutilized; they said it was for the good of the students. But no one doubted that they would keep opening privately managed charter schools as they closed public schools.

As in so many debates about education issues, there were dueling interpretations and dueling facts. My own view, as should be clear by now, is that public schools are rooted in their communities. They exist to serve the children of the communities. If they are doing a poor job, the leadership of the school system must do whatever is necessary to improve the schools—supply more staff, more specialists, more resources—not close them and replace them with new schools and new names. Accountability must begin at the top, with the leadership of the school system. It is the leadership that has the power to allocate resources and personnel to needy schools, and it is their responsibility to do so. I also believe that when a public school has the strong support of parents and the local community, the citywide school board should not disregard their views; it should work with them to support their local public school and make it better.

A careful study in California described how difficult it is to achieve a lasting "turnaround" of a low-performing school. The researchers started with a clear definition: a true turnaround school was one that ranked in the bottom third of the state for three consecutive years; it showed a specified level of growth over three years for all subgroups; it sustained its improvement into a fourth year; it improved relative to other schools in the state; and its student population remained demographically similar over time. The researchers identified 2,407 schools in the bottom third of the state rankings. Only 44 schools, or 2 percent, met all their criteria. Few of these schools made "dramatic" progress; typically, it was "slow and steady." The successful schools described the elements that contributed to their improvement: instructional strategies focused on subgroups (such as English-language learners or students with disabilities) that need extra help; professional development; teacher collaboration; instructional leadership; wise use of data; district support; and parent involvement.[5]

The California study showed that deep change is never accomplished in a year or two. It requires patience, persistence, good leadership, and collaboration, not mass firings.

But the Obama administration was unfazed and remained committed to its belief that the best way to turn around a school was to fire the principal and half or more of the staff.

In 2012, a few weeks after the Chicago school board's decision to close more schools, the Education Writers Association discussed the federal turnaround policy. The Department of Education insisted that great progress was being made, but others saw the results as disappointing. Anthony Cody, who attended the meeting, listened to speakers who thought that the federal government was too lenient and that harsher steps must be taken to "break the culture" of low-performing schools. They said that more teachers must be fired to make even greater progress.

Cody disagreed. Anthony Cody taught middle school science for nearly twenty years in the public schools of Oakland, California. He is a National Board Certified Teacher who blogs regularly for *Education Week,* the leading K–12 journal. In 2011, he helped organize a national march on Washington to protest punitive federal policies associated with high-stakes testing. As an experienced teacher in a high-poverty school district, Cody was skeptical of the quick fixes that are popular with reformers and policy makers.

Cody read the dueling papers describing the turnaround efforts in Chicago. He was aware of new research showing that teacher turnover, or churn, had a bad effect on schools, a phenomenon that he had observed in his own school. When he challenged the currently popular "fire and replace" strategy of turnaround, a speaker said to him, "That depends on whether you think old dogs can learn new tricks."[6]

In his own presentation at the conference, Cody told the story of what happened to his school. He was chair of the science department, and the principal asked him what the department's biggest problem was. He said it was teacher turnover. His department of ten lost two or three teachers every year, which made improvement hard to sustain. Veteran teachers wondered why they should spend time training the new teachers, when they were likely to move on. This attitude undermined collaboration and made it even harder to reduce teacher turnover. It was even worse in some other Oakland schools, where 50–60 percent of teachers left every year, discouraged by the low salaries (compared with affluent districts) and the problems of a high-poverty school.

Cody's department obtained a grant to encourage teacher retention. Every new teacher was assigned a mentor, who shared lesson plans, strategies, and curriculum with the newcomer. The department met regularly to exchange ideas and resources. The following year, the department retained every one of its teachers. The approach worked so well that it was extended to the math department, and soon all the teachers were working together, not just to mentor new teachers but to deepen their teaching skills and assessment practices. The model worked so well that the district adopted it in a program called Team-Science, pairing novice science teachers with experienced mentors.

Cody writes, "We found that we did NOT need to fire anyone in order to improve. Instead of trying to ferret out the weakest links, we sought to RETAIN everyone. Can 'old dogs learn new tricks'? Yes. And old dogs KNOW a lot of valuable tricks," which they can build on and share, if they are honored for what they know.

But then comes the sad denouement. As all these developments were unfolding, the school made steady progress, but not big enough gains to satisfy the constantly rising demands of No Child Left Behind. The school did not meet the goals set by Congress, years ago and three thousand miles away: "It broke the school's spirit to be cast as failures year after year. Staff meetings were taken over by data experts telling us how to target the students most likely to yield statistical gains. Just as school culture can be purposefully built, it also can be destroyed, and it was. Only one science teacher remains there from the team we built."

The theory of turnarounds, Cody wrote, assumes there is "little of value" in schools with low test scores, so it is a simple matter to discard the administrators, the teachers, and the school culture and start over. He concluded that the U.S. Department of Education had made "a fundamental error" by pushing the turnaround strategy. Instead of firing teachers, he wrote, "we are likely to gain much more by creating schools capable of supporting, developing and retaining them." Certainly there will still be teachers who should be fired, but that is the job of an effective principal, not state or federal policy.

The federal government bet nearly $5 billion that the Chicago strategy of closing schools and replacing them with new schools would work if applied to the entire nation. Chicago had been closing schools and opening schools for more than a decade. Had it transformed the schools of Chicago? Not many would consider Chicago a national model of school reform. The only thing that is certain is that the turnaround strategy has demoralized teachers and principals and created a climate of fear in the present and uncertainty about the future.

Arne Duncan had initiated the strategy of closing low-performing schools in 2002. At that time, he closed three elementary schools, fired their staffs, and started over. Two years later, he and Mayor Richard M. Daley made this strategy the centerpiece of their reform plan, called Renaissance 2010. President-elect Barack Obama chose one of the three schools, Dodge Elementary (renamed Dodge Renaissance Academy), as the place to announce his selection of Arne Duncan as secretary of education in 2008. He said of Duncan, "He's shut down failing schools and replaced their staffs, even when it was unpopular . . . This school right here, Dodge Renaissance Academy, is a perfect example. Since this school was revamped and reopened in 2003, the number of students meeting state standards has tripled." But somehow the miraculous turnaround evaporated. By 2013, Chicago school officials closed Dodge Renaissance Academy again, along with the other two elementary schools that Duncan had closed and "revamped" in 2002.[7]

Surely there are better ways to improve the education of students who have low scores in reading and mathematics than by closing their schools. They may need smaller classes, intensive tutoring, highly skilled teachers. Closing a school is not a reform. It is an admission of failure by those in charge, an acknowledgment that they do not have the knowledge and experience to evaluate the needs of the school, help the students, strengthen the staff, and provide the essential ingredients needed for a good school.

CHAPTER 21

Solutions: Start Here

Reformers frequently say that poverty is just an excuse, that poverty is not destiny, and that a child's education should not be determined by his or her zip code.

Poverty is not an excuse. It is a harsh reality. No one wants poverty to be any child's destiny. Public schools exist to give all children equal educational opportunity, no matter what their zip code.

Schools fail when they lack the resources to provide equal educational opportunity. And they fail not because of lack of will but because poverty often overwhelms the best of intentions.

Poverty persists not because schools are bad and teachers don't care but because society neglects its root causes. Concentrated poverty and racial segregation are social problems, not school problems. Schools don't cause poverty and racial segregation, nor can schools solve these problems on their own. W. E. B. DuBois said during the depths of the Great Depression that "no school, as such, can organize industry, or settle the matter of wage and income, can found homes or furnish parents, can establish justice or make a civilized world."[1] DuBois was not "making excuses." He was placing the blame for poverty and inequality where it belongs: on the shoulders of those who control industry and government.

DuBois recognized that schools alone cannot create equality or eliminate poverty. They can help highly motivated students escape poverty. Many thousands of personal stories attest to the power of one teacher, one principal, one school, that saved a student from his or her parents' life of hardship. Educators and schools do have remarkable power to change lives.

As important and inspiring as those stories are, they are atypical.

There is no example in which an entire school district eliminated poverty by reforming its schools or by replacing public education with privately managed charters and vouchers. If the root causes of poverty are not addressed, society will remain unchanged. Some poor students will get the chance to go to college, but the vast majority who are impoverished will remain impoverished. The current reform approach is ineffective at eliminating poverty or improving education. It may offer an escape hatch for some poor children, as public schools always have, but it leaves intact the sources of inequality. The current reform approach does not alter the status quo of deep poverty and entrenched inequality. After more than a decade of No Child Left Behind, we now know that a program of testing and accountability leaves millions of children behind and does not eliminate poverty or close achievement gaps. The growing demand for more testing and more accountability in the wake of NCLB is akin to bringing a blowtorch to put out a fire. More of the same is not change. The testing, accountability, and choice strategies offer the illusion of change while changing nothing. They mask the inequity and injustice that are now so apparent in our social order. They do nothing to alter the status quo. They preserve the status quo. They *are* the status quo.

Will it be expensive to address the root causes of poor academic performance? Of course, but probably not as expensive as the cost of doing nothing.

We need broader and deeper thinking. We must decide if we truly want to eliminate poverty and establish equal educational opportunity. We must decide if we truly want to build a society with liberty and justice for all. If that is our true purpose, then we need to move on two fronts, changing society and improving schools at the same time.

Linda Darling-Hammond of Stanford University reminds us that we know full well how to improve schools:

> It's not as though we don't know what works. We could implement the policies that have reduced the achievement gap and transformed learning outcomes for students in high-achieving nations where government policies largely prevent childhood poverty by guaranteeing housing, healthcare and basic income security. These same strategies were substantially successful in our own nation through the programs and policies of the war on poverty and the Great Society, which dra-

matically reduced poverty, increased employment, rebuilt depressed communities, invested in preschool and K–12 education in cities and poor rural areas, desegregated schools, funded financial aid for college and invested in teacher training programs that ended teacher shortages. In the 1970s teaching in urban communities was made desirable by the higher-than-average salaries, large scholarships and forgivable loans that subsidized teacher preparation, and by the exciting curriculum and program innovations that federal funding supported in many city school districts.[2]

These policies were hugely successful from the 1960s into the 1980s. Darling-Hammond points out that "the black-white reading gap shrank by two-thirds for 17-year-olds, black high school and college graduation rates more than doubled, and, in 1975, rates of college attendance among whites, blacks and Latinos reached parity for the first and only time before or since."

Thus, those who throw up their hands and say that nothing works are wrong. Those who say that public schools are obsolete and broken are wrong. Those who say that we must abandon public education and replace it with free-market schooling and for-profit vendors are wrong. When the public schools have the appropriate policies, personnel, resources, and vision to achieve attainable goals, they respond with positive achievement.

If we know where we want to go, we can begin to discuss the strategies that will move us in the right direction.

We need solutions based on evidence, not slogans or reckless speculation.

CHAPTER 22

Begin at the Beginning

SOLUTION NO. 1 *Provide good prenatal care for every pregnant woman.*

Chapter 10 reviewed research documenting the importance of prenatal care. Babies born to women who did not get prenatal care early in their pregnancies or who got none at all are at risk of being born preterm. Prematurity is the leading cause of death among newborns. Those who survive are at heightened risk of having learning disabilities and other impediments to their full development. Ban Ki-moon, secretary-general of the United Nations, wrote that "newborn deaths—those in the first month of life—account for 40 per cent of all deaths among children under five years of age. Prematurity is the world's single biggest cause of newborn death, and the second leading cause of all child deaths, after pneumonia. Many of the preterm babies who survive face a lifetime of disability."[1]

A report published by the March of Dimes, the World Health Organization, the Partnership for Maternal, Newborn, and Child Health, and Save the Children gave a low grade to the United States for its failure to prevent premature births. Of 184 countries assessed, the United States ranked 131st. As *Time* magazine put it in describing the study, this is "a worrisome distinction the U.S. shares with Somalia, Turkey and Thailand." Twelve of every 100 live births in the United States are preterm, about 500,000 each year. Only a handful of countries in sub-Saharan Africa, Pakistan, and Southeast Asia rank below us. The best country in the world when measured by the rate of preterm births was Belarus, where fewer than 5 of every 100 children were born prematurely.[2]

The March of Dimes global report shows that the average rate for preterm births among developed nations is 8.3 percent. Astonishingly, the U.S. rate of 12 percent was approximately the same as that of nations in sub-Saharan Africa, which lack our vast resources.

Now, here is an interesting question: Why do reformers brandish international test scores, whose validity is uncertain, yet ignore the global report on preterm babies, in which the United States ranks shamefully low in comparison to other developed nations? The human, financial, and academic costs of preterm births are real. Number 131 out of 184 nations in the world: remember that dismal statistic the next time you see or hear a claim by a reformer that we are number 12 or 14 or whatever on international tests of mathematics or science. Why not a sustained national campaign to make the United States first in the world in ensuring that every woman receives the prenatal care she and her baby need?

Reducing preterm births would improve the life chances of half a million children in the United States every year. It would guarantee that more children arrive at school healthy and ready to learn. It would improve academic performance by preventing many cognitive and emotional disabilities. It is far less expensive to prevent learning disabilities at the beginning of pregnancy than to remediate those disabilities for many years into the future.

The March of Dimes report has specific recommendations. They include well-constructed programs to improve nutrition, family planning services, and health education and to reduce substance abuse, sexually transmitted diseases, and exposure to environmental pollution. Women need access to comprehensive prenatal care, as well as quality childbirth services and emergency obstetric care. The global report set a goal of a 50 percent reduction in the preterm birthrate for every country by 2025. In the United States, that means driving the rate down to 6 percent, which would bring us closer to the rate in other developed nations.

Frankly, it is shocking that the world's richest nation has such a high preterm birthrate. It is shocking as a matter of humanity, because so many young lives will be needlessly lost or damaged. It is shocking from a financial standpoint because of the long-term costs of preterm births to society.

This is an excellent place to begin a genuine program of social reform. The research is clear. The need for action is clear. The short-term and long-term benefits are clear. There is a widespread consensus on how to address and remedy the problem.

Children will be healthier. They will have fewer disabilities. There will be fewer referrals to special education in the future. The costs to society will be reduced, far more than the cost of the medical care provided at the right time.

Our society, our children, our families, our communities, and our schools will reap the rewards.

CHAPTER 23

The Early Years Count

SOLUTION NO. 2 *Make high-quality early childhood education available to all children.*

The achievement gaps among different groups of students begin before the first day of school. Gaps exist between African American and white students; between Hispanic and white students; and between advantaged and disadvantaged students, because they have been exposed to very different environments. Some children hear many words and have a large vocabulary; others do not. Some children have parents who are college educated; others do not. Some get regular visits to the doctor and the dentist; others do not. Some live in comfortable homes in safe neighborhoods; others do not.

These differences affect children's readiness to learn. They influence their vocabulary and background knowledge. Access to health care and nutrition affect their physical and mental development. Of course, all children can learn, but some have a head start because of their socioeconomic circumstances, while others start far behind.

By itself, early childhood education cannot completely close the gaps caused by inequality of wealth and inequality of opportunity, but researchers have concluded that it is more successful in narrowing the gap than most other interventions. Early childhood education programs have abundant research to support them, unlike the currently fashionable "reforms," which have very little or no research or experience to back them up.

One of the most prominent advocates of early childhood education is James Heckman, a Nobel Prize–winning economist at the University of Chicago. Heckman approaches the subject as an economist, in search of the most cost-effective way to heal economic and social dysfunction. In the past few decades, he says, the proportion of children born into disadvantaged environments has been increasing, putting them at risk of teen pregnancy, crime, poor health, and a lifetime of low earnings. He observed that the accident of birth powerfully affects one's life chances; this is bad not only for the individuals but for society, which loses their potential contributions. He assembled evidence to demonstrate that "the absence of supportive family environments harms child outcomes." The good news, however, is that "if society intervenes early enough, it can improve cognitive and socio-emotional abilities and the health of disadvantaged children." Early intervention not only enhances the life prospects of children but also has a high benefit-cost ratio and rate of return for society's investment. Heckman argues that early intervention is more cost-effective than later interventions that target older students and adults. Building a strong foundation for learning in the early years is crucial: "Skill begets skill; motivation begets motivation." He writes that "if a child is not motivated to learn and engage early on in life, the more likely it is that when the child becomes an adult, it will fail in social and economic life. The longer society waits to intervene in the life cycle of a disadvantaged child, the more costly it is to remediate disadvantage."[1]

Heckman believes that noncognitive skills are as important for success in life as cognitive skills. But federal education policy, represented by No Child Left Behind, prioritizes cognitive skills and ignores noncognitive skills like motivation, self-discipline, and the ability to work with others, even though these skills are highly valued in the workplace. The growing divide in American society, Heckman writes, is attributable in large part to the decline of the American family, the growing proportion of children raised in disadvantaged families, the dramatic rise in the proportion of single-parent families and never-married mothers, who are less likely to invest in their children as they are growing up. This phenomenon, he says, is "especially pronounced for African American families." Compared with poorly educated women, more educated women are less likely to have children out of wedlock and more likely to be married, have fewer children, and invest more time and resources in the upbringing of their children. The children who lack these circumstances start far behind. Heckman insists that poverty is not destiny and that society can effectively intervene to change the early environment in which children are raised. Heckman cites longitudinal studies like the Nurse-Family Partnership program, the Perry Preschool Project, and the Abecedarian Project to demonstrate that investment in early childhood education improves noncognitive skills, has significant, lasting effects, and thus represents the best return on society's investment. Heckman recommends that when center-based programs end, they should be followed up by home-visiting programs that encourage a permanent change in the child's home environment and improved parenting. Such interventions, he recognizes, must be sensitive to cultural differences.[2]

Heckman's work was influenced by major longitudinal studies of preschool education. The most important of these studies was the Perry Preschool Project. David Weikart, who had just earned a PhD at the University of Michigan, started the project in 1961 at Perry Elementary School in Ypsilanti, Michigan. At the time, many people assumed that IQ was fixed and that interventions made no difference. Weikart set out to prove they were wrong.[3]

The project enrolled fifty-eight poor African American children, beginning at age three. Most of the children attended for three hours a day for two years. The school developed its own active-learning curriculum that encouraged children to plan their own daily activities. Most of the Perry teachers had master's degrees in child development. There was one teacher for every six children. They received salaries similar to public school teachers. Teachers made weekly home visits, teaching parents how to turn everyday activities into learning experiences for their children.

The project tracked the progress of these fifty-eight students until they were adults, well into their forties. They were "less likely than students in the control group to skip school, be assigned to a special education class, or have to repeat a grade. By age nineteen, 66 percent of them had graduated from high school, as compared to 45 percent of those who hadn't gone to Perry." As adults, they earned more, paid more taxes, were less likely to be on welfare, and were less likely to have been incarcerated. They were more likely to own a home and a car. On average, those who had the benefit of the Perry Preschool Project were contributors to society. Of the control group, 52 percent spent some time in jail for various offenses, as compared with 28 percent of those who had been in the preschool program. From the perspective of economists, an investment in high-quality preschool education improved the lives of those who were in the program and paid handsome returns to society.[4]

It is important to note important aspects of the Perry Preschool Project that contributed to its stellar record:

One, the teachers were professionals, very well trained for their work.

Two, class sizes were small so that each child received the time and attention needed from the teacher.

Three, parent education was integral to the work of the project. Teachers paid weekly home visits to teach the parents to engage their children and support what they were learning each day.

Knowing what we know from research about the value of early childhood education, how do we compare to other nations in providing it to our population? *The Economist* magazine surveyed the condition of early childhood education in forty-five nations in terms of availability and quality. The Nordic countries led the pack: Finland, Sweden, and Norway were at the top, "thanks to sustained, long-term investments and prioritization of early childhood development, which is now deeply embedded in society. In general, Europe's state-led systems perform well, as the provision of universal preschool has steadily become a societal norm." The United States, the wealthiest nation in the world, ranked twenty-fourth, in a tie with the United Arab Emirates. Compared with the top European nations, where preschool was near universal, only 54 percent of U.S. children in the relevant age group attended preschool.[5]

Since we know as a matter of fact that the achievement gap begins in the earliest years, reformers should be demanding an expansion of early childhood education of high quality with well-prepared teachers. I want to stress the second part of the last sentence: *high quality with well-prepared teachers.* Few Head Start centers meet those requirements. Is it not a scandal that we rank twenty-fourth among the world's most advanced nations? Reform could make a difference here if we mean to reduce the achievement gaps and improve the lives of children.

The case for early childhood education is based on sound research, conducted over many years. The evidence is overwhelming. Early childhood education works. Early intervention can make a lasting difference in children's lives. It's expensive to do it right. It's even more expensive to do half measures or not to do it at all.

CHAPTER 24

The Essentials of a Good Education

SOLUTION NO. 3 *Every school should have a full, balanced, and rich curriculum, including the arts, science, history, literature, civics, geography, foreign languages, mathematics, and physical education.*

Since the advent of No Child Left Behind, many schools have cut back on every subject that was not tested. The federal law demanded that all students be proficient in mathematics and reading by 2014, and every state was required to test those subjects. Nothing counted other than mathematics and reading. Schools expanded the time available to teach these subjects, which determined whether they would be honored or humiliated, whether they would live or die. More time was allotted to take practice tests in mathematics and reading. Because there are only so many hours in a day, there was less time for subjects that were not tested. When the economic recession of 2008 began, many schools experienced budget cuts. The combination of budget cuts and high-stakes testing meant that something had to go. When cutbacks were necessary, it was in the nontested subjects. When teachers were laid off, they were usually those who did not teach the tested subjects.

Our policy makers today think that what matters most is getting high test scores in reading and mathematics. They don't show any regrets if a school spends inordinate amounts of time and money on test preparation materials. They will pin an A label on a school that gets high scores, even if its students spend all day every day practicing to take tests in mathematics and reading. But such a school is really not a good school, even if it gets high scores and the state awards it an A.

So we must look for other indicators, not just test scores, and not the official grade offered by the state or the district, which is unduly tied to test scores.

Let us consider two other ways of evaluating schools. One is to ask what the most demanding families seek in a school. The other is to consider the school in relation to the purposes of public education.

What do the most demanding families seek in a school? Whether they are parents in an affluent suburb or parents whose children attend an expensive private school, they expect their children to have much, much more than training in basic skills. They expect their children to study history and literature, science and mathematics, the arts and foreign languages. They would never tolerate a school that did not have dramatics, art, music, and science laboratories. They would insist that the school have up-to-date technology that their children could use every day. They would expect excellent athletic facilities and daily physical education. If their child is unusually bright, they would expect advanced courses to keep her curiosity and zest for learning alive. If their child has disabilities of any kind, they would expect the school to have appropriately trained personnel to offer the help and support the child needs. They would correctly anticipate small classes, projects, and frequent writing assignments. They would want a full range of student activities, including student government, a newspaper, clubs, after-school activities, and plays.

In affluent communities today, such schools are the norm in the public sector, not just the private sector. They were once the norm in ordinary American public schools. Today, however, the No Child Left Behind law and the Race to the Top program have undermined this ideal curriculum and restricted it to only the most affluent communities. Because federal policies value only test scores, they have unleashed an almost fanatical obsession with data based on test scores. Today, almost every state has received federal funding to create a data "warehouse," where information about all students and teachers will be stored for future retrieval. What is the purpose of the data warehouse? No one knows for sure, but it will enable all students to be tracked throughout their lifetimes in relation to their test scores, graduation dates, future earnings, and who knows what else. Even now, the Gates Foundation and Rupert Murdoch's Amplify division have joined to create a $100 million database called inBloom to collect confidential student information from several states and districts and put it on an electronic "cloud" managed by Amazon.com. This data will include students' names, birthdates, addresses, social security numbers, grades, test scores, disability status, attendance, and other confidential information. The database may be made available to vendors for marketing purposes. Why the modern state should collect and share so much confidential information about its citizens is baffling.[1]

In contrast to federal policy, which is obsessed with test-based data, educated consumers of schooling want their children to have a full, balanced, and rich curriculum. They may look into outcome data about a school (for example, how many of its students graduate, how many go to college, which colleges admit its graduates), but their first concern is "inputs": What educational experiences will my child have? How experienced are the teachers? How small are classes? Are there a variety of athletic programs that are right for my child? Will my child have a broad curriculum? If she needs extra help, will she get it? Does the school have a warm and welcoming climate? Will this school take good care of my child?

An educated parent would not accept a school where many weeks of every school year were spent preparing for state tests. An educated parent would not tolerate a school that cut back or eliminated the arts to spend more time preparing for state tests. If you want to know what an educated parent-consumer would insist upon, go online and look at the curricula in schools such as Sidwell Friends in the District of Columbia; Lakeside School in Seattle; Deerfield Academy in Deerfield, Massachusetts; Phillips Academy in Andover, Massachusetts; and Maumee Valley Country Day School in Toledo, Ohio. Every one of these schools has a curriculum with extensive offerings in the arts, languages, world cultures, history, sciences, mathematics, and athletics.

A similar curriculum may be found in affluent suburban communities, richly endowed by their strong tax bases and committed parents. Families in communities like Plano, Texas, Deerfield, Illinois, and Scarsdale, New York, would accept nothing less for their children.

The typical public school today cannot afford the same offerings. It cannot afford the small classes and rich curriculum available only to the richest citizens. And yet I can personally attest that in the past American public schools routinely offered a varied curriculum, even if the class sizes were not 1:15 as they are in many elite private schools.

Why today are public schools unable to afford the curriculum they once offered? Why is the richest nation in the world unable to provide a full curriculum for all students in public schools? Why are budget cuts in the wake of the Great Recession of 2008 falling so heavily on the public schools? Why are states willing to spend hundreds of millions on testing and test preparation materials even as they cut back on teachers of the arts and foreign languages and on librarians and counselors?

We cannot provide equal educational opportunity if some children get access to a full and balanced curriculum while others get a heavy dose of basic skills. This is one instance where no research is needed. The fact of inequality is undeniable, self-evident, and unjustifiable. This inequality of opportunity may damage the hearts and minds of the children who are shortchanged in ways that may never be undone.

We know that those who can afford the best for their children demand a full curriculum. Another way to judge the importance of a high-value curriculum is to consider what it should be in light of the purposes of public education. Communities and states established public education as a public responsibility in the nineteenth century to educate future citizens and to sustain our democracy. The essential purpose of the public schools, the reason they receive public funding, is to teach young people the rights and responsibilities of citizens. As citizens, they will be expected to discuss and deliberate issues, to choose our leaders, to take an active role in their communities, and to participate in civic affairs. A secondary purpose was to strengthen our economy and our culture by raising the intelligence of our people and preparing them to lead independent lives as managers, workers, producers, consumers, and creators of ideas, products, and services. A third purpose is to endow every individual with the intellectual and ethical power to pursue his or her own interests and to develop the judgment and character to survive life's vicissitudes.

Today, policy makers think of education solely in terms of its secondary purposes. They speak of children as future global competitors. They sometimes refer to children in rather ugly terms as "human assets," forgetting that they are unique people and they are not fungible. They want all students to be "college and career ready." They tend to speak only of preparation for the workforce, not education for citizenship. But this is misguided. Workforce training may take place in schools; it may take place in the workplace. It is not unimportant.

Nor is college preparation unimportant. But getting ready for college is not the central purpose of education. Nor is workforce training. The central purpose of education is to prepare everyone to assume the rights and responsibilities of citizenship in a democracy.

What does this mean for schooling?

It means first of all that all citizens need the essential tools of learning, which are reading and mathematics. Knowing how to read and knowing how numbers are used (and misused) to characterize almost everything are basic necessities for citizens.

Basic skills are necessary, but they are not enough to prepare the citizen.

A citizen of a democratic society must be able to read critically, listen carefully, evaluate competing claims, weigh evidence, and come to a thoughtful judgment. In their hands will be the most important responsibilities of citizenship: choosing our leaders and serving on juries. One determines the fate of our nation and the other determines the fate of other humans.

To come to a thoughtful judgment about political affairs, citizens need a solid grounding in history, economics, and statistics. They will hear candidates make conflicting claims about what history proves and what the economy needs. Citizens need to understand the great issues in American and world history. They should know about Jim Crow, the Progressive movement, Prohibition, the Great Depression, the McCarthy era, the *Brown* decision, the Cold War, and the other events and issues that shaped our world today. They need to understand the measures that have helped or harmed the economy. They need to recognize how conflicts have started and ended. They need to know and understand enough to reach their own judgments about candidates and issues and proposed legislation.

To know the evil and the goodness of which men are capable, they must study history. To know the mechanisms that have been created to protect our rights and freedoms, they must study the Constitution and other founding documents. To learn about the many struggles that others have waged to improve our imperfect democracy, they must study history.

To be prepared for their weighty responsibilities, they need to study government, economics, and civics. These studies teach them how their society functions and how it may be changed. To be prepared to judge issues on the world scene, they need to study world history and world geography to learn about other forms of government and other ways of organizing society than the one that is most familiar to us.

As citizens, our students will be expected to come to judgments about complex scientific issues. They need to understand science and to bring their critical judgment to bear on questions such as global warming, cloning, evolution, the effects of smoking or sugar, regulation of drilling for natural gas and oil, and debates about maintaining clean air and clean water. As candidates debate these issues, voters must be informed and ready to make their own judgments. They must know how to research the issues and assess contesting claims. As advocates for industry advance their interests, citizens must be able to weigh their assertions. Their knowledge of science and their understanding of scientific method will prepare them to reach their own judgments in matters of public dispute.

As citizens, our students will be called upon to judge the character of those who seek to persuade them. They will need that judgment when casting a vote, when serving on a jury, when deciding whom to trust. They will gain insight into character through the study of literature. By reading good and great works of fiction, students learn about character, motivation, kindness, greatness of spirit, imagination, the depths of evil, chicanery, and other aspects of human nature. Literature provides students with the opportunity to experience life through the eyes of other people in other times and other places. Literature, like history, is a superb way to travel through time, to be transported into another world. A good education steps outside the world of textbooks and work sheets and introduces students to worlds that they never dreamed of and to ideas that change their way of thinking. It introduces them to authors who use language imaginatively and beautifully and to cultural experiences that they can enjoy and share.

To function effectively in the world of the twenty-first century, students should learn a foreign language. They should use their language skills to learn about the culture, literature, history, and arts of other societies. They should broaden their knowledge of the world so that they recognize that other people think differently; by doing so, they may abandon narrow provincialism and get a clearer understanding of other cultures.

All of these studies are important parts of a rich and balanced curriculum. They may be taught separately, or they may be taught as integrated studies of society. There is no single right way. Teachers are best equipped to judge how to teach, how to inspire young minds with a thirst to learn more.

None of these studies should be subject to budget cuts. They are fundamental ingredients of a liberal education.

All are enriched and enhanced by the arts. The arts are essential for everyone. Life is enhanced by the arts. No student should be denied the opportunity to participate in the arts or to learn about the arts as practiced here and in other cultures. All students should have the chance to sing, dance, draw, and paint in school. They should have the resources for video production and for chorus, band, orchestra, and dramatics. The arts are a source of joy, a means of self-expression and group expression. To master a musical instrument or to participate in choral music requires self-discipline and practice; no one can do it for you. Every school should have the resources to enable students to express their individuality or to take pleasure in joyful communal activity.

The ancients spoke of a healthy mind in a healthy body, and in our time we have forgotten the wisdom of that maxim. Children and adolescents need physical activity. They need recess during the day, to relax and run and shout and play. They need structured play and games where they can learn physical discipline, whether in gymnastics or sports. Their youthful energy should be channeled into track and field, basketball, cycling, swimming, volleyball, and other activities.

School provides a place for mental, physical, and ethical development. Character is taught and learned in many settings: in the classroom, in the hallways, in the lunchroom, and on the sports field. One of the reasons that online schools do not succeed is that children and youths need social interaction to develop the soft skills that are needed in life and work. They must learn the skills of democratic society, the give-and-take of participation in shared activities. They learn together to put on a play, to organize a game, to collaborate on a science project or a mock trial. All of these activities prepare them for life in ways unmeasured by standardized tests. These skills of interaction cannot be learned on a computer. They are learned together with others in shared tasks.

For the past two decades, even before No Child Left Behind, the U.S. educational system has had an unhealthy focus on testing and accountability—unhealthy because it has driven public policy to concentrate on standardized tests of uneven quality at the expense of the more important goals of education, like character and love of learning. Sadly, the growing obsession with data has shoved aside these important goals. Consequently, children are tested again and again, compelled to select a box on a multiple-choice test, which is then turned into a definitive judgment about their value and their intelligence. Today, we accord to standardized test scores the same power that was once granted to intelligence tests. They are taken to be a measure of the worth of boys and girls and ultimately a measure of their teachers as well.

Anyone who truly cares about children must be repelled by the insistence on ranking them, rating them, and labeling them. Whatever the tests measure is not the sum and substance of any child. The tests do not measure character, spirit, heart, soul, potential. When overused and misused, when attached to high stakes, the tests stifle the very creativity and ingenuity that our society needs most. Creativity and ingenuity stubbornly resist standardization. Tests should be used sparingly to help students and teachers, not to allocate rewards and punishments and not to label children and adults by their scores.

We cheat children when we do not give them the chance to learn more than basic skills. We cheat them when we evaluate them by standardized tests. We undervalue them when we turn them into data points.

If we mean to educate them, we must recognize that all children deserve a full liberal arts curriculum. All children need the chance to develop their individual talents. And all need the opportunity to learn the skills of working and playing and singing with others. Whatever the careers of the twenty-first century may be, they are likely to require creativity, thoughtfulness, and the capacity for social interaction and personal initiative, not simply routine skills. All children need to be prepared as citizens to participate in a democratic society. A democratic society cannot afford to limit the skills and knowledge of a liberal education only to children of privilege and good fortune.

CHAPTER 25

Class Size Matters for Teaching and Learning

SOLUTION NO. 4 *Reduce class sizes to improve student achievement and behavior.*

Most teachers and parents agree about the importance of small classes. Parents care about class size because they know that the amount of individual attention their child will receive depends on the size of the class. When Scholastic and the Gates Foundation surveyed teachers in 2012, 90 percent said that having fewer students in their classes would have a strong or very strong impact on academic achievement. The desire for smaller classes was greatest among teachers in the elementary grades. A large majority of teachers—ranging from 83 percent in high school to 94 percent in the elementary grades—agreed that reducing class size would have a strong or very strong impact on student achievement. In contrast, only 26 percent of teachers responded that performance pay would make a strong or very strong impact on student achievement. Teachers said that having a smaller class meant more to them than the chance to earn extra money.[1]

In another Gates-funded survey, only 4 percent of veteran teachers and 6 percent of newer teachers (less than ten years' experience) said they would be willing to accept larger classes in exchange for a higher salary.[2]

Although most parents and teachers are enthusiastic about class size reduction, policy makers and elected officials sometimes argue against it because it is seen as too costly. Some make the case that when they attended school, classes were larger, and yet they succeeded. Mayor Michael Bloomberg of New York City has said that when he went to school, there were forty students in each class, and if it was in his power to redesign the school system, he would cut the number of teachers in half, "weed out all the bad ones," double class size, and double the pay of the remaining teachers. He maintained that to "double the class size with a better teacher is a good deal for the students."[3]

However, when older people remember the supposedly "good old days" of forty or more students in a class, they are evoking a different time in American history. They are recalling a time when most schools had classes of homogeneous students. They are remembering a time before court decisions and federal legislation ended legal segregation. They are remembering a time before students with disabilities were included in public schools and before all but the most severely disabled were mainstreamed into regular classes. They are remembering a time before massive immigration from non-English-speaking nations in Latin America, Africa, Asia, and elsewhere. Many of those who fondly remember the "good old days" were in classrooms that included few, if any, students who did not speak English, had disabilities, or were of a race different from their own. Moreover, even in those supposedly good old days, the schools with many poor or immigrant children had low achievement (far lower than now) and high dropout rates (far higher than now), but this wasn't seen as consequential, because there were jobs available for those who did not graduate.

It is a different world now. Teachers may have students in their classes who have mental or emotional disabilities or behavioral problems, who speak little or no English, or who live in extreme poverty and may be homeless. Classes are seldom homogeneous and are more likely to have children with a range of backgrounds and achievement levels. Students in need of substantial individual attention are unlikely to get it when they are in large classes. Because of budget cuts, class sizes have increased in many districts, with teachers reporting classes as large as forty or more, especially in the large urban districts with the highest-need students.

The Scholastic-Gates survey asked teachers who had been teaching in the same school for at least five years about the changes they observed in their classes. Nearly two-thirds said they now had more students with behavioral problems; about half said they have more students living in poverty, more who were English-language learners, and more who arrived at school hungry. Thirty-six percent reported an increase in homeless students. These are not the sorts of students that many of the old-timers recall from their childhoods. The increased numbers of at-risk students make it especially difficult to teach large classes.[4]

When the Scholastic-Gates survey asked teachers what they considered the ideal class size, elementary teachers estimated eighteen to nineteen students; middle school teachers of grades 6–8 estimated twenty to twenty-one students; and high school teachers estimated twenty to twenty-one students. Teachers who were working in urban districts had significantly larger classes on average. Because of sharp state and local budget cuts, most teachers today have larger classes than before the economic recession. In New York City, for example, class sizes in grades K–3 are now the largest in fourteen years. Class sizes have risen sharply in all grades, and nearly half of middle school students and more than half of high school students are in classes that average thirty or more. In some urban districts, classes are closer to forty. In California, Michigan, and Oregon, some classes hold close to fifty students.[5]

One of the high school teachers surveyed for the Scholastic-Gates report unknowingly answered Mayor Bloomberg's comment about doubling class size: "I could teach larger numbers of students. But which class would you prefer to have your kid in?" No parent would prefer to have her child in a class of forty-eight if she could choose a class of twenty-four. And the teacher who is rated "highly effective" with twenty-four children would likely have a far lower value-added rating if the class size doubled. Yet the growth score models used to evaluate teachers rarely if ever take the critical factor of class size into account.

In response to the Scholastic-Gates survey, an elementary school teacher said, "I am a general education teacher but at least 50 percent of my class each year has special needs. At least 25 percent of these students have extreme behavior problems which interfere with teaching the other students to learn."

A middle school teacher pointed out, "We have larger classes, more behavioral problems, increased numbers of special education students, limited technology, and no teacher aides. It's not easy, but I do it. I'm not sure how much longer I can do it, though."[6]

As classes become more diverse, students require more time. Teachers can't give them the time they need if the classes are unmanageable. A salient finding of the class size research is that children tend to be more engaged and less disruptive when they are enrolled in a smaller class.

If a teacher has a large class, his or her job becomes an exercise in management and control rather than instruction. If the same teacher has twenty students in a class, he or she has more time to know each of them and give them the help they need, and they are less likely to act out and become problems for the teacher and the rest of the class.

Reducing class size is costly. It is an expensive intervention because it means hiring more teachers for the same number of students. But the benefits of class size reduction are so large that the cost is well worth it, in terms of higher achievement levels, higher graduation rates, and lower special education referrals, especially if the reductions are targeted to the students who need it most. Schools and districts have a choice: they can reduce class sizes now and reap the benefits for years; or they can increase class sizes and pay the cost of remediation, disruptive behavior, and failure for many years. Both routes are costly, but one involves spending to produce early and lasting success, and the other involves spending to compensate for failure.

The research on class size is extensive. Some researchers argue against it, but they are in a minority. The Institute of Education Sciences of the U.S. Department of Education has identified class size reduction as one of the few evidence-based reforms that has been proven effective.[7]

Class size reduction has many beneficial effects. Large-scale experiments have demonstrated that it has a significant positive effect on minority children in the early grades. Children who are in smaller classes in the early grades get higher test scores and better grades, behave better in school, are more likely to graduate from high school, and are more likely to go to college. Longitudinal research shows that the benefits of having smaller classes in elementary school last into adulthood.[8]

Not surprisingly, attending smaller classes helps to develop the non-cognitive skills that the economist James Heckman says are so important to success in work, in college, and later in life, like persistence, motivation, and self-esteem. Smaller classes offer more opportunities for social cooperation, participating in discussion and debate, and developing the sort of critical thinking that is increasingly recognized to be essential in college and most careers. The smaller group promotes positive behaviors and interactions, as compared with the larger classes, where the emphasis is likely to be on order and compliance.[9]

Experiments in class size reduction have been conducted in the early grades, but not in middle school or high school. However, controlled studies in middle school and high school have reported that reduced class sizes there make a positive difference and that students in smaller classes had higher test scores and were less likely to drop out of school than their peers in larger classes. A study of 2,561 schools released by the U.S. Department of Education found that student achievement was closely linked to class size, even in the upper grades.[10]

Class size reduction has been shown to have a significant impact on the black-white achievement gap. Low-income students who spend four years in a smaller class in the early grades are far more likely to graduate from high school on time. In addition, black students who were in small classes eventually get higher scores on their college-entrance tests than those who were not. Paul Barton of the Educational Testing Service has speculated that national decreases in class size during the 1970s and 1980s may have been a major factor in the significant narrowing of the achievement gap that occurred at that time.[11]

Students are not the only ones to benefit by having smaller classes. Teachers also benefit. They are less likely to leave teaching or to change schools if they have small, manageable classes.[12] With smaller classes, they are able to devote more time to reading and commenting on essays and other student work. Reducing teacher turnover—or churn—is important, because experienced teachers are more effective and because students and schools function best when there is a strong collaborative culture and a stable staff.

It is odd that so many prominent business, political, and foundation leaders think that class size is not an important element in school reform. When they select a public or private school for their own children, they invariably demand schools with small class sizes. The catalogs of the best private schools seldom fail to mention their 12:1 ratio of students to teachers, or even 8:1. The best suburban public schools seldom have classes larger than eighteen. And yet those who would accept nothing less for their own children find it hard to imagine the same conditions for poor and minority children.

Critics complain about the cost of reducing class size. But it is even more expensive to continue to have large classes, especially for disadvantaged and at-risk students who benefit the most from class size reduction. Whatever may be saved today by laying off teachers and increasing class sizes will be offset many times by the costs of remediation and special services for children who fall behind and suffer the consequences of high dropout rates and unemployment that result. If as a society we really want our schools to improve and all children to succeed, we will guarantee that they are provided with the benefits of small classes that are now reserved primarily for the children of the wealthy.

CHAPTER 26

Make Charters Work for All

SOLUTION NO. 5 *Ban for-profit charters and charter chains and ensure that charter schools collaborate with public schools to support better education for all children.*

In the world of contemporary school reform, charters are considered the silver-bullet solution for children who live in poverty, but the results have been mixed and disappointing. Numerous studies by independent researchers have found that the achievement levels of charters vary widely, when judged by test scores, from highly successful at one extreme to highly unsuccessful at the other.[1]

Typically, in most states and districts, charters on average do not get different test scores from public schools if they enroll the same kinds of students. Many studies show that charters enroll a disproportionately small share of students who are English-language learners or who have disabilities, as compared with their home district. A survey of expulsion rates in the District of Columbia found that the charters—which enroll nearly half the student population of the district—expel large numbers of children; the charters' expulsion rate is seventy-two times the expulsion rate in the public schools. The students who are kicked out of the charters return to the public schools. As the charters shun these students, the local district gets a disproportionately large number of the students who are most expensive and most challenging to educate; when public students leave for charters, the budget of the public schools shrinks, leaving them less able to provide a quality education to the vast majority of students. In effect, a cycle of decline is set in motion: the charter school enrolls the most motivated students, avoids the students with high needs, and boasts of its higher scores; the test scores in the public school decline as some of its best students leave for the charter, and the proportion of needy students increases.[2]

Meanwhile, there is a growing for-profit charter sector and a proliferation of charter chains, which are akin to chain stores that open in malls and either thrive or close. For-profit online charter schools are booming, even though they get poor results, whether judged by test scores, graduation rates, or attrition. And yet they are very profitable for investors because of their low costs. The for-profit charter chains are doing what businesses do in a competitive environment: they are practicing risk management, keeping the winners and discarding the losers. That may work in business, where the goal is profitability. But it is wrong in education, where public schools are expected to educate all children, not just the easiest to teach.

Charters have become very controversial as they expand because the few that have high test scores tend to be boastful of their superiority, which does not create goodwill among educators. Further, in districts that place charters into existing public schools, there is usually hostility and jostling for space between an underfunded public school and a richly endowed charter school, which enjoys abundant financial support from its private board of trustees and exhibits an air of condescension toward its host school. Co-locations, as they are called in New York City, have been especially contentious because of the predatory practices of some of the aggressive charter chains that enter as tenants but do not hesitate to monopolize facilities and eventually try to push out the host school. Many of these charters are staffed by young college graduates who work unusually long hours, burn out, and leave for other careers, which creates constant teacher turnover.

With two million students now attending charter schools, charters are here to stay. Is it possible to make them a productive part of American public education, rather than a disruptive force? The problem with charters as currently configured is that they have strayed so far from the original intention of their founding fathers, Ray Budde and Albert Shanker. These men, who did not know each other, both envisioned the charter idea in 1988. They saw charters as a way to empower public school teachers to devise their own innovative curricula and methods and to free them from excessive regulation and bureaucracy. Neither man thought of charters as a way to transfer control of public schools to private hands or to create profit-making enterprises for stockholders or to destroy teachers' rights and their unions. Their good ideas were distorted by quirks of fate and the entrepreneurial drive to expand and make money.

If charters continue to expand aggressively in districts across the nation, there is a risk of reverting to a publicly funded dual school system, especially in our nation's cities. Instead of being based solely on racial lines, this dual school system would be based on both racial and class lines. Charter schools would recruit and enroll students who are motivated and willing, while public schools would serve the rejects, the students who didn't make it into a charter school, those who were unwanted by charters because they didn't speak English, had disabilities, or threatened in some other way to lower the charter's test scores. A dual school system is inherently discriminatory, especially when one sector is privately run, deregulated, unsupervised, and free to write its own rules and avoid or eject students it does not want, and the other must take all students and abide by all state laws and regulations, no matter how burdensome and costly. At present, the most successful of the charters spend substantially more than the public schools, while the public schools enroll the students that are most costly to educate.[3] When fully evolved, such a system would turn the public schools into schools of last resort rather than institutions that reflect and serve their communities.

Charters could become a positive force in American education if the conditions under which they are authorized are changed. Given the money and political power of the charter movement, it will be difficult politically to alter the authorizing laws. But as charters move into affluent districts, putting admired public schools in jeopardy, there is a chance that public resistance will increase and make political changes possible. To make such changes will require leadership and legislative majorities that recognize the importance of public education as a basic democratic institution. Charters should become collaborators with public schools in a shared mission to serve the needs of all children. But to understand where they should go, we need to understand their original purpose, which is now long forgotten.

Ray Budde, a University of Massachusetts professor, envisioned charters as a way to reorganize district management and free teachers from unnecessary bureaucracy. He thought of them as self-governing schools, liberated to find new solutions to pedagogical problems. He did not imagine them as for-profit enterprises operating chains across the nation, nor as organizations aggressively entering districts to build market share. He did not see them as a way to extinguish teachers' unions or to regiment children with rigid discipline codes.

Albert Shanker, the president of the American Federation of Teachers, wanted to find alternative ways to educate disengaged students. In his vision of charters, teachers would bring their plan to their colleagues and their district for approval. The new charter school, as he saw it, would seek out and enroll the most difficult-to-educate students, the dropouts, and those at risk of dropping out. The teachers in the charter would be free to make up their own curriculum and try whatever they thought might work. They would share whatever they learned with their colleagues in the regular public school.

As I described in chapter 16, Shanker turned against the charter concept in 1993, when he realized that it was embraced by conservative governors and would advance privatization.

How can charters now work for the common good instead of competing with public schools for students, for facilities, and for resources? How can they collaborate instead of driving into bankruptcy the public schools that educate the great majority of students?

The answer lies in the charter schools' origins.

Imagine the following changes in state laws.

First, no public school should be operated for profit. At present, for-profit corporations compete to lower costs, and they do this by replacing experienced teachers with inexperienced teachers and by replacing teachers with computer instruction. The primary goal of a for-profit organization is to maximize profit, not to produce great education. Tax dollars for education should be spent entirely on the operation of schools and the provision of instruction and school activities. Not a penny should go to pay investors or stockholders. Certainly, some tax revenues will necessarily go to profit-making corporations that sell supplies and services to schools, but the schools themselves should always be operated as nonprofits.

Second, charter schools should be managed by local educators and nonprofit organizations, not by charter chains. They should be stand-alone, community-based schools designed and managed by parents, teachers, and members of the local community for the children of that district. They should not be run like Walmart or Target. By allowing schools to operate like chain stores, states have encouraged a chain-store mentality, with standardized management and standardized practices, run from another city or state. Schooling is not a commodity that can be packaged and distributed across the nation, a standard product that is not responsive to individual children and local needs. The ideal charter school would be created by the community, to serve the community, reflecting the goals and needs of the community.

Third, charter schools would still be privately managed with a private board of directors, as at present, but the salaries of charter school principals and executives should be aligned with those of local district principals and superintendents. This would eliminate the practice of paying exorbitant executive salaries and would eliminate charter leaders who have a pecuniary interest. It would keep the focus where it should be, on creating a superior and innovative educational program that serves a public purpose, not on cashing in with public funding.

Fourth, state law should closely regulate online virtual charter schools to provide oversight for recruitment practices, attrition rates, misrepresentation, and quality. The reimbursement of virtual charter schools should be reduced to reflect their actual costs of instruction; when students leave the online school in midyear, their funding should follow them to their next school. For-profit schools would be banned, and salaries would be regulated to prevent fraud and abuse. Students who wish to enroll in an online school should be interviewed by guidance counselors and have legitimate reasons for home instruction.

Fifth, a significant proportion of charter schools should enroll and educate the children who are not succeeding in public school, for whatever reason. They should seek out and recruit dropouts or children with behavioral problems or students with special needs whose parents do not want them to be mainstreamed, such as those with profound autism or profound deafness. Charter schools would explore new ways to educate these students. They should develop strategies and curricula to benefit all schools and regularly share what they have learned. If charter schools sought to enroll the neediest students, they would become an integral part of public education and a valued partner of public schools. Instead of fighting with each other over space and resources, the two sectors would have a common goal of educating all children well and a genuine basis for shared responsibility.

These changes are far removed from where we are now. But as the facts on the ground change, our laws can change to adapt to what we have learned and what we hope to accomplish. Charter schools and public schools should not compete; they should work together. Charters can be redesigned to serve the common good. Together, public schools and charter schools can collaborate to pursue equal educational opportunity.

CHAPTER 27

Wraparound Services Make a Difference

SOLUTION NO. 6 *Provide the medical and social services that poor children need to keep up with their advantaged peers.*

Nearly one of every four children in the United States lives in poverty. This is a far higher proportion than in any other advanced nation. There are children of all racial and ethnic backgrounds who live in poverty, but a disproportionate number are black and Hispanic. One of the main goals of educational and social policy is the narrowing of the gap between children who are advantaged and those who are disadvantaged. School reformers in our era believe that we can "fix" the schools before doing anything directly about poverty, but there is no precedent in history for their belief.

If we don't act to remedy the social and economic conditions that cause disadvantage, we are unlikely to see any large-scale change in the achievement gaps. While the test scores of poor, black, and Hispanic students have increased in the past twenty years or more and are now at a historical high point, the gaps remain stubbornly large. The gaps are caused by handicapping conditions associated with poverty and grow larger when children from impoverished circumstances attend schools that lack the personnel, resources, programs, and curricula to meet their needs. Other nations have figured out how to remedy or ameliorate or change the conditions in children's lives so that they are likely to grow up healthy and ready to learn. They make sure that children get off to a good start in life before they begin formal schooling. We pay lip service to the goal but skimp on implementation. In 1990, the nation's governors and the U.S. Department of Education endorsed an ambitious set of national goals, and the first goal was that by the year 2000 all children would be "ready to learn." We did not meet that goal, and it is now long forgotten. But the unaddressed needs remain.

In a projection of the feasibility of reducing the achievement gaps, Tamara Wilder, Whitney Allgood, and Richard Rothstein summarized the handicaps that poor children live with daily:

> Low-income children often have no routine or preventive medical, dental or optometric care, resulting in more school absences as a result of illness and even an inability to see well enough to read. Children in low-income families are more prone to asthma, resulting in more sleeplessness, irritability, and lack of exercise, as well as poorer attendance. Children born to low-income mothers have lower birth weight as well as more lead poisoning and iron deficiency anemia, each of which leads to diminished cognitive ability, more behavioral problems and more special education placement. Their families frequently fall behind in rent and move, so children switch schools more often, losing continuity of instruction. Poor children are, in general, not read to aloud as often or exposed to complex language and large vocabularies in their homes, so they begin school far behind in verbal ability, reasoning skills, and reading readiness. Their parents have low-wage jobs and are more frequently laid off, causing family stress that often leads to more arbitrary discipline at home and "acting out" in school. The neighborhoods through which these children walk to school and in which they play have more crime and drugs and fewer adult role models with professional careers. Children whose mothers are poorly educated are more often in single-parent families and so get less adult attention. They have fewer cross-country trips, visits to museums and zoos, music or dance lessons, and organized sports leagues to develop their ambition, cultural awareness, and self-confidence.[1]

A previous chapter reviewed the importance of providing good prenatal care to every pregnant woman to avoid the consequences of preterm births, such as lower birth weight and diminished cognitive ability. Another chapter showed the necessity of supplying high-quality early childhood education to help children begin school with a larger vocabulary, socialization skills, and broader experience with language and the world beyond their immediate neighborhoods. Other chapters argued that poor children benefit by being in small classes and having access to the kind of curriculum always found in the best schools and districts.

Here I propose interrelated solutions that are known as wraparound services. They should be integrated into and around the school and readily available to students as needed.

WRAPAROUND SOLUTION: *Every school should have a nurse, doctor, or health clinic to ensure that children get regular medical checkups and prompt treatment for illnesses.* All children should get regular screening for health problems. Such screening is routine among middle- and upper-income families. No child should be denied access to health care because of his family's economic status. Improving the health of children will improve their academic performance. Children who are sick, who have asthma, who have untreated illnesses, who can't hear the teacher or see the front of the room, are unlikely to keep up with their peers. Healthy children are more alert, more attentive, and less likely to miss days of school due to illness. There is no body of research that discounts the importance of good health. Improving the health of all children should be a national priority and a focus of educational and social reform.

Every child should have regular access to medical care. Families should not have to use the hospital emergency room for routine medical problems. Is research needed to demonstrate that every child should have a regular medical checkup, regular vision screening, and regular dental care? Just as children in middle-class and affluent circumstances receive preventive care, to avoid problems later, so should poor children. Just as middle-class and affluent children get care and medicine when they are ill, so should poor children.

WRAPAROUND SOLUTION: *Disadvantaged children should have summer programs that give them enrichment activities, sports, the arts, tutoring, and literacy activities to maintain the gains of the previous academic year.* A major study at the Johns Hopkins University by Karl L. Alexander, Doris R. Entwisle, and Linda Steffel Olson found that summer learning loss among lower-income students contributes significantly to the academic achievement gap. Children of higher-income groups start school with a large advantage due to the inequality of home and com-

munity environments. The researchers argued that "the early years of
schooling are foundational in that the skills acquired then support all
later learning." What happens in school matters in subsequent years. By
the time students start high school, most of what they learn is an accu-
mulation of previous years in school. "But with respect specifically to
the year 9 achievement gap by SES [socioeconomic status] background,
experiences outside school apparently make an even bigger difference,
as that gap substantially originates over the years before first grade and
summer periods during the elementary school years."[2]

Summer learning matters, whether it is formal or informal. Children from higher socioeconomic groups learn more over the summer
than children from lower-income groups, which widens the achievement gap. Because better-off children get more opportunity to learn in
the summer, their advantage increases in relation to poor students who
do not have comparable summer experiences. This accumulated disadvantage over the years causes low-income students to be more likely to
have low test scores, less likely to finish high school, and less likely to
enroll in a four-year college. The Johns Hopkins study reached a startling conclusion: "Summer shortfall over the five years of elementary
school accounts for more than half the difference [between high- and
low-socioeconomic-status youths by grade 9], a larger component than
that built up over the preschool years. And, too, these learning differences from the early years that present themselves in 9th grade reverber-
ate to constrain later high school curriculum placements, high school
dropout, and college attendance. This lasting legacy of early experience
typically is hidden from view."[3]

The authors conclude that interventions should begin early, before
the disadvantages grow even larger, and "the earlier the better," with
a high priority for preschool programs. Once disadvantaged children
are in school, they "need year-round, supplemental programming to
counter the continuing press of family and community conditions that
hold them back." While upper-income parents are working with their
children on letters and numbers and embarking on family trips with
educational value, lower-income students often lack the same advantages. The authors' study attributes fully two-thirds of the achievement gap between lower- and higher-income youths to differences in
summer learning opportunities. They find that children from low-
socioeconomic-status homes "come closer to keeping up with better-
off students during the school year than they do during the summer

months." They discovered a "school-year pattern of achievement gain parity (or near parity) across social lines," which "flies in the face of widely held (if only whispered) assumptions about the learning abilities of poor and minority youth. It also flies in the face of widely held assumptions about the failures of public schools and school systems burdened by high minority enrollments. Perhaps these schools and school systems are doing a better job than is generally recognized, with family disadvantages mistaken for school failings."[4]

The Johns Hopkins study is part of a large literature that documents the effects of summer learning loss. If disadvantaged students had access to high-quality summer programs, where their learning is sustained while they are enjoying drama and athletics and nature study, summer learning loss could be reduced or eliminated. That would substantially narrow the achievement gap.[5]

WRAPAROUND SOLUTION: *Disadvantaged children benefit if they have the opportunity to participate in excellent after-school enrichment programs.*

More than seven million children are without any adult supervision after school. Those who have the opportunity to be involved in after-school programs are less likely to use drugs, less likely to have behavioral problems at school, and more likely to have self-confidence, self-efficacy, and better academic outcomes at school.[6]

Children who live in poverty lack access to the programs that middle-class and affluent children take for granted. Better-off children get swimming lessons, tennis lessons, attend science camps, have tutoring, and visit museums and libraries with their families. After-school programs give all children and adolescents a chance to have some of the same experiences.

Organized after-school activities have a long history in this country. They began in settlement houses, when women such as Jane Addams opened large welcoming establishments in poor immigrant neighborhoods to offer arts and crafts, counseling, English-language classes, and assistance to children and families.

Today, many children do not have a safe place to play or adult supervision at the end of the school day. Some funders think of after-school programs solely as time for remediation and tutoring, but these are voluntary programs, so they should include activities that students want to do, not just provide more time for test prep. After-school programs like LA's Best, which serves nearly thirty thousand children in

Los Angeles, are safe havens for children, where they may engage in athletics, dramatics, tutoring, music, dance, poetry, writing, and visual arts. They teach conflict resolution and healthy eating habits. They offer classes where children learn typing and computer skills; they have science programs and Junior Achievement, where young people learn how businesses work. LA's Best gives preference to activities that interest children, and it promotes the development of both cognitive and noncognitive skills.

In his book *How Children Succeed*, Paul Tough wrote about the chess program at I.S. 318, a racially and economically diverse middle school in the Williamsburg section of Brooklyn, which was also featured in a film called *Brooklyn Castle*. The school has won more chess championships than any other school in the nation, public or private. The students work incredibly hard at learning and mastering chess. They develop habits of self-discipline and concentration. Chess is their passion. This is an excellent example of the power of an after-school program to motivate students to work hard, do their best, and develop the persistence that they need to succeed in school and in life. Sadly, the funding for the team's travel to national chess tournaments is in jeopardy every year.[7]

After-school programs are not a cure-all, but they fill a valuable role. They give children the chance to learn under adult supervision without the stress of grades and test scores, to play, to strengthen their bodies, to be active, to try out new skills, to make new friendships, to learn how to get along with others in a nonacademic environment. Without them, the millions of children now in after-school programs would be hanging out with nothing to do, their parents at work, susceptible to the influence of the street and of gangs. Why wouldn't we provide the same opportunities to all children who lack them?

I would add this caution. Adults no longer work a nine-hour day, and children should not be expected to study nine hours a day, fifty-two weeks a year. They need time for recreation, athletics, music, dramatics, and unstructured play.

WRAPAROUND SOLUTION: *Parent education will support and intensify the impact of all other interventions.*

Parents are their children's first and most important educators.

Parents—whether there is one or two of them—determine the conditions of their child's upbringing, given their knowledge and their means.

Families have a greater influence on children's success in school than teachers.

Many parents need no outside assistance to raise their children well. But some do, either because they do not know how to parent well or because they are under enormous financial or emotional stress.

All of the other interventions are reinforced by parent involvement. Some parents need support when they first bring home a newborn. High-quality preschool works best when parents get involved and learn how to help their child when he or she is not in school. Good programs teach parents to converse with their children in a way that builds vocabulary, to refrain from harsh disciplinary methods, to resolve conflicts amicably, to read to their children, and to engage them in thinking about the consequences of their actions. Some parents learn to help their children have a healthy lifestyle with a good diet and good hygiene, to limit their television-watching time, and to get them to do their homework.

When parents are actively involved in their children's lives, their children feel their support and their love. When they express interest in their schoolwork, children understand that their schoolwork matters to their parents. When they read to them, children learn to value language. When they smile and nod approval, children take pride in what they have done.

Not every parent knows how to feed and care for a newborn. One of the exemplary national programs is the Nurse-Family Partnership, which helps young women during their pregnancies and even after. In this program, now active in forty states, registered nurses make regular home visits to poor women during their pregnancies and for two years after the child is born. The nurse visits once a week during the second trimester of pregnancy, then every other week. After the child is born, the nurse pays a weekly visit for six weeks to be sure the mother gets the advice and support she needs for her baby. The visits are then scheduled every other week until the baby reaches twenty months and continue once a month until the baby is two years old.

During the pregnancy, the nurses "complete 24-hour diet histories, plot weight gains, coordinate visits with physicians, assess use of cigarettes, alcohol, and illegal drugs, and, if necessary, devise behavioral-

change strategies to reduce use of such substances." After the birth of
the child, the nurses help mothers "improve the physical and emotional
care of their children." They work to "enhance parent-child interactions. Nurses help parents to understand their infants' and toddlers'
communicative signals, enhance parents' interest in playing with their
children in ways that promote emotional and cognitive development,
and help to create safer households for children. Nurses also help
women establish and clarify their own goals, to solve problems that
may interfere with their educations, finding work, and planning future
pregnancies."[8]

Evaluations of the Nurse-Family Partnership found "significant
positive effects on pregnancy outcomes, child health and development,
and family economic self-sufficiency." Randomized field trials reported
"improved prenatal health, fewer subsequent pregnancies, increased
maternal employment, and increased intervals between births for
mothers, and fewer childhood injuries and improved school readiness
for children."

In their recommendations for narrowing the achievement gap,
Wilder, Allgood, and Rothstein recommend that the Nurse-Family
Partnership model be continued until the age of three, when preschool
begins, so there is no gap in promoting the well-being of children who
grow up in low-income homes.

Not every parent knows how to help a child grow and develop in
healthy ways. Not every parent has had a good example to follow. Not
every parent has the background knowledge to help a child succeed in
school.

If we help them, we help our society.

CHAPTER 28

Measure Knowledge and Skills with Care

SOLUTION NO. 7 *Eliminate high-stakes standardized testing and rely instead on assessments that allow students to demonstrate what they know and can do.*

Everyone interested in education knows about Finland. It is the counterexample to our own practices and policies. That nation determined to overhaul its educational system in the 1970s. It raised the admission standards for its teacher education colleges. They became so selective that today only 10 percent of those who apply are accepted. Every teacher has five years of education and training, including a master's degree. Teachers are highly respected, as respected as any other profession. As professionals, they exercise broad autonomy in their classrooms and their schools, where they make decisions about pedagogy and curriculum. Because they are held in high regard, no one questions their professionalism. There is a broad national curriculum, but it leaves considerable room for every school to make its own decisions about what to teach and how to teach it. And here is the kicker: *Finnish students never take a standardized test until they apply to college.* Teachers prepare their own tests. They are trusted to determine whether their students are making progress and to decide what additional help they need.

Finland has a national sampling system akin to our National Assessment of Educational Progress. There are no scores for individual students. Teachers are not judged by their students' test scores, because students don't take standardized tests and there are no scores. There is no merit pay based on scores because there are no scores. All teachers belong to a union; all principals belong to the same union. Oh, and one thing more: Less than 5 percent of children in Finland are growing up in poverty, compared with 23 percent in this country. That makes a huge difference.

Finland has built a strong and successful public school system. There are no charter schools and no vouchers. Finland has built a strong education profession. There is no Teach for Finland. Finns boast that there are good public schools in every city, every town, and every village.

For the past decade, Finland has performed well on every international assessment in reading, mathematics, and science, without making that performance its goal. The Finns improved their schools without testing their students, without merit pay, without privatization, without competition among schools, and without waving carrots and sticks at their teachers. They built a strong education profession, a trusted corps of career educators, and a high-quality public school system. Every child gets three meals a day and medical care. Pasi Sahlberg, the leading exponent of the Finnish school system, describes the approach now in vogue in the United States as the "global education reform movement," or GERM, a virus characterized by testing, accountability, choice, and competition.[1]

The Finnish answer is starkly different from our own education policies. The Finns say, select good recruits for the teaching profession; educate them well; prepare them well for the work they will be expected to do; trust their judgment; respect the profession; make sure that children grow up healthy and ready to learn; forget about standardized testing; forget about accountability; saturate children in the early years with whatever help they need to keep up with their peers; provide a curriculum that is balanced with academics, arts, and physical activity.

Perhaps this is too great a leap for most Americans to take. How will we hold students and teachers and schools accountable without test scores? We tend to forget that the United States somehow managed to become the world's leading economic and technological power before the advent of test-based accountability.

Since the passage of No Child Left Behind, public education has been caught up in a frenzied effort to raise test scores. The legislative authors of NCLB assumed that a regime of punishments and rewards would make teachers work harder, which would in turn produce higher test scores.

The assumption of the law's framers that students would learn more if their teachers were enticed with carrots and threatened with sticks never made sense. After all, it is students, not teachers, who ultimately decide whether they want to learn more. And the law's assumption that standardized tests are the best way to measure learning has never been established. If that were true, all private and independent schools in the nation would be devoted to standardized testing, but they are not.

The entire edifice of No Child Left Behind and its successor, Race to the Top, sits on the shaky foundation of standardized testing. The tests label, rank, and grade students, teachers, principals, and schools. They are ubiquitous. Schools that enroll mostly middle-income and affluent students get high scores and "succeed," while schools that enroll large numbers of impoverished black and Hispanic students and students with disabilities are stigmatized as "failing" schools. Schools that test students before admitting them are "successful" schools. The tests turn out to be a fairly reliable measure of advantage and disadvantage, of family income and education.[2]

Tests may be useful when they are used appropriately. They should be used to gather information about schools and districts so that programs may be assessed. They should be used for diagnostic purposes, to determine which students need more help with specific problems. They should be used to establish trends. The best tests have no stakes attached to them. The National Assessment of Educational Progress is an exemplar. It tests samples of students. No one knows who will take it. No one can prepare for it. No single student takes the entire test. No individual or school is punished or rewarded because of the scores on NAEP.

High-stakes testing can sometimes be useful for students because the prospect of a test encourages them to study the material the test will cover. But much of the test's usefulness depends on its quality. Tests that ask students to explain or demonstrate what they know elicit thoughtful responses. Multiple-choice tests may gauge little more than students' ability to guess the right answer. A steady diet of multiple-choice questions over a dozen years may impair students' ability to think critically and to reflect on alternate solutions to problems; instead, they are taught to guess "the right answer."

The tests should be a measure, not a goal of instruction. Standard-ized tests are not designed to measure school or teacher quality; they are designed to assess how well a student can read or do mathematics in comparison to others in the same grade. The tests are a snapshot on one day of what students know or remember or can figure out. They provide a means of comparing students, schools, and districts. But they are an imperfect measure.

The tests are not scientific instruments, like a thermometer. They are social constructions whose questions and answers are written by fallible human beings. Multiple-choice questions are scored by com-puters, but written responses are typically graded by hourly, low-wage workers. Even though many of those test graders have no background in education, their decisions affect the fate of students, the reputations of teachers, and the survival of entire schools.

Frankly, anyone who reads Todd Farley's *Making the Grades: My Misadventures in the Standardized Testing Industry,* would never again believe the results of standardized tests. Farley worked in the testing industry for fifteen years, scoring state tests and NAEP tests. Having seen the industry from the inside, he became completely cynical about it. In his book, he goes into elaborate detail about the hourly workers who grade standardized tests, the pressure they are under to complete their work quickly, and the arbitrary decisions that determine how they grade student answers. He writes, "I would say standardized testing is akin to a scientific experiment in which everything is a variable. Every-thing. It seems to me the score given to every response, and ultimately the final results given to each student, depended as much on the vaga-ries of the testing industry as they did on the quality of the student answers." He maintains that it is "absolute folderol" to believe that a standardized test is capable of making fine distinctions about any stu-dent's skills and abilities or that it is better to trust the testing industry instead of classroom teachers.

Based on his career in the testing industry, Farley concludes that it is wrong to entrust the fate of students, teachers, and schools to an industry that is

> unashamedly in the business of making money instead of listening to the many people who went into education for the more altruistic desire to do good. It means giving credence to the thoughts of mobs

of temporary employees who only dabble in assessment while ignoring the opinions of the men and women who dedicate themselves daily to the world of teaching and learning . . . It means ignoring the conclusions about student abilities of this country's teachers—the people who instruct and nurture this country's children every single day—to instead heed the snap judgments of bored temps giving fleeting glances to student work.[3]

Another writer, Dan DiMaggio, described his experience as a test grader for a major corporation:

Test-scoring companies make their money by hiring a temporary workforce each spring, people willing to work for low wages (generally $11 to $13 an hour), no benefits, and no hope of long-term employment—not exactly the most attractive conditions for trained and licensed educators. So all it takes to become a test scorer is a bachelor's degree, a lack of a steady job, and a willingness to throw independent thinking out the window and follow the absurd and ever-changing guidelines set by the test-scoring companies. Some of us scorers are retired teachers, but most are former office workers, former security guards, or former holders of any of the diverse array of jobs previously done by the currently unemployed. When I began working in test scoring three years ago, my first "team leader" was qualified to supervise, not because of his credentials in the field of education, but because he had been a low-level manager at a local Target.[4]

The tests today are a club, a sword held over the heads of teachers and principals. This places too much emphasis on the tests. It distorts the purposes of education. We no longer speak of education as a process of human development. We no longer discuss the role of education in preparing citizens for our democracy. We no longer consider how education builds character. We focus only on one thing: test scores. The truly important goals of education are neglected.

Even if state and federal test scores go up, and they have gone up in recent years (though less than they did prior to the implementation of NCLB), it is likely that students are getting a worse education. If they are not learning to think, to interpret, and to understand, then they are not getting a good education. If they are learning to pick the right answer rather than ask the right question, they are not getting a good education. If they are learning to take state tests but not learning the underlying skills and knowledge needed for unanticipated situations, they are getting a bad education. The standardized tests don't measure the ability to interpret ambiguous situations or to understand complex issues.

Worse, the heavy reliance on multiple-choice tests is itself deeply antagonistic to true learning. It teaches false lessons. It teaches students that questions have one right answer, and in life that is seldom correct. It is true that two plus two is always four. But many questions that people encounter on the job or in real life have answers shaded in gray. To figure out a complex social or political issue, adults must be able to assess the validity of the information they were given, to weigh alternatives, and to choose among courses of action that may or may not be right. In real life, people do not always agree on the right answer. The tests we now value don't teach what matters most, which is the ability to think for oneself.

There is a dubious assumption behind the entire testing mania. The testing advocates say that students who get higher test scores will get more education and will get better jobs and make more money. So, if everyone gets higher test scores, then everyone will get better jobs and make more money. But test scores don't change the shape of the economy. No matter how high test scores go, they will not restore the good middle-class jobs that disappeared in the recession of 2008. Schools don't control the economy. They prepare people with the skills and knowledge to qualify for jobs, but schools don't create jobs. In the 1930s, school enrollments increased, and people were better educated, but the schools and their graduates did not end the Great Depression. Public policy and events did.

Even more curious is the unwarranted belief that more testing and accountability will close the achievement gaps between rich and poor, blacks and whites, and Hispanics and whites. Since the source of the gaps is socioeconomic inequality, it is sheer fantasy to believe that the test scores of these groups will converge if only there are higher standards plus more testing and accountability. The assumption is that those who teach the low-performing groups are not really trying, and a carrot or a stick will motivate them to try harder.

Since the tests are scored around norms with a bell curve, there will always be some students at the top of the curve and others at the bottom, with most clustered in the middle. The bell curve is statistically unforgiving. There was never a time when all or almost all test takers were in the top half. And there is this nagging fact about standardized tests: they are highly correlated with family income and education. On every test ever administered, the children whose families have the highest income are overrepresented at the top, and the children whose families have the lowest income are overrepresented at the bottom. Of course, there are some poor kids at the top and some rich kids at the bottom, but on average family income is a reliable predictor of test scores. This is true of the National Assessment of Educational Progress, the SAT, the ACT, state tests, and international tests. And it is true in every other nation.

This being the case, why would anyone expect to close the achievement gap by imposing more testing and accountability? Those at the top will still be at the top and imagine that they deserve their exalted position, and those at the bottom will remain at the bottom, convinced that the tests have certified their lesser achievement and their lesser value. The test scores grade, rank, and brand students, who believe that they deserve the labels they receive. After all, the tests are supposedly "objective."

But there is another problem with the testing regime in which we are now immersed. It does not acknowledge that noncognitive dimensions of development are as important as cognitive ones. They may even be more important. The ability to read and count matters, but so do the ability to work with other people, the ability to persevere when confronted with a difficult task, and the ability to listen and communicate well. Whether on the job or as a citizen, a person needs many traits of character and many kinds of behavior to be successful, and these are not measured by standardized tests. Being able to select the right bubble of four possibilities is not a skill of great value once one leaves school. But the ability to collaborate with others to get a task accomplished matters very much. And so too do such qualities of character as honesty, responsibility, determination, integrity, and care for others.

The economist James Heckman has repeatedly made the case for noncognitive skills. He and a colleague at the University of Chicago wrote that "it is common knowledge outside of academic journals that motivation, tenacity, trustworthiness, and perseverance are important traits for success in life." This is the lesson of the fable "The Tortoise and the Hare" and of the book *The Little Engine That Could,* they said. Everyone knows of people with high IQs and high test scores who failed in life because they lacked self-discipline and drive, and of people who succeeded not because of their IQs but because they were persistent, reliable, and self-disciplined.[5]

Building on the work of Heckman and others, Paul Tough writes in his book *How Children Succeed* that what matters most, as his subtitle declares, is "grit, curiosity, and the hidden power of character." Children don't need more tests; they need the attitudes and values that help them succeed in the face of powerful adversity. What enables them to succeed is character. Schools don't do a very good job of teaching character, but at the very least they should not ignore it or discount it or save all the accolades for the kids with high test scores.

In a scholarly critique of the international focus on test scores, Henry M. Levin, a prominent economist of education, reviewed the importance of noncognitive skills. The idea of an international "race to the top" based solely on test scores makes little sense, he argued. For an individual to succeed, he or she needs interpersonal skills, the ability to relate well to others in different situations, teamwork, good judgment, problem-solving skills, motivation, the ability to listen and communicate, and the ability to plan the use of one's time, to control one's impulses, and to defer gratification. These attitudes and values may be even more important to employers than test scores. Indeed, employers place a high value on "punctuality, attendance, setting of goals, taking responsibility, and listening skills." Standardized tests do not measure these attitudes and values. What matters most in life are "effort, self-discipline, persistence, cooperation, self-presentation, tolerance, respect, and other noncognitive dimensions." Levin warns that "far from being harmless, the focus on test scores and the omission of the noncognitive impact of schools can create far-reaching damage." As more and more pressure is exerted on schools to raise test scores, less time and attention are available to encourage the important noncognitive goals. He writes, "The instructional strategies used to raise test results, such as test preparation, cramming, tutoring, and endless memorization, may have little effect on the broader cognitive and noncognitive skills that people need if they are to perform as competent adults contributing to a dynamic economy."[6]

Leading scholars have warned that tying incentives to test scores is not a useful strategy for improving education or even test scores. A seventeen-member panel of the National Research Council conducted a nine-year study of test-based accountability and concluded that it is ineffective. "Test-based incentive programs, as designed and implemented in the programs that have been carefully studied, have not increased student achievement enough to bring the United States close to the levels of the highest-achieving countries. When evaluated using relevant low-stakes tests, which are less likely to be inflated by the incentives themselves, the overall effects on achievement tend to be small and are effectively zero for a number of programs."[7]

Referring to No Child Left Behind, the committee identified some school-level effects, "but the measured effects to date tend to be concentrated in elementary grade mathematics, and the effects are small compared to the improvements the nation hopes to achieve." Dan Ariely, a behavioral economist at Duke, said, "We went ahead, implementing this incredibly expensive and elaborate strategy for changing the education system without creating enough ways to test whether what we are doing is useful or not." He added, "We're relying on some primitive intuition about how to structure the education system without thinking deeply about it." Kevin Lang of Boston University's economics department, said, "None of the studies that we looked at found large effects on learning, anything approaching the rhetoric of being at the top of the international scale." He said that the most successful effects of NCLB, according to the committee's calculations, "moved student performance by eight-hundredths of the standard deviation, or from the 50th to the 53rd percentile." Ariely said the report "raises a red flag for education. These policies are treating humans like rats in a maze. We keep thinking about how to reorganize the cheese to get the rats to do what we want. People do so much more than that." Even worse, he said, was the idea that teachers could be motivated by bonuses: "That's one of the worst ideas out there . . . In the process of creating No Child Left Behind, as people thought about these strategies and rewards, they actually undermined teachers' motivations. They got teachers to care less, rather than more . . . [because] they took away a sense of personal achievement and autonomy."[8]

How can we escape this counterproductive approach to education, which in fact is antithetical to education itself? How can we break free of the failed belief that people can be "incentivized" to teach and to learn by threats and rewards? How can we stop relying on methods that crown some children as winners and stigmatize others as losers? Life may do that, but schools should not.

Suppose schools used standardized tests only for purposes of information and diagnostics. One can envision a teacher requesting that a student take a specific test to determine her facility with fractions or vocabulary or grammar. The information gleaned from testing should inform the teacher about the students' needs, not supply data to the state for meting out rewards and punishments. The primary assessments in schools should be designed to gauge the quality of student learning, such as essays, problem-solving exercises, teacher-made tests, research papers, book reports, scientific projects, computer simulations, and other demonstrations of skills and knowledge.

Schools should treat the test scores of individual students as confidential information available only to students, parents, teachers, and, if need be, the principal. Just as doctors maintain confidentiality about their patients' medical records, schools should view test scores as a personal record pertaining to each student. That is what the best private schools do. Student report cards should contain qualitative judgments written by children's teachers, describing their accomplishments and their weaknesses, commending them where commendation is due and offering suggestions about how they might improve and where they need to apply greater effort. Written report cards offer the opportunity for teachers to evaluate students' behavior and noncognitive traits as well. Do they participate in class activities? Do they complete their assignments on time? Do they work well with others? Are they good citizens of the school?

We should have learned several lessons from the unfortunate experience of the No Child Left Behind era. First, tests are most valuable when they have no stakes attached to them; high stakes—punishments and rewards—must be used with caution as they encourage negative consequences, such as score inflation, cheating, and curriculum narrowing. Second, a good evaluation system should ask students to demonstrate and explain what they know and can do, not simply pick a right answer to a preset question. Third, the testing system should not prioritize basic skills over other school studies. Fourth, testing should not determine what is taught and learned; tests are a measure, not the overriding goal of education.

Much of the current demand for testing centers on evaluating teachers, not evaluating students. States are devising many new tests in every subject area, even in the arts and physical education, even in kindergarten and pre-kindergarten, so that teachers may be judged by how much their students' test scores have gone up from September to May. The new tests are intended to measure teachers' ability to raise test scores.

Given what we know about the limitations of standardized tests, it is predictable that this method will not improve teaching and learning. It is predictable that reliance on this method will promote teaching to the test and narrowing the curriculum, even the occasional resort to cheating.

There are better ways to hold teachers accountable, and they don't involve high-stakes testing.

Montgomery County, Maryland, has a well-established evaluation program called Peer Assistance and Review, or PAR. The county public schools enroll 145,000 students, one-third of whom are low income. PAR should be a national model of teacher evaluation, but Race to the Top has diverted attention from this successful method. It provides extra support for teachers who are struggling, both new teachers and experienced teachers, and it removes teachers who are unable or unwilling to improve. PAR engages senior teachers who are master teachers to mentor those who need help. After serving as mentors for three years, the master teachers return to their teaching assignments.[9]

The system works with two groups of teachers: new teachers with no teaching experience and experienced teachers who received poor ratings from their principal. These teachers are assigned a "consulting teacher" to help them improve. The consulting teachers help teachers plan their lessons and review student work; they model lessons and identify research-based instructional strategies; they team teach with them and find appropriate resources. A panel of eight teachers and eight principals reviews the performance of the new and experienced teachers who have received one year of PAR support. The panel decides whether to offer the struggling veterans another year of PAR, to confirm their success, or to terminate their employment. The PAR panel has fired more than two hundred low-performing teachers for failure to improve. In the decade previous to PAR, only five teachers had been removed from their jobs.[10]

This method of teacher evaluation has the support of teachers and principals. It works. It identifies teachers who are doing a poor job and helps them get better or removes them from the classroom. It relies on trust and professionalism. It does not rely on test scores.

Can we hold teachers, principals, and schools accountable without the current regime of standardized testing? Yes, we can.

Here is another model. New York City has a group of nearly thirty schools that banded together to try a different approach to teaching and learning in the mid-1990s. They did not want their students to be subject to the standardized-testing regime. They preferred performance assessment, where students were expected to demonstrate what they knew and could do to the satisfaction of a review panel of teachers, parents, and other observers. Classes at these schools emphasize teaching through discussion and inquiry. A dozen years after the New York Performance Standards Consortium began its work, it reported on its findings. The schools in the consortium have served a representative enrollment of the city's children, with the same demographics as other public schools. Compared with students in other public schools, its students are less likely to drop out, more likely to graduate, more likely to go to college, and more likely to stay in college. The consortium schools are unusually successful in educating students who are English-language learners and students with disabilities. Such long-term, real-life outcomes are better indicators of school success than test scores.[11]

Here is another possible model. Just imagine that every school district and state had a team of expert educators who regularly visited and inspected schools. They would review student work and meet with a school's principal, teachers, parents, and students. They would analyze the demographics, the curriculum, the staff, the resources, and the condition of the school. They would gauge the readiness and progress of students who advanced to the next level of schooling, from elementary school to middle school, from middle school to high school, and from high school to postsecondary studies. Schools that are struggling to meet the needs of their students would get frequent visits. Schools that are successful would require fewer inspections; some might get a visit only once in three or four years. The evaluation team would make recommendations to help schools improve and send in support personnel when needed. It would prod the authorities to make sure the school got the resources and support it needed. The goal of the evaluation should be continuous improvement, not a letter grade or a threat of closure.

There may be other models that would work. States and districts should be enabled to devise their own approaches, free from the perverse incentives and stigmatization of the high-stakes testing regime.

Accountability should be turned into responsibility. Those in charge of state and local systems should be accountable and responsible for supporting schools in their care, not for closing them down. If they don't know how to help them, they should not be in charge. Accountability begins at the top, not the bottom. Those in charge of school systems should have the experience and wisdom to make helpful changes in public policy, and they should respect the professionals in the schools. Adults should take responsibility for making schools work better to meet the needs of children and young people and to uphold high standards for the quality of education. Professional educators should be treated as professionals whose judgment matters, not as cogs in a machine, nor as compliant civil servants bound to obey their superior.

The overemphasis on standardized testing in the past decade and more has undermined the quality of education and demoralized professional educators. Our standards and expectations for our students must be much higher and more complex than the skills needed to pass a standardized test. If we want students to be creative, if we want them to be ingenious, if we want them to be thoughtful and serious of purpose, then we must realign our means and our ends.

CHAPTER 29

Strengthen the Profession

SOLUTION NO. 8 *Insist that teachers, principals, and superintendents be professional educators.*

One of the most disheartening aspects of the current reform movement is its disdain for the education profession. In many states, governors and mayors have sought out non-educators, or people with meager experience in education, for positions of leadership. They have at times selected non-educators as state commissioners of education and district superintendents. Sometimes they choose a business leader, assuming that education should operate like any commercial enterprise, recording gains every quarter. Or they choose a lawyer, assuming that he or she has the legal skills to negotiate with others. Or they choose a military leader, assuming that command authority may overcome all barriers to change. Some of the worst education policies today, especially those that rely exclusively on standardized testing, have been imposed by non-educators who were wrongly hired as state or city commissioners of education. People who have devoted their careers to education are rightly offended when someone with little knowledge or experience of education is chosen to rule over them and redesign the conditions of their work.

To raise the quality of education in our schools, states and districts must strengthen the education profession.

Ideally, teachers should have a four-year degree with a major in the subject or subjects they plan to teach. Those who enter teaching should be well educated. They should be able to pass qualifying examinations for entry into professional education programs by demonstrating their command of reading, writing, and mathematical skills, as well as mastery of their subject or discipline.

Once they are admitted into a professional education program, they should engage in a year of study of such subjects as cognitive science, literacy, child development and adolescent psychology, the sociology of the family and the community, cultural diversity, the needs of students with disabilities, the nature of testing, and the history, politics, and economics of education. They should deepen their knowledge of the subject or subjects they plan to teach, with opportunities to plan lessons and work with mentors. They should practice teaching under the guidance of an experienced teacher. No one should be allowed to teach who has not spent a year in the study and practice of the profession.

Once hired, they should work closely with a mentor teacher. The school and the district should provide frequent opportunities for professional development, collaboration, and intellectual stimulation for teachers, giving them opportunities to learn more about their field as well as to work with colleagues who share their interests.

Principals should be chosen from the ranks of master teachers. Before they become principals, they should have at least seven or eight years of experience in the classroom. Their most important job as principal will be to evaluate and help teachers. They can't do that unless they are accomplished teachers themselves.

Superintendents should be experienced educators. In order to have the respect of those they lead, they should have a strong background as a teacher and a principal. It is foolish to choose non-educators to run school systems because they don't know as much as those they lead. This is a recipe for hit-or-miss leadership. The superintendent should be knowledgeable about teaching and learning, about children, about curriculum, about building relationships with parents and communities, and about defusing conflict. Working with a business manager, the superintendent should make decisions about the budget and capital planning from the perspective of an educator who puts the core mission of the schools first.

Teachers, principals, and superintendents should work closely with parents, enlisting their support and explaining how they can help their children do well in school. Knowing how important parents are in the education of their children, educators should cultivate respectful and cooperative relationships with parents.

Other advanced nations recognize the importance of the education profession. Finland, for example, would not allow anyone to teach or to be a principal or superintendent who was not a professional educator.

It is unfortunate that many states are actually lowering standards for teachers, principals, and superintendents while claiming to be raising standards for students. This is inconsistent. It makes no sense. Students need well-prepared, professional teachers; teachers need experienced principals whom they trust; and the school system needs a steady and wise hand at the helm.

Colleges of education should raise their standards for entry and enrich their curricula. They should develop partnerships with colleges that teach the liberal arts so that future teachers may work to strengthen their subject matter knowledge as well as the pedagogical skills to teach it.

States should raise their standards for certifying teachers. They should not accept credentials earned online. Future teachers need practical, hands-on experience in real classrooms with real children, not a point-and-click virtual experience.

Governors and state boards of education should appoint experienced educators to manage the state education department and educational institutions.

Members of the public should insist that those who teach and lead the schools enrolling their children be well qualified, well prepared, and experienced.

The education profession must become more professional, not less so. In a professional environment, professionals have the autonomy to do their work and are not expected to follow scripted programs or orders written by nonprofessionals. Good schools cannot be mass-produced like automobiles; every good school has its own culture, reflecting the character of the community and competence of its staff. All past efforts to make schools "teacher-proof" have failed. Schools should not operate like factories that turn out identical products. Good schools are akin to families, in which every member of the family is different and every member of the family matters; they are akin to orchestras, a cooperative effort that requires skilled performers in every role, guided by a skilled conductor.

Teachers must be free to express their concerns without fear of reprisal. Principals should be free to question district policy when they believe it is harmful to students and staff morale. Superintendents should be free to challenge the school board. There should be healthy dialogue about education issues. No one should fear to speak openly about issues of concern to all.

In a healthy profession, all those who engage in its practice are professionals. They are well prepared. They are responsible to do their best and to adhere to the expectations and the ethics of their profession. To have a great educational system, we must build a respected profession. And politicians should stop telling educators how to do their work.

CHAPTER 30

Protect Democratic Control of Public Schools

SOLUTION NO. 9 *Public schools should be controlled by elected school boards or by boards in large cities appointed for a set term by more than one elected official.*

In the past decade, reformers have sought to centralize control over education policy so that the reforms they favor may be imposed without debate or delay. They say, "We can't wait." They argue that school boards are obstacles to speedy reform. They want national standards, national tests, weak unions, and performance pay tied to test scores; they want the freedom to open privately managed charter schools without having to take local opinion into account; they want the freedom to close public schools without listening to the parents or communities that oppose the closing of their schools; and they want the freedom to fire teachers without being slowed down by due process or hearings.

Matt Miller, an advocate of the new reforms at the Center for American Progress, argued, not entirely facetiously, "First, kill all the school boards."[1] He recommended the nationalization of education policy as well as mayoral control of urban districts. He claimed that the elimination of school boards would make it possible to install the new reform ideas, which would promptly lift test scores and graduation rates. His view reflected the common belief among reformers that checks and balances get in the way of their preferred policies.

The United States has an unusually decentralized school system. There are about 14,000 school districts, each with its own local school board. There are 50 state school boards, plus the school boards of the

District of Columbia and various territories. And there is the federal Department of Education. If this seems like a lot of decentralization, consider that in 1940 there were about 117,000 local school boards.[2]

Education in this nation operates on the basis of federalism. Federalism refers to a system of shared power, a balance of power among local school boards, state authorities, and the federal government. In this sharing of power, the federal government sets the basic ground rules protecting the civil rights of students but by law has no role in setting curriculum or instructional standards. Education is not mentioned in the Constitution. It has long been a state and local function. The states have primary responsibility for maintaining and funding public education. The federal government acts in a supportive role. It supplies about 10 percent of total funding; the states and localities provide the other 90 percent.

American education is a patchwork quilt, with responsibility for funding and managing education parceled out among the various jurisdictions.

The federal role in education began modestly in 1867, when the U.S. Office of Education was established to collect information about the "condition and progress of education" in the nation. This was the historic role of the federal government, to gather and publish accurate information about the schools, the students, the funding, and the programs available in the nation. In 1914 and 1917, Congress passed legislation to fund and encourage vocational and industrial education in the schools. During the Depression of the 1930s, the federal government established the National Youth Administration and the Civilian Conservation Corps as independent agencies to provide jobs and training for young people, but these agencies were eliminated after World War II began.

Although there were periodic efforts to pass federal aid to education, Congress did not enact it until 1965, because neither party trusted the other to control education. Each feared that the other might use its power to impose partisan ideas. The region that needed federal aid the most, because it was the poorest, was the South, but southern members of Congress wanted to avoid federal interference in their racially segregated school systems. Local control in this era meant the freedom to segregate students by race and to fund the two systems inequitably.

In 1965, Congress enacted the Elementary and Secondary Education

Act at the behest of President Lyndon B. Johnson. ESEA, as it is known, is the basic framework for distributing federal aid to the schools. The primary purpose of the federal role in education, Congress then agreed, was equity for needy children. ESEA allocated federal funds to schools and districts based on the proportion of poor children enrolled in their schools. The purpose of federal aid was to grant those schools extra funding so that poor children would have smaller classes, textbooks, and the additional teachers and resources they needed. ESEA enabled the federal government to take an aggressive role in enforcing the Civil Rights Act of 1964, by threatening to withhold federal funds from districts that failed to desegregate their schools.

In 1964, Congress created Head Start—a preschool program for poor children—as part of the Johnson administration's War on Poverty. Over the years, Congress authorized many other programs for needy students, such as aid for students with disabilities. Congress initially authorized the National Assessment of Educational Progress to administer tests to national and regional samples of students, and the first assessment was offered in 1969; in 1992, NAEP began reporting the scores of states that volunteered to be assessed. Most states participated, but not all. Participation in NAEP testing did not become mandatory for all states until the passage of NCLB.

In 1979, Congress established the U.S. Department of Education. Its advocates, primarily the National Education Association, thought that education would assume greater importance and perhaps greater funding if it had a cabinet-level position. That legislation passed while President Jimmy Carter, a Democrat, was in office. His successor, Ronald Reagan, was not at all pleased to have a department of education.

As the federal role grew, both parties agreed that the federal government should not tell states and districts how to run their schools. Together they maintained an understanding that the department would grant financial aid but not take a directive role, other than to ensure that the money was spent in accordance with the law. A decade before the establishment of the department, Congress enacted a specific prohibition to prevent federal officials from interfering in matters of curriculum and instruction.[3]

Both by tradition and with respect to funding, the states are—or have been—the primary actors in providing and overseeing public education. Every state has its own laws and regulations, but most are committed by their state constitutions to provide a free public education to their children. Most states have specific provisions in their constitutions prohibiting any public funding of sectarian schools.

State legislatures regulate the operation of public schools, but the actual day-to-day oversight rests with local school boards. Across the nation, 95 percent of local school boards are elected by popular vote. In some urban districts, school boards are appointed by the mayor or by a combination of different elected officials.

All of this is background to the current debates about who should control the schools. As a result of President Bush's No Child Left Behind and President Obama's Race to the Top, the federal role changed dramatically in only a decade. Its powers expanded far beyond the imaginings of the legislators who passed ESEA in 1965 or who created the Department of Education in 1979.

No Child Left Behind put the federal government, with its relatively minor financial contribution, in the driver's seat. The law requires all public schools to test all students in grades 3 through 8 in reading and mathematics, and it mandates specific sanctions for schools that do not make what the law defines as "adequate yearly progress." No Child Left Behind passed with strong bipartisan support. For many years afterward, no one in Congress looked back to wonder why it had ditched federalism. After NCLB, the federal government assumed a command-and-control role that was never envisioned in 1965 or in 1979. For the first time in history, school districts and states had to ask permission from the U.S. Department of Education to change their plans to meet federal goals.

Race to the Top elevated the U.S. Department of Education into the equivalent of a national ministry of education. Building on the precedent established by NCLB, the Department of Education aggressively took charge of the nation's education agenda and forcefully demanded that states and districts enact certain policies if they wanted to win a share of $5 billion in economic stimulus funds. If states wanted the money, they had to accept the conditions spelled out by Secretary Duncan. In 2009, the states were in deep fiscal distress and of course they wanted the money. So they accepted the conditions and they applied. The Obama administration pretended that states participated of their own volition, thus maintaining the fiction that Race to the Top was "voluntary" and that the federal government was not calling the tune.

Many states rewrote their laws—agreeing to expand the number of charter schools, to evaluate teachers by test scores, and to adopt Common Core standards—in hopes of winning federal money.

Long before 2014, it was obvious that no state would meet the NCLB target; no state could claim that all of its students were proficient. Since Congress repeatedly failed to reauthorize NCLB (but extended it annually), Duncan offered waivers to states that agreed to accept his conditions. He canceled the 2014 deadline and substituted his own conditions. To obtain waivers, states had to agree to comply with the same conditions included in Race to the Top. They had to agree to adopt "college and career-readiness standards," which most states understood as the Common Core State Standards that were funded mainly by the Gates Foundation and promoted by the Obama administration. They had to agree to test students to measure progress toward meeting the goals of college and career readiness; these were the tests funded by the Obama administration to assess the Common Core standards. They had to agree to submit their standards and assessments to the U.S. Department of Education for review. They had to agree to evaluate teachers and principals using student test scores as a significant part of their evaluation. They had to agree to establish a system of recognizing schools as "reward," "focus," and "priority," with a plan to intervene aggressively in the "priority" schools, which were the lowest performing. They had to develop a plan to establish measurable objectives for all their schools.[4]

The combination of NCLB and Race to the Top changed the role of the federal government in American education. The Bush administration and the Obama administration, with the active (and in the case of Race to the Top, passive) consent of Congress, put the federal government in a dominant position. Federalism—understood as a balancing of powers among three levels of government—was eviscerated. The U.S. Department of Education took charge of driving school reform, imposing the policies it preferred. It gave directions to the state departments of education. The U.S. secretary of education became the nation's superintendent of schools, telling every district and every school what was required of them to receive federal funding. For the first time in history, the federal government took control of the nation's public schools.

As 2014 neared, many states applied for waivers to avoid the sanctions in NCLB. The states that won waivers had to accept the same conditions as states that won millions in Race to the Top funding, but the waivers brought no new funding, only new mandates. Among other conditions attached to the NCLB waivers, states agreed to rank schools by their test scores and to evaluate teachers to a significant degree by student test scores. As states began identifying "reward" schools at the top and "priority" schools at the bottom, they discovered an unremarkable fact. Schools in well-off districts were doing very well. The "priority" schools were overwhelmingly located in poor neighborhoods, serving high proportions of African American and Hispanic students. Perhaps as many as five thousand schools would be eligible for aggressive interventions, staff firings, even closures. Most were in impoverished neighborhoods, serving children of color. Where would thousands of new principals be found? Where would tens of thousands, or hundreds of thousands, of "great" teachers be found?

For the first time in American history, states would rate teachers and principals by their students' test scores to comply with federal directives. How many will be fired? Will they be correctly identified? Will they be the worst teachers, or will they be victims of a flawed method or teachers who had the bad luck to teach students with high needs? Will there be a game of musical chairs in which educators fired by one district are hired by another district? Or is there somewhere a huge cadre of new educators, waiting their turn to enter the profession and willing to take their chances at being next in line to be fired?

This, for now, is the federal role: The federal government controls the agenda. It issues requirements for those who want federal money; that money may be only 10 percent of the district budget, but no district or state can afford to walk away from millions of dollars in federal aid. To underline the federal government's insistence on test scores as the measure of all things, the U.S. Department of Education informed colleges of education, both public and independent, that they would be held accountable for the test scores of the students taught by their graduates. This was a stretch indeed, and there was no research evidence to support this demand.

What happened to the state role? The states are now in a reactive mode, scrambling to comply with the new federal mandates and regulations. The state education departments have become the go-betweens, making sure that districts comply with the blizzard of federal requirements. There is no room for creativity or innovation. The state education departments now exist to enforce compliance and to add their own rules and mandates.

Under the present setup, local school boards are nearly irrelevant. The most important decisions are increasingly made by politicians and bureaucrats in Washington, D.C. To an extent unknown before in United States history, the federal Department of Education and its grantees are deciding what to teach, how to teach, who should teach, how to evaluate teachers, when to fire teachers, what kind of organization may qualify for public funding, and which education institutions will be allowed or not allowed to train teachers. Power over education has shifted decisively to the federal government. If these projections seem extreme, consider how improbable it would have been in 1980 or 1990 to imagine that the federal government would now be setting the rules for testing students and evaluating teachers.

We are headed in the wrong direction. American education should not be standardized and controlled by federal bureaucrats and congressional mandates. We achieved national greatness without a ministry of education regulating every school, every district, and every state. This is a big and diverse nation. The needs of schools in rural Nebraska are not the same as the needs of schools in District 10 in the South Bronx in New York City. For that matter, there is great variation in the needs of schools within the same state and often within the same district. One size does not fit all.

The very notion of a "Race to the Top" betrays the equity mission of the historic federal role in education. A "race" implies winners and losers. Equity implies a commitment to the education of every child. The reason that the federal government became involved in funding education was to promote equity, not to select winners and losers. Competition inevitably favors the strong and disadvantages the weak. The role of the federal government is not to honor the strong but to level the playing field for those students who have the least and need the most.

The U.S. Department of Education should reclaim its mantle as an agency whose fundamental mission is to promote equality of educational opportunity. At a time when nearly one-quarter of the children in this nation live in poverty, the U.S. Department of Education should promote equity for needy children, sponsor first-rate research, and advance educational policies that are supported by research and evidence. It should award grants based on need, not on competitions among districts and states. It should defend the civil rights of all children. It should advocate for early childhood education, class size reduction, social services, and other research-based policies for all students. It should provide research and information about the best programs across the country and around the world. It should inform the public and the profession about appropriate and inappropriate uses of assessment. It should continue its periodic national assessments of subjects taught in school, based on samples of the student population. It should provide research-based information to assist teachers and parents of children with special needs. The secretary of education should use his bully pulpit to keep before the public a vision of good education.

It should never again attempt to control every school in the United States. No one in Congress or the U.S. Department of Education has the knowledge, experience, or wisdom to impose his or her ideas and plans on every school and community in the nation. Just as we do not expect the U.S. military to police the streets of every city, town, and hamlet, we should not expect the Department of Education to direct the education of every child in every public school.

What, then, of the state education departments? They should resume their roles as agencies that serve the schools and districts of their states. They should provide technical assistance, resources, professional development, and other forms of support that districts may need. They should work together with teachers and scholars to develop curriculum frameworks so that there is continuity in teaching history, science, and other subjects in districts across the state. It should not be left to every district whether or when to teach science, the arts, civics, and history; state curricula should reflect modern scholarship, not religious or local opinion.

Every state should have teams of inspectors who visit schools and provide expert advice, who are empowered to send the schools whatever support services and resources the students need. Those who work in state education departments should see themselves as co-equals to those who work in schools and district offices, as partners and colleagues who collaborate to reach a shared goal: the education of the children of the district and the state. The state education commissioner should see himself or herself as an employee of the state board, not as the person who gives orders to schools that everyone must obey. In many states, there is more experience in the schools and in the district offices than in the state offices. The state commissioners should respect the wisdom of those who are closest to the schools of their community and should intervene only when a local board or district leadership is corrupt, irresponsible, or incompetent.

Then we come to local school boards. The corporate reformers don't like school boards. They think they should be abolished or rendered toothless. In urban districts, the reformers want the mayor to have absolute control, unchecked by a school board with the power to question or overrule his decisions. In recent times, mayoral control began in Boston in 1992, in Chicago in 1995, in Cleveland in 1998, in New York City in 2002, and in the District of Columbia in 2007. Detroit tried mayoral control in 1999, but voters abandoned it in 2004 (which was probably just as well, since one of the mayors after 2004 went to jail).

The results of mayoral control have been mixed at best. From the reformers' perspective, mayoral control is a success because it enables the mayor to close schools irrespective of community opinion and to open privately managed charter schools. The reformers consider it essential to sever any connection between the schools and any democratic control that might impede privatization. But the downside of mayoral control is that it eliminates the role of the public in public education. It eliminates the democratic nature of public education. It produces disengagement and anger among parents and community members, whose opinions are excluded from any decisions affecting their children and their communities. When people appear at hearings about school closings and their voices are disregarded, it erodes trust and civic engagement. Community anger about school reform was a leading cause of the defeat of Washington, D.C., mayor Adrian Fenty when he sought reelection in 2010. Mayor Michael Bloomberg's school reform policies featured school closings, opening of more than a hundred charter schools, and a relentless emphasis on standardized tests to evaluate schools and teachers; by the end of the mayor's third term, only 22 percent of New York City voters wanted his style of autocratic control to continue. Chicago's system of mayoral control and its unending parade of reforms stoked the anger of the Chicago Teachers Union, which went on strike in 2012 for the first time in twenty-five years. When voters in most precincts in Chicago were asked whether they favored mayoral control of the schools, a resounding 87 percent said no.[5]

There is a reason that 95 percent of school districts in the United States have an elected board. Schools are a central part of the fabric of life in communities, villages, towns, and small cities. In big cities, the school boards are supposed to represent the interests of the communities that are served, whether by election or by appointment. Parents and members of local communities should have a voice in the democratic process of decision making. They should be heard. The purpose of the board in major urban districts should be to allow public participation, not to shut it out. Most people don't like the idea of autocracy. Most Americans think that when it is their children and their tax dollars, they should be able to choose the people making the decisions or at the very least to be heard respectfully.

The reformers are correct when they say that school boards are an obstacle to radical change. They move slowly. They argue. They listen to different points of view. They make mistakes. They are not bold and transformative. They prefer incremental change. In short, they are a democratic forum. They are a check and balance against concentrated power in one person or one agency. The same complaints may be justly lodged against state legislatures and against Congress. They debate, they move slowly, one house checks the impulses of the other, they listen to their constituents. That's democracy.

Authoritarian governments can move decisively. They listen to no one outside their inner circle. They are able to make change without pondering or taking opposing views into account. But they too make mistakes. And because they do not listen to the opposition, they may make even larger mistakes than democratic bodies. There is an arrogance to unchecked power. There is no mechanism to vet its ideas, so it plunges forward, sometimes into disastrous schemes.

Local control of the public schools is a venerable American tradition. American public schools should have elected local school boards. Their power is not absolute: they work within the context of federal and state law regarding civil rights and curriculum standards. The local board should be a forum for public opinion. The reason for this is clear. The school board picks the superintendent, and the superintendent works for the school board. When she makes a major policy decision, she must stand up in public and explain that decision. When she decides on a budget, she must stand up in public and explain it. Members of the public get to comment. If the decision or the budget meets overwhelming public rejection, the superintendent must rethink the decision. She cannot do whatever she wants or whatever the mayor wants without a thorough public airing. If the school board flouts public opinion, its members may go down to defeat.

In major cities that have an appointed board, different officials—not just the mayor—should select the board. The appointed board should serve for set terms, not at the pleasure of the appointing authority, so that members have a measure of independence. In big cities with an appointed board, there should be local school councils where parents can become involved, work with school staff to review the budget, and have a say in the education of their children.

If we believe in democracy, and if we believe that public schools must act in concert with the principles of democracy, then we must reject authoritarianism from any quarter, be it the mayor, the state education department, or the federal government. No one should exercise untrammeled control over education policy and have the power to ignore public opinion. The children belong to the parents, and the schools belong to the public, not to the mayor or the governor or the president. Public officials are elected to serve the public, not to control it.

No reform idea is so compelling and so urgent that it requires the suspension of democracy. Supporters of top-down reforms say that the situation is so dire that "we cannot wait." Their ideas are not good enough to require the sacrifice of democracy. Only in wartime do we willingly suspend our right to have a say about how we are governed, and even then we lose our liberties at our peril. The rise or fall of test scores and graduation rates is not a sufficient reason to eliminate democratic participation by the people. Elected officials should respect the judgment of professional educators about how to run schools and work cooperatively with them to make sure that the needs of students are met and that the budget is sufficient and responsibly managed, but educators too ultimately work for the public.

Schools need the support of the entire community, including parents, educators, community leaders, civic leaders, business leaders, and the mayor. Two decades of experimentation with the governance of public schools has demonstrated certain fundamental truths: Some decisions should be made at the national level; some at the state level; and some at the local level. Every school should be able to respond to the needs of the children it enrolls and have the resources to do it well.

Because public schools need the support of the public that funds them, they should have the widest possible community support. Community support means democratic governance. School districts should be governed by those who are willing to work diligently to improve them and by those who have the greatest stake in the success of the children and the community.

CHAPTER 31

The Toxic Mix

SOLUTION NO. 10 *Devise actionable strategies and specific goals to reduce racial segregation and poverty.*

There is one certain conclusion that can be drawn from studies of educational achievement: poverty has a negative effect on student learning. On every test, whether in reading or in mathematics, the results are stratified by family income. Students from the wealthiest families tend to have the highest scores, and students from the poorest families tend to have the lowest scores. Every standardized test produces this result, whether it is the SAT, the ACT, state tests, the National Assessment of Educational Progress, or international tests.

This does not mean that poor children can't learn. Even though they start school far behind their advantaged peers, some poor children will overcome the odds and achieve academic success. But make no mistake: the odds of success are against them. Children who live in poverty have less access to health care, are more likely to have undiagnosed illnesses, are more likely to miss school because of illness, are less likely to have educated parents, are less likely to have books in the house, are more likely to live in unsafe neighborhoods, are more likely to be hungry and homeless, are more likely to change schools because of their family's inability to pay the rent, and are less likely to have economic security than their peers who grow up in middle- and upper-income families.

Nearly a quarter of children in the United States are now growing up in poverty. By the Census Bureau's calculation, the percentage of children living in poverty today is about the same as it was in 1964. For children who are white, the current poverty rate is 12.5 percent. For children who are Asian, the poverty rate is 13 percent. For children who are Hispanic, it is 34 percent. For children who are black, it is 37 percent. This should be considered a national scandal.

Cognitive scientists recognize that poverty damages children's lives. A report prepared by the National Scientific Council on the Developing Child concluded that children's brain development is affected by excessive stress. A certain amount of stress and challenge is "essential to survival." But, the report said, "severe, uncontrollable, chronic adversity . . . can have an adverse impact on brain architecture." Children who have been subject to abuse or neglect, children who have been exposed to drugs and alcohol, children whose parents face economic hardship, children whose mothers are depressed, may be subject to "toxic stress." The report suggests specific ways to reduce toxic stress: allow parents to have family leave to take care of newborns and infants; make sure that low-income parents who want to care for their young children have the means to do so rather than seek immediate employment; reduce the turnover of staff in programs that promote stable relationships between children and caregivers; provide expert help to parents who are struggling to deal with their child's behavioral problems or developmental delays; provide qualified clinicians to help young children and their mothers deal with the consequences of toxic stress; change public policies that force mothers of young children to return to the workforce as a condition of receiving public assistance. It is humane and cost-effective for society to help all young mothers learn nurturing skills, enable them to spend more time with their children, and help them to raise them well.[1]

Poverty is the most important factor contributing to low academic achievement. Even high expectations, as important as they are, are unlikely to be enough to overcome the adversity that results from not having enough money to meet life's basic needs.

Poverty is not the only factor that affects academic achievement. Racial segregation also contributes to low academic achievement. As the U.S. Supreme Court said in the *Brown v. Board of Education* decision of 1954, "To separate them [children in grade and high schools] from others of similar age and qualifications solely because of their race generates a feeling of inferiority as to their status in the community that may affect their hearts and minds in a way unlikely ever to be undone." At the time of the *Brown* decision, seventeen states and many districts had laws requiring the segregation of students by race. The Supreme Court decision overturned such laws in 1954, but segregation as a matter of fact has long survived the demise of de jure segregation. Today, racial segregation remains a pervasive fact of life for millions of black children, primarily as a result of residential segregation. The only difference is that today they are often in schools with equally impoverished Hispanic children. Children who are black or Hispanic suffer from higher rates of poverty and segregation than white or Asian children.

School segregation is increasing, according to the Civil Rights Project at the University of California in Los Angeles, which cites the expansion of charter schools as one of the causes. Sadly, desegregation is no longer a priority for the federal government. Few federal programs mention desegregation as a prerequisite or even a goal when allocating competitive grants. The project reports that segregation has recently intensified for Latino students, "who are attending more intensely segregated and impoverished schools than they have for generations. The segregation increases have been the most dramatic in the West. The typical Latino student in the region attends a school where less than a quarter of their classmates are white; nearly two-thirds are other Latinos; and two-thirds are poor." The most segregated schools for students of Latino or Hispanic origin are in California, New York, and Texas.[2]

According to the project, 80 percent of Latino students and 74 percent of black students attend majority-nonwhite schools. Forty-three percent of Latinos and 38 percent of black students attend intensely segregated schools, where fewer than 10 percent of the students are white. Fifteen percent of black and Latino students attend what the project calls "apartheid schools," where white students make up 1 percent or less of the population.

Segregation is most concentrated in the nation's cities. Half of the more than sixteen hundred schools in New York City are more than 90 percent black and Hispanic. Half of the black students in Chicago and one-third of the black students in New York City attend apartheid schools.[3]

Many black students are doubly segregated, by race and by poverty. The report finds that "the typical black student is now in a school where almost two out of every three classmates (64 percent) are low-income, nearly double the level in schools of the typical white or Asian student (37 percent and 39 percent, respectively)." The most segregated schools for black students are in New York, Illinois, and Michigan, the least segregated in Washington, Nebraska, and Kansas. The project reports that resegregation of black students is on the rise in the South. While great progress was made in the 1970s and 1980s, the South began backsliding in the 1990s after the Supreme Court allowed districts to abandon their desegregation commitments.

The greatest forward movement for desegregation—and the most significant narrowing of the achievement gap—occurred when the federal government and the federal courts worked in concert to integrate schools. However, for at least the past decade, the federal government and the courts have abandoned their interest in desegregation as a national priority. In the absence of committed leadership by elected officials, desegregation has disappeared from the national agenda and from public consciousness as a valuable goal. Now the media unthinkingly celebrate the seemingly miraculous (and isolated) successes of all-black or all-minority schools without questioning whether racially segregated schools should exist.

The proliferation of charter schools contributes to the problem. Minnesota is the state with the longest history of charter schools. The Institute on Race and Poverty at the University of Minnesota Law School issued critical reports on the state's charter schools in 2008 and 2012, questioning both their performance and their high levels of segregation. The reports concluded that charter schools in Minneapolis and St. Paul, the Twin Cities, consistently underperformed comparable public schools. The charter schools make bold promises to minority parents, but those promises are broken. The 2008 report found that "most offer low income parents and parents of color an inferior choice—a choice between low-performing traditional public schools and charter schools that perform even worse." The charters are characterized by intense racial and economic segregation: "The data show that charter schools are . . . even more segregated than the already highly-segregated traditional public schools. In some predominantly white urban and suburban neighborhoods, charter schools also serve as outlets for white flight from traditional public schools that are racially more diverse than their feeder neighborhoods." In its 2012 update, the Institute on Race and Poverty found that charter school enrollment had grown sharply and that these damaging trends continued: charter school students were severely segregated, and the performance of students in charter schools lagged behind that of students in traditional public schools.[4]

John Hechinger of Bloomberg News visited the charter schools of the Twin Cities, including an all-black school in St. Paul dedicated to children of East Africa, where students learn Arabic and Somali; a German-immersion school that was 90 percent white, where children studied with interns from Germany, Austria, and Switzerland and learned to waltz; and other schools that were nearly all Asian, Hispanic, or Native American. Referring to national trends, he observed that "six decades after the U.S. Supreme Court struck down 'separate but equal' schools for blacks and whites, segregation is growing because of charter schools, privately run public schools that educate 1.8 million children."[5]

The UCLA Civil Rights Project noted that "the Obama Administration, like the Bush Administration, has taken no significant action to increase school integration or to help stabilize diverse schools as racial change occurs in urban and suburban housing markets and schools. Small positive steps in civil rights enforcement have been undermined by the Obama Administration's strong pressure on states to expand charter schools—the most segregated sector of schools for black students."

Despite loud cries about the need to reduce achievement gaps related to race, ethnicity, and income, the one issue that few in the corporate reform community discuss is desegregation. This is odd because, as the Civil Rights Project notes, "schools of concentrated poverty and segregated minority schools are strongly related to an array of factors that limit educational opportunities and outcomes. These include less experienced and less qualified teachers, high levels of teacher turnover, less successful peer groups and inadequate facilities and learning materials. There is also a mounting body of evidence indicating that desegregated schools are linked to important benefits for all children, including prejudice reduction, heightened civic engagement, more complex thinking and better learning outcomes in general."[6]

In the absence of active leadership by federal officials and the judiciary, the public is apathetic about racial and ethnic segregation, as well as socioeconomic segregation. The more that public officials assume nothing can be done, nothing is done, and these problems grow worse. Neither of the major federal efforts of the past generation—No Child Left Behind and Race to the Top—has even mentioned segregation, let alone attempted to reduce persistent racial and ethnic isolation. Both programs are silent on the subject. While these programs directed billions of federal aid, they did not leverage any funding to promote desegregation of schools or communities, and in their demand to expand the charter sector, they may have worsened the problem. As black and Hispanic students remain segregated in large numbers, their academic achievement remains low. Then federal law stigmatizes their schools as "failing" and recommends firing their principals and their teachers and closing their schools. By punishing those who teach low-performing students of color, these federal programs contribute more instability to the students' lives and discourage educators who might want to work with these students.

The evidence for the value of integration has grown stronger with the perspective of time. Social science research shows that peer effects matter. When students go to school with others who are highly motivated, it lifts their performance as well. Schools attended by affluent and academically successful students not only tend to have a richer curriculum and smaller classes but also have the benefits of a better school climate and positive peer effects. The schools for the poor are likeliest to sacrifice time for the arts and other studies to make more time for standardized testing and test prep, for fear that if scores don't improve, the staff will be fired and the school will close. Segregated schools are also more likely to have harsh discipline policies, higher rates of suspension and expulsion, metal detectors, and high rates of teacher and student turnover.

As the Civil Rights Project report notes, nearly all of the nation's two thousand so-called dropout factories are "doubly segregated by race and poverty."[7]

The Civil Rights Project summarizes a rich body of research that demonstrates the positive value of desegregation on academic achievement, fostering critical thinking skills, and learning to work and communicate with people from different backgrounds. Black students who attended desegregated schools are more likely to have higher test scores and graduate from high school and college, in part because of the quality of their schooling but also because of the positive effects of having friends and associates who are academically engaged and headed to college.

Rucker Johnson, an economist at the University of California at Berkeley, has identified specific lifetime gains for blacks who attended desegregated schools. He examined the outcomes for children born between 1950 and 1970, throughout their lives, up to the year 2007. Johnson found that "school desegregation and the accompanied increases in school quality resulted in significant improvements in adult attainments for blacks . . . school desegregation significantly increased educational attainment and adult earnings, reduced the probability of incarceration, and improved adult health status; desegregation had no effects on whites across each of these outcomes. The results suggested that the mechanisms through which school desegregation led to beneficial adult attainment outcomes for blacks include . . . reductions in class size and increases in per-pupil spending."[8] Based on his longitudinal studies, Johnson concluded that the positive effects of school desegregation endure across generations: "I find a considerable impact of school desegregation that persists to influence the outcomes of the next generation, including increased math and reading test scores, reduced likelihood of grade repetition, increased likelihood of high school graduation and college attendance, improvements in college quality/selectivity, and increased racial diversity of student body at their selected college."[9]

David L. Kirp, referring to Johnson's studies, laments that our society has "turned away from one tool that has been shown to work: school desegregation." This approach, he argued, "has been unceremoniously ushered out, an artifact in the museum of failed social experiments." He regretted that the current crop of school reformers treats integration as "at best an irrelevance," a contrivance that diverts attention from their obsessive focus on bad teachers. He cited the latest research to show how the black-white achievement gap narrowed between 1970 and 1990, the high-water mark for integration, and how black children benefited. "The experience of an integrated education made all the difference in the lives of black children—and in the lives of their children as well."

Kirp cited recent studies that show how African American students who attended integrated schools fared better academically than those left behind in segregated schools and graduated at greater rates from high school and college. The analysis of his colleague Rucker Johnson revealed that "black youths who spent five years in desegregated schools have earned 25 percent more than those who never had that opportunity. Now in their 30s and 40s, they're also healthier—the equivalent of being seven years younger."[10]

Kirp pointed out that after the federal courts retreated from enforcing desegregation in the 1990s and allowed districts to abandon their desegregation efforts, the black-white gap stalled and, by some measures, widened. He concluded that "the failure of the No Child Left

Behind regimen to narrow the achievement gap offers the sobering lesson that closing underperforming public schools, setting high expectations for students, getting tough with teachers and opening a raft of charter schools isn't the answer. If we're serious about improving educational opportunities, we need to revisit the abandoned policy of school integration."[11]

Richard Rothstein, one of our nation's leading authorities on race, class, and schooling, points out that schools alone can never substantially narrow the achievement gap. He maintains that many of the allegedly "failing" schools are doing as well as they can in the light of enormous challenges of educating black children who live in poverty. He is convinced that the possibility of changing their life trajectory depends on "breaking up heavy concentrations of low-income minority children in urban schools, giving these children opportunities to attend majority middle-class schools outside their distressed neighborhoods." It is not busing that he wants, but residential integration. In his recent work, he reviewed the history of efforts in the 1970s to increase residential integration. As it happens, the most outspoken proponent for this idea was George Romney, first as governor of Michigan and then as secretary of the Department of Housing and Urban Development (HUD) under President Richard M. Nixon. George Romney recognized that the intense segregation experienced by blacks in urban districts was not the result of choice or accident; it was the consequence of decades of discrimination, of federal, state, and local policies permitting or ignoring racial restrictions in public housing, zoning ordinances, urban renewal programs, and highway construction projects that intentionally isolated blacks in cities and kept them out of the suburbs. He became convinced that only the federal government could break up residential segregation and enable or compel communities to desegregate. Romney and his staff shaped a program called Open Communities, with the intent of denying HUD funding to communities unless they agreed to accept subsidized low-income housing. Unfortunately, Nixon did not endorse Romney's bold idea, and it was quickly forgotten.[12]

Just as school integration proved to be politically unpalatable, so too did efforts to integrate housing. Faced with political intransigence, our leaders have dropped both goals. Instead, they promote ideas like the Common Core, increased testing, privatization, and competition. They offer Band-Aid solutions through No Child Left Behind and Race to the Top.

But the wounds caused by centuries of slavery, segregation, and discrimination cannot be healed by testing, standards, accountability, merit pay, and choice. Even if test scores go up in a public or charter school, the structural inequality of society and systematic inequities in our schools remain undisturbed. For every "miracle" school celebrated by the media, there are scores of "Dumpster schools," where the low-performing students are unceremoniously hidden away. This is not school reform, nor is it social reform. It is social neglect. It is a purposeful abandonment of public responsibility to address deep-seated problems that only public policy can overcome.

The tragic legacy of our history cannot be overcome by inexperienced college graduates who volunteer for a tour of duty in Harlem or Watts or the Mississippi Delta or by billions of public dollars diverted to vouchers and charters. We may look back, twenty or thirty years from now, and wonder why we abandoned public education and why we thought that privatization would end poverty.

What can we do?

We should set national goals to reduce segregation and poverty. In combination, these are the root causes of the achievement gaps between economic and racial groups. No child should grow up without medical care, go to bed hungry, or arrive in school without the necessary clothing. Our families need basic economic security. A child poverty rate in excess of 20 percent is shameful in one of the world's richest nations.

Education is a basic human right. It is impossible to imagine a modern society that does not educate its children, equitably and systematically. Our goal should be to provide a good school in every community. The quality of one's education should not be determined by one's zip code or by one's ability to pay taxes, fees, or tuition. To assure that all children arrive in school prepared for learning, we should provide universal high-quality preschool education. To meet the needs of children, every school should have a nurse, a social worker, after-school programs, and a library. Every school, regardless of its location, should offer small classes—small enough to allow teachers a chance to teach and students a chance to learn. Poor children need even more personal attention from their teachers and more academic support than affluent children. Instead, most of the large urban schools that children of the poor attend have classes of thirty or more students.

All children deserve a curriculum that includes the arts, history, civics, geography, the sciences, foreign languages, mathematics, and literature. Children of the poor need good schools and adequate resources as much as—perhaps even more than—children of the affluent, especially since they are far less likely to have their education supplemented by private art or music lessons after school or in the summer, as afforded the children in well-to-do families.

Federal, state, and local policy should be designed to remove every vestige of racial and ethnic discrimination from our public institutions. Public policy should leverage federal and state funding to reduce poverty and racial isolation in schools and housing and reduce the income inequality that has increased rapidly in recent years and is a plague on our society.

We cannot expect the schools alone to shoulder the burden of social change. They are part of the solution, but only a part. Neither addressing poverty alone nor focusing solely on schools is likely to transform children's lives sufficiently and give them the opportunities they need to succeed.

Are all of these changes expensive? Yes, but not nearly as expensive as the social and economic costs of crime, illness, violence, despair, and wasted human talent.

To accomplish these ambitious goals, we need leadership. We need leadership by the president, Congress, the judiciary, governors, state legislatures, and all our elected leaders at the state and local levels. We need the business community, foundations, academia, and the media to recognize that they have roles to play, that preserving public education and strengthening it rather than privatizing it is critically important to preserve our democracy. And that blaming and punishing the people who work in our neediest public schools for the persistence of social, economic, and educational inequities is not just wrong, but will further damage the children in whose interest the corporate reformers claim to be acting. We do not help children by demoralizing those who do the most difficult work with them under the most difficult conditions, every day.

Without a vision for a better society, without the leadership to turn the vision into reality, any talk of reform is empty verbiage.

CHAPTER 32

Privatization of Public Education Is Wrong

SOLUTION NO. 11 *Recognize that public education is a public responsibility, not a consumer good.*

In 1991, a businessman named Jamie Vollmer gave a speech to a group of teachers in Indiana. He was an executive at an ice cream company who had come to conduct an in-service program for educators. He told them they needed to operate more like his company, whose blueberry ice cream had been recognized by *People* magazine in 1984 as the "Best Ice Cream in America." He told the assembled teachers, "If I ran my business the way you people operate your schools, I wouldn't be in business for long."[1]

As he later told the story, he explained to the teachers that the schools were obsolete and that educators resist change because tenure protects them from accountability. Business, he thought, had it right. It operates on principles of "Zero defects! TQM [total quality management]! Continuous improvement!"

Not surprisingly, the teachers reacted with sullen hostility. When he finished his speech, a teacher innocently asked about his company's method of making the best ice cream. He boasted of its "super-premium" ingredients, nothing but the best. Then she asked a question:

"Mr. Vollmer," she said, leaning forward with a wicked eyebrow raised to the sky, "when you are standing on your receiving dock and you see an inferior shipment of blueberries arrive, what do you do?"

In the silence of that room, I could hear the trap snap . . . I was dead meat, but I wasn't going to lie.

"I send them back."

She jumped to her feet. "That's right!" she barked, "and we can never send back our blueberries. We take them big, small, rich, poor, gifted, exceptional, abused, frightened, confident, homeless, rude, and brilliant. We take them with ADHD, junior rheumatoid arthritis, and English as their second language. We take them all! Every one! And that, Mr. Vollmer, is why it's not a business. It's school!"

In an explosion, all 290 teachers, principals, bus drivers, aides, custodians, and secretaries jumped to their feet and yelled, "Yeah! Blueberries! Blueberries!"

Jamie Vollmer had an epiphany. From that day forward, he realized that schools could never operate like a business because they do not control their "raw material." They cannot sort the blueberries and reject those that are bruised or broken. They take them all.

He did not conclude that schools are fine the way they are. He concluded that they "must change what, when, and how we teach to give all children maximum opportunity to thrive in a post-industrial society. But educators cannot do this alone; these changes can occur only with the understanding, trust, permission, and active support of the surrounding community. For the most important thing I have learned is that schools reflect the attitudes, beliefs and health of the communities they serve, and therefore, to improve public education means more than changing our schools, it means changing America."

Vollmer understood what today's reformers do not. Public schools must accept all children. They cannot pick and choose among them. They cannot reject those who are homeless and those who don't speak English. They cannot "counsel out" those with low test scores or those with profound disabilities. They must find a place for students with behavioral problems. They are responsible for educating them all. Obviously, schools with selective admissions policies and schools with lotteries, whether they are public or private or charter, will have higher test scores and fewer discipline problems. It is easy to get high test scores when the students are ready, willing, and able to learn.

When corporate executives look at the public schools, they cannot understand why they move slowly; they want them to produce rapid and dramatic changes. They demand results, not explanations. They want scores to rise overnight. They believe in transformative change and disruptive innovation. They see this kind of lightning change in their own businesses. A hedge fund manager may place a bet and make millions of dollars in a few days, perhaps even overnight. An executive in the high-technology sector may introduce a new design or application that takes the market by storm in a matter of weeks or even days and changes the industry. Why can't schools work like that? Why can't we just break up the existing system, reinvent it, and start fresh?

Business leaders talk a lot about innovation and creative disruption. Sometimes it works; sometimes it produces spectacular failures. They accept the risk because they want the rewards, the possibility of hitting it big in the marketplace. Creative disruption does not work well in education, however, because education is a slow and incremental process of human development. Children learn one day at a time. Test scores are only one metric, the one that is easiest and cheapest to obtain, but they say more about the background of the student body than about the quality of the school or its teachers.

Whatever the flaws of the tests, they determine whether a school remains open or is closed. But any method designed to boost test scores in a short time will depend on memorization and rote drill and will not be educationally sound. Answers to multiple-choice questions may come quickly, but understanding comes slowly. Real education is about understanding and knowledge, about habits of mind and the ability to think independently, not the ability to click quickly through test questions and find the right answer. The current obsession with test scores is educational malpractice; it discourages creativity, thoughtfulness, ingenuity, and risk taking. These values, habits, and character traits matter far more in life than test scores.

Today, many private sector leaders feel sure, as Jamie Vollmer once did, that business has the right approach. Focus relentlessly on quality control, keep close watch on the metrics, manage the process, rank and rate the workers, reward the workers who get results, and fire those who don't. The formula for success in the competitive global marketplace of the twenty-first century requires businesses to pay close attention to their bottom lines. They must cut costs to succeed, and usually the highest cost is labor. To succeed, they must cut the number of employees, replace them with technology, or outsource their jobs to lower-wage nations. The equity investor Steven Rattner said in an interview with Fareed Zakaria: "Every company in America or, for that matter, every part of the world, they're tasked with looking at their costs and always say to themselves, is there a way to lower our costs? You, better than many—if not everybody in the world, knows we are living in a global world and companies have to produce efficiently in order to compete. And if you don't have the lowest costs, you will simply fail in the marketplace."[2]

Business leaders expect schools to compete by cutting their costs. The only way to do this is to reduce the number of teachers or lower the cost of teachers. That means schools must have larger classes or must replace teachers with technology or substitute low-wage, inexperienced teachers for costly experienced teachers. But does this produce better education? Small classes matter, especially for minority students in the elementary grades, students who don't speak English, students with disabilities, and students who can't keep up with the pace of instruction. There is no evidence that students learn more or better when taught on computers. Computers have many exciting uses in the classroom as a supplement to good teaching, as a vehicle for research and exploration, as a means for cooperative learning and student projects. But computers are not a satisfactory substitute for a human teacher.

What does the business model mean in educational terms? It means an obsessive devotion to testing, accountability, and data. Devotees of the business approach like to say, "You measure what you treasure." Believing this, they have fastened a pitiless regime of testing on the nation's schools that now reaches down as low as kindergarten, where children of five who should be playing and using their imaginations are being assessed for their "readiness" skills, sometimes several times a year. Some states even have standards and assessments for prekindergarten students. This is developmentally inappropriate. Children of this age need nurturing and play, not testing.

But is it true that we "measure what we treasure"? I would argue the contrary. What we treasure most are human relationships, friends and family, and we would never subject those relationships to any kinds of metrics. We do not measure how much we love our parents or spouses or children or friends. We may love some more than others, but we don't have a standardized gauge for that love, and if we did, we would never publish it to them or to the world. It would be cruel if we did something so foolish. If we treasure music or art or travel or home or a pet, how do we measure it? Why should we? Can anyone honestly say that a test score in reading or math is what they "treasure" more than anything else? The things we treasure most are the very things that cannot be measured with a yardstick or a scale or a test.

The current obsession with data and data-based decision making is not twenty-first-century thinking. It reflects the views of early-twentieth-century efficiency experts like Frederick Winslow Taylor, who carefully monitored the output of laborers, developed time-and-motion studies, and created benchmarks by which to judge the productivity of workers. Taylorism, as it is now known, encouraged educators to think of students as raw material to be shaped by the demands of the school, exposed to instruction, then tested for their powers of retention. Students, like laborers, were ranked and sorted, some fit for work on farms or in factories or in offices, some for college, others for menial labor. In the industrial age, this model met the needs of the economy. Young people, whether they knew it or not, were sorted for their "place" in society. Today, our society expects all students to be equipped with the skills and knowledge demanded by an advanced postindustrial society. Today, no one knows what the jobs of the future will be, so all people must be equipped with the ability to think for themselves, to solve problems, to make informed decisions, and to carry out the responsibilities of citizenship in a democratic society. They need a sound education, with the vocabulary and background knowledge in fields such as history, mathematics, and science, to adapt to a changing world.

The free market works well in producing goods and services, but it produces extreme inequality, and it has a high rate of failure. That is not the way we want our schools to work. The core principle of American public education is supposed to be equality of educational opportunity, not a race to the top or a free market of choices with winners and losers. Our goal as a society, which we have never achieved, is to provide an education of equal quality to every child so that each of them has an equal chance to succeed in the world. The business model of choice and competition, testing and accountability, moves us even further away from that goal; as communities dissolve, students and families sort themselves into schools that reflect differences in race, ethnicity, and class. As communities and schools become more segregated, they become more, not less, inequitable. The goal of equality of educational opportunity is impossible to achieve to the extent that we remain in thrall to standardized testing, which calculates the gaps among different groups but does nothing to close them.

The business world is rife with innovation and failure. Every year, hundreds of thousands of new businesses open, and every year hundreds of thousands of businesses fail. Businesses come and go. Over the years, household names disappear, like Woolworth's, Pan Am, Bethlehem Steel, Polaroid, TWA, and Borders. Some disappeared because they became obsolete. Some lost to the competition. Others disappeared because of corrupt activities, like Enron and Madoff. Many thousands of restaurants open and close every year. Big national corporate chain stores eliminate mom-and-pop stores; Internet businesses eliminate national corporate chain stores. Business leaders accept instability and risk and hope not to be caught in the next round of closures. They call it "creative destruction," as one enterprise replaces another. They pride themselves on their ability to "reinvent" themselves every two or three years, with new products, new services, and new ideas. They engage in risk management and cut their losses; they must discard the damaged blueberries, close the failing chain stores, get rid of the losers in their portfolios.[3]

But children do not thrive on turmoil and instability. Chaos is not good for children. Chaos and disruption are not good for families and communities. There is nothing creative about closing a school that is a fixture in its community. If it is struggling, it needs help. It may need extra staff, extra resources, and expert supervision. It doesn't need to be shuttered like a shoe store. No school was ever saved or improved by closing it.

Schools should be places that provide a respite from the uncertainty in children's lives. They should be safe havens from what is often a heartless world. They should be institutions that change with the times when it is necessary to change. They should be up-to-date with technology, they should welcome evidence-based innovation, and they should be receptive to the best ideas about meeting the needs of children, but they should not be treated like fast-food franchises. Businesses come and go, but families should not, nor should schools. Schools should be the center of the community, akin to the public library and the public park, stable institutions that serve the needs of the community.

Privatization does not work well in providing public services. The need to cut costs and generate a profit for shareholders is inconsistent

with the need to assure a reliable, dependable, and equitable public service. Deregulation unleashes enterprise, but it also means less oversight
of funds and practices. Sometimes privatization of public service produces efficiency, but it may also produce corruption and a low quality
of service, due to the lack of oversight and lack of regulation of private
vendors. When *The New York Times* surveyed prison privatization, it
concluded that privately run prisons cost more than state-run prisons
and avoided the sickest and the costliest prisoners.[4]

When New York State's comptroller general audited the state's privately run program for preschool students with disabilities, he discovered numerous examples of fraudulent practices. The owner of one
company pleaded guilty to defrauding the state of $800,000; among
other abuses, he had hired his wife at a salary of $150,000, even though
she already earned $90,000 a year as a full-time professor at a local
university. Other private vendors had billed the state for jewelry and
expensive clothing, vacations, and no-show jobs. Some had "funneled
public money into expensive rents paid by their preschools to entities
they personally control." The cost of the program in New York State
had doubled in only six years to $2 billion. The bulk of the spending
was in New York City, which was spending about $40,000 per child,
or $1 billion for twenty-five thousand children. By contrast, Massa-
chusetts spent less than $10,000 per child for what experts considered
a "resource-rich" program. The state of New York allowed the private
vendors both to evaluate the children and to provide the services that
they prescribed. According to *The New York Times,* the private contractors, "who have their tuition rates set by the state, have become an
influential lobbying force in Albany, where they have regularly rallied
parents of disabled children to protest spending curbs in the program."
Privatization was a boon to the vendors but was far more costly to the
taxpayers and of a lesser quality than the same program offered by public agencies in other states.[5]

Just as the private contractors expanded and protected their program
by lobbying and putting pressure on legislators, charter operators have
persuaded legislators to increase the number of charters by lobbying
and by mobilizing their students and their parents to lobby for them.

When charter schools were first opened, they claimed they would
provide better education at a savings to the taxpayers. To date, there is
no evidence that charter schools provide better education than public

schools when they enroll the same kinds of students. And the promised savings have never materialized; once they are established, charters
demand equal funding. Meanwhile, the charter sector has become a
formidable political force. Charter corporations, both for-profit and
nonprofit, and members of their boards of directors make contributions
to candidates for school board races, for the legislature, for the gover-
norship, and for referenda about the future of charter schools. When
public hearings are conducted about charter schools in New York City
and Los Angeles, charter operators send busloads of their students and
parents wearing identical T-shirts to the hearings to demand more
charter schools, more funding, and less regulation and oversight. When
New York City held public hearings about closing public schools, the
same brigades of charter students and parents arrived in buses to support the school closings to provide more free space for charters. If public schools used their students to engage in the same political lobbying,
their principals would be brought up on charges and fired.

Despite the problems associated with privatizing public services,
some elected officials insist on turning public dollars over to private
organizations and businesses. In the spring of 2012, Governor Bobby
Jindal of Louisiana pushed a "reform" bill through the state legislature that made more than half the children in the state eligible for
vouchers and encouraged the creation of numerous boards to authorize
new charter schools. In addition, his legislation authorized payment
of public funds to private vendors. The costs of these alternatives to
public schooling were supposed to be paid from the state's "minimum
foundation budget" for public schools. Because the state constitution
says that the money in the minimum foundation budget is dedicated
specifically to public schools, teachers' organizations and local school
boards sued to block the funding of the vouchers and vendors. In 2013,
the state's highest court ruled that it was unconstitutional to divert
money dedicated to public schools to vouchers and private vendors.
Even after the funding was put on hold by the court, the state board
of education authorized forty-five vendors, all of whom would be paid
from the state's public education budget. Only thirteen of the forty-
five were "face-to-face" programs; twenty were virtual programs, and
twelve were a blend of online and face-to-face classes. The vendors
included a program to teach barbering, cosmetology, and "oil and
gas production"; one was a course to prepare young people to work in

construction trades; some offered to teach test preparation or credit recovery for failing students; some were courses offered either online or in person by a single tutor; and there were applications from the online for-profit corporation K12.[6]

Two of Louisiana's eleven board members voted against authorizing the vendors. They objected not only because a judge had ruled that their funding was unconstitutional but because at least five of the other state board members had accepted campaign contributions from some of the vendors. A spokesperson for the state board of ethics said those board members did not have a conflict of interest because they were not employees of the vendors.[7]

As the privatization movement in education gained momentum, its wealthy supporters poured large contributions into state and local political races to elect like-minded allies and to pass initiatives. In 2011, out-of-state donors gave unprecedented sums of money to elect a state board committed to Governor Jindal's sweeping privatization plan. Jindal's slate was buoyed by contributions from some of America's richest people, including Eli Broad, Michael Bloomberg, and the Walton family, outspending supporters of public education by twelve to one to gain control of the state board. The director of Teach for America in New Orleans won a seat on the state board by outspending her opponent by thirty-four to one. The amount spent to elect unpaid state board members—$2.6 million—was ten times greater than the total spent for the same races only four years earlier.[8]

In Georgia, contributions of millions of dollars from outside the state ensured the passage of a constitutional amendment empowering the governor to create a commission to authorize charter schools over the objections of local school boards. This proposal, which echoed model legislation by the right-wing ALEC organization, demonstrated that the free-market reformers valued privatization over local control of schools. They are free-market radicals, not conservatives. According to *The New York Times*, donors to the pro-charter campaign included "Alice Walton, the daughter of the founder of Walmart, Sam Walton; Americans for Prosperity, the Tea Party group founded by the billionaire Koch brothers; and several companies that manage charter schools and stood to benefit directly by passage of the amendment. Supporters of the amendment outspent opponents by about 15 to 1."[9]

In the state of Washington, a handful of billionaires, led by Bill Gates,

Alice Walton, and the Bezos family of Amazon.com, in 2012 raised $11 million to support a charter school initiative that had previously been rejected three times by the state's voters. This time, although the initiative was opposed by the League of Women Voters, the NAACP, teachers' unions, local school boards, and parents' associations across the state, it passed by a small margin.[10]

In Tennessee, Michelle Rhee's StudentsFirst spent $900,000 in 2012 to enable conservative Republicans to attain a supermajority of the state legislature. Their agenda included vouchers and the creation of a state charter board to override local school boards. Nationally, Rhee's organization supported 105 candidates, of whom 90 were Republicans and supporters of charters and vouchers.[11]

In some political contests, the champions of privatization were defeated, despite their huge financial advantage, by voters who saw through their rhetoric and rejected their goals. The veteran educator Glenda Ritz defeated Indiana's state superintendent of education Tony Bennett, even though he outspent her by ten to one. Bennett was a national hero to conservatives for his advocacy of privatization and his antagonism to collective bargaining.

In Idaho, the reddest of red states, Republicans swept to victory in every statewide office, yet voters repealed three "reform" laws passed by the legislature in 2011 at the behest of the conservative state superintendent, Tom Luna. The Luna laws, as they were known, were intended to tie educators' evaluations to student test scores, to cripple teachers' unions, and to digitize the schools by requiring every student to take two online courses to graduate.[12]

In Santa Clara County, California, the charter lobby targeted a school board member, Anna Song, who had voted in 2011 against authorizing twenty new Rocketship charters in the district. Wealthy out-of-district contributors gave nearly $250,000 to Song's opponent. Song spent less than $10,000. Despite the twenty-five-to-one imbalance against her, Song was reelected.[13]

In Bridgeport, Connecticut, corporations and wealthy donors funded a campaign to eliminate the local school board and turn the schools over to the mayor. Voters were asked in a referendum to give up their right to elect their local school board, and they said no.

When Los Angeles held its election for school board in 2013, a small group of very wealthy people raised nearly $4 million, with half the amount targeted to defeat Steve Zimmer, a one-term incumbent. Zimmer began his career in Teach for America but remained as a classroom teacher in the Los Angeles public schools for seventeen years. After his election to the city's school board, he became concerned that the district had more charter schools than any other city in the nation but no policy for oversight. He proposed that the school board create such a policy and, until it was finalized, set a moratorium on new charters. This angered the charter school lobby, which determined to unseat him. Mayor Antonio Villaraigosa assembled a fund with large contributions from Eli Broad, Michelle Rhee's StudentsFirst, Rupert Murdoch, the California Charter Schools Association, and others; New York City's mayor Michael Bloomberg added $1 million. Zimmer was supported by the United Teachers Los Angeles, even though he was not a reliable supporter of the union. Outspent by at least two to one, Zimmer pulled an upset and won by a margin of fifty-two to forty-eight.[14]

While the media noticed the large contributions from out-of-state donors to high-profile races in Los Angeles and Louisiana, little notice was paid to out-of-state contributions to local and state school board races in less-prominent races. A candidate for local school board in Perth Amboy, New Jersey, received nearly $50,000 to run in a contest that normally costs $5,000; most of the donors to the Perth Amboy race were residents of California. Why the sudden interest in Perth Amboy? Bloggers discovered that many of the same California donors made campaign contributions to school board races in Nevada, Colorado, Oregon, New York, and Indiana. It is a troubling pattern that raises questions about who is bundling the money and why it is sent to certain races. It is not illegal to give campaign contributions to races in other districts and states, but local and state school board races should be determined by those who live in those districts and states, not by the organized power of big donors.[15]

The issue for the future is whether a small number of very wealthy entrepreneurs, corporations, and individuals will be able to purchase educational policy in this nation, either by funding candidates for local and state school boards, for state legislatures, for governor, and for Congress or by using foundation "gifts" to advance the privatization of public education.

If we take seriously our national commitment to equality of educational opportunity, then we must reject the effort to privatize public education. Privatization will not produce equality of opportunity, nor is it "cost-effective," in business terms, to provide the high-quality education needed for children whose families are poor, who have disabilities, and who struggle to learn.

At present, our national policy relies on the belief that constant testing will improve the education of children in the poorest neighborhoods. But this is the cheapest way to supply schooling, not the best way or the right way. The children with the greatest needs are the most expensive to educate. They will not have equality of educational opportunity if their schools focus relentlessly on preparing them to take state tests. Like children in elite private schools and affluent suburbs, they need the arts and sports and science laboratories and libraries and social workers; they need school nurses and guidance counselors. They need to learn history and civics, to read literature and learn foreign languages. They need the latest technology and opportunities to learn to play musical instruments, to sing in groups, to make videos, and to perform in plays. They need beautiful campuses too. It will not be cost-effective to give them what they need. It is expensive. What is needed most cannot be achieved by cutting costs, hiring the least experienced teachers, increasing class size, or replacing teachers with computers.

The movement toward a free market is inconsistent with our commitment to provide high-quality public education for all. The more that policy makers promote choice—charters and vouchers—the more they sell the public on the idea that their choice of a school is a decision they make as individual consumers, not as citizens. As a citizen, you become invested in the local public school; you support it and take pride in its accomplishments. You see it as a community institution worthy of your support, even if you don't have children in the school. You recognize that the school is educating the children of the community and that this is good for everyone, not just for the child and his or her parents. You think of public education as an institution that educates citizens, future voters, members of your community.

But as school choice becomes the basis for public policy, the school becomes not a community institution but an institution that meets the needs of its customers. The school reaches across district lines to find customers; it markets its offerings to potential students. Districts poach students from each other, in hopes of getting more dollars. The customers choose or reject the school, as they would choose or reject a restaurant; it's their choice. The community no longer feels any ties to the school, because the school is not part of the community. The community no longer feels obliged to support the school, because it is not theirs. It belongs to its board and to its customers, not to the community. When a bond issue comes up for a vote, will the public support schools that belong to corporations and private boards?

We must pause and reflect on the wisdom of sundering the ties between communities and schools. Choice erodes those ties. It creates and reinforces a consumer mentality. It encourages instability as parents shop for schools after scanning the latest report cards and test scores. It encourages school districts to waste precious tax dollars advertising their wares in hopes of luring student "customers" from other school districts. This is American consumerism run amok. This is American consumerism at war with the need to establish stable communities.

The principles of competition and choice sound good, because they echo what we expect when we shop for clothing or automobiles. Competition is expected on the sports field or in science fairs and debates. But competition among schools for students does not improve the quality of education. Nothing inherent in competition guarantees that students will learn about history and government or the principles of democracy, nor will it assure that young people are prepared to vote wisely or to assume the responsibilities of citizenship. Competition and choice erode trust and community. Competition and choice exacerbate inequality and segregation by race and class. "Creative disruption" is certainly disruptive, but it is not creative. It is not what children and adolescents need. It is not what families and communities need. It sacrifices social and human values that are more important to children and to society than consumerism, competition, and choice.

The best schools value quality over cost. They honor experienced teachers. They do not judge them by their students' scores on tests. They do not substitute computers for teachers. Nor do they subject their students to multiple bouts of standardized testing. Nor are they focused on data. The best schools in the nation have small classes, experienced teachers, ample resources, a rich curriculum, well-maintained facilities, many opportunities for students to engage in the arts, and daily physical education. These are ideal conditions for a good education. This is what we should want for all children.

CHAPTER 33

Conclusion: The Pattern on the Rug

When I wrote *The Death and Life of the Great American School System,* I thought that two very different reform movements just happened to converge in some sort of unanticipated and unfortunate accident. There was the testing and accountability movement, which started in the 1980s and officially became federal policy in 2002 as part of the No Child Left Behind law. Then there was the choice movement, which had been simmering on the back burner of education politics for half a century, not making much headway. Though it had been a cherished belief of the far-right wing of the Republican Party for decades, it had never achieved a popular base. Some supporters of testing and accountability were not supporters of school choice; some supporters of school choice were not supporters of testing and accountability. Each thought its own approach was the cure-all for public education.

NCLB breathed new life into the choice movement by decreeing that schools persistently unable to meet its impossible goal of 100 percent proficiency be handed over to private management, undergo drastic staff firings, or be closed. For the first time in history, federal law decreed that privatization was a viable remedy to improve low-performing public schools.

Now the two movements are no longer separate. They have merged and are acting in concert. Many of the original sponsors of NCLB might not have intended to encourage the privatization of the nation's public schools, but that has been its outcome. Supporters and critics of the law may argue about whether it has produced higher scores and whether the scores represent anything other than intense test preparation and rote learning. But no one thinks that the law was a success other than the handful of people who designed it. Even supporters of the law recognize that it is so unpopular that it should be "rebranded." The fact that the nation remains gripped by increasingly shrill and increasingly radical demands for "reform" indicates how little NCLB accomplished.

With the distance of nearly a dozen years, we can see the damage done by NCLB to the nation's educational system. Race to the Top actually doubled down on the wrongheaded assumptions of NCLB and further promoted its demoralizing and punitive policies. The practice of closing schools because of low test scores has become routine, barely getting notice in the media; before the year 2000, it was a rare occurrence. In the past, those in charge of school systems were expected to fix troubled schools, not shut them down.

NCLB centralized control of public education in Washington to an extent that was unimaginable when the U.S. Department of Education was established in 1979. When Congress debated whether to create a cabinet-level department of education, opponents warned that the mere fact of having a department would lead to federal control of education, but its proponents insisted this would never happen and federalism— a calibrated balance among federal, state, and local governments— would always prevail. Today, however, thanks to the philosophical and political alignment of No Child Left Behind and Race to the Top, federalism has been all but abandoned. The Department of Education now routinely imposes its preferred reforms on states and districts, using the bait of billions of federal dollars to win supposedly "voluntary" assent to its decrees.

The Common Core State Standards are an example of the Department of Education's muscular use of federal funds to push a policy on the states that may or may not be wise. Nonfederal organizations led the effort to develop the standards over an eighteen-month period, although it was well understood by all concerned that these groups (the National Governors Association and Achieve) had the strong support of the U.S. Department of Education and heavy funding from the Gates Foundation. When the Obama administration put forward the criteria for Race to the Top grants, one of the primary requirements was that the state adopt a common set of high-quality standards, in collaboration with other states, that were internationally benchmarked and led to "college and career readiness."[1] These were widely understood to be the Common Core standards. In short order, almost every state agreed to adopt them, even states with clearly superior standards like Massachusetts and Indiana, despite the fact that these new standards had never been field-tested anywhere. No one can say with certainty whether the Common Core standards will improve education, whether they will reduce or increase the achievement gaps among different groups, or how much it will cost to implement them. Some scholars believe they will make no difference, and some critics say they will cost billions to implement; others say they will lead to more testing. But the pressure by the federal government to adopt these standards was intense, and many states adopted the standards even though they won no Race to the Top money. The states wanted to be eligible for the money that was on offer, not recognizing that the federal funds could be used only for the purposes approved by the federal government, not to plug holes in the state budget.

NCLB created the unrealistic expectation that all students should be proficient, as judged by state tests, and Race to the Top built on that assumption—while encouraging a shift to "value-added" measures to rate schools and teachers. Secretary Arne Duncan allowed states to get waivers from the goal that all students should be proficient but replaced it with an equally unrealistic measure: that students must improve their test scores every year. If they don't, then someone must be "held accountable." Someone must be blamed and punished. Heads must roll. No consideration would be given to the possibility that test scores may not go up every year, often for reasons beyond teachers' control. Some students will not be proficient on the standardized tests no matter how hard they try, no matter how talented their teachers or how dedicated their principal. Some students will be distracted by crises in their lives; some will lack motivation or interest; some will inevitably land in the bottom half of the bell curve because the bell curve always has a bottom half. There is no way that schools and their staffs can control for all the external factors that contribute to test results.

NCLB created—and Race to the Top sustained—the unwarranted belief that standardized tests are an accurate, scientific gauge of educational achievement. They are not. They provide information about whether students on one particular day answered particular questions in the way the test makers decided was correct, which may or may not be useful to the teacher in assessing what students know and can do, let alone provide help in addressing deficiencies. Often the test results arrive too late to be helpful to the teacher in addressing the needs of students. Different tests in the same subject, or even the same test on different days, often yield different results. The test scores provide a way to rank children, but the labeling in and of itself serves no valid educational purpose. The tests do not measure the many dimensions of intelligence, judgment, creativity, and character that may be even more consequential for the student's future than his or her test score.

NCLB validated the patently false narrative that American education was failing. Year after year, the number of "failing schools" increased in every state as more and more schools failed to meet the unreachable goal of 100 percent proficiency that NCLB demanded. Race to the Top and the Obama administration's associated School Improvement Grants program imposed harsh penalties on schools that may indeed be struggling, due to serving at-risk students in overcrowded conditions with scarce resources, by sentencing them to additional chaos, disruption, and, in some cases, closure.

Together, these federal programs have fueled and accelerated the privatization movement. The constant barrage of bad news, based on unrealistic goals, was used to justify hostile takeovers, profiteering, mass layoffs, and a death sentence for too many schools, in an effort to convince the public that this was the only way to address low achievement. The stories of escalating failure acted as a sort of "shock doctrine" that made almost any remedy seem palatable. The promoters of privatization promised miracles that would shame snake-oil salesmen. Their remedies, they claimed, would produce a dramatic increase in test scores and graduation rates. The media, always suckers for "miracle" claims, retailed stories of charter schools or so-called turnaround schools where everyone succeeded, without bothering to examine even the most obvious evidence suggesting exclusionary policies, expulsions, or attrition rates.

The charter movement paved the way for the resurgence of the voucher movement, as its advocates insisted that "choice" was far more important than investing in public education. This was precisely what the far-right wing of the Republican Party had been saying for decades, without winning public support. When the evidence for the superiority of charter schools or voucher schools was scant, shaky, or even nonexistent, the champions of the free market insisted that choice itself was an important value. They held that as long as parents chose to send their children to schools that taught creationism or that global warming was a hoax, their choices should be respected, over the time-honored value of public responsibility for a well-run system of public education.

The free-market reform movement had more than federal mandates on its side. It had big money. The billions dangled before cash-hungry states by Obama's Race to the Top made states compete to accept market-based, test-driven policies. The nation's largest foundations— Walton, Broad, Gates, and dozens of others—used their billions as well to reinforce the free-market agenda, subsidizing the operations of schools and districts that implemented privatization and high-stakes testing, hired their favored administrators, and put in place the policies they favored. They funded think tanks in Washington, D.C., to put out reports and host conferences, spinning the benefits of such programs, despite the lack of any solid research evidence. The privateers produced slick movies to disseminate their message and found willing supporters in the mass media, such as NBC's annual "Education Nation" program.

Though the partisans of choice and privatization may have political power and money, their cause lacks one crucial ingredient: it does not have a popular base. Its proponents, most of them extremely wealthy, number in the thousands, yet they aim to control the fate of a national school system with many millions of students, parents, and teachers. To overcome this significant handicap, the corporate reform movement has used the vast wealth of its members to contribute to political campaigns to elect its allies to state and local offices and to pass referenda on behalf of privatization. A small number of billionaires have poured millions of dollars into political campaigns across the nation, using the positive rhetoric of "reform" and images of happy children in neat uniforms to advance their agenda. And always, the reformers speak of "putting children first," "students first," "kids come first," as though the teachers and principals were only concerned with their own selfish interests, and only the reformers really care about the children. Such rhetoric is divisive and hollow, because parents know that most teachers work hard every day and do their best to help their children learn. The horrific massacre at Sandy Hook Elementary School in Newtown, Connecticut, in December 2012 dented that absurd image, at least temporarily, and reminded the public that educators are willing to die for their students, as several did on that terrible day.

Across the nation, in state after state, and in city after city, parents and community leaders are beginning to realize that education policy has been hijacked. They are starting to organize against high-stakes testing and privatization. Parent organizations, educators, students, and local school boards are rebelling against the amount of time given over to prepare children for the tests and the resulting loss of time for the arts and other programs. As more of the public understands that charter schools do not produce miracles, their luster will fade; one hopes that only those that are truly devoted to the local community will survive. As more stories appear about corruption and self-dealing by charter operators, the public will realize the risks of deregulation. As more journalists ask questions about attrition rates and low numbers of students with special needs and English-language learners, their mystique will dissolve. The public is beginning to understand, to see the pattern on the rug, and to realize that they are being fooled into giving up what belongs to them.

In the fall of 2012, the Chicago Teachers Union (CTU) took action against the agenda of the privatization movement. More than 90 percent of the union's members voted to strike a school system run by the Democratic mayor, Rahm Emanuel, who had served as President Obama's chief of staff. The union was striking not for more money but for improvements in the schools for their students. The city's public schools had been a playground for corporate reform for nearly twenty years, accomplishing little. The reformers placed their bets on closing schools and opening schools but paid little attention to deteriorating conditions within the schools, intense segregation within the school system, and gang violence that took the lives of many adolescents. Many public schools had no libraries, no art or music teachers, no social workers, and overcrowded classes. The CTU decided enough is enough. The union won some concessions from the mayor, and it shone a bright light on the essentially elitist indifference of the mayor, his school board, and by implication the Obama administration. But the CTU's main victory was the example of unity and militancy that it offered to dispirited educators across the nation.

However, the CTU was unable to dissuade the mayor from his plan to close scores of public schools. Rahm Emanuel, like Arne Duncan, Joel Klein, Michelle Rhee, and other proponents of privatization, continued to be wedded to the belief that the private sector has a "secret sauce" (Emanuel's term) for school success, not realizing (or pretending not to realize) that the great results he admired were usually obtained by skimming the students they want and exclusion, attrition, and expulsion of those they don't want. More of this "secret sauce," and the nation's cities will be left with a dual school system of haves and have-nots, reinforcing the structural inequalities of American society, leaving many children not only behind but hopeless, and destroying public education in the bargain.

In time, perhaps, legislators will demand proper oversight of charters so that they are expected to collaborate with the public schools, so they take a fair share of the neediest students, and so their finances are transparent. If charters could be freed from corporate control and freed from the profit motive, if they became stand-alone, community-based organizations that meet the needs of the community, they might yet become a useful part of the landscape of public education.

The overwhelming majority of the American public were themselves educated in public schools and, once informed, will not readily hand these valuable public assets over to entrepreneurs, profit-making organizations, or well-intentioned amateurs. They want better neighborhood public schools, not chain-store schools that pick and choose their students. Despite the grandiose promises made by charter corporations and their political allies, the public is awakening to the threat posed by privatization.

The corporate reform movement has capitalized on the American public's infatuation with consumerism. Consumerism is as American as apple pie. People shop for their shoes and their jeans and their homes, say reformers, why not shop for their children's schools? Competition may produce better shoes and jeans, but there is no evidence that it produces better schools.

The advance of privatization depends on high-stakes testing. The federally mandated regime of annual testing generates the data to grade not only students and teachers but schools. Given unrealistic goals, a school can easily fail. When a school is labeled a "failing school" under NCLB or a "priority" or "focus" school according to the metrics of the Obama administration's program, it must double down on test preparation to attempt to recover its reputation, but the odds of success are small, especially after the most ambitious parents and students flee the school. The federal regulations are like quicksand: the more schools struggle, the deeper they sink into the morass of test-based accountability. As worried families abandon these schools, they increasingly enroll disproportionate numbers of the most disadvantaged students, either children with special needs or new immigrants who can barely speak English. Low grades on the state report card may send a once-beloved school into a death spiral. What was once a source of stability in the community becomes a school populated by those who are least able to find a school that will accept them.

Once the quality of the neighborhood school begins to fall, parents will be willing to consider charter schools, online schools, brand-new schools with catchy, make-believe names, like the Scholars Academy for Academic Excellence or the School for Future Leaders of Business and Industry. In time, the neighborhood school becomes the school of last resort, not the community school. When the neighborhood school is finally closed, there is no longer any choice. Then parents will be forced to travel long distances and hope that their children will be accepted into a school; the school chooses, not the student.

Does it matter?

Yes, it does.

Public education is an essential part of the democratic fabric of American society. Nearly 90 percent of American students attend public schools, whose doors are open to all, without regard to race, ethnicity, language, gender, disability status, national origin, or economic class. Control of public education is democratic, subject to decisions made by elected or appointed officials, rather than by private boards and for-profit corporations. Community schools are controlled by residents of the community, not by corporate chains. In 95 percent of the school districts in the United States, if the public does not like the decisions of their school boards, they can vote them out of office.

The goal of our public educational system, evolved over many decades, is equality of opportunity. Have we met our goal? Absolutely not. But choice will not bring us any closer. Choice does not produce equality; choice exacerbates inequality, as a free market produces winners and losers. Choice intensifies racial and ethnic segregation, as well as segregation by class. Both choice and high-stakes testing erode equity by encouraging self-segregation and by ranking that reifies socioeconomic status.

Liberals should be at the forefront of the effort to defend public education, because public education has been a force for social and intellectual progress, a force to achieve a more just society. Liberals should understand that the public schools are an integral part of the commons that belong to us all and should oppose any efforts to give them away to entrepreneurs.

Conservatives should be at the forefront of the effort to oppose privatization because the public school is a source of community, stability, and local values. Conservatives do not tear down established institutions and hand them over to the vagaries of the free market or the whims of financial and political elites. Conservatives do not destroy communities. What we are witnessing today is the Walmartization of American education, an effort to uproot neighborhood schools and Main Street businesses and outsource their management to chain schools and chain stores run by anonymous corporations. If they do not make their bottom line, they may pull up their stakes and abandon the community, leaving it bereft, as many chain stores and charter chains have already done. Conservatives protect their community and its institutions. There is nothing conservative about the chain-store mentality that is now being introduced into the control of schooling.

Ours is a diverse nation that respects the choices that people make about their children's education. We respect the right of parents to send their children to private and religious schools. We respect the right of families to homeschool their children. Yet more than a century ago, our nation decided to separate church and state, to restrict the allocation of public funds to public schools, and to keep religious doctrine out of public school classrooms. The public schools became the schools where children of all religions and no religion could learn together. Those who wanted a religious education for their children were free to seek it elsewhere, at their own expense. Catholic education has been especially valuable for the families and children it serves; the best way to maintain Catholic schools is to keep them independent. Where public funding goes, public accountability must follow. Here is a principle that might be useful in our present debates: public money for public schools; private money for nonpublic schools. If Catholic and other religious schools received even half of the munificent private philanthropy now directed to charter schools, they would have the financial stability they require to continue their mission for many decades into the future. Meanwhile, the principle of separation of church and state that has served our nation well would remain intact.

Why do we have public schools? In the early decades of the nineteenth century, most children were schooled at home by their parents, by tutors if their parents could afford it, in private academies, or in church schools. The children of the poor were schooled, if they were lucky, by charitable and religious organizations. As communities grew, parents and concerned citizens realized that educating children was a shared public responsibility, not a private one. The private, religious, and charitable schools were largely replaced by public schools, paid for with taxes raised by the entire community. For many years, the public schools were known as common schools, because they were part of the public commons. Like parks, libraries, roads, and the police, they were institutions that belonged to the whole people. Some people complained that they didn't want to pay taxes for other people's children either because their own children were in private school or because they had no children. But most people understood that paying for the education of the community's children was a civic duty, an investment in the future, in citizens who would grow up and become voters and take their place in society.

Public education has enlarged our democracy since the mid-nineteenth century. It was the public schools that assimilated millions of immigrant children from Europe in the nineteenth and early twentieth centuries, by teaching them how to speak English and how to participate in American democracy. The public schools were the immigrants' ladder of social and economic mobility into the middle class. The *Brown* decision of 1954 ended the rigid, legally mandated segregation of public schools in the South, a historic change that eventually desegregrated not only schools but other public institutions, and eventually most of American society. The integration of large numbers of African Americans into the middle class began in the public schools. Similarly, the public schools were the first major public institution to insist upon gender equality in American society. At the same time, the public schools opened their classrooms to students with disabilities of all kinds, which paved the way for their integration into other sectors of our society.

None of these advances happened without court orders and legislation, but no other institution could have done it except the public schools. A century ago, John Dewey explained the connection between democracy and education. He wrote:

A democracy is more than a form of government; it is primarily a mode of associated living, of conjoint communicated experience. The extension in space of the number of individuals who participate in an interest so that each has to refer his own action to that of others, and to consider the action of-others to give point and direction to his own, is equivalent to the breaking down of those barriers of class, race, and national territory which kept men from perceiving the full import of their activity. These more numerous and more varied points of contact denote a greater diversity of stimuli to which an individual has to respond; they consequently put a premium on variation in his action. They secure a liberation of powers which remain suppressed as long as the incitations to action are partial, as they must be in a group which in its exclusiveness shuts out many interests.[2]

What Dewey taught us, which we have spent the past century trying to incorporate into our way of life, is that democracy is more than the institutional arrangements for governing and voting. It requires that decisions be made with the involvement and participation of those who are affected by them. Democracy functions most effectively when people from different backgrounds interact, communicate their interests, and participate in shaping the purposes by which they live. Perhaps Abraham Lincoln put it best when he described American democracy as that "government of the people, by the people, for the people."

More than any other institution in American life, the public schools have broken down the barriers of class, race, religion, gender, ethnicity, language, and disability status that separate people. They have not eliminated those divisions, but they have enabled people from different walks of life to learn from one another, to study together, play together, plan together, and recognize their common humanity. More than any other institution in our society, the public schools enable the rising generation to exchange ideas, to debate, to disagree, and to take into account the views of others in making decisions.

Over time, as the public schools opened their doors to all, they expanded opportunity to more people, distributed the benefits of knowledge to more people, and strengthened our nation. Public education has been an American melting pot, an American salad bowl, an American orchestra, an American mosaic. The public schools have taught us how to be one society, not a collection of separate enclaves, divided by race, language, and culture. They have contributed directly to the growth of a large middle class and a dynamic society. Our nation's public schools have been a mighty engine of opportunity and equality. They still are.

But no matter how much we improve our public schools, they alone cannot solve the deeply rooted, systemic problems of our society. Federal, state, and municipal policies have isolated many children, especially in urban districts, into schools that are segregated by race, class, and income. Many of our public schools have also been badly underfunded and regularly pummeled by budget cuts, rising class sizes, and damaging mandates that have undermined their mission. The inevitable result of such segregation and underfunding is low academic performance, which is then blamed on the schools. The failure of public policy is not the failure of the public schools. The challenge to our society today is to repair public policy and to give our public schools the care and support they need to thrive, in all communities and for all children, rather than abandon them to the idiosyncrasies of the free market.

Our communities created public schools to develop citizens and to sustain our democracy. That is their abiding purpose. This unique institution has the unique responsibility of developing a citizenry, making many peoples into one people, and teaching our children the skills they need to prepare for work and further education.

The public schools have made real the promise of *e pluribus unum*, without sacrificing either the *pluribus* or the *unum*.

When public education is in danger, democracy is jeopardized.

We cannot afford that risk.

The way forward requires that education policy be shaped by evidence and by the knowledge and wisdom of educators, not by a business plan shaped by free-market ideologues and entrepreneurs.

We must take care not to reestablish a dual school system, with privately managed charters for the most motivated, most able students and public schools as the repositories for those unable to get into the charter system. We must take care to avoid a future in which the rich have small classes with teachers, while the poor are taught by computers.

If we take seriously the charge to improve education, we must improve both schools and social conditions for children and families. To reduce the achievement gap, we must reduce the opportunity gap. We must invest in early childhood education and make sure that all children have the medical care they need.

If we mean to lift the quality of education, we should insist that all children have a full curriculum, including history, civics, literature, foreign languages, physical education, mathematics, and science. We should make sure that every child has the chance to sing, dance, write, act, play instruments, sculpt, design, and build. Students need a reason to come to school, not as duty, but for the joy that comes from performance and imagination.

If we truly care about the welfare of the most vulnerable children in our society, we will turn our efforts to reducing segregation and poverty. These are the root causes of poor academic performance. We must lower the child poverty rate. It is a national scandal. Other nations have figured out how to protect the well-being of children and families, and we have not. It's time to get to work on policies and programs that address root causes.

Only well-qualified, well-prepared teachers should be hired to work in our schools. We must stop giving them orders and scripts and let them teach. In turn, teachers need to be evaluated by human beings, including their principals and their peers, rather than computer-driven metrics.

Yes, we must improve our schools. Start now; start here, by building the bonds of trust among schools and communities. The essential mission of the public schools is not merely to prepare workers for the global workforce but to prepare citizens with the minds, hearts, and characters to sustain our democracy into the future.

Genuine school reform must be built on hope, not fear; on encouragement, not threats; on inspiration, not compulsion; on trust, not carrots and sticks; on belief in the dignity of the human person, not a slavish devotion to data; on support and mutual respect, not a regime of punishment and blame. To be lasting, school reform must rely on collaboration and teamwork among students, parents, teachers, principals, administrators, and local communities.

Despite its faults, the American system of democratically controlled schools has been the mainstay of our communities and the foundation for our nation's success. We must work together to improve our public schools. We must extend the promise of equal educational opportunity to all the children of our nation. Protecting our public schools against privatization and saving them for future generations of American children is the civil rights issue of our time.

Appendix

Graphs 1–4 appear in the text in chapter 5. For graphs 1 and 2, see p. 46; for graph 3, see p. 51; for graph 4, see p. 52.

5. Trend in Fourth-Grade NAEP Reading Achievement-Level Results

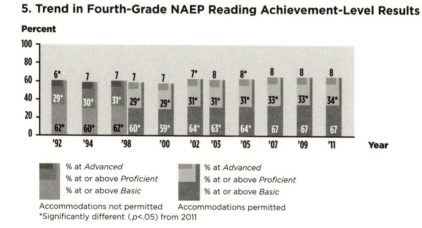

Percent

% at *Advanced*
% at or above *Proficient*
% at or above *Basic*
Accommodations not permitted

% at *Advanced*
% at or above *Proficient*
% at or above *Basic*
Accommodations permitted

*Significantly different (p<.05) from 2011

6. Trend in Fourth-Grade NAEP Reading Average Scores

Scale score

- - - - Accommodations not permitted
——— Accommodations permitted
*Significantly different (p<.05) from 2011

7. Trend in Fourth-Grade NAEP Reading Average Scores and Score Gaps for White and Black Students

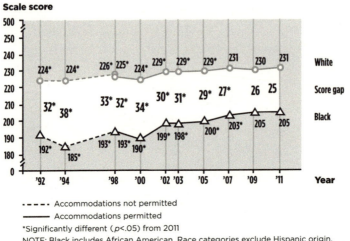

- - - - Accommodations not permitted

——— Accommodations permitted

*Significantly different ($p<.05$) from 2011

NOTE: Black includes African American. Race categories exclude Hispanic origin.
Score gaps are calculated based on differences between unrounded average scores.

8. Trend in Fourth-Grade NAEP Reading Average Scores and Score Gaps for White and Hispanic Students

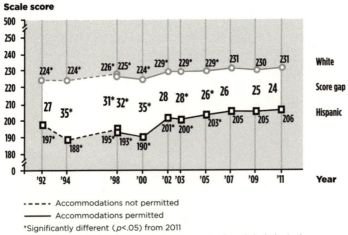

- - - - Accommodations not permitted

——— Accommodations permitted

*Significantly different ($p<.05$) from 2011

NOTE: White excludes students of Hispanic origin. Hispanic includes Latino.
Score gaps are calculated based on differences between unrounded average scores.

9. Trend in Fourth-Grade NAEP Reading Average Scores and Score Gaps for Asian/Pacific Islander and White Students

Scale score

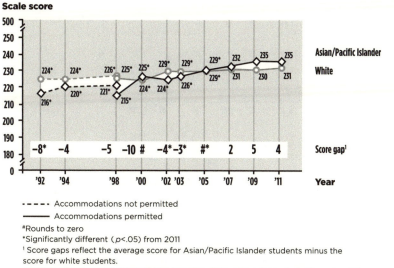

- - - - Accommodations not permitted
——— Accommodations permitted

#Rounds to zero

*Significantly different (*p*<.05) from 2011

[1] Score gaps reflect the average score for Asian/Pacific Islander students minus the score for white students.

NOTE: Pacific Islander includes Native Hawaiian. Race categories exclude Hispanic origin. Score gaps are calculated based on differences between unrounded average scores. Score differences between Asian/Pacific Islander and white students were not found to be statistically significant in 1994, 1998, 2000, 2005, and 2007.

10. Trend in Fourth-Grade NAEP Reading Average Scores and Score Gaps for White and American Indian/Alaska Native Students

Scale score

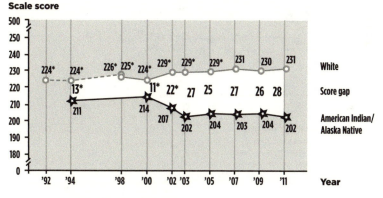

- - - - Accommodations not permitted
——— Accommodations permitted

*Significantly different (*p*<.05) from 2011

NOTE: Sample sizes were insufficient to permit reliable estimates for American Indian/Alaska Native students in 1992 and 1998. Race categories exclude Hispanic origin. Score gaps are calculated based on differences between unrounded average scores. Score differences between white and American Indian/Alaska Native students were not found to be statistically significant in 1994 and 2000.

11. Trend in Eighth-Grade NAEP Reading Achievement-Level Results

Percent

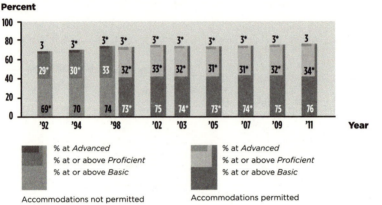

% at *Advanced*
% at or above *Proficient*
% at or above *Basic*

Accommodations not permitted

% at *Advanced*
% at or above *Proficient*
% at or above *Basic*

Accommodations permitted

*Significantly different (*p*<.05) from 2011

12. Trend in Eighth-Grade NAEP Reading Average Scores and Score Gaps for White and Black Students

Scale score

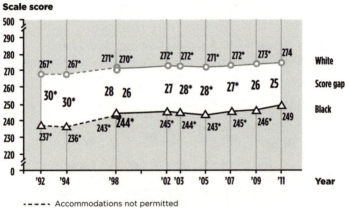

----- Accommodations not permitted

—— Accommodations permitted

*Significantly different (*p*<.05) from 2011

NOTE: Black includes African American. Race categories exclude Hispanic origin.
Score gaps are calculated based on differences between unrounded average scores.

13. Trend in Eighth-Grade NAEP Reading Average Scores and Score Gaps for White and Hispanic Students

Scale score

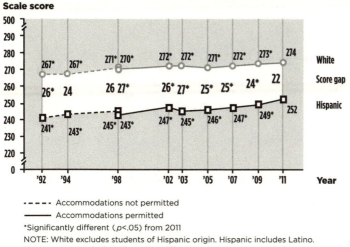

- - - - Accommodations not permitted
——— Accommodations permitted
*Significantly different (*p*<.05) from 2011
NOTE: White excludes students of Hispanic origin. Hispanic includes Latino.
Score gaps are calculated based on differences between unrounded average scores.

14. Trend in Eighth-Grade NAEP Reading Average Scores and Score Gaps for Asian/Pacific Islanders and White Students

Scale score

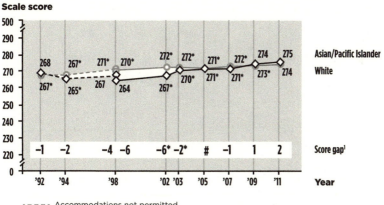

- - - - Accommodations not permitted
——— Accommodations permitted
#Rounds to zero
*Significantly different (*p*<.05) from 2011
[1] Score gaps reflect the average score for Asian/Pacific Islander students minus the score for white students.
NOTE: Pacific Islander includes Native Hawaiian. Race categories exclude Hispanic origin.
Score gaps are calculated based on differences between unrounded average scores.
Score differences between Asian/Pacific Islander and white students were not found to be statistically significant in 1992, 1994, 1998, 2003, 2005, 2007, 2009, and 2011.

15. Trend in Eighth-Grade NAEP Reading Average Scores and Score Gaps for White and American Indian/Alaska Native Students

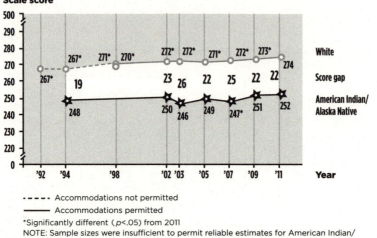

- - - - - Accommodations not permitted
———— Accommodations permitted
*Significantly different (*p*<.05) from 2011
NOTE: Sample sizes were insufficient to permit reliable estimates for American Indian/
Alaska Native students in 1992 and 1998. Race categories exclude Hispanic origin.
Score gaps are calculated based on differences between unrounded average scores.

16. Trend in Fourth-Grade NAEP Mathematics Average Scores and Score Gaps for White and Black Students

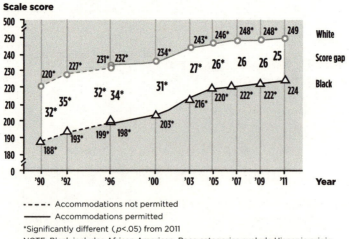

- - - - - Accommodations not permitted
———— Accommodations permitted
*Significantly different (*p*<.05) from 2011
NOTE: Black includes African American. Race categories exclude Hispanic origin.
Score gaps are calculated based on differences between unrounded average scores.

17. Trend in Fourth-Grade NAEP Mathematics Average Scores and Score Gaps for White and Hispanic Students

Scale score

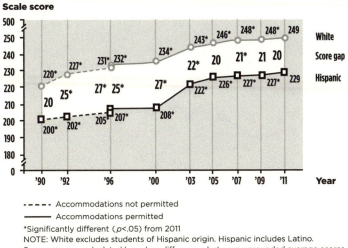

- - - - Accommodations not permitted
——— Accommodations permitted

*Significantly different (*p*<.05) from 2011
NOTE: White excludes students of Hispanic origin. Hispanic includes Latino.
Score gaps are calculated based on differences between unrounded average scores.

18. Trend in Fourth-Grade NAEP Mathematics Average Scores and Score Gaps for Asian/Pacific Islanders and White Students

Scale score

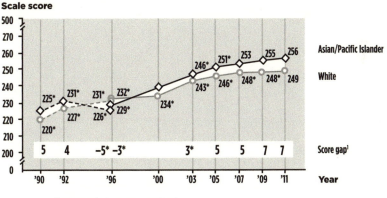

- - - - Accommodations not permitted
——— Accommodations permitted

*Significantly different (*p*<.05) from 2011
[1]Score gaps reflect the average score for Asian/Pacific Islander students minus the score for white students.
NOTE: Special analyses raised concerns about the accuracy and precision of the results for Asian/Pacific Islander students in 2000; therefore, they are omitted from this figure. Pacific Islander includes Native Hawaiian. Race categories exclude Hispanic origin. Score gaps are calculated based on differences between unrounded average scores. Score differences between Asian/Pacific Islander and white students were not found to be statistically significant in 1990, 1992, and 1996.

19. Trend in Fourth-Grade NAEP Mathematics Average Scores and Score Gaps for White and American Indian/Alaska Native Students

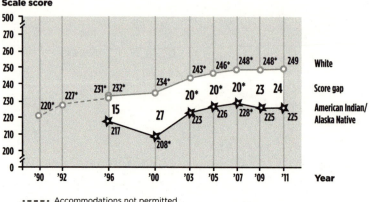

Scale score

----- Accommodations not permitted

——— Accommodations permitted

*Significantly different (*p*<.05) from 2011

NOTE: Sample sizes were insufficient to permit reliable estimates for American Indian/Alaska Native students in 1990, 1992, and 1996 (accommodations-not-permitted sample). Race categories exclude Hispanic origin. Score gaps are calculated based on differences between unrounded average scores. The score difference between white and American Indian/Alaska Native students was not found to be statistically significant in 1996.

20. Trend in Fourth-Grade NAEP Mathematics Achievement-Level Results, by Race/Ethnicity

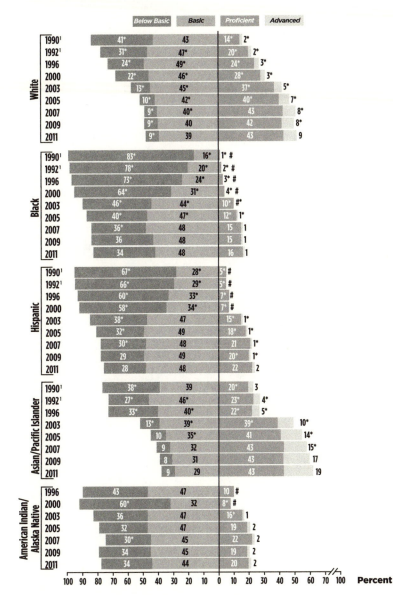

Rounds to zero
* Significantly different (*p*<.05) from 2011
[1] Accommodations not permitted
NOTE: Special analyses raised concerns about the accuracy and precision of the results for Asian/ Pacific Islander students in 2000; therefore, they are omitted from this figure. Sample sizes were insufficient to permit reliable estimates for American Indian/Alaska Native students in 1990 and 1992. Black includes African American, Hispanic includes Latino, and Pacific Islander includes Native Hawaiian. Race categories exclude Hispanic origin. Results are not shown for students whose race/ ethnicity was unclassified or two or more races. Detail may not sum to totals because of rounding.

21. Trend in Eighth-Grade NAEP Mathematics Average Scores

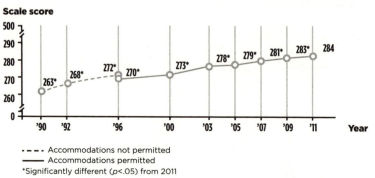

- - - Accommodations not permitted
—— Accommodations permitted
*Significantly different (*p*<.05) from 2011

22. Trend in Eighth-Grade NAEP Mathematics Achievement-Level Results

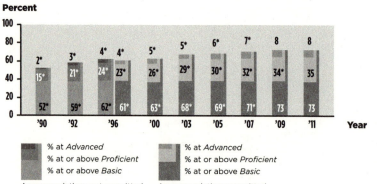

% at *Advanced*
% at or above *Proficient*
% at or above *Basic*

% at *Advanced*
% at or above *Proficient*
% at or above *Basic*

Accommodations not permitted   Accommodations permitted
*Significantly different (*p*<.05) from 2011

23. Trend in Eighth-Grade NAEP Mathematics Average Scores and Score Gaps for White and Black Students

Scale score

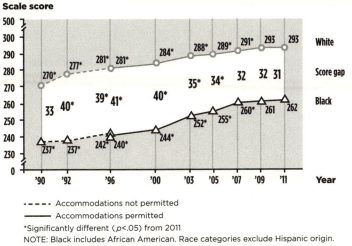

- - - - Accommodations not permitted
———— Accommodations permitted
*Significantly different ($p<.05$) from 2011
NOTE: Black includes African American. Race categories exclude Hispanic origin.
Score gaps are calculated based on differences between unrounded average scores.

24. Trend in Eighth-Grade NAEP Mathematics Average Scores and Score Gaps for White and Hispanic Students

Scale score

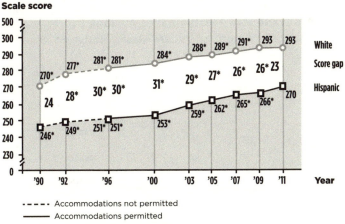

- - - - Accommodations not permitted
———— Accommodations permitted
*Significantly different ($p<.05$) from 2011
NOTE: White excludes students of Hispanic origin. Hispanic includes Latino.
Score gaps are calculated based on differences between unrounded average scores.

25. Trend in Fourth-Grade NAEP Mathematics Average Scores and Score Gaps for Asian/Pacific Islanders and White Students

Scale score

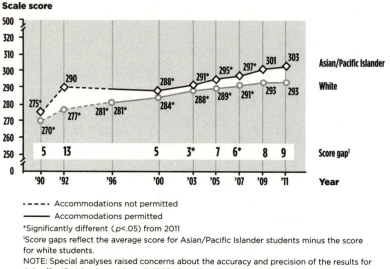

----- Accommodations not permitted

——— Accommodations permitted

*Significantly different (*p*<.05) from 2011

[1]Score gaps reflect the average score for Asian/Pacific Islander students minus the score for white students.

NOTE: Special analyses raised concerns about the accuracy and precision of the results for Asian/Pacific Islander students in 1996; therefore, they are omitted from this figure. Pacific Islander includes Native Hawaiian. Race categories exclude Hispanic origin. Score gaps are calculated based on differences between unrounded average scores. Score differences between Asian/Pacific Islander and white students were not found to be statistically significant in 1990, 1992, and 2000.

26. Trend in Eighth-Grade NAEP Mathematics Average Scores and Score Gaps for White and American Indian/Alaska Native Students

Scale score

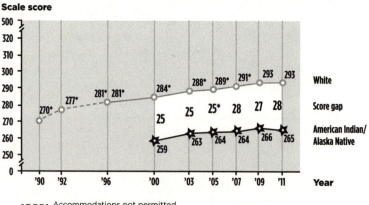

----- Accommodations not permitted

——— Accommodations permitted

*Significantly different (*p*<.05) from 2011

NOTE: Sample sizes were insufficient to permit reliable estimates for American Indian/Alaska Native students in 1990, 1992, and 1996. Race categories exclude Hispanic origin. Score gaps are calculated based on differences between unrounded average scores.

27. Trend in Eighth-Grade NAEP Mathematics Achievement-Level Results, by Race/Ethnicity

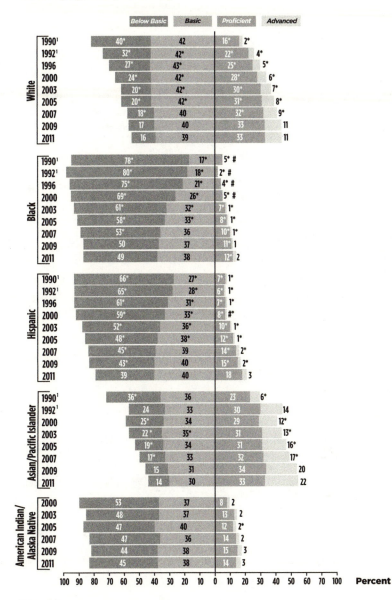

Rounds to zero

* Significantly different (*p*<.05) from 2011

[1] Accommodations not permitted

NOTE: Special analyses raised concerns about the accuracy and precision of the results for Asian/Pacific Islander students in 1996; therefore, they are omitted from this figure. Sample sizes were insufficient to permit reliable estimates for American Indian/Alaska Native students in 1990, 1992, and 1996. Black includes African American, Hispanic includes Latino, and Pacific Islander includes Native Hawaiian. Race categories exclude Hispanic origin. Results are not shown for students whose race/ethnicity was unclassified or two or more races. Detail may not sum to totals because of rounding.

28. Trend in NAEP Reading Average Scores for Nine-, Thirteen-, and Seventeen-Year-Old Students

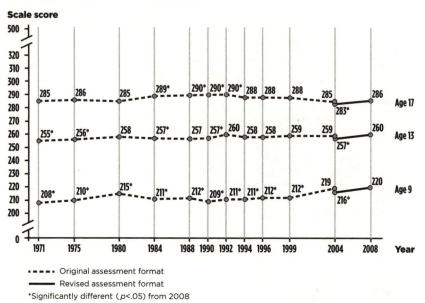

29. Trend in NAEP Mathematics Average Scores for Nine-, Thirteen-, and Seventeen-Year-Old Students

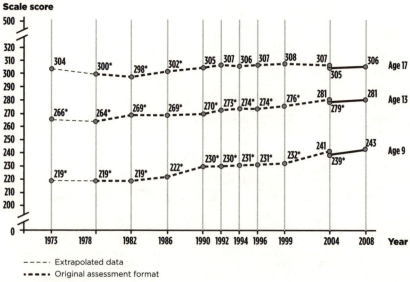

30. Trend in Fourth-Grade NAEP Reading Achievement-Level Results, by Race/Ethnicity

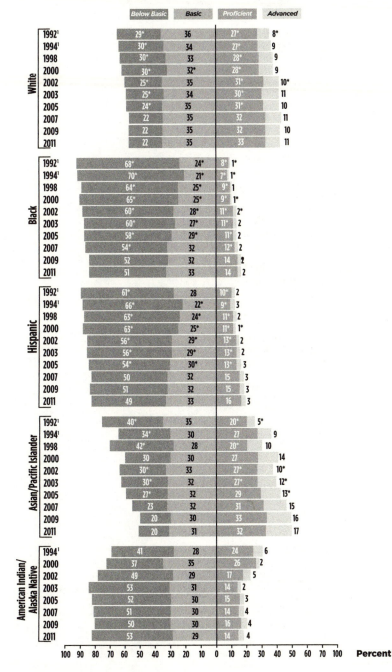

Legend: Below Basic | Basic | Proficient | Advanced

White
Year	Below Basic	Basic	Proficient	Advanced
1992[1]	29*	36	27*	8*
1994[1]	30*	34	27*	9
1998	30*	33	28*	9
2000	30*	32*	28*	9
2002	25*	35	31*	10*
2003	25*	34	30*	11
2005	24*	35	31*	10
2007	22	35	32	11
2009	22	35	32	10
2011	22	35	33	11

Black
Year	Below Basic	Basic	Proficient	Advanced
1992[1]	68*	24*	8*	1*
1994[1]	70*	21*	7*	1*
1998	64*	25*	9*	1
2000	65*	25*	9*	1*
2002	60*	28*	11*	2*
2003	60*	27*	11*	2
2005	58*	29*	11*	2
2007	54*	32	12*	2
2009	52	32	14	2
2011	51	33	14	2

Hispanic
Year	Below Basic	Basic	Proficient	Advanced
1992[1]	61*	28	10*	2
1994[1]	66*	22*	9*	3
1998	63*	24*	11*	2
2000	63*	25*	11*	1*
2002	56*	29*	13*	2
2003	56*	29*	13*	2
2005	54*	30*	13*	3
2007	50	32	15	3
2009	51	32	15	3
2011	49	33	16	3

Asian/Pacific Islander
Year	Below Basic	Basic	Proficient	Advanced
1992[1]	40*	35	20*	5*
1994[1]	34*	30	27	9
1998	42*	28	20*	10
2000	30	30	27	14
2002	30*	33	27*	10*
2003	30*	32	27*	12*
2005	27*	32	29	13*
2007	23	32	31	15
2009	20	30	33	16
2011	20	31	32	17

American Indian/Alaska Native
Year	Below Basic	Basic	Proficient	Advanced
1994[1]	41	28	24	6
2000	37	35	26	2
2002	49	29	17	5
2003	53	31	14	2
2005	52	30	15	3
2007	51	30	14	4
2009	50	30	16	4
2011	53	29	14	4

Percent: 100 90 80 70 60 50 40 30 20 10 0 10 20 30 40 50 60 70 100

* Significantly different (*p*<.05) from 2011
[1] Accommodations not permitted

NOTE: Sample sizes were insufficient to permit reliable estimates for American Indian/Alaska Native students in 1992 and 1998. Black includes African American, Hispanic includes Latino, and Pacific Islander includes Native Hawaiian. Race categories exclude Hispanic origin. Results are not shown for students whose race/ethnicity was unclassified. Detail may not sum to totals because of rounding.

31. Trend in Eighth-Grade NAEP Reading Achievement-Level Results, by Race/Ethnicity

Race/Ethnicity	Year	Below Basic	Basic	Proficient	Advanced
White	1992¹	23*	42	32*	4
White	1994¹	23*	42	32*	4*
White	1998	19*	42	36	3*
White	2002	16	43*	37	4*
White	2003	17*	42	37*	4
White	2005	18*	43	35*	4*
White	2007	16*	43*	36*	4*
White	2009	16	43	38	4*
White	2011	15	42	38	5
Black	1992¹	55*	36*	9*	#
Black	1994¹	57*	34*	9*	#
Black	1998	47*	40	12	#
Black	2002	45*	42	13	1
Black	2003	46*	41*	12*	1
Black	2005	48*	40*	12*	#
Black	2007	45*	42	12*	#*
Black	2009	43*	43	13	#
Black	2011	41	44	14	1
Hispanic	1992¹	51*	36*	12*	1
Hispanic	1994¹	49*	36*	14*	1
Hispanic	1998	47*	39	14*	1
Hispanic	2002	43*	42	15*	1
Hispanic	2003	44*	41*	15*	1
Hispanic	2005	44*	41*	14*	1
Hispanic	2007	42*	43*	15*	1
Hispanic	2009	39*	44	16	1
Hispanic	2011	36	45	18	1
Asian/Pacific Islander	1992¹	24	39	30	7
Asian/Pacific Islander	1994¹	28*	38	29	5
Asian/Pacific Islander	1998	25	42	30	3*
Asian/Pacific Islander	2002	24*	41	32*	4*
Asian/Pacific Islander	2003	21*	39	35	5
Asian/Pacific Islander	2005	20*	40	35*	6
Asian/Pacific Islander	2007	20	39	36	5*
Asian/Pacific Islander	2009	17	38	39	6
Asian/Pacific Islander	2011	17	36	39	8
American Indian/Alaska Native	1994¹	42	39	17	2
American Indian/Alaska Native	2002	39	44	17	1
American Indian/Alaska Native	2003	43	40	16	1
American Indian/Alaska Native	2005	41	41	16	1
American Indian/Alaska Native	2007	44*	38	16	2
American Indian/Alaska Native	2009	38	41	19	2
American Indian/Alaska Native	2011	37	41	20	2

100 90 80 70 60 50 40 30 20 10 0 10 20 30 40 50 60 70 100   **Percent**

\# Rounds to zero

* Significantly different ($p<.05$) from 2011

¹ Accommodations not permitted

NOTE: Sample sizes were insufficient to permit reliable estimates for American Indian/Alaska Native students in 1992 and 1998. Black includes African American, Hispanic includes Latino, and Pacific Islander includes Native Hawaiian. Race categories exclude Hispanic origin. Results are not shown for students whose race/ethnicity was unclassified. Detail may not sum to totals because of rounding.

32. Averaged Freshman Graduation Rate for Public High School Students: Selected School Years 1990–91 Through 2008–9

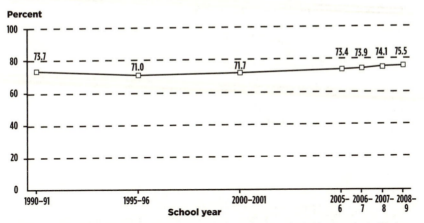

NOTE: The averaged freshman graduation rate is the number of graduates divided by the estimated freshman enrollment count four years earlier. This count is the sum of the number of eighth graders five years earlier, the number of ninth graders four years earlier, and the number of tenth graders three years earlier, divided by 3. Ungraded students were allocated to individual grades proportional to each state's enrollment in those grades. Graduates include only those who earned regular diplomas or diplomas for advanced academic achievement (e.g., honors diplomas) as defined by the state or jurisdiction. The 2005-6 national estimates include imputed data for the District of Columbia, Pennsylvania, and South Carolina. The 2007-8 estimate for Maine includes graduates from semiprivate schools. The 2008-9 national estimates include imputed data for California and Nevada.
SOURCE: U.S. Department of Education, National Center for Education Statistics, Common Core of Data (CCD), "NCES Common Core of Data State Dropout and Completion Data File," school year 2007-8; 2008-9, Version 1a; and "State Nonfiscal Survey of Public Elementary/Secondary Education," 1990-91, Version 1b; 1995-96, Version 1b; 2000-2001, Version 1b; 2005-6, Version 1b; and 2006-7, Version 1b.

33. Status Completion Rates of Eighteen- Through Twenty-Four-Year-Olds Not Currently Enrolled in High School or Below, by Race/Ethnicity: October 1972 Through October 2009

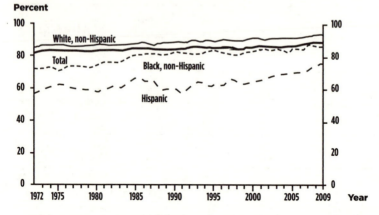

Percent

NOTE: Status completion rates measure the percentage of eighteen- through twenty-four-year-olds who are not enrolled in high school and who also hold a high school diploma or alternative credential, such as a General Educational Development (GED) certificate. Those still enrolled in high school are excluded from the analysis. Beginning in 2003, respondents were able to identify themselves as being two or more races. The 2003 through 2009 categories for white, non-Hispanic, and black, non-Hispanic contain only respondents who indicated just one race. The Hispanic category includes Hispanics of all races and racial combinations. Due to small sample sizes for some or all of the years shown in the figure, Asians/Pacific Islanders and American Indians/Alaska Natives who are not Hispanic are included in the totals but not shown separately. The "two or more races, non-Hispanic" category is also included in the total in 2003 through 2009 but not shown separately due to small sample sizes. The variability of Hispanic status rates reflects, in part, small sample size of Hispanics in earlier years of the Current Population Survey (CPS). Beginning with 1987, estimates reflect new editing procedures for cases missing school enrollment item data. Estimates beginning with 1992 reflect new wording of the educational attainment item. Estimates beginning with 1994 reflect changes due to newly instituted computer-assisted interviewing. For details about changes in the CPS over time, please see P. Kaufman, M. N. Alt, and C. Chapman, *Dropout Rates in the United States: 2001* (NCES 2005-046) (Washington, D.C.: National Center for Education Statistics, Institute of Education Sciences, U.S. Department of Education, 2004).
SOURCE: U.S. Department of Commerce, Census Bureau, Current Population Survey (CPS), October 1972–2009.

34. Status Completion Rates of Eighteen- Through Twenty-Four-Year-Olds Not Currently Enrolled in High School or Below, by Race/Ethnicity and Sex: October 2009

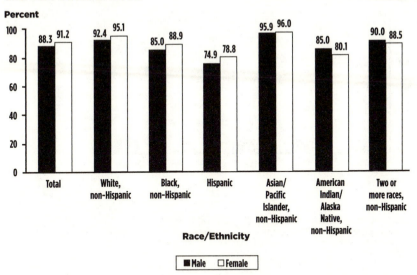

NOTE: Status completion rates measure the percentage of eighteen- through twenty-four-year-olds who are not enrolled in high school and who also hold a high school diploma or alternative credential, such as a General Educational Development (GED) certificate. Those still enrolled in high school are excluded from the analysis. Respondents were able to identify themselves as being two or more races. The white, non-Hispanic; black, non-Hispanic; Asian/Pacific Islander, non-Hispanic; and American Indian/Alaska Native, non-Hispanic categories consist of individuals who considered themselves to be one race and who did not identify as Hispanic. Non-Hispanics who identified themselves as multiracial are included in the "two or more races, non-Hispanic" category. The Hispanic category consists of Hispanics of all races and racial combinations.
SOURCE: U.S. Department of Commerce, Census Bureau, Current Population Survey (CPS), October 2009.

Appendix

35. Public High School Event Dropout Rate for Grades 9-12, by Race/Ethnicity: School Year 2009-10

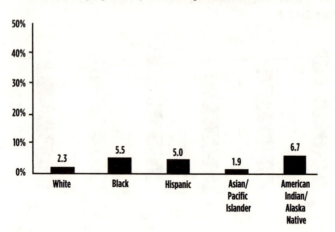

SOURCE: U.S. Department of Education, National Center for Education Statistics, Common Core of Data (CCD, NCES), Common Core of Data State Dropout and Completion Data file, School Year 2009-10, Version 1a.

36. Status Dropout Rates of Sixteen- Through Twenty-Four-Year-Olds by Race/Ethnicity: October 1972 Through October 2009

Percent

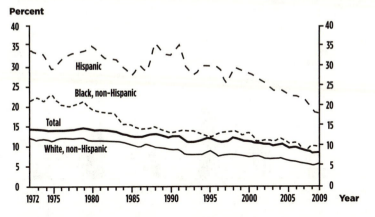

NOTE: The status dropout rate indicates the percentage of sixteen- through twenty-four-year-olds who are not enrolled in high school and who lack a high school credential. High school credentials include high school diplomas and alternative credentials, such as a General Educational Development (GED) certificate. Beginning in 2003, respondents were able to identify themselves as being two or more races. The 2003 through 2009 categories for white, non-Hispanic, and black, non-Hispanic contain only respondents who indicated just one race. The Hispanic category includes Hispanics of all races and racial combinations. Due to small sample sizes for some or all of the years shown in the figure, Asians/Pacific Islanders and American Indians/Alaska Natives who are not Hispanic are included in the totals but not shown separately. The "two or more races, non-Hispanic" category is also included in the totals in 2003 through 2009 but not shown separately due to small sample sizes. The variability of Hispanic status rates reflects, in part, small sample size of Hispanics in earlier years of the Current Population Survey (CPS). Beginning with 1987, estimates reflect new editing procedures for cases with missing data on school enrollment items. Estimates beginning with 1992 reflect new wording of the educational attainment item. Estimates beginning with 1994 reflect changes due to newly instituted computer-assisted interviewing. For details about changes in the CPS over time, please see P. Kaufman, M. N. Alt, and C. Chapman, *Dropout Rates in the United States: 2001* (NCES 2005-046) (Washington, D.C.: National Center for Education Statistics, Institute of Education Sciences, U.S. Department of Education, 2004).
SOURCE: U.S. Department of Commerce, Census Bureau, Current Population Survey (CPS), October 1972–2009.

37. Status Dropout Rates of Sixteen- Through Twenty-Four-Year-Olds, by Race/Ethnicity and Sex: October 2009

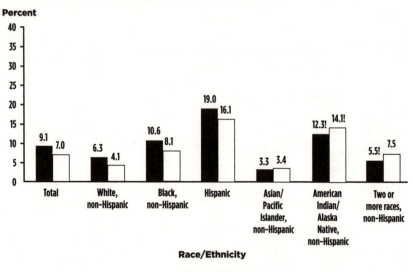

Percent

! Interpret data with caution. The coefficient of variation (CV) for this estimate is 30 percent or greater.
NOTE: The status dropout rate indicates the percentage of sixteen- through twenty-four-year-olds who are not enrolled in high school and who lack a high school credential. High school credentials include high school diplomas and alternative credentials, such as a General Educational Development (GED) certificate. Respondents were able to identify themselves as being two or more races. The white, non-Hispanic; black, non-Hispanic; Asian/Pacific Islander, non-Hispanic; and American Indian/Alaska Native, non-Hispanic categories consist of individuals who considered themselves to be one race and who did not identify as Hispanic. Non-Hispanics who identified themselves as multiracial are included in the "two or more races, non-Hispanic" category. The Hispanic category consists of Hispanics of all races and racial combinations.
SOURCE: U.S. Department of Commerce, Census Bureau, Current Population Survey (CPS), October 2009.

38. Population That Has Attained at Least Upper Secondary Education, 2010

This figure shows the percentage of twenty-five- to thirty-four-year-olds and fifty-five- to sixty-four-year-olds who have been through at least upper secondary education. The rapid expansion of education in recent decades means younger people tend to have higher levels of education.

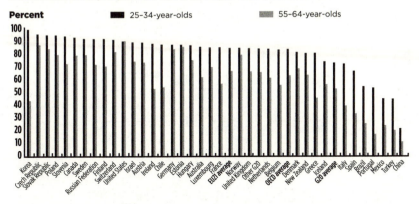

SOURCE: OECD, *Education at a Glance 2012* (2012), Table A1.2a, available at http://dx.doi.org/10.1787/888932664176.

39. Percentage of Population That Has Attained Tertiary Education, by Age Group, 2009

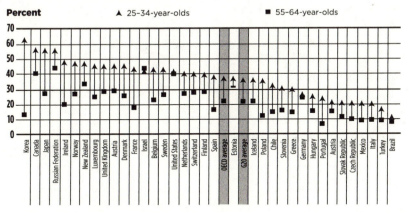

NOTE: Countries are ranked in descending order of the percentage of twenty-five- to thirty-four-year-olds who have attained tertiary education.
SOURCE: OECD, Table A1.3a. See Annex 3 for notes (www.oecd.org/edu/eag2011).

Appendix

40. Trend in White-Black NAEP Reading Average Scores and Score Gaps for Nine-, Thirteen-, and Seventeen-Year-Old Students, 1971–2008

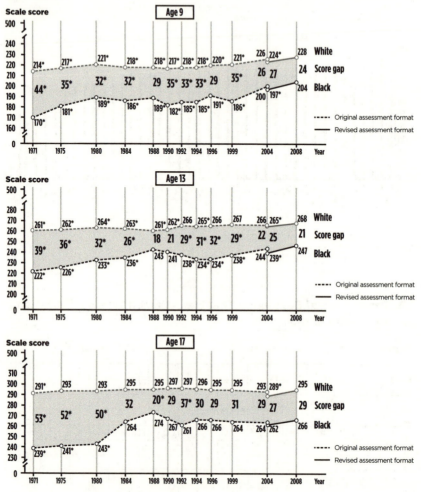

* Significantly different (*p*<.05) from 2008
NOTE: Score gaps are calculated based on differences between unrounded average scores.
Black includes African American. The white and black race categories exclude Hispanic origin.

41. Trend in White-Black NAEP Mathematics Average Scores and Score Gaps for Nine-, Thirteen-, and Seventeen-Year-Old Students, 1971–2008

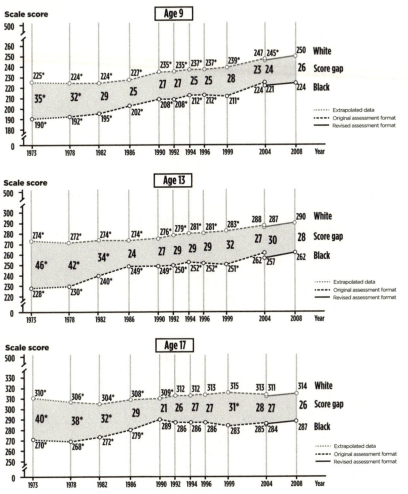

* Significantly different (*p*<.05) from 2008

NOTE: Score gaps are calculated based on differences between unrounded average scores. Black includes African American. The white and black race categories exclude Hispanic origin.

Acknowledgments

In writing this book, I incurred many debts. I wish above all to thank my dear friend and partner, Mary Butz, whose patience and support sustained me during long hours of reading, writing, and revising.

I thank the other members of my family, who have been understanding and supportive of my passion to write this book, including my children, Joseph, Lisa, Michael, and Daniel, and my grandchildren, Nico, Aidan, and Elijah.

I am grateful to those on whom I relied for ideas, inspiration, reflections, research, and suggestions, including Bruce Baker, Jennifer Berkshire, Carol Burris, Anthony Cody, Linda Darling-Hammond, Matthew Di Carlo, Stephen Dyer, Leonie Haimson, Noel Hammatt, Lance Hill, Daniel Hurewitz, Jeannie Kaplan, Rita Kramer, Larry Lee, Karen Miller, Jonathan Pelto, Bill Phillis, Michael Ravitch, Janice Resseger, Richard Rothstein, Gary Rubinstein, Pasi Sahlberg, Carla Sanger, Mercedes Schneider, Diana Senechal, Mark Weber, Elaine Weiss, and Yong Zhao. I thank my dear friend Sandra Priest Rose, who has been a source of encouragement and wisdom for many years. I thank the many teachers, principals, superintendents, parents, school board members, scholars, and friends who sent me articles and ideas about what was happening in their schools and communities.

I thank my literary agents, Lynn Chu and Glen Hartley, for believing in my work over many years.

And I thank Victoria Wilson, my editor. Knopf published my 2003 book, *The Language Police*. It aslo published the work of my mentor, the late Lawrence A. Cremin, and I am happy to see this book on the same list with his great works on the history of American education.

Notes

CHAPTER 2 The Context for Corporate Reform

1. Walt Haney, "The Myth of the Texas Miracle in Education," *Education Policy Analysis Archives* 8, no. 41 (August 19, 2000); Stephen P. Klein et al., "What Do Test Scores in Texas Tell Us?" RAND Issue Paper IP-202, RAND, Santa Monica, Calif., 2000, 2, 9–13.
2. Jennifer Brown, "Cost Doesn't Spell Success for Colorado Schools Using Consultants to Improve Achievement," *Denver Post*, February 19, 2012.
3. Rick Hess, "The Common Core Kool-Aid," *Education Week*, November 30, 2012.
4. Joanne Weiss, "The Innovation Mismatch: 'Smart Capital' and Education Innovation," *Harvard Business Review*, HBR Blog Network, March 31, 2011.
5. Stephanie Simon, "Privatizing Public Schools: Big Firms Eyeing Profits from U.S. K–12 Market," *Huffington Post*, August 2, 2012.
6. Daniel Taub, "Andre Agassi Forms Charter-School Fund with Canyon Capital," Bloomberg News, June 2, 2011; Brian Toporek, "Billionaire Donates $18 Million to Agassi's Charter School," *Education Week*, October 31, 2011.
7. Tierney Plumb, "Movie-House Investor Dives into the Charter-School Space," *The Motley Fool*, August 16, 2011; Capital Roundtable, For-Profit Education Roundtable Brochure, July 16, 2012, http://capitalroundtable.com/masterclass/Capital-Round table-For-Profit-Education-Private-Equity-Conference-2012.html; Juan Gonzalez, "Albany Charter Cash Cow: Big Banks Making a Bundle on New Construction as Schools Bear the Cost," *New York Daily News*, May 7, 2010.

CHAPTER 3 Who Are the Corporate Reformers?

1. Rick Snyder, "A Special Message from Rick Snyder: Education Reform" (memorandum), April 27, 2011, http://www.michigan.gov/documents/snyder/SpecialMessage onEducationReform_351586_7.pdf.
2. Sam Dillon, "Behind Grass-Roots School Advocacy, Bill Gates," *New York Times*, May 21, 2011; Sam Dillon, "Foundations Join to Offer Online Courses for Schools," *New York Times*, April 27, 2011; Stephanie Simon, "K–12 Student Database Jazzes Tech Startups, Spooks Parents," *Reuters*, March 3, 2013.
3. The National Education Association and the American Federation of Teachers

together gave a total of $330 million to political campaigns and civil rights groups over a six-year period from 2005 to 2011. Alicia Mundy, "Teachers Unions Give Broadly," *Wall Street Journal,* July 12, 2012. During the same period of time, the major foundations supporting test-based accountability and choice spent many times that amount. Gates spends $300–$400 million each year on education. Ken Libby, "A Look at the Education Programs of the Gates Foundation," *Shanker Blog,* March 2, 2012, http://shankerblog.org/?p=5234. In 2011, the Walton Family Foundation spent $159 million on education grants: http://www.waltonfamilyfoundation.org/mediacenter/walton-family-foundation-invests-$159-million-in-k12-education-reform-in-2011. These figures do not include political contributions made by either Gates or the Walton family.

4. Steven Brill, *Class Warfare: Inside the Fight to Fix America's Schools* (New York: Simon & Schuster, 2011), 131–32, 224–25.
5. "Chiefs for Change Statement on Louisiana's Bold Education Reforms," Foundation for Excellence in Education Web site, April 18, 2012, http://www.excelined.org/Reform News/2012/Chiefs_for_Change_Statement_on_Louisianas_Bold_Education _Reforms.aspx.
6. Andrew Ujifusa, "Policy Shop Casts Long K–12 Shadow," *Education Week,* April 25, 2012; Julie Underwood and Julie F. Mead, "A Smart ALEC Threatens Public Education," *Education Week,* February 29, 2012.
7. Anthony Cody, "Obama Blasts His Own Education Policies," *Living in Dialogue* (blog), *Education Week,* March 29, 2011.
8. Sunlen Miller, "Obama on Wisconsin Budget Protests: 'An Assault on Unions,'" ABC News, February 17, 2011; Nia-Malika Henderson and Peter Wallsten, "Obama Praises Jeb Bush on Education Reform," *Washington Post,* March 4, 2011; "Struggling Florida Schools Get More Time," WCTV, July 19, 2011, http://www.wctv.tv/news/headlines/Struggling_Schools_Ask_to_Remain_Open_125809473.html?ref=473.
9. Adam Peshek, "ALEC Responds to Ravitch Blog Post," *Education Week,* May 15, 2012.

CHAPTER 4 The Language of Corporate Reform

1. Jeffrey M. Jones, "Confidence in U.S. Public Schools at New Low," *Gallup Politics,* June 20, 2012.
2. William J. Bushaw and Shane Lopez, "Betting on Teachers: The 43rd Annual Phi Delta Kappa/Gallup Poll of the Public's Attitudes Toward the Public Schools," *Phi Delta Kappan,* September 2011, 18–19.
3. Bill Gates, "America's High Schools Are Obsolete" (speech to the National Governors Association, February 26, 2005).
4. Melinda Gates, interview with Jeffrey Brown and Hari Sreenivasan (video and transcript), *NewsHour, PBS,* June 4, 2012.
5. Diane Ravitch, "The Myth of Charter Schools," *New York Review of Books,* November 11, 2010.
6. Joel I. Klein, Condoleezza Rice, and others, *U.S. Education Reform and National Security* (New York: Council on Foreign Relations, 2012).
7. Tom Loveless, *The 2012 Brown Center Report on American Education,* Brookings Institution, Washington, D.C., February 16, 2012; Tom Loveless, "Does the Common Core Matter?," *Education Week,* April 18, 2012; Diane Ravitch, "Do Our Public Schools Threaten National Security?," *New York Review of Books,* June 7, 2012.

CHAPTER 5   The Facts About Test Scores

1. Robert Rothman, "NAEP Board Urged to Delay Standard-Setting Plan," *Education Week,* January 16, 1991.
2. Ravitch, "Myth of Charter Schools."
3. A screen shot of the StudentsFirst Web site: http://msteacher65.tumblr.com/post/24901512311/michelle-rhee-no-friend-to-educators.
4. National Center for Education Statistics, *The Nation's Report Card: Reading 2011* (Washington, D.C.: Institute of Education Sciences, U.S. Department of Education, 2011), 15, 44; National Center for Education Statistics, *The Nation's Report Card: Mathematics 2011* (Washington, D.C.: Institute of Education Sciences, U.S. Department of Education, 2011), 16, 41.
5. Gerald Bracey pointed out how education statistics are misreported by ignoring Simpson's paradox. See Gerald Bracey, "On Knowing When You're Being Lied to with Statistics," *Huffington Post,* January 27, 2007. He explained: "Simpson's Paradox occurs whenever the whole group shows one pattern but subgroups show a different pattern." Thus, the whole group may show a flat line at the same time that every subgroup shows gains because of increased numbers of those in the lowest-scoring groups.
6. NAEP began reporting data for American Indian/Alaska Native in 2000.
7. B. D. Rampey, G. S. Dion, and P. L. Donahue, *NAEP 2008 Trends in Academic Progress* (Washington, D.C.: National Center for Education Statistics, U.S. Department of Education, 2009). Progress stopped in 2008, the high-stakes testing era of NCLB and Race to the Top. The update of this report in 2013 showed virtually no change in scores between 2008 and 2012. See http://www.nationsreportcard.gov/ltt_2012/.

CHAPTER 6   The Facts About the Achievement Gap

1. Martin Carnoy and Richard Rothstein, *What Do International Tests Really Show About U.S. Student Performance?* (Washington, D.C.: Economic Policy Institute, 2013).
2. Paul E. Barton and Richard J. Coley, *The Black-White Achievement Gap: When Progress Stopped* (Princeton, N.J.: Educational Testing Service, 2010).
3. National Center for Education Statistics, *Nation's Report Card: Reading 2011,* 11.
4. National Center for Education Statistics, *Nation's Report Card: Mathematics 2011,* 12.
5. Sean F. Reardon, "The Widening Academic Achievement Gap Between the Rich and the Poor: New Evidence and Possible Explanations," in *Whither Opportunity? Rising Inequality, Schools, and Children's Life Chances,* ed. Greg J. Duncan and Richard J. Murnane (New York: Russell Sage Foundation, 2011).
6. Thomas B. Timar and Julie Maxwell-Jolly, eds., *Narrowing the Achievement Gap: Perspectives and Strategies for Challenging Times* (Cambridge, Mass.: Harvard Education Press, 2012), 230.
7. Ibid., 240–41.

CHAPTER 7   The Facts About the International Test Scores

1. Klein, Rice, et al., *U.S. Education Reform and National Security.*
2. Http://www.aip.org/fyi/2010/121.html.
3. Yong Zhao, "A True Wake-Up Call for Arne Duncan: The Real Reason Behind

Chinese Students Top PISA Performance," December 10, 2010, http://zhaolearning .com/2010/12/10/a-true-wake-up-call-for-arne-duncan-the-real-reason-behind -chinese-students-top-pisa-performance/.

4. H. L. Fleischman, P. J. Hopstock, M. P. Pelczar, and B. E. Shelley, *Highlights from PISA 2009: Performance of U.S. 15-Year-Olds in Reading, Mathematics, and Science Literacy in an International Context* (NCES 2011-004), U.S. Department of Education, National Center for Education Statistics (Washington, D.C.: U.S. Government Printing Office, 2011), 16, 21, 27.

5. Ibid., 15; Carnoy and Rothstein, *What Do International Tests Really Show About U.S. Student Performance?*.

6. Torsten Husen, ed., *International Study of Achievement in Mathematics: A Comparison of Twelve Countries*, 2 vols. (New York: John Wiley & Sons, 1967), 2:21–25.

7. L. C. Comber and John P. Keeves, *Science Education in Nineteen Countries* (New York: John Wiley & Sons, 1973); Elliott A. Medrich and Jeanne E. Griffith, *International Mathematics and Science Assessments: What Have We Learned?* (Washington, D.C.: U.S. Department of Education, 1992), 79–81.

8. Curtis C. McKnight et al., *The Underachieving Curriculum: Assessing U.S. Mathematics from an International Perspective* (Champaign, Ill.: Stipes, 1987), 17, 26–27; Willard J. Jacobson and Rodney L. Doran, *Science Achievement in the United States and Sixteen Countries: A Report to the Public* (New York: Teachers College Press, 1988), 30, 37, 45.

9. Motoko Rich, "U.S. Students Still Lag Globally in Math and Science, Tests Show," *New York Times,* December 11, 2012; Lyndsey Layton and Emma Brown, "U.S. Students Continue to Trail Asian Students in Math, Reading, Science," *Washington Post,* December 11, 2012.

10. National Center for Education Statistics, Trends in International Mathematics and Science Study, 2012, http://nces.ed.gov/timss/. All the TIMSS statistics that follow are drawn from this government report.

11. Ina V. S. Mullis, Michael O. Martin, Pierre Foy, and Kathleen T. Drucker, *PIRLS 2011 International Results in Reading* (Chestnut Hill, Mass.: TIMSS & PIRLS International Study Center, Boston College, 2012).

12. Http://nces.ed.gov/timss/results07_math95.asp; http://nces.ed.gov/timss/table07_4 .asp.

13. Yong Zhao, "The Grass Is Greener: Learning from Other Countries," September 18, 2011, http://zhaolearning.com/2011/09/18/the-grass-is-greener-learning-from-other -countries/.

14. Yong Zhao, *Catching Up or Leading the Way: American Education in the Age of Globalization* (Alexandria, Va.: ASCD, 2009), vii, xi.

15. Yong Zhao, "Reforming Chinese Education: What China Is Trying to Learn from America," *Solutions,* April 2012, 38–43.

16. Vivek Wadhwa, "U.S. Schools Are Still Ahead—Way Ahead," *Bloomberg Businessweek,* January 12, 2011.

17. Keith Baker, "Are International Tests Worth Anything?," *Phi Delta Kappan,* October 2007.

CHAPTER 8 The Facts About High School Graduation Rates

1. U.S. Department of Education, *The Condition of Education, 2012* (Washington, D.C.: National Center for Education Statistics, 2012), fig. 32-2; U.S. Department

of Education, *Public School Graduates and Dropouts from the Common Core of Data: School Year 2009–10* (Washington, D.C.: National Center for Education Statistics, 2013).

2. Federal data about graduation rates and dropout rates are drawn from the most recent report: C. Chapman, J. Laird, N. Hill, and A. KewalRamani, *Trends in High School Dropout and Completion Rates in the United States: 1972–2009* (NCES 2012-006) (Washington, D.C.: U.S. Department of Education, National Center for Education Statistics, 2011), 13.

3. Lawrence Mishel and Joydeep Roy, *Rethinking High School Graduation Rates and Trends* (Washington, D.C.: Economic Policy Institute, 2006), 49.

4. Mishel and Roy conclude that the exclusion of these two groups—those who are in the military and those who are incarcerated—tends to neutralize any effect on the overall graduation rate, since the graduation rate for one group is high and the other is low. The exception, they say, is black males, who have a higher incarceration rate than other groups. Thus, "the black-white gap in high school completion may be higher than the official statistics show." Ibid., 38, 10.

5. Chapman, Laird, Hill, and KewalRamani, *Trends in High School Dropout and Completion Rates in the United States: 1972–2009*, 24, 44.

6. Ibid., 5.

7. Cameron Brenchley, "High School Graduation Rate at Highest Level in Three Decades," *Homeroom: The Official Blog of the U.S. Department of Education,* http://www.ed.gov/blog/2013/01/high-school-graduation-rate-at-highest-level-in-three-decades/, fig. 2.

8. Chapman, Laird, Hill, and KewalRamani, *Trends in High School Dropout and Completion Rates in the United States: 1972–2009*, 8.

9. OECD, *Education at a Glance 2011* (Paris: Organization for Economic Cooperation and Development, 2011), table A1.2a.

10. U.S. Department of Education, *The Condition of Education, 2011* (Washington, D.C.: National Center for Education Statistics, 2011), 76–77.

11. Russell W. Rumberger, "Solving the Nation's Dropout Crisis," *Education Week,* October 26, 2011.

CHAPTER 9   The Facts About College Graduation Rates

1. Thomas D. Snyder, ed., *120 Years of American Education: A Statistical Portrait* (Washington, D.C.: U.S. Department of Education, 1993), 66–69.

2. U.S. Department of Education, *Condition of Education, 2012,* http://nces.ed.gov/pubs2012/2012045.pdf, p. 109, fig. 45-1.

3. OECD, *Education at a Glance 2011,* http://www.oecd.org/education/higheredu cationandadultlearning/48630299.pdf, Table A1.3A, p. 30; OECD, *Education at a Glance 2012* (Paris: Organization for Economic Cooperation and Development, 2012), p. 13, fig. 1.2.

4. U.S. Department of Education, *Condition of Education, 2012,* table A-48-1.

5. College Board Commission on Access, Admissions, and Success in Higher Education, http://completionagenda.collegeboard.org/about-agenda.

6. U.S. Department of Education, *Condition of Education, 2011,* p. 68, indicator 21.

7. Paul Krugman, "Degrees and Dollars," *New York Times,* March 7, 2011.

8. Hope Yen, "In Weak Job Market, One in Two College Graduates Are Jobless or Underemployed," *Huffington Post,* April 22, 2012.

9. Bureau of Labor Statistics, http://www.bls.gov/opub/mlr/2009/11/art5full.pdf, 88, 93.

10. Andrew Martin and Andrew W. Lehren, "A Generation Hobbled by the Soaring Cost of College," *New York Times,* May 12, 2012.

CHAPTER 10   How Poverty Affects Academic Achievement

1. Joel I. Klein, "Urban Schools Need Better Teachers, Not Excuses, to Close the Education Gap," *U.S. News,* May 4, 2009.

2. Http://www.billgateswindows.com/ms/817/bill-gates-improving-education-is-the-best-way-to-solve-poverty/.

3. Wendy Kopp with Steven Farr, *A Chance to Make History: What Works and What Doesn't in Providing an Excellent Education for All* (New York: PublicAffairs, 2012), 5, 8.

4. UNICEF, *Measuring Child Poverty: New League Tables of Child Poverty in the World's Rich Countries* (Florence, Italy: UNICEF Innocenti Research Centre, 2012), p. 3. The league tables did not include Asian nations.

5. John L. Kiely and Michael D. Kogan, "Prenatal Care," in *Reproductive Health of Women: From Data to Action: CDC's Public Health Surveillance for Women, Infants, and Children,* http://www.cdc.gov/reproductivehealth/ProductsPubs/DatatoAction/pdf/rhow8.pdf.

6. James N. Martin, "Facts Are Important: Prenatal Care Is Important to Healthy Pregnancies," American Congress of Obstetricians and Gynecologists, February 21, 2012, http://www.acog.org/-/media/Departments/Government%20Relations%20and%20Outreach/20120221FactsareImportant.pdf?dmc=1&ts=20120701T1119268833.

7. Ibid.

8. Richard Rothstein, *Class and Schools: Using Social, Economic, and Educational Reform to Close the Black-White Achievement Gap* (New York: Teachers College Press, 2004), 16.

9. Ibid., 19–32; U.S. Department of Education, *Condition of Education, 2012,* 18.

10. Rothstein, *Class and Schools,* 37–47.

11. R. Balfanz and V. Byrnes, *Chronic Absenteeism: Summarizing What We Know from Nationally Available Data* (Baltimore: Johns Hopkins University Center for Social Organization of Schools, 2012).

12. Helen F. Ladd, "Education and Poverty: Confronting the Evidence," *Journal of Policy Analysis and Management* 31, no. 2 (2012): 203–27.

CHAPTER 11   The Facts About Teachers and Test Scores

1. Evan Thomas and Pat Wingert, "Why We Must Fire Bad Teachers," *Newsweek,* March 5, 2010.

2. William L. Sanders and June C. Rivers, "Cumulative and Residual Effects of Teachers on Future Student Academic Achievement" (Knoxville: University of Tennessee Value-Added Research and Assessment Center, 1996); William L. Sanders et al., "The Tennessee Value-Added Assessment System: A Quantitative, Outcomes-Based Approach to Educational Assessment," in *Grading Teachers, Grading Schools: Is Student Achievement a Valid Evaluation Measure?,* ed. Jason Millman (Thousand Oaks, Calif.: Corwin Press, 1997). Matthew Di Carlo debunked the "three great teachers in

a row" claim in "How Many Teachers Does It Take to Close an Achievement Gap?," *Shanker Blog,* March 17, 2011, http://shankerblog.org/?p=2156.

3. Http://www.takepart.com/article/2011/05/06/michelle-rhee-how-nations-gone-soft-great-teachers-and-politics-education.

4. Http://blog.thedaily.com/post/3233869778/three-great-teachers-in-a-row-and-the-average.

5. Eric A. Hanushek, "The Economic Value of Higher Teacher Quality" (NBER working paper 16606, December 2010).

6. Eric A. Hanushek, "The Tradeoff Between Child Quantity and Quality," *Journal of Political Economy* 100, no. 1 (February 1992): 84–117; http://garyrubinstein.teachforus.org/2012/06/09/do-effective-teachers-teach-three-times-as-much-as-ineffective-teachers/.

7. Joel Klein, Michelle Rhee, et al., "How to Fix Our Schools: A Manifesto," *Washington Post,* October 10, 2010.

8. Http://www.whitehouse.gov/the-press-office/remarks-president-arnold-missouri-town-hall.

9. Richard Rothstein, "How to Fix Our Schools," Economic Policy Institute, October 14, 2010.

10. Eric A. Hanushek, John F. Kain, and Steven G. Rifkin, "Teachers, Schools, and Academic Achievement" (NBER working paper 6691, August 1998); Matthew Di Carlo, "Teachers Matter, but So Do Words," *Shanker Blog,* July 14, 2010, http://shankerblog.org/?p=74; Matthew Di Carlo, "Teacher Quality on the Red Carpet; Accuracy Swept Under the Rug," *Shanker Blog,* September 16, 2010, http://shankerblog.org/?p=799.

11. Http://www.studentsfirst.org/pages/last-in-first-out-a-policy-that-hurts-students-teachers-and-communities. The source of this claim was Eric Hanushek: http://www.studentsfirst.org/blog/entry/why-an-effective-teacher-matters-a-q-a-with-eric-hanushek/.

12. Http://www.pbs.org/newshour/bb/education/jan-june12/melindagates_06-04.html.

13. Eric A. Hanushek, "Valuing Teachers: How Much Is a Good Teacher Worth?," *Education Next* 11, no. 3 (Summer 2011).

14. Annie Lowry, "Big Study Links Good Teachers to Lasting Gain," *New York Times,* January 6, 2012.

15. Bruce D. Baker, "Fire First, Ask Questions Later? Comments on Recent Teacher Effectiveness Studies," *School Finance 101* (blog), January 7, 2012, http://schoolfinance101.wordpress.com/2012/01/07/fire-first-ask-questions-later-comments-on-recent-teacher-effectiveness-studies/. In the next post on Baker's blog (January 19, 2012), John Friedman wrote to Baker that his comment about firing teachers was taken out of context. He also said that Baker had not adjusted for discounting, and that the study actually projected a lifetime gain per person of about $1,000 per year, or $20 per week; http://schoolfinance101.wordpress.com/2012/01/19/follow-up-on-fire-first-ask-questions-later/. Another reviewer, Moshe Adler of Columbia University, maintained that the Chetty study contradicted itself about future earnings and proved nothing, except that big studies should be peer-reviewed before they are released to the media. Moshe Adler, "Findings Vs. Interpretations in 'The Long-Term Impacts of Teachers,'" *Education Policy Analysis Archives* 21, no. 10 (February 1, 2013).

16. Matthew Di Carlo, "How Many Teachers Does It Take to Close an Achievement Gap?," *Shanker Blog,* March 17, 2011, http://shankerblog.org/?p=2156.

17. American Educational Research Association and National Academy of Education, "Getting Teacher Evaluation Right: A Brief for Policymakers" (2011).
18. Linda Darling-Hammond, "Value-Added Evaluation Hurts Teaching," *Education Week,* March 20, 2012.
19. John Ewing, "Mathematical Intimidation: Driven by the Data," *Notices of the American Mathematical Society* 58, no. 5 (May 2011): 671.
20. Fernanda Santos and Robert Gebeloff, "Teacher Quality Widely Diffused, Ratings Indicate," *New York Times,* February 24, 2012; Georgett Roberts, "Queens Parents Demand Answers Following Teacher's Low Grades," *New York Post,* February 26, 2012; Diane Ravitch, "How to Demoralize Teachers," *Bridging Differences* (blog), *Education Week,* February 28, 2012.
21. Leo Casey, "The True Story of Pascale Mauclair," *Edwize,* February 28, 2012.

CHAPTER 12 **Why Merit Pay Fails**

1. Richard J. Murnane and David K. Cohen, "Merit Pay and the Evaluation Problem: Understanding Why Most Merit Pay Plans Fail and a Few Survive," *Harvard Educational Review* (Spring 1986).
2. M. G. Springer, D. Ballou, L. Hamilton, V. Le, J. R. Lockwood, D. McCaffrey, M. Pepper, and B. Stecher, *Teacher Pay for Performance: Experimental Evidence from the Project on Incentives in Teaching* (Nashville, Tenn.: National Center on Performance Incentives at Vanderbilt University, 2010).
3. Sarah D. Sparks, "Study Leads to End of New York City Merit-Pay Program," *Education Week,* July 20, 2011.
4. David W. Chen and Anna M. Phillips, "Mayor Takes On Teachers' Union in School Plans," *New York Times,* January 12, 2012.
5. Steven Glazerman and Allison Seifullah, "An Evaluation of the Chicago Teacher Advancement Program (Chicago TAP) After Four Years" (Washington, D.C.: Mathematica Policy Research, March 7, 2012); Nora Fleming, "Some Efforts on Merit Pay Scaled Back," *Education Week,* September 21, 2011.
6. Debra Viadero, "Texas Merit-Pay Pilot Failed to Boost Student Scores, Study Says," *Education Week,* November 4, 2009; "Texas Takes Another Stab at Teacher Merit Pay," *Education News,* August 22, 2009.
7. Andrea Gabor, *The Man Who Discovered Quality: How W. Edwards Deming Brought the Quality Revolution to America—the Stories of Ford, Xerox, and GM* (New York: Times Books, 1990), 250–53.

CHAPTER 13 **Do Teachers Need Tenure and Seniority?**

1. Sam Dillon, "Gates Urges School Budget Overhauls," *New York Times,* November 19, 2010.
2. Bruce D. Baker, *Revisiting the Age-Old Question: Does Money Matter in Education?* (Washington, D.C.: Albert Shanker Institute, 2012).
3. Richard M. Ingersoll, "Beginning Teacher Induction: What the Data Tell Us," *Education Week,* May 16, 2012; Ken Futernick, "Incompetent Teachers or Dysfunctional Systems?: Re-framing the Debate on Teacher Quality and Accountability" (San Francisco: WestEd, 2010), http://www.wested.org/tippingpoint/downloads/incompetence_systems.pdf.

4. Richard Ingersoll and Lisa Merrill, "The Changing Face of the Teaching Force," *@PennGSE: A Review of Research* (Fall 2010), http://www.gse.upenn.edu/review/feature/ingersoll.

CHAPTER 14 The Problem with Teach for America

1. "The Story of Teach for America," *Harvard Magazine,* July–August 2012; Wendy Kopp, "In Defense of Optimism in Education," *Huffington Post,* March 13, 2012.
2. Teach for America Web site: http://www.teachforamerica.org/our-mission/a-solvable -problem.
3. Teach for America, 990 tax forms: http://www.guidestar.org/FinDocuments/2011/ 133/541/2011-133541913-08746967-9.pdf.
4. Wendy Kopp, *One Day, All Children . . .: The Unlikely Triumph of Teach for America and What I Learned Along the Way* (New York: Public Affairs: 2003), 185.
5. Kopp, "In Defense of Optimism."
6. Http://www.fastcompany.com/social/2008/profiles/teach-for-america.html.
7. Paul T. Decker, Daniel P. Mayer, and Steven Glazerman, "The Effects of Teach for America on Students: Findings from a National Evaluation" (Washington, D.C.: Mathematica Policy Research, June 9, 2004), xiv.
8. Julian Vasquez Heilig and Su Jin Jez, "Teach for America: A Review of the Evidence" (Boulder, Colo.: National Education Policy Center, June 2010).
9. Http://garyrubinstein.teachforus.org/2011/10/31/why-i-did-tfa-and-why-you -shouldnt/.
10. Bruce D. Baker, "Ed Schools," *School Finance 101* (blog), December 3, 2010, http:// schoolfinance101.wordpress.com/2010/12/03/ed-schools/.
11. Cowen Institute for Public Education Initiatives, "School Choice: Parent Opinions on School Selection in New Orleans" (New Orleans: Tulane University, January 2013), http://www.coweninstitute.com/wp-content/uploads/2013/01/Choice-Focus-Groups-FINAL-small.pdf, p. 7; Raynard Sanders, "Why the Education Reforms in New Orleans Failed and Will Never Work," Research on Reforms, February 2012, http://www.researchonreforms.org/html/documents/RSWhyEducRefmsFail.pdf; Charles J. Hatfield, "Should the Educational Reforms in New Orleans Serve as a National Model for Other Cities?," Research on Reforms, New Orleans, Louisiana, 2012, http://www.researchonreforms.org/html/documents/ResponsetoNSNO_001. pdf; Kari Dequine Harden, "Report Says New Orleans Parents Need Better Information for School Choice to Work," *The Advocate,* February, 11, 2013.
12. Barbara Miner, "Looking Past the Spin: Teach for America," *Rethinking Schools* (Spring 2010); see also Andrew Hartman, "Teach for America: The Hidden Curriculum of Liberal Do-Gooders," *Jacobin* (Winter 2012); Rachel Levy, "Teach for America: From Service Group to Industry," *All Things Education,* May 28, 2011.
13. Barbara Torre Veltri, *Learning on Other People's Kids: Becoming a Teach for America Teacher* (Charlotte, N.C.: Information Age Publishing, 2010), 190 and jacket copy.
14. Matthew Ronfeldt, Susannah Loeb, and Jim Wyckoff, "How Teacher Turnover Harms Student Achievement," http://cepa.stanford.edu/sites/default/files/TchTrnSt Ach%20AERJ%20RR%20not%20blind.pdf.
15. Http://blogs.edweek.org/teachers/living-in-dialogue/2012/04/deepening_the _debate_over_teac.html.
16. William V. Healey, "Heal for America," *Wall Street Journal,* September 12, 2009.

CHAPTER 15 The Mystery of Michelle Rhee

1. To learn more about Baltimore's short-lived experiment in privatization, see http:// articles.baltimoresun.com/keyword/tesseract.

2. Richard Whitmire, *The Bee Eater: Michelle Rhee Takes on the Nation's Worst School District* (San Francisco: Jossey-Bass, 2011).

3. Bill Turque, "Rhee Deploys 'Army of Believers,'" *Washington Post,* July 5, 2008.

4. Clay Risen, "The Lightning Rod," *Atlantic,* November 2008.

5. Valerie Strauss, "Michelle Rhee's Greatest Hits," *The Answer Sheet* (blog), *Washington Post,* October 14, 2010, quoting a statement Rhee made at an Aspen Institute summit in Washington in September 2008.

6. Bill Turque, "Many Teachers Pass on IMPACT Bonuses," *Washington Post,* January 28, 2011.

7. Bill Turque, "Michelle Rhee's D.C. Schools Legacy Is in Sharper Focus One Year Later," *Washington Post,* October 15, 2011.

8. Jack Gillum and Marisol Bello, "When Standardized Test Scores Soared in D.C., Were the Gains Real?," *USA Today,* March 30, 2011.

9. Bill Turque, "Ex-Noyes Principal Wayne Ryan Resigns," *Washington Post,* June 20, 2011.

10. Jay Mathews, "D.C. Keeps Ignoring Its Test Erasure Scandal," *Washington Post,* June 22, 2012; Emma Brown, "Investigators Find Test Security Problems at a D.C. School," *Washington Post,* August 8, 2012; Jay Mathews, "D.C. Schools' Test-Score Fantasyland," *Washington Post,* September 23, 2012; Michael Winerip, "Ex-Schools Chief in Atlanta Is Indicted in Testing Scandal," *New York Times,* March 29, 2013.

11. Whitmire, *Bee Eater,* 222.

12. Http://gfbrandenburg.wordpress.com/2011/02/09/i-got-scooped-by-more-than -three-years/.

13. Http://gfbrandenburg.files.wordpress.com/2011/01/cohort-effects-at-harlem-park -jpg.jpg; Jay Mathews, "Michelle Rhee's Early Test Scores Challenged," *Washington Post,* February 8, 2011.

14. "Rhee's Response to Blogger's Allegations," *Washington Post,* February 9, 2011.

15. Http://gfbrandenburg.wordpress.com/2011/02/13/an-interview-with-dr-lois-c -williams-principal-investigator-for-the-umbc-tesseract-report/#comments.

16. Bill Turque, "'Creative . . . Motivating' and Fired," *Washington Post,* March 6, 2012.

17. Emma Brown, "Study Chides D.C. Teacher Turnover," *Washington Post,* November 8, 2012; New Teacher Project, "Keeping Irreplaceables in D.C. Public Schools: Lessons in Smart Teacher Retention," http://tntp.org/assets/documents/TNTP_DC Irreplaceables_2012.pdf; Bill Turque, "D.C. Principals: 'Class of '08' Continues to Dwindle," *Washington Post,* June 5, 2012. Personal communication from Mary Levy to author, December 3, 2012.

18. Daniel Denvir, "Michelle Rhee's Right Turn," *Salon,* November 17, 2012. On Rhee's role in Tennessee, see http://blogs.knoxnews.com/humphrey/2013/01/michelle-rhee -on-tn-spending-t.html.

19. Http://www.studentsfirst.org/pages/about-michelle-rhee/.

20. Alan Ginsburg, "The Rhee DC Record: Math and Reading Gains No Better Than Her Predecessors Vance and Janey," January 2011, http://therheedcrecord.wikispaces .com/file/view/The+Rhee+DC+Math+And+Reading+Record+.pdf; see the response to Ginsburg by Paul E. Peterson, "The Case Against Michelle Rhee," *Education Next* 11, no. 3 (Summer 2011); and Ginsburg's response to Peterson: "Michelle Rhee vs. Her

Critics," April 2011, http://therheedcrecord.wikispaces.com/file/view/Final+Peterson +Educationnext+Michelle+Rhee+v.+Her+Critics.pdf.

21. National Center for Education Statistics, *The Nation's Report Card: Trial Urban District Assessment: Reading 2011* (NCES 2012-455) (Washington, D.C.: Institute of Education Sciences, U.S. Department of Education, 2011).

22. National Center for Education Statistics, *The Nation's Report Card: Trial Urban District Assessment: Mathematics 2011* (NCES 2012-452) (Washington, D.C.: Institute of Education Sciences, U.S. Department of Education, 2011).

23. John Merrow, "Michelle Rhee's Reign of Error," *Taking Note: Thoughts on Education from John Merrow,* April 11, 2013, http://takingnote.learningmatters.tv/?p=6232.

CHAPTER 16   The Contradictions of Charters

1. National Alliance for Public Charter Schools, "Unionized Charter Schools: Data from 2009–2010," http://www.publiccharters.org/data/files/Publication_docs/NAPCS %20Unionized%20Charter%20Schools%20Dashboard%20Details_20111103 T104815.pdf.

2. Albert Shanker, "Students Paid the Price When Private Firm Took Over School" (paid advertisement), *New York Times,* February 22, 1996.

3. Albert Shanker, "Goals, Not Gimmicks" (paid advertisement), *New York Times,* November 7, 1993; "Noah Webster Academy" (paid advertisement), *New York Times,* July 3, 1994; "Beyond Magic Bullets" (paid advertisement), *New York Times,* March 19, 1995.

4. Chris Cerf, "Charter Schools: A Single Strand in the Tapestry of New Jersey's Great Public Schools," *NJSpotlight,* July 16, 2012.

5. The states that had not passed legislation authorizing charter schools by the end of 2012 were Alabama, Kentucky, Montana, Nebraska, North Dakota, South Dakota, Vermont, and West Virginia. Voters in Washington State narrowly passed a charter referendum in 2012, after having rejected it three times earlier; the fourth time was a charm, facilitated by a multimillion-dollar campaign fund.

6. National Alliance for Public Charter Schools, "A Growing Movement: America's Largest Charter School Communities," 6th ed., October 2011, 1.

7. Julian Vasquez Heilig, "Why Do Hedge Fund Managers Adore Charters?," http:// cloakinginequity.com/2012/12/07/why-do-hedge-funds-adore-charters-pt-ii-39 -return/.

8. Juan Gonzalez, "Albany Cash Cow: Big Banks Making a Bundle on New Construction as Schools Bear the Cost," *New York Daily News,* May 7, 2010.

9. Stephanie Simon, "The New U.S. Visa Rush: Build a Charter School, Get a Green Card," Reuters, October 12, 2012.

10. Valerie Strauss, "The Big Business of Charter Schools," *Washington Post,* August 17, 2012. See also Stephanie Strom, "For Charter School Company, Issues of Spending and Control," *New York Times,* April 24, 2010.

11. Center for Media and Democracy, "ALEC Exposed," http://alecexposed.org/w/ images/5/57/2D4-Next_Generation_Charter_Schools_Act_Exposed.pdf; see also http://www.edreform.com/wp-content/uploads/2011/09/NextGenerationCharter SchoolsAct.pdf.

12. Http://mediamatters.org/research/2012/05/09/how-alec-is-quietly-influencing -education-refor/184156; Salvador Rizzo, "Some of Christie's Biggest Bills Match Model Legislation from D.C. Group Called ALEC," *Star-Ledger,* April 1, 2012.

13. Lindsay Wagner, "Senate Considers New Public Charter School Board," *The Progressive Pulse* (blog), March 27, 2013 http://pulse.ncpolicywatch.org/2013/03/27/senate-considers-creation-of-new-public-charter-school-board/; http://pulse.ncpolicywatch.org/wp-content/uploads/2013/03/SB-337-NC-Public-Charter-Schools-Board.pdf.

14. U.S. Court of Appeals for the Ninth Circuit, *Caviness v. Horizon Community Learning Center Inc.; Lawrence Pieratt,* January 4, 2010.

15. Preston C. Green, Erica Frankenberg, Steven L. Nelson, and Julie Rowland, "Charter Schools, Students of Color, and the State Action Doctrine," *Washington and Lee Journal of Civil Rights and Social Justice* (Spring 2012): 254–75. See also Julian Vasquez Heilig, "Why Judges Say Charters Are NOT Public Schools—Students and Parents Should Be Nervous," *Cloaking Inequity,* January 2, 2013.

16. New York Charter Schools Association, "Charters Prevail over State Comptroller," *Chalkboard,* June 25, 2009.

17. Martha Woodall, "Phila.'s New Media Charter School Contends It's Not a Public School," philly.com, July 2, 2011; Julie Shaw, "Two Ex-Charter Officials Accused of Taking Money from School," philly.com, April 15, 2011; Martha Woodall, "Former Head of Philadelphia Charter School Admits Fraud," philly.com, April 4, 2012; Martha Woodall, "Charter School Founder Gets 2-Year Term for Fraud," philly.com, July 14, 2012.

18. Becky Vevea, "Chicago Charter School Subject to Private-Sector Labor Laws," WBEZ, January 2, 2013, http://www.wbez.org/news/chicago-charter-school-subject-private-sector-labor-laws-104660; National Labor Relations Board, "Chicago Mathematics and Science Academy Charter School, Inc., Employer and Chicago Alliance of Charter Teachers & Staff, AFT, AFL-CIO," Petitioner, Case 13-RM-001768, December 14, 2012 (359 NLRB No. 41).

19. Bruce D. Baker, "Charter Schools Are . . . [Public? Private? Neither? Both?]," *School Finance 101* (blog), May 2, 2012; Bruce D. Baker, Ken Libby, and Kathryn Wiley, "Spending by the Major Charter Management Organizations: Comparing Charter School and Local Public District Financial Resources in New York, Ohio, and Texas" (National Education Policy Center, May 2012); KIPP challenged these findings: http://www.kipp.org/news/kipp-statement-nepc-report-by-bruce-d-baker-on-spending-by-the-major-charter-management-organizations.

20. Gary Miron, Jessica L. Urschel, Mayra A. Yat Aguilar, and Breanna Dailey, *Profiles of For-Profit and Nonprofit Education Management Organizations, Thirteenth Annual Report, 2010–2011* (Boulder, Colo.: National Education Policy Center, 2012), i–ii.

21. Julian Vasquez Heilig, Amy Williams, Linda McSpadden McNeil, and Christopher Lee, "Is Choice a Panacea? An Analysis of Black Secondary Student Attrition from KIPP, Other Privately Operated Charters, and Urban Districts," *Berkeley Review of Education* 2, no. 2 (2011); KIPP, "Statement by KIPP Regarding Report: 'Is Choice a Panacea?' by Dr. Julian Vasquez Heilig and Colleagues," April 12, 2012, http://www.kipp.org/news/statement-by-kipp-regarding-report-is-choice-a-panacea-by-dr-julian-vasquez-heilig-and-colleagues.

22. Sharon Higgins, "Largest Charter Network in U.S.: Schools Tied to Turkey," *Washington Post,* March 27, 2012; Greg Toppo, "Objectives of Charter Schools with Turkish Ties Questioned," *USA Today,* August 17, 2010; Dan Bilefsky and Sebnem Arsu, "Turkey Feels Sway of Reclusive Cleric in the U.S.," *New York Times,* April 25, 2012; Stephanie Saul, "Charter Schools Tied to Turkey Grow in Texas," *New York Times,* June 6, 2011; Stephanie Saul, "Audits for 3 Georgia Schools Tied to Turkish Movement," *New York Times,* June 5, 2012.

23. Matthew Di Carlo, "The Evidence on Charter Schools and Test Scores," Albert Shanker Institute, December 2011, http://shankerblog.org/wp-content/uploads/2011/12/CharterReview.pdf.

24. David Arsen and Yongmei Ni, "Resource Allocation in Charter and Traditional Public Schools: Is Administration Leaner in Charter Schools?," National Center for the Study of Privatization in Education, March 2012, http://www.ncspe.org/publications_files/OP201.pdf.

25. Miron, Urschel, Yat Aguilar, and Dailey, *Profiles of For-Profit and Nonprofit Education Management Organizations,* ii.

26. Erik Kain, "80% of Michigan Charter Schools Are For-Profits," *Forbes,* September 29, 2011.

27. "A Political Education," *Toledo Blade,* July 9, 2006.

28. "White Hat Management: Ohio Charter School Giant," State Impact Ohio, http://stateimpact.npr.org/ohio/tag/white-hat-management/; "Judge Says White Hat Must Open Its Books," State Impact Ohio, http://stateimpact.npr.org/ohio/2011/12/28/judge-says-white-hat-must-open-its-books/; Ida Liezkovsky, "Making Money on Education: The For-Profit Charter School," State Impact Ohio, http://stateimpact.npr.org/ohio/2011/10/12/charters-schools-part-iii-cashing-in-on-education/.

29. Http://www.plunderbund.com/2012/02/24/white-hat-management-nears-one-billion-dollars-in-charter-school-funding-in-ohio/.

30. Stephanie Strom, "For School Company, Issues of Money and Control," *New York Times,* April 23, 2010; A. D. Pruitt, "Entertainment Company Is Tested by Charter Schools," *Wall Street Journal,* June 26, 2012; Elisa Crouch, "Shuttering of Imagine Charter Schools in St. Louis Is Daunting," *St. Louis Post-Dispatch,* April 20, 2012.

31. Office of the State Comptroller Thomas P. DiNapoli, "Oversight of Financial Operations: Brooklyn Excelsior Charter School," New York State Division of State Government Accountability, Report 2011-S-14, December 2012; Yoav Gonen, "Charter Management Firm Charging Huge Rent Markups to Charter Schools," *New York Post,* April 30, 2012.

32. Julie Dunn, "Agassi Hopes Charter School Will Be a Model," *New York Times,* April 21, 2004; Bryan Toporek, "Billionaire Donates $18 Million to Andre Agassi's Charter School," *Education Week,* October 31, 2011; "Andre Agassi Launches Charter School Building Fund," *Huffington Post,* June 2, 2011.

33. Amy Kingsley, "Learning Curve," *Las Vegas Citylife,* March 14, 2012; Adrian Arambulo, "Agassi Prep Cheerleading Coach Charged in Prostitution Sting," KLAS-TV, Las Vegas, http://www.8newsnow.com/story/6634246/agassi-prep-cheerleading-coach-charged-in-prostitution-sting; Gary Rubinstein, http://miracleschools.wikispaces.com/Agassi+Prep; "Cheer Coach at Agassi's Academy Charged in Prostitution Sting," *USA Today,* June 8, 2007; Alan Dessoff, "High Stakes Cheating," *District Administration,* April 1, 2011. For the school's report card, see http://www.nevadareportcard.com/.

34. "New York Success Academy Network to Receive 50 Percent Increase in Per Student Payment," *Huffington Post,* June 25, 2012.

35. Anne Ryman, "Insiders Benefiting in Charter Deals," *Arizona Republic,* November 17, 2012.

36. Mitchell Landsberg, "Spitting in the Eye of Mainstream Education," *Los Angeles Times,* May 31, 2009; Jill Tucker, "Oakland Charter School Accused of Fraud May Close," *San Francisco Chronicle,* April 3, 2012; Jill Tucker, "Oakland School Official May Face Criminal Probe," *San Francisco Chronicle,* June 14, 2012; Ellen

Cushing, "Are American Indian Public Charter School's Scores Inflated?," *East Bay Express,* June 13, 2012; David Whitman, *Sweating the Small Stuff: Inner-City Schools and the New Paternalism* (Washington, D.C.: Thomas B. Fordham Institute, 2008), 71; Katy Murphy, "High-Scoring Oakland Charter Schools Facing Growing Threat of Closure," *Contra Costa Times,* January 24, 2013; Oakland Unified School District Report, Superintendent's Recommendation to Revoke American Indian Model School (AIMS) Charter, March 20, 2013, http://www.ousd.k12.ca.us/Page/10160.

37. John Merrow, "Can Rocketship Launch a Fleet of Successful Schools?," *NewsHour,* PBS, December 28, 2012, http://learningmatters.tv/blog/on-pbs-newshour/watch -rocketship-schools/10645/.

38. Matt Richtel, "A Silicon Valley School That Doesn't Compute," *New York Times,* October 22, 2011.

39. Benjamin Herold, "'Significant Barriers' to Entry at Many Philadelphia Charters, District Report Says," *Notebook,* July 31, 2012; Benjamin Herold, "Questionable Application Practices at Green Woods, Other Philly Charter Schools," *Notebook,* September 14, 2012.

40. U.S. Government Accountability Office, *Charter Schools: Additional Federal Attention Needed to Help Protect Access for Students with Disabilities* (Washington, D.C.: U.S. GAO, June 2012).

41. Matthew DiCarlo, "Do Charter Schools Serve Fewer Special Education Students?," *Shanker Blog,* June 21, 2012, http://shankerblog.org/?p=6107; Alleen Brown, "Cityview Leaves Special Education Students Behind," *Twin Cities Daily Planet,* July 24, 2012; Cindy Chang, "New Orleans Special Needs Students File Federal Lawsuit Against Louisiana Department of Education," *New Orleans Times-Picayune,* October 29, 2010.

42. Sean Cavanaugh, "Catholic Schools Feeling Squeeze from Charters," *Education Week,* August 29, 2012; *Who Will Save America's Urban Catholic Schools?,* ed. Scott Hamilton (Washington, D.C.: Thomas B. Fordham Institute, 2008); Scott Waldman, "Parochial Schools Feel Pinch," *Albany Times-Union,* September 24, 2012. Abraham Lackman, a scholar in residence at Albany Law School, studied the effect of charters on Catholic schools in New York. He concluded, "We've wound up replacing a good system with a system that is inferior, and it's cost the taxpayer a good deal of money." Lackman found that "for every charter school that has opened in New York in the past decade, a parochial school has closed." Lackman served as chief of staff for the New York State Senate Committee on Finance at the time that charters were authorized in 1998. Abraham Lackman, "The Collapse of Catholic School Enrollment," http://www.scribd.com/doc/106930920/Abe-Lackman-Draft.

43. Samuel Casey Carter, *No Excuses: Lessons from 21 High-Performing, High-Poverty Schools* (Washington, D.C.: Heritage Foundation, 2000), 43–46; Lance T. Izumi, *They Have Overcome: High-Poverty, High-Performing Schools in California* (San Francisco: Pacific Research Institute for Public Policy, 2002); Rob Kuznia, "Inglewood School District Teeters on Verge of State Takeover," *Daily Breeze,* November 3, 2011; Rob Kuznia, "State Takes Over Financially Strapped Inglewood Unified School District," *Daily Breeze,* September 14, 2012; Rob Kuznia, "Inglewood Unified Begins Making Deep Cuts Amid Howls of Protest," *Daily Breeze,* March 15, 2013.

44. Keystone State Education Coalition, http://keystonestateeducationcoalition.blog spot.com/2011/06/follow-money-contributions-by-vahan.html, last updated June 28, 2012; Tony West, "Charter Schools: A School for Scandal?," *Philadelphia Public Record,* August 3, 2012.

CHAPTER 17 Trouble in E-land

1. Stephanie Simon, "Private Firms Eyeing Profits from U.S. Public Schools," Reuters, August 2, 2012; Rick Hess, "The Common Core Kool-Aid," *Education Week,* November 30, 2012.

2. John Hechinger, "Education According to Mike Milken," *Bloomberg Businessweek,* June 2, 2011; Alexandra Starr, "Bill Bennett: The Education of an E-school Skeptic," *Bloomberg Businessweek,* February 13, 2001. Bennett resigned as chairman of K12 in 2005 to avoid causing problems for K12 after he made racist remarks on his radio show.

3. Stephanie Saul, "Profits and Questions at Online Charter Schools," *New York Times,* December 12, 2011.

4. Jeb Bush and Bob Wise, *Digital Learning Now!* (Foundation for Excellence in Education, December 1, 2010), 10.

5. Barbara Means, Yukie Toyama, Robert Murphy, Marianne Bakia, and Karla Jones, *Evaluation of Evidence-Based Practices in Online Learning: A Meta-analysis and Review of Online Learning Studies* (Washington, D.C.: U.S. Department of Education, 2010). The study team found no studies between 1996 and 2006. "By performing a second literature search with an expanded time frame (through July 2008), the team was able to greatly expand the corpus of studies with controlled designs and to identify five controlled studies of K–12 online learning with seven contrasts between online and face-to-face conditions. This expanded corpus still comprises a very small number of studies, especially considering the extent to which secondary schools are using online courses and the rapid growth of online instruction in K–12 education as a whole. Educators making decisions about online learning need rigorous research examining the effectiveness of online learning for different types of students and subject matter as well as studies of the relative effectiveness of different online learning practices" (53).

6. Center for Media and Democracy, "ALEC Exposed," http://alecexposed.org/w/images/4/4a/2D23-Virtual_Public_Schools_Act_Exposed.pdf; Center for Media and Democracy, PR Watch, http://www.prwatch.org/news/2012/07/11652/energy solutions-and-connections-education-are-27th-and-28th-corporations-leave-al.

7. Lee Fang, "How Online Learning Companies Bought America's Schools," *Nation,* December 5, 2011.

8. Gene V. Glass and Kevin G. Welner, *Online K–12 Schooling in the U.S.: Uncertain Private Ventures in Need of Public Regulation* (Boulder, Colo.: National Education Policy Center, 2011), 3.

9. Saul, "Profits and Questions at Online Charter Schools."

10. Colin Woodard, "Special Report: The Profit Motive Behind Virtual Schools in Maine," *Maine Sunday Telegram,* September 3, 2012.

11. Lyndsey Layton and Emma Brown, "Virtual Schools Are Multiplying, but Some Question Their Educational Value," *Washington Post,* November 26, 2011.

12. Ibid.

13. Fang, "How Online Learning Companies Bought America's Schools."

14. Hechinger, "Education According to Mike Milken"; Jack Wagner, "Charter and Cyber Charter Education Funding Reform Should Save Taxpayers $365 Million Annually," Pennsylvania Department of the Auditor General, June 20, 2012.

15. Hechinger, "Education According to Mike Milken."

16. Saul, "Profits and Questions at Online Charter Schools."

17. Ibid.

18. Jason Tomassini, "Virtual Ed. Company Faces Critical Press and a Recent Lawsuit," *Education Week,* February 22, 2012.

19. Layton and Brown, "Virtual Schools Are Multiplying, but Some Question Their Educational Value."

20. Gary Miron and Jessica L. Urschel, *Understanding and Improving Virtual Full-Time Schools: A Study of Student Characteristics, School Finance, and School Performance, in Schools Operated by K12 Inc.* (Boulder, Colo.: National Education Policy Center, 2012), v–vi; press release.

21. Burt Hubbard and Nancy Mitchell, "Troubling Questions About Online Education," *EdNews Colorado,* October 4, 2011.

22. "Tuning In, Dropping Out: Online Schools Troubled?," *Denver Post,* October 9, 2011.

23. *Charter School Performance in Pennsylvania* (Stanford, Calif.: CREDO, April 2011).

24. Http://www.pacyber.org/about.jsp?pageId=216139224060129129784 6033.

25. Http://www.huffingtonpost.com/2012/07/13/fbi-agents-raid-office-of_n_1671829 .html; Rich Lord and Eleanor Chute, "Cyber Charter Is a Magnet for Money," *Pittsburgh Post-Gazette,* July 17, 2012; Rich Lord, "PA Cyber Condo Deal in Florida Defies Math," *Pittsburgh Post-Gazette,* October 12, 2012.

26. Federal Bureau of Investigation, "Charter School Founder Dorothy June Brown Charged in $6 Million Scheme," U.S. Attorney's Office, Eastern District of Pennsylvania, July 24, 2012, http://www.fbi.gov/philadelphia/press-releases/2012/charter -school-founder-dorothy-june-brown-charged-in-6-million-fraud-scheme; Damon C. Williams, "Fraud Case Proceeds Against Charter School Founder," phillytrib.com, July 27, 2012; Betsy Hammond, "Oregon Charter School Founders Charged in $20 Million Racketeering Lawsuit," *Oregonian,* January 4, 2013.

27. "Ohio's E-schools: Funding Failure; Coddling Contributors," Innovation Ohio, May 12, 2011, http://innovationohio.org/wp-content/uploads/2011/05/IO.051211 .eschools.pdf.

28. German Lopez, "School's Out: Data Suggests Internet-Based Education Isn't Living Up to the Hype," *CityBeat,* August 1, 2012.

CHAPTER 18   Parent Trigger, Parent Tricker

1. California Charter School Association, "California Charter Schools Grow to Over 1,000 for the 2012–13 School Year," press release, October 12, 2012. When Jerry Brown was elected governor in 2010, he replaced several of Schwarzenegger's appointees to the state board of education who had not yet been confirmed, including Ben Austin of Parent Revolution.

2. Http://parentrevolution.org/content/passing-parent-trigger.

3. "Lessons of 'Parent Trigger,'" *Los Angeles Times,* November 14, 2011; Caroline Grannan, "Beyond the Parent Trigger Hype and Propaganda: Just the Facts," Parents Across America, August 13, 2012.

4. Teresa Watanabe, "Ruling Supports Adelanto Charter School Effort," *Los Angeles Times,* July 24, 2012; Mark Gutglueck, "Adelanto Charter School's Demise Involved Postmus and DeFazio," *San Bernardino County Sentinel,* May 27, 2011.

5. Http://www.commoncause.org/atf/cf/%7BFB3C17E2-CDD1-4DF6-92BE-BD 4429893665%7D/ed_35daymailing-dc.pdf; http://www.prwatch.org/node/11612.

6. Http://parentsacrossamerica.org/2012/01/parents-watch-out-for-parent-trigger-proposals-in-your-state/.
7. Steve Bousquet, "Legislature Approves $70 Billion Budget," *Miami Herald,* March 10, 2012.
8. "Promote Charter Schools, but Don't Stack the Deck," *Orlando Sentinel,* March 10, 2012.
9. Http://www.usmayors.org/80thAnnualMeeting/media/proposedresolutions2012.pdf.
10. Stephanie Simon, "Mayors Back Parents Seizing Control of Schools," Reuters, June 18, 2012.
11. "No Magic Bullet for Schools," *Los Angeles Times,* April 8, 2012.
12. Bill Berkowitz, "Meet the Christian Right-Wing Billionaire Out to Frack Our World," *AlterNet,* May 13, 2012.
13. Http://parentsacrossamerica.org/wp-content/uploads/2011/03/PAA_Parent_Trigger-position-final.pdf.

CHAPTER 19   The Failure of Vouchers

1. Https://webspace.utexas.edu/hcleaver/www/FriedmanRoleOfGovtEducation1955.htm.
2. John E. Chubb and Terry M. Moe, *Politics, Markets, and America's Schools* (Washington, D.C.: Brookings Institution, 1990), 2, 12; http://civilliberty.about.com/b/2007/06/28/school-integration-after-parents-v-seattle-district.htm.
3. Matthew DeFour, "DPI: Students in Milwaukee Voucher Program Didn't Perform Better in State Tests," *Wisconsin State Journal,* March 29, 2011; "Test Scores Improve for Milwaukee Voucher Schools, but Still Lag Public Schools," *Wisconsin State Journal,* March 27, 2012. On the state tests, there was no difference in the scores of low-income students, whether they attended Milwaukee public schools or voucher schools.
4. National Center for Education Statistics, *Nation's Report Card: Trial Urban District Assessment: Reading 2011,* 92–93; National Center for Education Statistics, *Nation's Report Card: Trial Urban District Assessment: Mathematics 2011,* 82–83.
5. Patrick J. Wolf, *The Comprehensive Longitudinal Evaluation of the Milwaukee Parental Choice Program: Summary of Final Reports* (Fayetteville: University of Arkansas, 2012); Casey D. Cobb, "Review of SCDP Milwaukee Evaluation Report #30" (Boulder, Colo.: National Education Policy Center, 2012), http://nepc.colorado.edu/files/ttr-mkeeval-ark-30.pdf. For an account of the alteration of the attrition rate, see "NEPC: Patrick Wolf Should Apologize," *Diane Ravitch's Blog,* April 2, 2013, http://dianeravitch.net/2013/04/02/nepc-patrick-wolf-should-apologize/. The "independent evaluator" of the Milwaukee and the District of Columbia voucher programs wrote an opinion piece in the *Minneapolis Star-Tribune* calling on his home state of Minnesota to offer more private school choice; see Patrick J. Wolf, "Minnesota Falls Behind on School Choice," *Minneapolis Star-Tribune,* January 28, 2013.
6. Matthew DuFour, "DPI: Students in Milwaukee Voucher Program Didn't Perform Better in State Tests," *Wisconsin State Journal,* March 29, 2011; Erin Richards, "Proficiency Plummets at Voucher Schools, MPS with New Test Scoring," *Milwaukee Journal Sentinel,* October 24, 2012; Alan J. Borsuk, "Scores Show Voucher Schools Need Accountability," *Milwaukee Journal Sentinel,* December 1, 2012.

7. Http://www.federationforchildren.org/leadership; http://alecexposed.org/wiki/Privatizing_Public_Education,_Higher_Ed_Policy,_and_Teachers.

8. National Center for Education Statistics, Nation's Report Card: *Reading 2011,* 72–73; National Center for Education Statistics, Nation's Report Card: *Mathematics 2011,* 62–63; Thomas Ott, "Cleveland Students Hold Their Own with Voucher Students on State Tests," *Cleveland Plain Dealer,* February 22, 2011; http://stateimpact.npr.org/ohio/2012/06/27/how-ohio-spent-103-million-a-year-on-private-school-vouchers/.

9. Patrick Wolf, Babette Gutmann, Michael Puma, Brian Kisida, Lou Rizzo, Nada Eissa, and Matthew Carr, *Evaluation of the DC Opportunity Scholarship Program: Final Report* (NCEE 2010-4018) (Washington, D.C.: National Center for Education Evaluation and Regional Assistance, Institute of Education Sciences, U.S. Department of Education, 2010). In 2013, Patrick Wolf, the evaluator for the Milwaukee and District of Columbia voucher programs, wrote an opinion piece expressing his support for school choice, specifically, for vouchers: Patrick J. Wolf, "Minnesota Falls Behind on School Choice," *Minneapolis Star-Tribune,* January 28, 2013. In the article, he chastised his home state of Minnesota for falling behind his adopted state of Arkansas in providing school choice.

10. Alan Richard, "Florida Supreme Court Finds State Voucher Program Unconstitutional," *Education Week,* January 6, 2006. A study of the Florida voucher program concluded that the test scores increased at the public schools most threatened by the loss of students. David Figlio and Cassandra Hart, "Competitive Effects of Means-Tested School Vouchers," Center for Analysis of Longitudinal Data in Education Research, Working Paper 46, June 2010.

11. Gus Garcia-Roberts, "McKay Scholarship Program Sparks a Cottage Industry of Fraud and Chaos," *Miami New Times,* June 23, 2011.

12. Andy VanDeVoorde, "VVM Writers Named National SPJ Winners," *Village Voice,* April 10, 2012.

13. Stephanie Simon, "Louisiana's Bold Bid to Privatize Schools," Reuters, June 1, 2012.

CHAPTER 20 Schools Don't Improve if They Are Closed

1. *The MetLife Survey of the American Teacher: Teachers, Parents, and the Economy, 2011,* http://www.metlife.com/assets/cao/contributions/foundation/american-teacher/MetLife-Teacher-Survey-2011.pdf; *Primary Sources: 2012: America's Teachers on the Teaching Profession* (Scholastic and Gates Foundation, 2012). *The MetLife Survey of the American Teacher: Challenges for School Leadership, 2012,* https://www.metlife.com/assets/cao/foundation/MetLife-Teacher-Survey-2012.pdf.

2. Marisa de la Torre, Elaine Allensworth, Sanja Jagesic, James Sebastian, and Michael Salmoniwicz for the Consortium; Coby Meyers and Dean Gerdeman for American Institutes for Research, *Turning Around Low-Performing Schools in Chicago* (February 2012).

3. *Chicago's Democratically-Led Elementary Schools Far Out-Perform Chicago's "Turnaround Schools"* (Chicago: Designs for Change, February 2012).

4. Rebecca Vevea, "Board Backs School Closings, Turnarounds at Raucous Meeting," Chicago News Cooperative, February 23, 2012, http://www.chicagonewscoop.org/board-backs-school-closings-turnarounds-at-raucous-meeting/.

5. American Institutes for Research, "Turnaround Schools in California: Who Are They and What Strategies Do They Use?" (Washington, D.C., 2012).

6. Anthony Cody, "Flipping the Script on Turnarounds: Why Not Retain Teachers Instead of Reject Them?," *Education Week,* March 29, 2012.

7. Becky Vevea, "CPS Wants to Close First Renaissance Schools," WBEZ91.5, May 8, 2013, www.wbez.org/news/education/cps-wants-to-close-first-renaissance-schools-107072; Stephanie Banchero, Joe Bermuska, and Darnell Little, "Daley School Plan Fails to Make Grade," *Chicago Tribune,* January 17, 2010.

CHAPTER 21 Solutions: Start Here

1. W. E. B. DuBois, Address to Georgia State Teachers Convention, April 12, 1935, cited in Kenneth James King, *Pan-Africanism and Education: A Study of Race Philanthropy and Education in the Southern States of America and East Africa* (New York: Oxford University Press, 1971), 257.

2. Linda Darling-Hammond, "Why Is Congress Redlining Our Schools?," *Nation,* January 30, 2012.

CHAPTER 22 Begin at the Beginning

1. March of Dimes, *Born Too Soon: The Global Action Report on Preterm Birth* (2012), vii.

2. Ibid.; http://www.marchofdimes.com/mission/globalpreterm.html; Bonnie Rochman, "The Cost of Premature Birth: For One Family, More Than $2 Million," *Time,* May 2, 2010.

CHAPTER 23 The Early Years Count

1. James J. Heckman, "Schools, Skills, and Synapses," NBER working paper 14064, June 2008, http://www.nber.org/papers/w14064.pdf?new window=1.

2. Ibid., 15–21.

3. David Weikart, *How High/Scope Grew: A Memoir* (Ypsilanti, Mich.: High/Scope, 1994). For more about the history of early childhood education, see David L. Kirp's excellent *The Sandbox Investment: The Preschool Movement and Kids-First Politics* (Cambridge, Mass.: Harvard University Press, 2007); and David L. Kirp, *Kids First: Five Big Ideas for Transforming Children's Lives and America's Future* (New York: PublicAffairs, 2011), chap. 2.

4. Kirp, *Kids First,* 68–69.

5. Economist Intelligence Unit, *Starting Well: Benchmarking Early Education Across the World* (Economist, 2012).

CHAPTER 24 The Essentials of a Good Education

1. Stephanie Simon, "K–12 Student Database Jazzes Tech Startups, Spooks Parents," Reuters, March 3, 2013.

CHAPTER 25 Class Size Matters for Teaching and Learning

1. *Primary Sources: 2012: America's Teachers on the Teaching Profession* (Scholastic and Gates Foundation, 2012), 10.

2. *Great Expectations: Teachers' Views on Elevating the Teaching Profession* (Teach Plus, 2012).

3. Mary Ann Giordano and Anna M. Phillips, "Mayor Hits Nerve in Remarks on Class Sizes and Teachers," *New York Times,* December 2, 2011.

4. *Primary Sources,* 46–49.

5. Darling-Hammond, "Why Is Congress Redlining Our Schools?"

6. *Primary Sources,* 20–21, 66.

7. Institute of Education Sciences, *Identifying and Implementing Educational Practices Supported by Rigorous Evidence: A User Friendly Guide* (December 2003). The other three reforms cited are one-on-one tutoring by qualified tutors for at-risk readers in grades 1–3, life-skills training for junior high students, and instruction for early readers in phonics.

8. Jeremy D. Finn et al., "The Enduring Effects of Small Classes," *Teachers College Record,* April 2001; Alan B. Krueger, "Experimental Estimates of Education Production Functions," *Quarterly Journal of Economics* 114, no. 2 (1999); Barbara Nye, Larry V. Hedges, and Spyros Konstantopoulos, "The Long-Term Effects of Small Classes: A Five-Year Follow-Up of the Tennessee Class Size Experiment," *Educational Evaluation and Policy Analysis* 21, no. 2 (1999); Jeremy D. Finn, "Small Classes in American Schools: Research, Practice, and Politics," *Phi Delta Kappan,* March 2002; Jeremy D. Finn et al., "Small Classes in the Early Grades, Academic Achievement, and Graduating from High School," *Journal of Educational Psychology* 97, no. 2 (2005); Alan B. Krueger and Diane Whitmore, "The Effect of Attending a Small Class in the Early Grades on College-Test Taking and Middle School Test Results: Evidence from Project STAR," *Economic Journal,* January 2001; Raj Chetty et al., "How Does Your Kindergarten Classroom Affect Your Earnings? Evidence from Project STAR," *Quarterly Journal of Economics* 126, no. 4 (2011).

9. Thomas Dee and Martin West, "The Non-Cognitive Returns to Class Size," *Educational Evaluation and Policy Analysis,* March 2011; Philip Babcock and Julian R. Betts, "Reduced-Class Distinctions: Effort, Ability, and the Education Production Function," *Journal of Urban Economics,* May 2009; James J. Heckman and Yona Rubinstein, "The Importance of Noncognitive Skills: Lessons from the GED Testing Program," *American Economic Review* 91, no. 2 (2001).

10. Donald McLaughlin and Gili Drori, *School-Level Correlates of Academic Achievement* (Washington, D.C.: U.S. Department of Education, 2000); also Sarah T. Lubienski et al., "Achievement Differences and School Type: The Role of School Climate, Teacher Certification, and Instruction," *American Journal of Education* 115 (November 2008). For more studies that show correlations between smaller classes in the middle and upper grades and improved academic outcomes, see Class Size Matters fact sheet, "The Importance of Class Size in the Middle and Upper Grades," http://www.classsizematters.org/wp-content/uploads/2011/04/fact-sheet-on-upper-grades.pdf.

11. Spyros Konstantopoulos and Vicki Chun, "What Are the Long-Term Effects of Small Classes on the Achievement Gap? Evidence from the Lasting Benefits Study," *American Journal of Education* 116 (November 2009); Krueger and Whitmore, "Effect of Attending a Small Class in the Early Grades on College-Test Taking and Middle School Test Results"; see, for example, Alan B. Krueger and Diane Whitmore, "Would Smaller Classes Help Close the Black-White Achievement Gap?," in *Bridging the Achievement Gap* (Washington, D.C.: Brookings Institution Press, 2002);

and Paul E. Barton and Richard A. Coley, *The Black-White Achievement Gap: When Progress Stopped* (Policy Information Report, Educational Testing Service, 2010).

12. Lawrence P. Gallagher, "Class Size Reduction and Teacher Migration: 1995–2000," in Technical Appendix of the Capstone Report, part C, 2002; Emily Pas Isenberg, "The Effect of Class Size on Teacher Attrition: Evidence from Class Size Reduction Policies in New York State," U.S. Bureau of the Census, February 2010.

CHAPTER 26   Make Charters Work for All

1. Matthew Di Carlo, "The Evidence on Charter Schools and Test Scores," Albert Shanker Institute, December 2011, http://shankerblog.org/wp-content/uploads/2011/12/CharterReview.pdf.

2. Emma Brown, "D.C. Charter Schools Expel Students at Far Higher Rates Than Traditional Public Schools," *Washington Post*, January 5, 2012; Ed Fuller, *Examining High-Profile Middle Schools in Texas: Characteristics of Entrants, Student Retention, and Characteristics of Leavers* (Texas Business and Education Coalition, 2012); Bruce D. Baker, "Effects of Charter Enrollment on Newark District Enrollment," http://schoolfinance101.wordpress.com/2012/08/06/effects-of-charter-enrollment-on-newark-district-enrollment/; Bruce D. Baker, "Misinformed Charter Punditry Doesn't Help Anyone (Especially Charters)," http://schoolfinance101.wordpress.com/2011/10/04/misinformed-charter-punditry-doesnt%E2%80%99t-help-anyone-especially-charters/.

3. Bruce D. Baker, Ken Libby, and Kathryn Wiley, "Spending by the Major Charter Management Organizations: Comparing Charter School and Local Public District Financial Resources in New York, Ohio, and Texas," National Education Policy Center, May 2012.

CHAPTER 27   Wraparound Services Make a Difference

1. Tamara Wilder, Whitney Allgood, and Richard Rothstein, *Narrowing the Achievement Gap for Low-Income Children: A 19-Year Life Cycle Approach* (2008), http://www.epi.org/page/-/pdf/wilder_allgood_rothstein-narrowing_the_achievement_gap.pdf.

2. Karl L. Alexander, Doris R. Entwisle, and Linda Steffel Olson, "Lasting Consequences of the Summer Learning Gap," *American Sociological Review* 72, no. 2 (2007): 171.

3. Ibid., 175.

4. Ibid., 171, 177.

5. National Summer Learning Association, *Summer Learning Can Help Close the Achievement Gap*, http://www.summerlearning.org/?page=TheAchievementGap; Johns Hopkins University School of Education, Center for Summer Learning, *Motivating Adolescent Readers: The Role of Summer and Afterschool Programs*, http://www.summerlearning.org/resource/resmgr/publications/2007.motivatingadolescentrea.pdf; http://breakingnewsbtc.files.wordpress.com/2010/05/summer-learning-loss-research-overview.pdf.

6. J. A. Durlak and R. P. Weissberg, "The Impact of After-School Programs That Promote Personal and Social Skills" (Chicago: Collaborative for Academic, Social, and

Emotional Learning; After-School Alliance, 2007), http://www.afterschoolalliance
.org/documents/2012/Essentials_4_20_12_FINAL.pdf.

7. Paul Tough, *How Children Succeed: Grit, Curiosity, and the Hidden Power of Character* (Boston: Houghton Mifflin Harcourt, 2012), 105–47.

8. Wilder, Allgood, and Rothstein, *Narrowing the Achievement Gap for Low-Income Children,* 25–28.

CHAPTER 28 Measure Knowledge and Skills with Care

1. Pasi Sahlberg, *Finnish Lessons* (New York: Teachers College Press, 2011).

2. Bruce D. Baker, "Ed Waivers, Junk Rating Systems & Misplaced Blame: Case 1—New York State," http://schoolfinance101.wordpress.com/2012/08/31/ed-waivers-junk-rating-systems-misplaced-blame-case-1-new-york-state/; Education Law Center, "NJDOE Intent on Closing Schools Serving Students of Color," http://www.edlaw center.org/news/archives/other-issues/njdoe-intent-on-closing-schools-serving-students-of-color1.html; Matthew Di Carlo, "Assessing Ourselves to Death," *Shanker Blog,* October 4, 2012.

3. Todd Farley, *Making the Grades: My Misadventures in the Standardized Testing Industry* (Sausalito, Calif.: PoliPoint Press, 2009), pp. 240, 242.

4. Dan DiMaggio, "The Loneliness of the Long-Distance Test Scorer," *Monthly Review,* December 2010.

5. Heckman and Rubinstein, "Importance of Noncognitive Skills."

6. Henry M. Levin, "More Than Just Test Scores," *Prospects: Quarterly Review of Comparative Education* 42, no. 3 (2012).

7. National Research Council, *Incentives and Test-Based Accountability in Education* (Washington, D.C., 2011).

8. Sarah D. Sparks, "Panel Finds Few Learning Gains from Testing Movement," *Education Week,* May 26, 2011.

9. MCEA/MCPS, *Peer Assistance and Review Program: Teachers Guide,* http://www .mceanea.org/pdf/PAR2012-13MCEAGuide.pdf.

10. Michael Winerip, "Helping Teachers Help Themselves," *New York Times,* June 5, 2011.

11. *Educating for the 21st Century: Data Report on the New York Performance Standards Consortium,* http://www.nyclu.org/files/releases/testing_consortium_report.pdf.

CHAPTER 30 Protect Democratic Control of Public Schools

1. Matt Miller, "First, Kill All the School Boards," *Atlantic,* January–February 2008.

2. Data obtained from Dottie Gray, research librarian, National School Boards Association.

3. Congress passed legislation in 1970 prohibiting federal control of education: "No provision of any applicable program shall be construed to authorize any department, agency, officer, or employee of the United States to exercise any direction, supervision, or control over the curriculum, program of instruction, [or] administration . . . of any educational institution." PL 103-33 General Education Provisions Act, 432.

4. *ESEA Flexibility Request* (Washington, D.C.: U.S. Department of Education, 2012).

5. Rebecca Harris, "Voters Approve Referenda on Elected Board, Teachers Pensions," *Catalyst,* November 7, 2012; Quinnipiac University Polling Institute, April 11, 2013,

http://www.quinnipiac.edu/institutes-and-centers/polling-institute/new-york-city/release-detail?ReleaseID=1880.

CHAPTER 31 The Toxic Mix

1. National Scientific Council on the Developing Child, "Excessive Stress Disrupts the Architecture of the Developing Brain" (working paper 3, 2005), www.developing child.harvard.edu.
2. Gary Orfield, John Kucsera, and Genevieve Siegel-Hawley, *E Pluribus . . . Separation: Deepening Double Segregation for More Students* (UCLA Civil Rights Project, September 19, 2012), http://civilrightsproject.ucla.edu/research/k-12-education/integration-and-diversity/mlk-national/e-pluribus . . . separation-deepening-double -segregation-for-more-students.
3. Ibid.; "A Portrait of Segregation in New York City," *New York Times,* May 11, 2012.
4. Institute on Race and Poverty, *Failed Promises: Assessing Charter Schools in the Twin Cities* (University of Minnesota Law School, 2008); Institute on Race and Poverty, *Update of "Failed Promises: Assessing Charter Schools in the Twin Cities"* (University of Minnesota Law School, 2012).
5. John Hechinger, "Segregated Charter Schools Evoke Separate but Equal Era in U.S.," Bloomberg.com, December 22, 2011.
6. Orfield, Kucsera, and Siegel-Hawley, *E Pluribus . . . Separation,* 7–8.
7. Ibid., 8.
8. Rucker C. Johnson, "Long-Run Impacts of School Desegregation & School Quality on Adult Attainments" (NBER working paper 16664, January 2011), http://www .nber.org/papers/w16664.
9. Rucker C. Johnson, "The Grandchildren of Brown: The Long Legacy of School Desegregation," http://socrates.berkeley.edu/~ruckerj/RJabstract_BrownDeseg_Grand kids.pdf.
10. David L. Kirp, "Making Schools Work," *New York Times,* May 19, 2012.
11. Ibid.
12. Richard Rothstein and Mark Santow, "A Different Kind of Choice" (Washington, D.C.: Economic Policy Institute, 2012).

CHAPTER 32 Privatization of Public Education Is Wrong

1. Jamie Robert Vollmer, "The Blueberry Story: A Businessman Learns His Lesson," *Education Week,* March 6, 2002.
2. Steven Rattner, interview with Fareed Zakaria, CNN, July 22, 2012, http://edition .cnn.com/TRANSCRIPTS/1207/22/fzgps.01.html.
3. Tim Holt, "Education and the Business Model," http://holtthink.tumblr.com/post/25291144880/education-and-the-business-model.
4. Richard A. Oppel Jr., "Private Prisons Found to Offer Little in Savings," *New York Times,* May 18, 2011; Sam Dolnick, "As Escapees Stream Out, a Penal Business Thrives," *New York Times,* June 17, 2012; Julie Creswell and Reed Abelson, "A Giant Hospital Chain Is Blazing a Profit Trail," *New York Times,* August 15, 2012.
5. David M. Halbfinger, "Cost of Preschool Special Education Is Soaring," *New York Times,* June 6, 2012. See also "Oversight for Preschool Special Education," *New York Times,* July 16, 2012.

6. "Course Choice Quality Control" (Louisiana Department of Education, 2012), http://boarddocs.com/la/bese/Board.nsf/files/92ETL277D2BF/$file/AG_3-2 _Course_Choice_Attachment_B_Dec12.pdf; Valerie Strauss, "Louisiana Supreme Court Rules School Voucher Funding Unconstitutional," *Washington Post,* May 7, 2013.

7. Jessica Williams, "BESE Approves Online Providers Despite Judge Nixing Pay Plan," *Lens,* December 4, 2012.

8. Matthew Cunningham-Cook, "Why Do Some of America's Wealthiest Individuals Have Fingers in Louisiana's Education System?," *Nation,* October 23, 2012.

9. Motoko Rich, "Charter Schools Win Support in Georgia," *New York Times,* November 7, 2012.

10. Washington State, Public Disclosure Commission, http://www.pdc.wa.gov/MvcQuery System/CommitteeData/contributions?param=WUVTIFdDIDUwNw====&year =2012&type=initiative.

11. Daniel Denvir, "Michelle Rhee's Right Turn," Salon.com, November 17, 2012.

12. State Impact, "Idaho Voters Resoundingly Reject Propositions 1, 2, and 3," http:// stateimpact.npr.org/idaho/tag/propositions-1-2-3/; Andrew Crisp, "Luna Laws Award $180 Million Laptop Deal to HP," *Boise Weekly,* October 23, 2012; Dan Popkey, "Tom Luna's Education Reform Plan Was a Long Time in the Making," *Idaho Statesman,* February 20, 2011.

13. Santa Clara County Office of Education, "County Board Approves 20 More Rocketship Charters" (press release), http://www.sccoe.k12.ca.us/newsandfacts/ newsreleases/2011-12/news121511.asp?CFID=15231363&CFTOKEN=34992529&j sessionid=843032e7a6176e9adf9a5b4a1758607767e2; Sharon Noguchi, "PAC Money Floods Local School Board Races," http://www.mercurynews.com/bay-area-news/ ci_21896419/pac-money-floods-local-school-board-races; Sharon Noguchi, "Santa Clara County School Board: Mah Wins Seat; Song Beats Neighbors," http://www .mercurynews.com/elections/ci_21943699/santa-clara-county-school-board-has -two-seats.

14. Howard Blume, "Big Money Doesn't Buy Much in L.A. School Races," *Los Angeles Times,* March 6, 2013.

15. Jersey Jazzman, "Who Runs the Reformy Campaign Money Machine?" April 2, 2013, http://jerseyjazzman.blogspot.com/2013/04/who-runs-reformy-campaign-money -machine.html.

CHAPTER 33 Conclusion: The Pattern on the Rug

1. Http://www2.ed.gov/programs/racetothetop/executive-summary.pdf.

2. John Dewey, *Democracy and Education* (New York: Macmillan, 1916), 101.

Index

Page numbers in *italics* refer to figures.

ILLUSTRATION CREDITS

Graphs 1, 2, 16, 17, 18, 19, 20, 21, 22, 23, 24, 25, 26, 27: National Center for Education Statistics, *The Nation's Report Card: Mathematics 2011* (Washington, D.C.: Institute of Education Sciences, U.S. Department of Education, 2011).

Graphs 3, 4, 28, 29, 40, 41: B. D. Rampey, G. S. Dion, and P. L. Donahue, *NAEP 2008 Trends in Academic Progress* (Washington, D.C.: National Center for Education Statistics, Institute of Education Sciences, U.S. Department of Education, 2009).

Graphs 5, 6, 7, 8, 9, 10, 11, 12, 13, 14, 15, 30, 31: National Center for Education Statistics, *The Nation's Report Card: Reading 2011* (Washington, D.C.: Institute of Education Sciences, U.S. Department of Education, 2011).

Graph 32: National Center for Education Statistics, *The Condition of Education, 2012,* indicator 32-2 (Washington, D.C.: U.S. Department of Education, 2012).

Graphs 33, 34, 36, 37: Chris Chapman, Jennifer Laird, and Angelina KewalRamani, *Trends in High School Dropout and Completion Rates in the United States: 1972–2009* (Washington, D.C.: U.S. Department of Education, National Center for Education Statistics, 2011), p. 23.

Graph 35: National Center for Education Statistics, *Public School Graduates and Dropouts from the Common Core of Data: School Year 2009–10, First Look (Provisional Data),* U.S. Department of Education (NCES 2013-309), January 2013, pp. 17–18.

Graph 38: OECD, *Education at a Glance 2012* (Paris: Organization for Economic Cooperation and Development, 2012), Table A1.2a, p. 13.

Graph 39: OECD, *Education at a Glance 2011* (Paris: Organization for Economic Cooperation and Development, 2011), Chart A1.1, p. 30.

A NOTE ON THE TYPE

This book was set in Adobe Garamond. Designed for the Adobe
Corporation by Robert Slimbach, the fonts are based on types first cut
by Claude Garamond (c. 1480–1561). Garamond was a pupil of Geoffroy
Tory and is believed to have followed the Venetian models, although he
introduced a number of important differences, and it is to him that we
owe the letter we now know as "old style." He gave to his letters a certain
elegance and feeling of movement that won their creator an immediate
reputation and the patronage of Francis I of France.

Composed by North Market Street Graphics, Lancaster, Pennsylvania

Printed and bound by Berryville Graphics, Berryville, Virginia

Designed by Maggie Hinders